SPSS for Psychologists

SPSS for Psychologists

A Guide to Data Analysis using SPSS for Windows

(Versions 12 and 13)

Third Edition

NICOLA BRACE
RICHARD KEMP
AND
ROSEMARY SNELGAR

palgrave
macmillan

SPSS Screen Images © SPSS Inc.

SPSS is a registered trademark and the other product names are trademarks of SPSS Inc.
For information about SPSS contact:
SPSS UK Ltd, St Andrew's House, Working, Surrey, UK, GU21 1EB
Tel: +44 1483 719200 Fax: +44 1483 719290 http:www.spss.com

First edition 2000
Reprinted five times
Second edition 2003
Reprinted seven times
Third edition 2006

Published by
PALGRAVE MACMILLAN
Houndmills, Basingstoke, Hampshire RG21 6XS and
175 Fifth Avenue, New York, N.Y. 10010
Companies and representatives throughout the world

Palgrave Macmillan is the global academic imprint of the Palgrave Macmillan division of St. Martin's Press, LLC and of Palgrave Macmillan Ltd. Macmillan® is a registered trademark in the United States, United Kingdom and other countries. Palgrave is a registered trademark in the European Union and other countries.

ISBN 1–4039–8787–4

This book is printed on paper suitable for recycling and made from fully managed and sustained forest sources.

A catalogue record for this book is available from the British Library.

10   9   8   7   6   5   4   3
13 12 11 10 09 08 07 06

Printed in China

Dedications

To my family: Graham, Hannah and Francesca
Nicky

To my family: Penelope, Joseph, Francesca (and the 'pigs)
Richard

To my sisters and brother: Sue, Meg and Tim
Rosemary

Contents

Preface

This book is designed to help you analyse psychological data on your own. With the exception of the first few sections in the first chapter, we recommend that you read the book whilst sitting at a computer that is running SPSS. The book is divided into different chapters and within each chapter there are several sections. Chapters 1, 2 and 6 cover issues related to research design, data entry and data handling, and Chapter 12 provides additional information that you will find useful once you are an experienced user of SPSS. The remaining chapters explain how to undertake a variety of statistical procedures using SPSS. The order of the statistical tests covered in Chapters 3–5 and 7 reflects the way in which many Psychology departments teach research methods and statistics. Chapters 8–11 explain how to conduct more complex analyses that may or may not be covered in undergraduate courses but that might be of use to postgraduate students or researchers.

Like all academic books, it is not necessary to read this book from cover to cover. In particular, if you are confident in your knowledge of statistics and research methods in psychology, then you may be able to skip straight to Section 4 of Chapter 1. If you have used previous versions of SPSS, then you may wish to proceed straight to the section covering the statistical test you wish to perform.

To provide you with an overview of the structure of this book, a summary of the material covered and the rationale underpinning each chapter is given below. Please note that we include a glossary after the last chapter, which may be of help should you come across a term that you do not understand.

Chapter 1

The first chapter provides a brief overview of the basic concepts and terminology used in psychological research and statistical analysis, and introduces SPSS. We describe some basic methods of data collection and the types of data that are collected in quantitative research. We then consider data analysis and provide you with an introduction to the windows and buttons you will use when analysing your data with SPSS. Finally, we show you how to start and exit SPSS.

In Chapter 2, we show you how to create and save a data file and how to obtain some simple descriptive statistics. Chapter 6 also focuses on the data file, showing you how data can be manipulated and modified in SPSS. Although a novice user may not need to use these techniques, they are valuable for more sophisticated analyses and when analysing larger data files, especially those resulting from surveys.

Chapters 3–5 and 7–11

In Chapter 3, we cover inferential statistical tests that can be used to determine whether a difference exists between two levels of an independent variable. In Chapter 4, we cover inferential statistical tests that can be used to determine whether a relationship exists between two variables. In Chapter 5, we consider tests that are suitable for use with nominal or categorical data. In Chapters 7–11, we look at tests that are appropriate for experiments involving more complex designs or for data obtained using non-experimental methods such as surveys or questionnaires.

In general, each chapter covers a family of related tests, each of which is described in its own section. We introduce each statistical test with a brief description. This description is not intended to replace that which you will find in a statistics text; rather it is intended to act as a reminder of when and how to use the test. We also include an example of a typical or real piece of research that might be analysed using the test, to give you a concrete example. We then give very detailed step-by-step instructions on how to perform the test using SPSS. In the earlier chapters, we include screen-shots (pictures) and a full description of every step required to perform the test. In later chapters, we assume that you will have become a little more familiar with the workings of SPSS, and therefore summarise some of the more simple operations. Each chapter includes an annotated example of the output produced by SPSS to help you understand the results of your analyses. Finally, we include a note on how you should report the results of your analyses.

The data we use to demonstrate the statistical tests can be found in Appendix I of this book, or can be downloaded from the Palgrave website (http://www.palgrave.com/psychology/brace/data.htm).

Chapter 12

This chapter is a little different. Here, we describe a range of procedures that our students have wanted to undertake, for example how to insert SPSS output into a text document. It is important to note that a full description of what SPSS can do is beyond any one book, but we show you here how to use the on-line help provided by SPSS, so that you can discover for yourself how to do something not covered in this book. For more experienced researchers, we also include some notes on the use of the Syntax window.

DIFFERENCES BETWEEN RECENT AND EARLIER VERSIONS OF SPSS

This book is written using SPSS Version 12 and 13. These two versions are very similar and where differences arise we show how to use both versions. You may find some small differences between our SPSS output pages and your own, such as the number of decimal places reported in the output, and these minor differences may relate to the way in which SPSS is set up on your computer.

In addition, you should find this book useful if you are using earlier versions of SPSS, although there are some differences between these two earlier versions and the more recent versions. The key differences are listed below and as some are important in terms of following this guide, we have included relevant information for you in Appendices II and III.

If you are using Version 8 or 9:

1. Data entry, in particular in how variables are defined, is different and to help users of earlier versions we explain how you will enter data in Appendix II.
2. The main menu bar in Version 8 shows a Statistics item rather than an Analyze item and Descriptive Statistics rather than Summarize.
3. Earlier versions list fewer options on the drop-down menus of the Analyze and the Data menu items.
4. You will not find an Exact button on the dialogue boxes associated with nonparametric tests. This was added as an option and we explain what it does in Chapter 5.
5. You will not find a Jonckheere–Tempstra button on the dialogue boxes associated with the Kruskal–Wallis test. This was added as an option; we don't explain it in this guide.
6. You will not see a test called Marginal Homogeneity, available now when selecting some of the non-parametric tests.

7. You will not find an option called Cochran's and Mantel-Haenszel statistics on the Crosstabs Statistics dialogue box. This was added as an option; we don't explain it in this guide.
8. You may notice some differences in the names given to some dialogue boxes.
9. You may also notice some differences in the number of decimal places included in the SPSS output.

If you are using Version 10 or 11 or an earlier version:

1. Adding regression lines to scattergrams is different and to help users of earlier versions we explain how to do this in Appendix III.
2. Earlier versions list fewer options on the drop-down menu of the Analyze menu item.
3. You will find differences in graphing, for example when creating bar charts or working in Chart Editor.
4. There are also some small differences in the dialogue boxes for certain statistical tests, including Crosstabs: Cell Display dialogue box, the Exact Tests dialogue box, the ANOVA Repeated Measures Define Factor(s) dialogue box.

Acknowledgements

Welcome to the third edition of our guide to SPSS.

As with our previous editions, we would like to take the opportunity to thank the many people who have contributed to this book. In particular, we would like to thank our colleagues, both past and present, who have provided such valuable advice and feedback on the earlier editions. We hope that they will be able to see where we have made amendments or additions in light of their comments. We would also like to thank the various colleagues, supervisors, students and friends who have contributed to our knowledge of statistics and data analysis either through formal teaching, through informal discussion or by presenting us with challenging data analysis problems. Some of these people were also kind enough to allow us to utilise their data to illustrate the use of particular statistical techniques. We would particularly like to thank Graham Pike for his continued support and advice.

We thought about writing a book on SPSS for 10 years before the first edition was published. We first taught students to use SPSS-PC, preparing new teaching notes with each new group of students and each new version of SPSS. When we finally got around to writing the first edition of this book we were overwhelmed by the very positive response it received. One of the things that gave us most pleasure was the emails we received from students who were using our guide. Our intention in writing this book has always been to enable students of psychology to actively engage in the discipline by undertaking their own research. Reading about psychology can be interesting but the real fun is in doing it – and, because psychology is a scientific discipline, that involves the collection and analysis of data. The students who contacted us told us that our book had enabled them to complete their own research, and it was this more than anything which persuaded us to update and expand our text in the second and third editions. Thank you for taking the time to contact us.

In the acknowledgements section of the second edition we dedicated the index to our readers who had used post-it notes to compensate for the lack of an index in the first edition. We hope that these readers will be even more excited by our considerably expanded index and glossary!

Finally, we would once again like to thank Frances Arnold and the ever expanding team at Palgrave for their support and good humour. Frances was instrumental in guiding the production of the first and second editions, and has once again made a valuable contribution to the production of this third edition. We also thank Jaime Marshall, Stephen Wenham, Anna van Boxel and Jo Digby who have worked with us on this edition.

Nicola Brace
Richard Kemp
Rosemary Snelgar

Chapter One

Introduction

Psychological research and SPSS
Some basic statistical concepts
Working with SPSS
Starting SPSS
How to exit from SPSS
Some useful option settings in SPSS

Section 1: Psychological research and SPSS

WHAT IS SPSS?

SPSS is a very widely used computer program designed to aid the statistical analysis of data, particularly data collected in the course of research. In various different forms SPSS has been around for many years, and has become the "industry standard" software for data analysis. SPSS is the program most widely used by university researchers, especially those working in psychology and the social sciences. SPSS is also widely used in private and government research organisations and many large private companies. Being able to describe yourself as a competent user of SPSS will enhance your employment prospects considerably.

Although at first sight SPSS might appear rather complex, it is not difficult to learn how to undertake a wide range of statistical analyses and, once you have mastered these basics, they will enable you to undertake far more sophisticated research than would be possible without the aid of such software.

BUT I AM STUDYING PSYCHOLOGY NOT STATISTICS – WHY DO I NEED TO LEARN TO USE SPSS?

This is a common question, and the answer lies in an understanding of the nature of psychology and the research that psychologists undertake. Psychology is a science, and like all sciences our discipline advances through research involving observation. That is, we learn new facts by making systematic observations about our subject matter – people. The problem is that people are not the easiest of things to observe because they vary both between individuals and over time. That is, you and I might differ in how we react in a particular situation, and how I react to a situation today might be quite different to how I react tomorrow. This means that the data collected by psychologists are much more "noisy" than that collected in some other sciences. Consider for example a chemist investigating the properties of magnesium. The chemist knows that, under constant conditions, every bit of magnesium will react in the same way as every other bit of magnesium, and that how the magnesium reacts today will be the same as how it reacts tomorrow. Thus, the chemist might only need to do an experiment once using one piece of magnesium and is unlikely to need to use statistics to help explain the results of the observations. The situation facing the psychologist is quite different, and in order to be able to determine how people in general react in a given situation, the psychologist will probably need to test several different individuals on several different occasions and then make use of statistical techniques to determine what trends are present in the data. So, psychologists are particularly likely to need to use statistics in their research. In recent years the complexity of the statistical techniques routinely used in psychological research, and taught to undergraduate students has increased considerably. This routine reliance on more complex statistical analysis is made possible by the widespread availability of sophisticated statistical analysis software such as SPSS. Thus, in order to be able to undertake psychological research, either as a student or a professional, you need to be able to use a software such as SPSS. This book is designed to introduce you to SPSS so that you can use the program to undertake the statistical analyses you need for your course or research.

Section 2: Some basic statistical concepts

Before we start to use SPSS we need to briefly revise some basic statistical concepts.

DATA, VARIABLES AND CASES

When conducting psychological research we make systematic observations and record the results of our observations. The records of our observations form the data on which our conclusions will be based. The data can be qualitative or quantitative – that is, they can be described in words and phrases or with numbers. SPSS is designed to aid the analysis of quantitative data.

Our quantitative data will probably consist of a series of measurements for each of one or more variables. A variable is simply some quantity which varies and can be measured – so height, time, weight, sex (male or female) and IQ test score are all examples of variables.

Variables are usually measured several times. These repeat observations form cases. In psychological research it is common to make observations of several different individuals or participants. Thus, for psychological research a case is almost always a unique individual. A typical data set in psychological research will consist of several variables each measured for each of several cases or participants.

LEVELS OF MEASUREMENT

We use a scale to make the measurements of a variable, and the characteristics of the scale we use determine the characteristics of the data we collect and ultimately what we can and cannot do with our data. Most statistics texts written for psychology students describe four different types of scales, or levels of measurement: *nominal*, *ordinal*, *interval* and *ratio*. SPSS doesn't differentiate between interval and ratio data, using the term "Scale" to describe both.

> **TIP**   Before we enter our data into SPSS, it is important to give careful consideration to what type of scale was used when measuring the data. SPSS distinguishes between just three types of variables, nominal variables, ordinal variables and scale (interval or ratio) variables.

Nominal variables

Nominal or categorical variables are measured using scales which only categorise the observations. The value of a nominal variable should not be taken to imply any more than a label (or a name, hence the term "nominal"). For example, we might decide to record the sex of our participants and adopt the coding scheme 1 = Male, 2 = Female. This coding scheme forms our scale for this nominal variable. When we record the values 1 or 2 we do not intend to suggest that women are more than men – just to record the difference between these two groups of participants. With nominal data just about the only thing we can do is count or measure frequency. We can report how many men and women we have, but there is little else we can do with these data and it would make no sense to calculate statistics such as the mean sex of our participants.

> **TIP**   SPSS does not automatically know about the level of measurement used to collect your data. It is up to you to make sure that you do not ask SPSS to undertake any inappropriate analysis, such as the mean of nominal data.

Ordinal variables

Ordinal variables are measured using a scale which allows us to imply order or rank. For example, suppose your lecturer gave your class a statistics test and then ranked the scores. The student coming top will have a rank of 1, the next best student a rank of 2 and so on. Performance recorded using such a rank scale will result in an ordinal variable. An ordinal variable tells you more than a nominal variable – it is legitimate to say that a rank of 1 is better than a rank of 2. However, what we can do with these data is still limited because we do not know how much better the rank 1 student performed than the rank 2 student, and because it is unlikely that the difference in ability indicated by ranks 1 and 2 will be the same as that between ranks 2 and 3, or ranks 101 and 102. Thus, an ordinal scale is still a rather limited measure of performance.

Interval and ratio variables – scale variables

Most psychology statistics texts differentiate between interval and ratio levels of measurement. An interval scale is a scale which has an arbitrary zero so that a value of zero doesn't indicate that you have none of the quantity being measured. In a ratio scale zero means that there is none of the quantity being measured. In practice the difference between these two types of data is not critical, which is fortunate because psychologists often disagree about whether a variable is measured using an interval or a ratio scale, especially when the variable is measuring a psychological construct such as an attitude.

SPSS does not attempt to distinguish between interval and ratio data, using the term **Scale** variable to describe both interval and ratio variables. In SPSS we classify variables as nominal, ordinal or scale.

RESEARCH METHODS IN PSYCHOLOGY

A variety of different methods can be used in psychological research. Methods commonly used include questionnaire studies, interviews, observation and experiments. Each of these methods can result in the collection of quantitative data suitable for analysis using SPSS. The experimental method is a particularly important method which allows us to draw conclusions regarding the cause–effect relationship between two variables. When using an experimental method we distinguish between the independent variable and the dependent variable. In a classic experiment we manipulate the independent variable and measure the consequence of this change on the dependent variable. For example, we can investigate how temperature affects memory by manipulating temperature to create at least two different temperature conditions, and measure memory performance under each of these conditions. In this experiment temperature is our independent variable and memory is our dependent variable.

Related and unrelated designs in psychological research

One important characteristic of any research method is whether it involves a *related* or *unrelated* design (also known as correlated and uncorrelated designs respectively). In a related research design two or more variables are linked in some way – typically because they are measured from the same participant. For example, if we measure the age and the reading ability of each of a group of 10 participants then our data set would be made up of these two related variables. The variables are related because each pair of observations came from the same participant. In contrast, if we compared the reading age of a group of male and female children, then we would make only one measurement from each participant – this would be an unrelated design. This distinction is important because data collected using related and unrelated designs are analysed using different techniques, and because the data collected using related and unrelated data are coded differently in SPSS data files (see Chapter 2).

When using an experimental method we use a special set of terms to describe related and unrelated designs. Independent groups designs, or between-subjects (between-participants) designs are the most common unrelated experimental designs in which we compare one group of participants with a different group of participants. Repeated measures or within-subjects (within-participants) designs are the most common related experimental designs in which we compare the performance of a single set of participants under two different sets of conditions. Another type of related design is the matched-subjects design, in which each participant is matched closely with another participant, to give a participant pair. Each member of the pair is then allocated by a random process to different levels of the independent variable.

TWO TYPES OF STATISTICAL ANALYSIS

Broadly there are two types of statistical procedure which serve two different roles in psychological research.

Descriptive statistics

Descriptive statistics are procedures used to summarise large volumes of data. The role of descriptive statistics is to provide the reader with an understanding of what the data look like by using a few indicative or typical values. Some descriptive statistics are used in everyday language; for example, when we talk about "average pay" we are employing a descriptive statistic to describe the pay of a large number of individuals.

Inferential statistics

Inferential statistics are procedures which allow us to go beyond simply describing the data; and ask questions about the data. For example, we can ask questions such as "is there a difference between the reading ability of the male and the female participants?" or "is there a relationship between participants' age and reading ability?" Questions such as these are answered through the use of a variety of different inferential statistical procedures. What all these statistical procedures have in common is that they use mathematical procedures to attempt to estimate the probability that the data we have collected support our hypothesis.

Hypotheses and null-hypotheses

A hypothesis is a prediction about the outcome of the research. The hypothesis, often known as research hypothesis, experimental hypothesis, or alternative hypothesis, predicts that there will be a difference between conditions, or that there is an association between variables. The null-hypothesis, by contrast, expresses the possibility that there is no effect or association. For example, if we are investigating the effect of temperature on memory, the hypothesis might state that an increase in temperature will have a negative impact on memory performance. The null-hypothesis states that there will not be an effect of temperature on memory. We should plan our research in an attempt to falsify the null-hypothesis. If we try but fail to falsify the null-hypothesis then it is likely that the hypothesis is true.

One- and two-tailed hypotheses

Research hypotheses can be of two types, one-tailed or two-tailed. A one-tailed hypothesis makes predictions regarding both the presence of a significant effect (e.g., there will be a difference in the performance of young and old participants on a memory test) and also of the direction of this difference or association (e.g., young participants will perform better on a memory test than elderly participants). In contrast, a two-tailed hypothesis predicts only the presence of a statistically significant effect, not its direction. This distinction can be critical because the nature of the hypothesis is one of the factors influencing the calculation of the outcome of an inferential statistical test.

UNDERSTANDING INFERENTIAL STATISTICS

Populations and samples

When we plan a piece of research we will have in mind a population. For statistical purposes, a population is the total set of all possible scores for a particular variable. For some research the population might be quite small. For example, if we are researching occupational stress amongst professional taxidermists then our population is the stress level of all professional taxidermists. Given that there are relatively few professional taxidermists, we might be able to interview them all and so measure the entire population of scores. However, for most research it would never be possible to collect the entire population of all possible scores for a variable, either because the population is too large, or because of practical limitations. In these situations we rely on testing a sample. That is, we collect a smaller sub-group of scores which we hope will be representative of the whole population. Inferential statistical techniques allow us to generalise from the sample to the population.

Parameters and statistics

If we measure the entire population of scores for a variable, then we can calculate a *parameter* of the population, such as the mean. However, usually we only sample the population and so can only calculate the mean of the sample. A measure, such as the mean or standard deviation, based on a sample is known as a *statistic*. The important distinction is that we can calculate a statistic, but usually can only estimate a parameter because we cannot measure the entire population of scores. Assuming that our sampling procedure was sound we would expect the mean of the sample to provide a fairly accurate estimate of the mean of the population. The bigger the sample, the more accurate our estimate is likely to be, but unless we test the entire population we will never know the true population parameter for certain.

Inferential statistics and probability

All inferential statistical tests calculate the probability that the pattern of results we have observed in our data could have arisen by chance alone. Suppose we want to know whether Australian children have superior hand–eye coordination to British children. Our research question relates to the hand–eye coordination of all Australian and all British children but, in order to make the research practical, we measure hand–eye coordination in a sample of 100 Australian and 100 British children. Clearly, hand–eye coordination varies greatly within both national groups and some children will be better than others, but our question is whether there are also some general differences between the two groups. If we find that the average level of hand–eye coordination is higher for the Australian than the British children, then this could be for one of two reasons. It could be that this reflects a real difference in hand–eye coordination that could arise for a variety of interesting reasons which could be the subject of future research. Alternatively, it could be that in reality there is no difference between the hand–eye coordination of Australian and British children and that our samples were unrepresentative. For example, by chance we might have selected a group of British children who never play sport and have especially poor hand–eye coordination. Inferential statistical tests allow us to decide which of these two possible explanations is the most likely; is it more likely that our sample was unrepresentative or that there really is a difference between the two groups? Inferential tests do this by calculating the probability that the apparent difference was just down to bad luck in our sampling. For this reason all inferential statistical tests will result in the computation of a probability value or a p value.

The probability value that is calculated by an inferential test tells us how likely it is that the pattern we can see in our data is just down to chance and is not indicative of a "real" effect. That is, the probability that the null-hypothesis is correct. But what do we do with this knowledge? Probability values never reach 0 (nothing is impossible) and never reach 1 (nothing is certain) so we can never be sure which of these possible explanations is correct. If the observed difference in hand–eye coordination of Australian and British school children is very unlikely to occur by chance alone, then we can probably argue that this is a real difference. But just how unlikely is "very unlikely"? There are two approaches we can take here – we can either inform the reader of the probability level and leave the reader to decide how to interpret this, or we can set a criterion below which we will declare that the probability is so low that we will dismiss the null-hypothesis and accept the hypothesis. This second approach is the one traditionally adopted in psychological research and is the basis of the concept of statistical significance. Psychologists usually set the criterion (also known as the Type I error rate) at $p=0.05$. If the probability that the result we have observed is due to chance alone is less than 0.05 (or 5%) then we reject the null-hypothesis, accept the alternative hypothesis and declare that we have a *statistically significant* result.

When using SPSS the output from inferential tests includes the information necessary to adopt this null-hypothesis significance testing approach, including the probability that the null-hypothesis is "true". In SPSS output this is often labelled the "Sig. Value".

Adjusting *p* values for one- and two-tailed hypotheses

By default SPSS usually calculates the p value for the two-tailed hypothesis, and this is the safest, most conservative option to adopt. However, if before undertaking the research we have established a one-tailed hypothesis, then it is possible to either request the calculation of a p value appropriate to a one-tailed hypothesis (e.g., see the tests of correlation described in Chapter 4) or to calculate the one-tailed p value by halving the two-tailed value.

Exact and asymptotic significance

SPSS provides the option of either exact or asymptotic significance for certain inferential statistical tests. Asymptotic significance is tested against an asymptotic distribution in which the probability of occurrence of extremely high or low values never reaches zero, so in a graph of the distribution the tails never touch the horizontal axis. The normal distribution is an example of an asymptotic distribution. In real distributions such extreme values do not occur, so real distributions are not asymptotic. If we have a large sample then it is safe to use the asymptotic distribution to calculate probability values. However, with small sample sizes this approach can be problematic. To overcome this problem versions of several inferential tests have been developed which give what is called the "exact" significance. One common example is Fisher's Exact test, used in Chi-square designs which involve small numbers of participants (see Chapter 5, Section 4). If you choose to make use of an exact test, then you should make this clear when reporting the results of your analysis.

> **TIP** The fact that the exact tests allow you to test hypotheses with small numbers of participants does not mean that it is acceptable to test few participants. The statistical power of your design (see below) will be greatly reduced by a small sample size.

CONFIDENCE INTERVALS, EFFECT SIZE AND STATISTICAL POWER

Some statisticians have argued that psychologists should make greater use of a range of measures which are deigned to provide the reader with more information about the results of the research being reported. In recent years, several influential bodies including the American Psychological Association (see the 5th edition of the APA Publication Manual (APA, 2001)) have suggested a change in the way in which psychological research is reported. In particular there has been a call for researchers to make greater use of confidence intervals and measures of effect size when reporting the results of their research. Recent versions of SPSS have begun to incorporate these measures into some, but not all statistical routines. In the following pages we provide a brief introduction to the use of confidence intervals and measures of power and effect size. We hope that this will be useful to researchers who are new to these measures.

Confidence intervals and point estimates

When estimating a statistic such as a mean, there are two approaches we could adopt. In psychological research the most common approach is to cite a single value, or point estimate, which represents the best estimate of the parameter. For example, we might estimate that the population mean height is 1.73m. Clearly it is very unlikely that the true value will be exactly 1.73m, but this point estimate represents our best guess. Although they are very widely employed in psychology, point estimates are limited because they do not tell us anything about the likely accuracy of our estimate. The alternative approach uses a device called a confidence interval which consists of two values, an upper and lower limit, which define the range within which we expect the true value to fall. For example if we estimate that the upper and lower limits of the 95% confidence interval are 1.6 and 1.8, then we are stating that the probability that the parameter will fall in the range 1.6 to 1.8 is 0.95 (95%). The confidence interval approach has several advantages over the point estimate approach. Firstly, it serves to remind us that the population estimate is just that – an estimate which has associated with it a certain level of error. Secondly, the confidence interval approach conveys information about the likely magnitude of the real value. If we only provide a point estimate value for the population mean then we have no way of knowing what the likely limits are. Another very valuable use of confidence intervals is in the graphing of results. By marking the confidence intervals when plotting means, we provide the reader with a clear indication of the extent to which the estimated means for different conditions overlap. This use of confidence intervals in graphing is illustrated in Chapter 2.

Confidence intervals and statistical inference

In the discussion above we have only considered the use of confidence intervals with descriptive statistics such as the sample mean. However, the confidence interval approach can also be employed to make statistical inference. If we return to our hypothetical study of the hand–eye coordination skills of Australian and British children, then it will be clear that we can calculate the *mean difference* in skill level of the two groups. This mean difference is an estimate of the real difference between the two population means, and so we can state this mean difference either using a point estimate or using a confidence interval. For example, if the upper and lower limits of the 95% confidence interval for the mean difference were 1.3 and 2.2, then this would tell us that, according to our estimates, there is a probability of .95 that the real mean difference in skill level will lie somewhere between these two values. Assuming that a positive score means that the Australian children have scored higher than the British children, then the fact that both the upper and lower limits of the 95% confidence interval are positive tells us that there is a 95% probability that the Australian children have better hand–eye coordination than the British children. This is equivalent to stating that there is a significant difference between the ability of the Australian and British children, but note that expressing the significant difference using confidence intervals has the advantage that it also gives us an indication of the magnitude of the likely difference between the two groups and the variability of the difference. Using the confidence interval approach, a difference is taken to be significant if the upper and lower limits of the confidence interval are either both positive, or both negative – that is if the range of values does not include zero. Using this method a non-significant difference is indicated when the range of values does include zero because in such a case the difference between the groups might be zero. Thus, upper and lower limits of −1.4

and +0.8 would indicate that either the Australian children may be better than the British children, or the British children may be better than the Australian children, or there may be no difference – clearly a non-significant result.

SPSS and 95% confidence intervals

The latest version of SPSS has increased the availability of measures of confidence intervals. However, confidence intervals are still not readily available for some of the routines covered in this book. At present SPSS provides confidence intervals for the mean difference as part of the default output for the *t*-test (see Chapter 3) and in this case these confidence intervals can be used to infer statistical significance. Confidence intervals for the mean are also available as optional output for ANOVA, ANCOVA and MANOVA. However, at present the use of confidence intervals to infer statistical significance in these routines is not well supported in SPSS and is beyond the scope of this book. Interested readers are advised to consult Bird (2004) which provides a very comprehensive coverage of this complex issue.

Effect size

Another, closely related, trend in the reporting of statistics in psychological research is the increased emphasis on measures of effect size. If we are undertaking research into the effectiveness of a new form of psychological treatment for depression, then we will not only want to know whether the new form of treatment is significantly more effective than the old, but also **how much** more effective the new treatment is. This is the role of a measure of effect size; it tells us how big an effect we can expect from an intervention, treatment, manipulation of an independent variable or difference between groups. Measures of effect size can be very useful, particularly when we are attempting to evaluate or interpret our results. For example, if our new treatment for depression has a very large effect size compared to the small effect size of the old treatment, we may choose to implement it even if it is much more expensive and time consuming than the old treatment. However, if the difference in effect size is very small, then even though the new treatment may be significantly more effective than the old one, we may decide that it is not worth implementing given the increased expense. Effect sizes are not only useful in applied research, they are also critical in interpreting the results of theoretical research, where an indication of the size of an effect may help us to understand its likely cause.

Effect sizes are measured and quoted using a variety of scales. The most basic, and sometimes most useful, measure of effect size is a raw difference of means expressed in the same units used to measure the dependent variable. For example, when reporting the results of an intervention for children with reading difficulties we could report that the mean difference between the treated and untreated group was 8.2 points on a standardised test of reading ability. Researchers familiar with this test of reading ability will be able to determine whether this is a large, medium or small effect size and thus whether the intervention is worthwhile. To give another example, research comparing the earnings of university graduates and non-graduates might reveal that the mean difference in earnings is $10,000 per year. This is an effect size measure expressed in the same units used to measure the dependent variable, and it provides you with some very useful information when it comes to planning your future.

Sometimes it is not very useful to express effect sizes in the units used to measure the dependent variable. For example, suppose a researcher measures how long it takes a group of elderly and a group of young participants to memorise a piece of text. The dependent variable is time measured in minutes, but the absolute time taken will depend on the passage selected and is therefore rather arbitrary and difficult to interpret. The most widely adopted solution in cases like this is to standardise the effect size measure by expressing it in standard deviation units, a procedure advocated by Cohen (1969). The resulting measure, called Cohen's d, tells us how big the difference in the means is relative to the spread of the scores. Cohen (1969) suggested a classification for effect sizes using this measure. He suggested that an effect size of 0.2 should be regarded as "small", 0.5 should be regarded as a "medium" sized effect, and an effect size of 0.8 should be regarded as "large". It is important to realise that there is nothing special about these values and the labels attached to them – this is merely the naming convention suggested by Cohen.

TIP   Very small effects can be very important. The effect size for many lifesaving medical treatments is less than 0.2 standardised units. Measures of effect size are valuable but we must consider them alongside other factors, including the "cost" of the treatment when assessing an effect.

Effect size measures, like confidence intervals, are a way of providing the reader with more meaningful information when reporting the results of inferential statistical analysis and many psychological journals now request that authors quote these statistics alongside the statement of whether the result is significant.

Statistical power

The power of an inferential statistical procedure is the probability that it will yield statistically significant results. Power is the ability of a procedure to accurately discriminate between situations where the null-hypothesis is true and situations where the null-hypothesis is false. Statistical power is influenced by several factors, including the effect size (see above) and the sample size (usually the number of participants tested). If we are hoping to find statistically significant evidence for a small effect, then we will need to test a large number of participants. It is possible to calculate, for a given effect size, how many participants we will need in order to have a good chance of achieving statistical significance. Cohen (1977) suggests that, in order to avoid wasting their own time and that of their participants, experimenters should aim to achieve a power of 0.8. That is, we should design our experiments so that we have at least an 80% chance of obtaining a significant result. Good practice would be to estimate the power that a particular design will achieve, and how many participants will be needed, to give a good chance of revealing a significant effect. There is little point in undertaking a piece of research if the probability of it revealing a significant result is only about 50%.

There is another reason to calculate the power of a given design. If we fail to obtain a significant result, then there are two possible explanations for this. It could be that the null-hypothesis is true – that is, that there is no difference or no association. Alternatively, it could be that there is a difference or an association but that we failed to detect it because we had insufficient statistical power. Unless you know about the power of your design there is no way you can distinguish between these two alternatives. If on the other hand you know that your design had a power of about 0.8 to detect a small effect size (d=0.2), then you know that the probability is .8 that either there is no effect or that if there is an effect it is small (d<0.2).

Practical equivalence of two samples

In advance of undertaking our research we might decide that we are only interested in an effect that exceeds a certain effect size. For example if comparing two treatments for depression we might decide that given the additional "costs" associated with our new treatment we are only interested in an effect size of at least d=0.15. In this situation we have decided in advance that an effect size of less than 0.15 is "trivial" and that two treatments that differ by less than this amount are of *practical equivalence*. Given this, if our power was 0.8 to detect an effect of size 0.15, then we can confidently conclude that there is no practical difference between the two treatments. If, on the other hand, the statistical power of our design to detect such a small effect was low, say perhaps 0.5, then we should conclude that the issue of whether this new treatment is worthwhile is still undecided (and we should chastise ourselves for having conducted such an important piece of research with such low statistical power!).

Statistical power calculations can appear daunting because they involve the interrelationship between four variables: the statistical power of the design, the sample size, the criterion p value and the effect size. However, there are several specialist software packages available to undertake these calculations for you. We particularly recommend a piece of software called G*Power which can be downloaded free from http://www.psycho.uni-duesseldorf.de/aap/projects/gpower

Statistical power and SPSS

As with confidence intervals, recent editions of SPSS have increased the availability of measures of power. For example, measures of "Observed power" are now available from the "Options" dialogue box for the ANOVA, ANCOVA and MANOVA routines. More advanced users may like to incorporate this additional information into their research reports.

CHOOSING THE CORRECT STATISTICAL PROCEDURES

SPSS will not tell you which descriptive statistic/s you should use to describe your data, or which inferential statistic to use to test your hypothesis. Broadly speaking, you need to consider the nature of the hypothesis being tested, the method and/or experimental design employed, the number of variables manipulated and/or measured, and the type of data collected.

Parametric and nonparametric tests

Parametric tests are inferential tests which have greater statistical power, and often can be used in more complex experimental designs, but which are limited to use in situations where the data meet certain requirements, including the following assumptions:
1. that the data are collected using an interval or ratio scale;
2. that the data are normally distributed;
3. that the samples being compared have equal variance.
As we will see, in some cases SPSS includes information that you can use to assess whether the data violate any of these assumptions.

There are many occasions in psychology when we collect data that do not satisfy all these requirements. *Nonparametric* tests are inferential tests that make very few assumptions about the data and in particular its distribution. However, they are less powerful than their parametric equivalents.

In the remaining sections of this chapter we introduce SPSS so that you are ready to enter data in the next chapter.

Section 3: Working with SPSS

SPSS (originally Statistical Package for the Social Sciences) is an enormously powerful program. Knowing how to use SPSS will allow you to perform a very wide range of statistical operations and, because the computer does all the calculations, you do not have to use formulae or carry out long operations on your calculator.

DATA ANALYSIS USING SPSS

There are three basic steps involved in data analysis using SPSS. Firstly, you must enter the raw data and save to a file. Secondly, you must select and specify the analysis you require. Thirdly, you must examine the output produced by SPSS. These steps are illustrated below. The special windows used by SPSS to undertake these steps are described next.

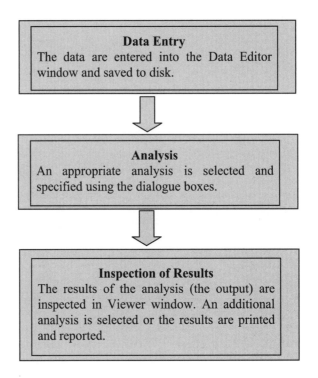

Data Entry
The data are entered into the Data Editor window and saved to disk.

Analysis
An appropriate analysis is selected and specified using the dialogue boxes.

Inspection of Results
The results of the analysis (the output) are inspected in Viewer window. An additional analysis is selected or the results are printed and reported.

THE DIFFERENT TYPES OF WINDOW USED IN SPSS

SPSS utilises several different window types. However, new users of SPSS only need to be familiar with two of these windows, the Data Editor window and the Viewer window. We will be using these two windows in this and the next chapter. The other window types are explained very briefly here and will be covered in more detail elsewhere in the book.

The Data Editor window

The Data Editor window (or data window) is the window you see when you start up SPSS. This window looks rather like a spreadsheet and is used to enter all the data that is going to be analysed. You can think of this window as containing a table of all your raw data. We will examine this window in more detail when we start up SPSS.

The Viewer window

The Viewer window is used to display the results or output of your data analysis. For this reason we will sometimes refer to it as the Output window. We will examine this window in more detail when we perform our first simple analysis in the next chapter.

Some other windows used in SPSS

1. The Syntax Editor window is used to edit special program files called syntax files. The use of this window is explained in Chapter 12 and will be of particular interest to more advanced users.
2. The Chart Editor window is used to edit standard (not interactive) charts or graphs. The use of this window is explained in Chapter 12.
3. The Pivot Table Editor window is used to edit the tables that SPSS uses to present the results of your analysis. The use of this window is explained in Chapter 12.
4. The Text Output Editor window is used to edit the text elements of the output shown in the Viewer window. The use of this window is described briefly in Chapter 12.

Section 4: Starting SPSS

Start up SPSS by double clicking on the icon on your desk top or selecting SPSS for Windows from the applications on your machine.

> **TIP** If you do not have an SPSS icon on your desktop then click on the Start button at the bottom left hand corner of the screen, then select **Programs** and then select **SPSS 13.0 for Windows** (or the latest version you have).

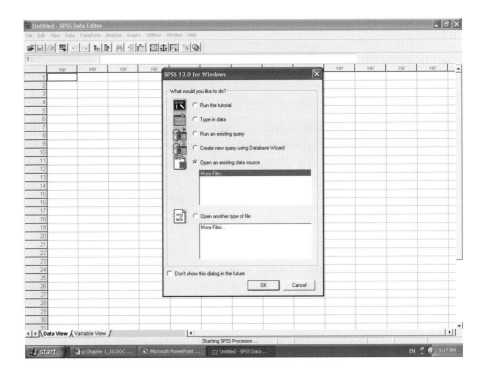

If SPSS opens in a smaller window, then click on the maximise button ▣ in the top right hand corner of the SPSS window. The image shown above is the opening screen for SPSS Version 13.0.

Unless a previous user has switched it off, the box shown below will appear in the centre of the opening screen. This box is an example of a dialogue box. SPSS makes extensive use of dialogue boxes to allow you to control the program.

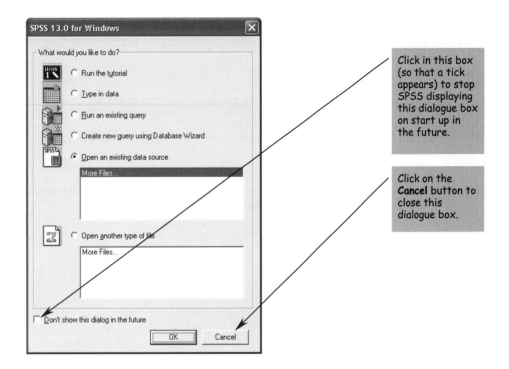

Click in this box (so that a tick appears) to stop SPSS displaying this dialogue box on start up in the future.

Click on the **Cancel** button to close this dialogue box.

We are not going to use this dialogue box, so click on the **Cancel** button to close it. We will now examine the Data Editor window.

THE DATA EDITOR WINDOW

You should now be looking at the Data Editor window. The basic components of this window are labelled on the illustration below. The words across the top of the window are the menu items. Below the menu items is the tool bar. This is a collection of special buttons that perform some of the most common operations. The scroll bars and buttons on the right hand side and bottom edge of the window allow you to move the window over the data table to view all your data. The text areas at the bottom of the window give you information regarding the current status of SPSS.

These are the menu items which give access to drop down lists of commands.

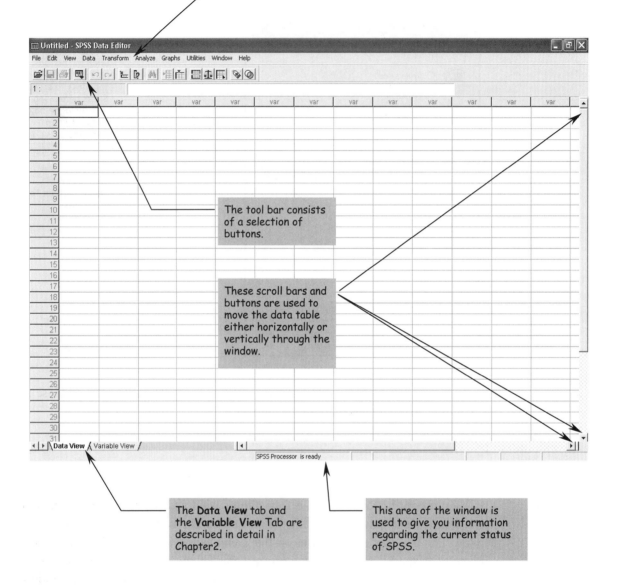

The tool bar consists of a selection of buttons.

These scroll bars and buttons are used to move the data table either horizontally or vertically through the window.

The **Data View** tab and the **Variable View** Tab are described in detail in Chapter2.

This area of the window is used to give you information regarding the current status of SPSS.

The menu and tool bars from the Data Editor windows

The menu and toolbars from the Data Editor window of SPSS Version 13 are shown below. The buttons duplicate functions that are also available from the menus. Some of the more useful buttons are explained below.

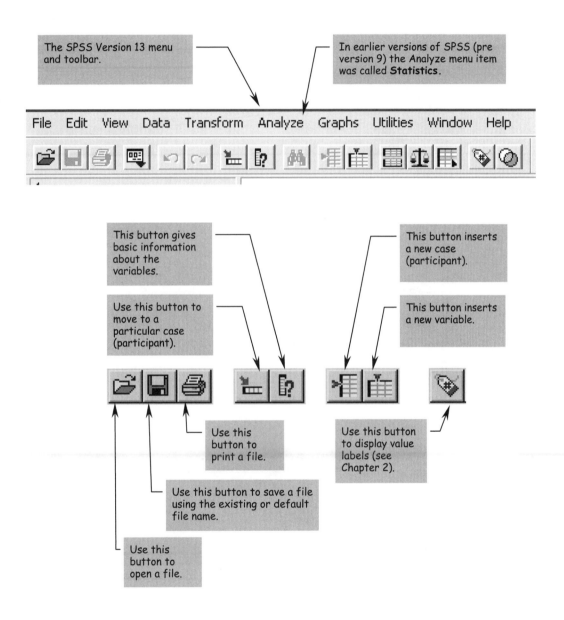

The SPSS Version 13 menu and toolbar.

In earlier versions of SPSS (pre version 9) the Analyze menu item was called **Statistics**.

This button gives basic information about the variables.

This button inserts a new case (participant).

Use this button to move to a particular case (participant).

This button inserts a new variable.

Use this button to print a file.

Use this button to display value labels (see Chapter 2).

Use this button to save a file using the existing or default file name.

Use this button to open a file.

Section 5: How to exit from SPSS

1. Click on the **File** menu item.
2. Select **Exit** from the **File** menu.

1. Click on the **File** menu item.
2. Select **Exit** from the **File** menu.

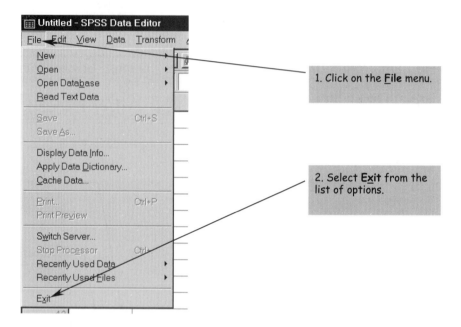

1. Click on the **File** menu.

2. Select **Exit** from the list of options.

If you have made any changes since you last saved the file, SPSS will ask you if you want to save the file before you exit (see below).

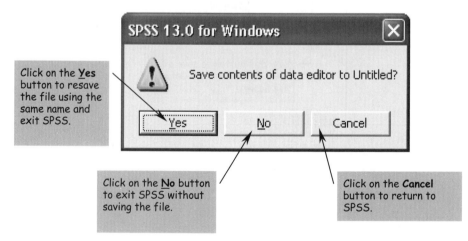

Click on the **Yes** button to resave the file using the same name and exit SPSS.

Click on the **No** button to exit SPSS without saving the file.

Click on the **Cancel** button to return to SPSS.

Section 6: Some useful option settings in SPSS

SPSS is a very flexible program which allows the user considerable control over a wide range of settings. In this section we briefly review a few of the options which you may like to adjust once you have become more familiar with SPSS. If you do not understand these setting options then leave them at their default values. Unless otherwise stated, all the screen images in this book were produced using SPSS version 13.0 with all options set to their default values. If you choose to change these or any other settings your system may not look like the images displayed in this book.

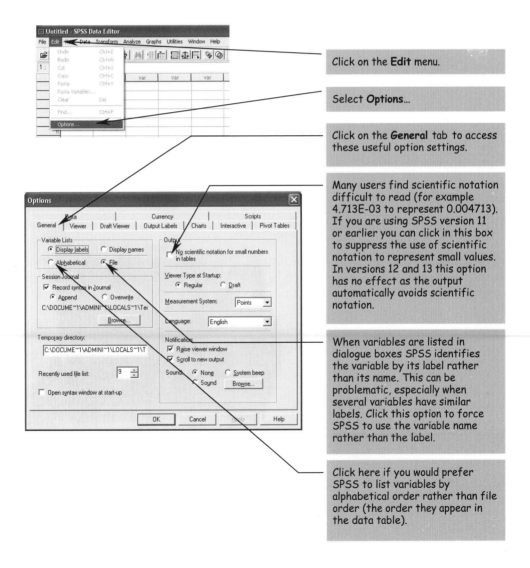

Click on the **Edit** menu.

Select **Options...**

Click on the **General** tab to access these useful option settings.

Many users find scientific notation difficult to read (for example 4.713E-03 to represent 0.004713). If you are using SPSS version 11 or earlier you can click in this box to suppress the use of scientific notation to represent small values. In versions 12 and 13 this option has no effect as the output automatically avoids scientific notation.

When variables are listed in dialogue boxes SPSS identifies the variable by its label rather than its name. This can be problematic, especially when several variables have similar labels. Click this option to force SPSS to use the variable name rather than the label.

Click here if you would prefer SPSS to list variables by alphabetical order rather than file order (the order they appear in the data table).

Chapter Two

Data entry in SPSS

The Data Editor window
Defining a variable in SPSS
Entering data
Saving a data file
Opening a data file
Data entry exercises
Answers to data entry exercises
Summary descriptive statistics and the
Viewer window

Section 1: The Data Editor window

When you start SPSS, the Data Editor window is the active window. We are going to use this window to record all the data we want to analyse. The window is arranged as a table with a large number of cells in rows and columns. If you have previously used a spreadsheet program then it should look familiar. In effect this window is a special sort of spreadsheet.

The table can be very large, and only a small part of it can be seen through the Data Editor window at any one time. You can use the scroll bars on the edges of the window to move round the table. Make sure that you are positioned at the beginning of the table – the top left hand corner.

In Psychology, we almost always enter data in the same way. Each *participant* normally occupies a *row* of the table whereas each *variable* (each thing about which we have recorded information from the participants) occupies a *column* of the table. You can think of the row numbers down the left hand side of the table as the participant numbers (SPSS refers to these as *case numbers*).

> **TIP** Normally each row represents an individual participant and each column represents a variable.

THE ARRANGEMENT OF THE DATA IN THE DATA EDITOR WINDOW

The precise way that the data are entered in the Data Editor window is critical and will depend, in part, on the details of your study. If you are entering data from an experiment, then you need to consider the design employed. In an independent groups design, each participant will provide one measure of performance. In addition, you will need to indicate which of your experimental groups each participant was assigned to. Thus, the most basic independent groups design will require that you use one column of your data table to record which group your participant was in, and a second column to record that participant's score. By comparison, in a repeated measures design each participant's performance will be assessed (at least) twice. Thus you will have a measure of performance under one set of conditions and a second measure of performance under different conditions. You will therefore need to use two columns of your data table to record these two performance levels.

> **TIP** In SPSS, the word "variable" means a column in the data table; it does not have the same meaning as it does in experimental design. For example, in a repeated measures design there is one dependent variable that is recorded across two columns of the data table.

Before you can enter any values you must first set up the Data window. That is, you need to tell SPSS what you are going to call each variable (i.e., you must give a name to each column in the table) and what sort of values you are going to put into that column. One of the changes introduced with Version 10 of SPSS made this process slightly easier but different from earlier versions. For this reason, if you are using an earlier version, the following sections of this chapter are not appropriate and you should refer to Appendix II.

Section 2: Defining a variable in SPSS

Before you can analyse your data, SPSS needs to know that name of each of your variables and other important information about each of your variables. This process of defining the variables is described here.

THE DATA VIEW AND VARIABLE VIEW

If you look at the bottom left hand corner of the Data Editor window you will notice two "tabs". One tab is labelled "Data View" and the other is labelled "Variable View". You can think of these as the index tabs for two different pages of information. When you first enter the Data Editor window, you will either find the Data View tab or the Variable View tab selected (version 13 opens showing Variable View). If you click on the Data View tab, you will be looking at the empty data table. If you click on the Variable View tab, a different screen of information will be displayed. These two different views are illustrated on the next page.

The Data View is the screen you will use when entering your data into SPSS. At present this view shows an empty data table in which each of the variables (columns) is labelled "var". Before you can type your data into this data table you must set it up so that it is ready to receive your data. SPSS needs to know the name of each of your variables so that these names can be inserted at the top of the columns of the data table. In addition, you need to give SPSS other important information about each of your variables. This process of defining the variables is undertaken in the Variable View. If you click on the Variable View tab you will notice that in this view the columns are headed **Name**, **Type**, **Width**, **Decimals** etc. In the Variable View of the data table the variables are arranged down the side of the table and each column gives information about a variable. For example, in the column headed **Name** we are going to type the name of each variable, in the **Type** column we are going to tell SPSS what type of variable this is and so on.

> **TIP** As explained earlier, in SPSS each row of the data table represents data from one case and each column contains data from one variable. However, in the Variable View of the Data Editor window, the columns and rows are used differently. In this view each row gives information about one variable. Don't let this confuse you – remember once you have set up all your variables and are ready to enter your data, you will return to the Data View where a row is a case (usually a participant) and a column is a variable.

This is the Data View of the Data Editor window.

Note that the Data View tab is at the front. This tells you that you are looking at the Data View.

Click on the Variable View tab to change to the Variable View– see below.

This is the Variable View of the Data Editor window.

Note that the Variable View tab is now at the front.

TIP   Henceforth, when we refer to "the Data Editor window" without specifying which view, we will be referring to the Data View.

If you are not already in the Variable View of the Data Editor, click on the Variable View tab to switch to that view. We will now use this view to set up each of the variables we need.

> **TIP** An alternative way to switch from the Data View to the Variable View is to double click on the grey header (which will probably be labelled "var") at the top of the column you wish to define. This will take you to the appropriate row of the Variable View.

Variable name

The first thing we need to do is to give the variable a meaningful name. Type the name of your first variable into the first row of the **Name** column. You should choose a variable name that makes sense to you and you are not likely to forget. Students often use the variable name "score". This is not a good choice as it tells us almost nothing about the variable. Examples of more useful variable names might include "memscore" (for participants' scores in a memory experiment), "introver" (a participant's introversion score), "sex" or "famfaces" (the number of famous faces named by a participant). Although earlier versions of SPSS restricted the length of variable names to 8 characters, this is not the case with versions 12 or 13. Nonetheless, we suggest you keep the length of the name you choose to something close to 8 characters (else it might not be legible in Data View) and it must start with a letter of the alphabet (i.e. not a number). Variable names cannot contain spaces or some special characters such as colons, semicolons, hyphens or commas (full stops, the @, #, $ and _ characters are allowed). If you enter an invalid variable name SPSS will warn you when you try to move from the **Name** column.

> **TIP** The underline character (_) can be used in place of spaces in variable names. For example the name "Q1_1" might be used for the scores from Question 1 Part 1.

We have given the first variable the variable name "Sex" as we are going to use this variable to code the sex of our participants.

Once you have entered the variable name, use either the mouse (point and click) or the tab key to move to the next column of the table. As you move the cursor, several of the other columns of the table will be filled with either words or numbers. These are the default settings for the variable "sex". You can leave these settings as they are, or you can change some or all of them before moving on to define your next variable. Below we explain each of the settings and how to adjust them.

Variable type

The second column in the Variable View table is headed **Type**. SPSS can handle variables of several different types. For example, variables can be numeric (containing numbers) or string (containing letters) or even dates. The **Type** column is used to indicate what type each variable is. The **Type** will now be set to **Numeric** (unless the default settings have been changed on your copy of SPSS). If you want to change the variable type, move to the **Type** column and click on the button that appears next to the default setting. This will call up the **Variable Type** dialogue box (see below).

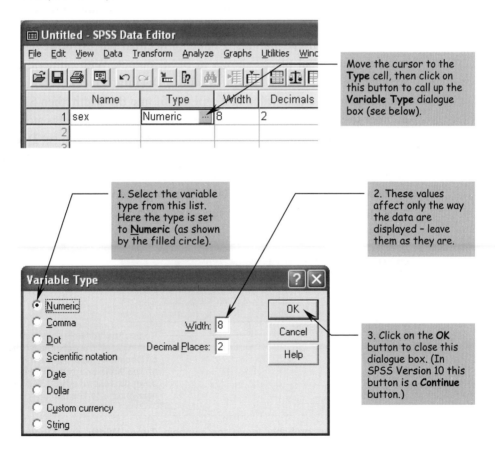

Move the cursor to the **Type** cell, then click on this button to call up the **Variable Type** dialogue box (see below).

1. Select the variable type from this list. Here the type is set to **Numeric** (as shown by the filled circle).

2. These values affect only the way the data are displayed – leave them as they are.

3. Click on the **OK** button to close this dialogue box. (In SPSS Version 10 this button is a **Continue** button.)

We strongly recommend that, until you are an experienced user, you only use numeric variables. It is very easy to use numbers to represent strings and this will save you trouble later (e.g., you can use the numbers 1 and 2 rather than "m" and "f" to record the sex of your participants). You are unlikely to need to use any of the other variable types.

> **TIP**   If at all possible avoid using string variables in SPSS – if you ignore this advice you will regret it later!

Variable width and decimal places

The **Variable Type** dialogue box also allows you to set the **Width** and **Decimal Places** of the variable (see above). Alternatively, these settings can be changed in the third and fourth columns of the Variable View (see below).

These settings adjust the number of characters before and after the decimal place used to display the variable in the Data Editor and Output Viewer windows. These settings do not affect the way the value is stored or the number of decimal places used in statistical calculations. Changing decimal places, however, does affect the number of decimal places shown in SPSS output. With numeric data the default settings are for a total **Width** of 8 with 2 **Decimal Places** (e.g., 12345.78). If you attempt to input a data value that will not fit into the width, then SPSS will round it in order to display the value. However, the value you entered is stored by SPSS and used in all calculations. One effect of this is that unless you set **Decimal Places** to zero, all values, even integers (whole numbers without decimal places) will be displayed with 2 decimal places. Thus if you enter a value of "2" in the Data Editor window, SPSS will display "2.00". This might look a little untidy, but is of little consequence and it is probably not worth altering these settings to stop this from happening.

To use the Variable View table to change the settings for the variable **Width** and number of **Decimals**, move to the appropriate column of the table and then either use the up and down buttons to adjust the value or type the new value into the cell.

> **TIP**   You can probably leave the variable **Type**, **Width** and **Decimals** settings at their default values.

Variable labels

The fifth column in the Variable View table is headed **Label**. This column is used to enter a variable label.

A variable label is simply a phrase that is associated with the variable name and which helps you to remember what data this variable contains. If you have called a variable something like "sex", then you probably do not need to be reminded about what it is describing. If, however, you have a large number of variables, then variable labels can be very useful. For example, if you are entering the data from a questionnaire, you might have a variable named "q3relbef". In this case a variable label might be invaluable, as it could remind you that this variable coded the responses to question 3 on your questionnaire which asked about religious belief. You can type in any phrase using any characters that you like, but it is best to keep it fairly short. SPSS will not try to interpret this label; it will simply insert it into the output next to the appropriate variable name when you perform any analysis.

To add a variable label, type it in to the column **Label**.

TIP   Variable labels are printed on the output produced by SPSS. Although they are not essential, they act as a reminder about the variables and can be very helpful when you are interpreting the output. We recommend you take the time to use them whenever appropriate.

Value labels

A value label is a label assigned to a particular value of a variable. You are most likely to use value labels for nominal or categorical variables. For example, we might want to use labels to remind ourselves that, when entering values for the religion of our respondents, we used the codes: 1 = Buddhist; 2 = Christian; 3 = Hindu; 4 = Muslim; 5 = Other; 0 = Atheist.

A second use for value labels is with a grouping or independent variable. For example, you might want to compare the reaction time of participants who were tested under one of several different doses of alcohol. You could use a value label to remind yourself that group 1 received no alcohol, group 2 received 1 unit of alcohol and group 3 received 2 units. Value labels will be inserted into the SPSS output to remind you what these values mean.

Value labels are entered using the **Val_ues** column of the Variable View table. At present this column will probably contain the word **None**. Click the mouse on this cell, or use the tab key to move to this cell. As you do so a button will appear at the right hand side of the cell. Click on this button to call up the **Value Labels** dialogue box (see below).

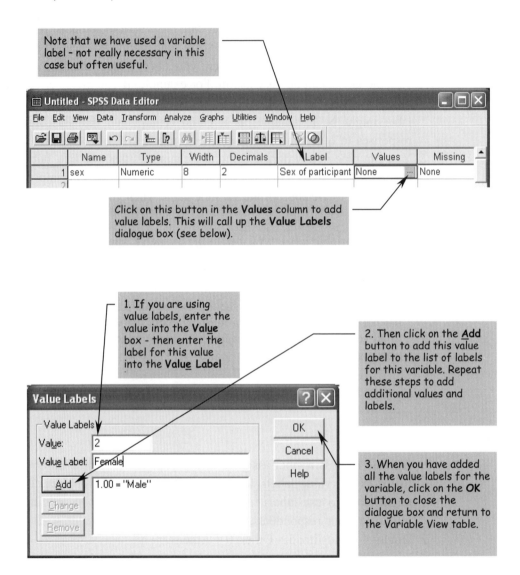

Note that we have used a variable label - not really necessary in this case but often useful.

Click on this button in the **Values** column to add value labels. This will call up the **Value Labels** dialogue box (see below).

1. If you are using value labels, enter the value into the **Val_ue** box - then enter the label for this value into the **Value Label**

2. Then click on the **Add** button to add this value label to the list of labels for this variable. Repeat these steps to add additional values and labels.

3. When you have added all the value labels for the variable, click on the **OK** button to close the dialogue box and return to the Variable View table.

Do not forget to click the **Add** button after typing the last label. If you do, SPSS will warn that "Any pending add or change operations will be lost" when you click on the **OK** button. When you return to the Variables View table, the first of your labels will be visible in the **Values** cell.

> **TIP** Value labels can be a great help when interpreting SPSS printout. Although they are not essential, we recommend that you use them when appropriate. It would not be appropriate to add value labels to some variables. For example, you would not want to add a label to every possible value of a continuous variable such as reaction time. A good rule-of-thumb is that you should add value labels to all nominal variables and should consider adding them to ordinal variables. They are unlikely to be needed for interval or ratio variables.

Missing values

Sometimes you will not have a complete set of data. For example, some participants might decline to tell you their religion or their age, or you might lose or be unable to collect data from some participants (e.g., as the result of equipment failure). These gaps in the data table are known as missing values.

When we have a missing value we need to be able to tell SPSS that we do not have valid data for this participant on this variable. We do this by choosing a value that cannot normally occur for this variable. In the religion example above, we might choose to code religion as 9 when the participant does not state their religion. Thus, 9 is the missing value for the variable religion. The missing value can be different for each variable. For age it could be 99 (unless you are testing very old people).

Before you specify any missing values, the cell in the **Missing** column of the Variable View table will contain the word **None**. To specify a missing value click in the **Missing** column of the Variable View table. A button will appear at the right hand end of the cell. Click on this button to call up the **Missing Values** dialogue box (see below).

Click on the button in the **Missing** cell to call up the **Missing Values** dialogue box (see below).

Missing Values

○ No missing values
● Discrete missing values
`9`

○ Range plus one optional discrete missing value
Low: [ ]   High: [ ]
Discrete value: [ ]

OK
Cancel
Help

1. To include up to three different missing values click on this circle (so that it becomes filled) then enter your missing value(s) in the box(es).

2. Click on the **OK** button to close the dialogue box and return to the Variable View table.

SPSS allows you to specify the missing values in several ways:

1. **No missing values**: This is the default setting for this dialogue box. If this option is selected, SPSS will treat all values for this variable as valid.
2. **Discrete missing values**: This option allows you to enter up to three discrete values. For example, 7, 9 and 11 could all be set as missing values by selecting this option and entering the values in the three boxes. If you have only one missing value enter it into the first of the three boxes (as we've done above).
3. **Range plus one optional discrete missing value**: This option allows you to indicate that a range of values is being used as missing values. For example, selecting this option and entering the values 7 and 11 in the **Low** and **High** value boxes would instruct SPSS to treat the values 7, 8, 9, 10 and 11 as missing values. If, in addition to this range of values, the value 0 were typed into the **Discrete value** box, then SPSS would treat the values 7, 8, 9, 10, 11 and 0 as missing.

In practice we rarely need more than one missing value for a variable (occasionally you might want more than one – for example, you might wish to distinguish between an unanswered question and an illegible answer as both are missing values). You will therefore almost always want to enter your missing value into the first of the **Discrete missing values** boxes. To do this, simply click on the circle next to the words **Discrete missing values** and then enter your missing value into the first of the three boxes. Now click on the **OK** button to return to the Variable View table.

> **TIP** **Missing Values** dialogue box does not allow you to label the missing values. Once you have entered them, however, you can label them in the **Value Labels** dialogue box: e.g. 9 = unanswered; 10 = illegible.

Column format

The next column of the Variable View table is labelled **Columns**. This entry in the table is used to specify the width of the column that the variable occupies in the Data View table of the Data Editor window. You can leave this value at its default setting unless you want to change the appearance of the Data View table. You may, for example, want to fit more columns onto the screen in order to see more variables without having to scroll. In this case you could reduce the width of each column. To adjust the settings, click on the cell and then use the up and down buttons that will appear at the right hand end of the cell to adjust the value. You can look at the effect of the change you have made by switching to the Data View.

TIP   Be careful when changing column widths – you might think that you only need a column width of 1 for a variable that contains numbers in the range 0–9. However, if the column width is set too small, the variable name that appears at the top of the column will not be legible. A good compromise, if you really need to change column widths, is to set the width equal to no less than the number of characters in the variable name (e.g., a column width of 3 for the variable "sex").

Column alignment

The column of the Variable View labelled **Align** allows you to specify the alignment of the text within the cells of the Data View of the Data Editor window. This setting has no effect on the operation of SPSS and only changes the appearance of the Data View table. The default setting is right alignment in which the decimal points of the values in the column are lined up. In left alignment the values are flush to the left hand end of the cell. In centre alignment the values are centred in the cell (and thus the decimal points will not necessarily line up).

If you wish to change the Column Alignment, click in the **Align** cell and then click on the menu button that will appear in the cell and select the required alignment from the drop-down list (see below).

Type	Width	Decimals	Label	Values	Missing	Columns	Align	Measure
Numeric	8	2	Sex of participant	{1.00, Male}...	9.00	8	Right	Scale

To change the column alignment, click on this button and select from the drop-down list.

Measurement

The final column of the Variable View table is labelled **Measure.** This column is used to specify the level of measurement for the variable. SPSS offers three options, **Nominal**, **Ordinal** and **Scale.**

Psychologists usually distinguish four levels of measurement, nominal, ordinal, interval and ratio (see Chapter 1). SPSS does not distinguish between interval and ratio data and uses the term **Scale** to cover a variable measured using either of these levels of measurement.

It is not essential to set the measurement option as it is only used in the creation of Interactive Charts (see Chapter 12). However, if you wish to set it, click in the **Measure** cell of the Variable View table and then click on the button that appears in the cell and select from the drop-down list (see below).

Missing	Columns	Align	Measure
9.00	7	Right	Scale
			Scale
			Ordinal
			Nominal

Select the **Scale** option for variables measured using either an Interval or Ratio scale.

Select the **Ordinal** option for variables measured using an ordinal scale.

Select the **Nominal** option for nominal variables (e.g., "sex" or "group").

Once you have completed the definition of your first variable, switch to the Data View (click on the Data View tab at the bottom right hand corner of the table). You will now see the name of your new variable appear at the top of the appropriate column of the Data Editor window (see below). If you changed the column width and/or alignment you will see the effect of these changes.

Now switch back to the Variable View of the Data Editor Window and repeat this process for each of the variables required for your data file.

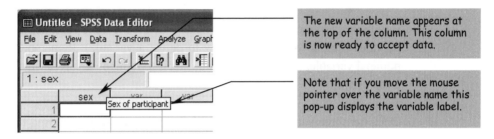

The new variable name appears at the top of the column. This column is now ready to accept data.

Note that if you move the mouse pointer over the variable name this pop-up displays the variable label.

TIP   Remember, for most variables you can accept the default settings. In practice all you need to do is to enter a variable name and, if appropriate, add variable and value labels.

COPYING VARIABLE SETTINGS

It is easy to copy the settings from one variable and "paste" these on to one or more new variables. This is one of the major advantages of the Variable View table that was introduced in Version 10 (in earlier versions of SPSS it was possible to copy variable settings, but this was a rather complex process).

Suppose, for example, that you have administered a questionnaire that contains 20 items. Each item consists of a printed statement to which the participant is asked to respond by choosing from one of several options such as "Strongly Disagree", "Disagree", "Neither Agree or Disagree", "Agree" and "Strongly Agree". In our SPSS data table, each question will be represented by a variable, which we might call Q1, Q2 etc. For each of these variables it would be useful to enter the value labels 1 = "Strongly Disagree", 2 = "Disagree" etc. This would be rather time consuming. However, if we enter these value labels for the first variable, we can then move the cursor to the **Values** cell of the Variable View table and select **Copy** from the **Edit** menu. If we now click in the cell (or select the range of cells) we want to copy these labels to, and select **Paste** from the **Edit** menu, the value labels will be copied to all the selected cells.

Section 3: Entering data

A FIRST DATA ENTRY EXERCISE

As a data entry exercise, we will enter the data from a very simple study in which we have recorded the sex (coded as 1 = male, 2 = female), the age and the memory score (number of words recalled from a list of 20) for each of five participants.

Before we can enter these data, we need to define the three variables to be used (see the previous section for details of how to define a variable). Remember that as sex is a nominal variable, we should use value labels to remind ourselves what the values 1 and 2 represent.

Once the three variables have been defined we can begin entering the data. You can copy the data from the screen-shot shown below.

Click on the top left hand cell of the table (ensure that you are at the top left hand corner of the window by checking the scroll bars). This cell will become highlighted (it will have a bold border). Any number you now type will appear in the bar above the variable names at the top of the window. If you press the Enter key or the Tab key, or use the mouse or cursor keys (up, down, left and right arrows) to move to another cell, this number will be inserted into the cell.

Moving around the Data Editor window

> **TIP**   Check that you are in Data View table before entering data.

This shows that a value is currently being entered for the fifth participant in the column called "memscore".

This value represents the memory score for the fifth participant. As you type in the number it appears both here and in the cell that was highlighted (which previously contained a dot indicating that no value has yet been entered).

These are the row or case numbers. You can think of them as participant ID numbers.

	sex	age	memscore
1	1.00	23.00	12.00
2	1.00	32.00	8.00
3	1.00	25.00	11.00
4	2.00	18.00	9.00
5	2.00	21.00	17
6	2.00	21.00	.
7			

You will probably find it easier to use the cursor keys rather than the mouse to move round the data table. Alternatively, you can press the Enter key to move down to the next participant for the current variable, or the Tab key to move across to the next variable for the current participant.

It is best to enter the data one participant at a time, working across the data table. For example, you should enter the sex, age and memory score for the first participant in row one, then for the second participant in row two and so on. If you enter the data a column at a time working down the columns (e.g., the sex of all the participants first, then their ages etc.), it is more likely that you will make a mistake. Such an error is likely to result in the data from one participant being assigned to another participant.

Once you have entered all your data into the data table, you should carefully check that you have entered it correctly. Cross-checking the data file against the original record of the data is a very important stage in the process of analysis. Either cross check the original records against the data on the screen, or against a printout of the data (see Chapter 12, Section 4, for details of how to print a copy of your data).

TIP   It is very easy to accidentally enter an extra row of data. This will appear as a row of cells filled with dots. If this has happened it is worth taking the time to remove the blank line(s) as SPSS will interpret each blank line as a participant for whom you have no data. Thus SPSS will tell you it has more cases than you expect. This "phantom participant" can affect some statistical calculations. To delete the blank case, click on the case number associated with the extra row; the case will become highlighted. Now click on the Edit menu and choose Cut or Clear. The blank case will now be deleted from the table.

Sometimes new SPSS users panic that they have "lost" their data because they cannot see it on the screen. This is often because the data have scrolled out of the window. Check that the scroll bars are set to the top left hand corner of the window.

The value labels button

If you have assigned value labels to one or more of your variables, you can choose whether you want SPSS to display the values you enter, or whether it should translate these values into the appropriate labels and display these labels. For example, in this file, we have assigned the value labels "Male" and "Female" to the values 1 and 2 of the variable "Sex". SPSS can either display the values (i.e., the numerals "1" or "2") or the labels "Male" or "Female". Clicking on the **Value Labels** button on the toolbar of the Data Editor window will toggle between these two display states (see below). Note, regardless of whether you choose to display values or labels, you must enter the data in the form of values (i.e., you must enter "1" or "2" and not "Male" or "Female"). This option affects only the way the data are displayed in the Data Editor window, and not the way they are entered or analysed.

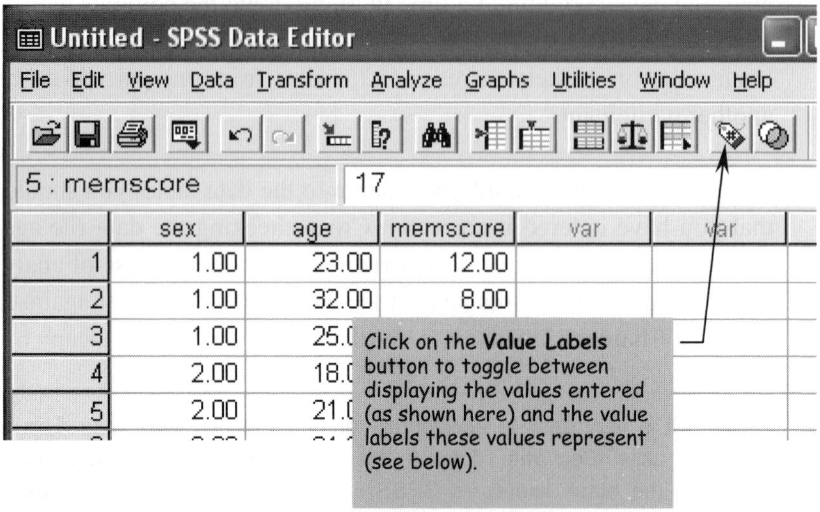

Click on the **Value Labels** button to toggle between displaying the values entered (as shown here) and the value labels these values represent (see below).

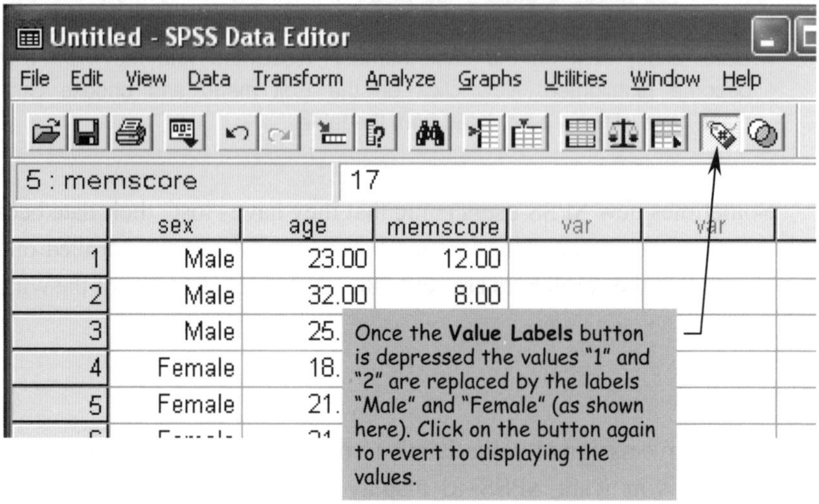

Once the **Value Labels** button is depressed the values "1" and "2" are replaced by the labels "Male" and "Female" (as shown here). Click on the button again to revert to displaying the values.

When your data are entered, checked and if necessary corrected, they should be saved to disk. We describe how to save the data file in the next section.

Section 4: Saving a data file

You will have spent a lot of time entering your data, so remember to save the data file as soon as you have checked it carefully. If you are entering a large amount of data it is a good idea to save the file every few minutes.

TO SAVE THE DATA TO A FILE

Click on the menu item (word) **File** at the top of the screen. Now click on either **Save** or **Save As**.

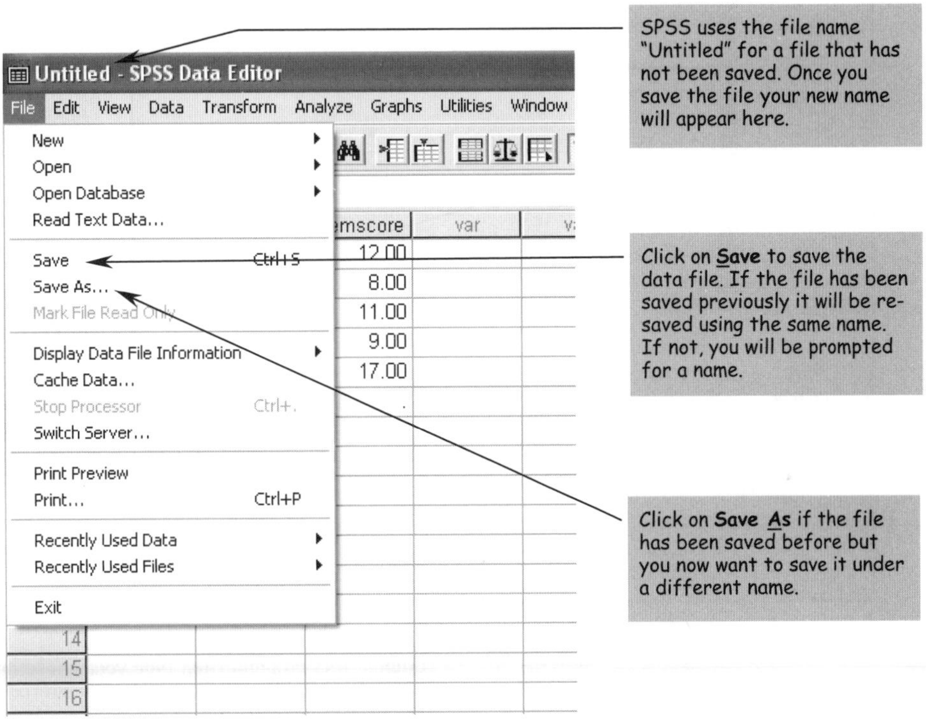

SPSS uses the file name "Untitled" for a file that has not been saved. Once you save the file your new name will appear here.

Click on **Save** to save the data file. If the file has been saved previously it will be re-saved using the same name. If not, you will be prompted for a name.

Click on **Save As** if the file has been saved before but you now want to save it under a different name.

Select **Save** to resave the file using the existing name. The resaved file will replace the old version. If the file has not been saved previously, or if you click on **Save As**, you will be presented with the **Save Data As** dialogue box (see below).

Type the name for the file into the **File name** box. The file name you choose should be reminiscent of the study from which the data originated (e.g., "memorystudy"). You should not use a full stop in the file name and should not attach a suffix to the file name. By default SPSS will attach the suffix ".sav" to any name you enter. Do not change this suffix, or SPSS might not recognise the file as a data file. Check which disk and which directory the file is going to be saved to, before you click the **Save** button. You may want to save the file to a different drive, or to a disk or USB stick. To do this follow the instructions given below ("Changing the drive or directory"). Alternatively you can put the drive letter at the start of the file name (e.g., "a:\mnemonic experiment").

This shows that the current directory (folder) is called SPSS data files.

Click here to change the Drive or Directory (see next page).

This box shows the names of existing data files in the current directory and also any sub-directories (here there aren't any sub-directories).

Click in this box and then type your chosen file name. By default SPSS uses the file suffix ".**sav**" for data files (as shown in the **Save as type** box). So if you just enter the name "**Mnemonic experiment**" for a data file, SPSS will save it as "**Mnemonic experiment.sav**".

Changing the drive or directory

To change the current drive or directory before saving a file, click on the button at the end of the **Save in** box, and select the drive or directory you require from the drop-down list that appears (see below).

Click here to reveal a list of drives and directories.

Select the drive or directory you require from the list. To save the file to a floppy disk select drive (A:).

TIP   Avoid using a dot in an SPSS file name. If you do use a dot, and if you include three characters after the dot, then SPSS will treat the characters after the dot as the suffix. For example, if you call the file "file name with a .dot" SPSS will treat the ".dot" part of the name as the suffix, and will not add the standard ".sav" suffix. This is important because when you come to reopen the file, SPSS will not list it as a data file. Students often tell us that the computer has "lost" their data file and this is usually the explanation. If you think this has happened to you, see the tip box at the end of the next section ("Opening a data file").

You can now enter and save data in SPSS. To practise your new skills enter the data from the experiments described in Section 7. We will be using this data file later to undertake some statistical procedures. First, though, we will tell you how to open a file that has been saved previously.

Section 5: Opening a data file

To open a data file follow the instructions below.

1. Ensure that the Data Editor window is the active window. If this is not the case, click on the **Goto Data** button on the toolbar at the top of the window (alternatively, select the Data Editor window from the list available under the **Window** menu).

1. If the Data Editor is not the active window, then click on this **Goto Data** button which is available on the toolbar of all other windows. This will return you to the Data Editor window.

2. Click on the **File** menu.
3. Select **Open** from the drop-down menu. This brings up another menu showing the different SPSS files that you can open.
4. Click on **Data**. The **Open File** dialogue box will now appear (see next page).

2. Click on the word **File** at the top of the screen.

3. Moving the mouse over **Open** will bring up another menu.

4. Click on **Data** to open the **Open File** dialogue box.

5. The current directory is indicated in the box labelled **Look in**. To change the directory or to select a different drive (such as drive **A:**), click on the button at the right hand end of this box, and select the drive or directory you require (as explained at the end of Section 4).

6. Examine the list of data files shown in the box, and click on the name of the file you want to open.

7. The name of the file you have selected will appear in the **File name** box. Alternatively, if you are sure you know it, you can type the name of the file directly into this box.

8. Finally, click on the **Open** button to open the file and load the data into the Data Editor window.

> **TIP**   If you double-click on the name of the file it will be opened immediately without the need to click on the **Open** button.

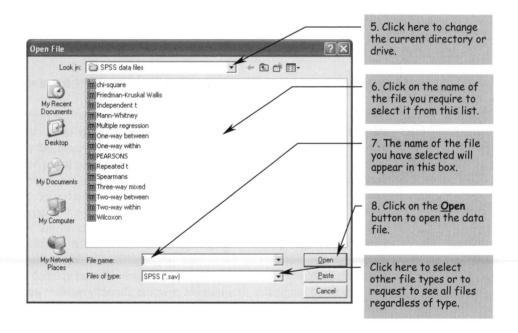

5. Click here to change the current directory or drive.

6. Click on the name of the file you require to select it from this list.

7. The name of the file you have selected will appear in this box.

8. Click on the **Open** button to open the data file.

Click here to select other file types or to request to see all files regardless of type.

> **TIP**   If the file you are looking for has a suffix other than "**.sav**", SPSS will not recognise it as a data file and will not display it in the dialogue box. If you can't find the file you are looking for, and think that it may have been saved with some other file name suffix, click on the button at the right hand end of the **Files of type** box and select "**All files *.***" from the list of file types offered. All the files in the current directory, regardless of type or suffix name will now be displayed in the dialogue box. If you find that your data file was saved with some other suffix, load it and then immediately resave it with the "**.sav**" suffix.

Section 6: Data entry exercises

In this section, we are going to practise entering data from two different types of experimental design. Later in this chapter and in subsequent chapters we will use these data files to demonstrate other procedures. Take the time to complete these exercises, as they will help you to appreciate the way that the design employed in a study influences the shape of the data file. When you have completed these two data files, compare them to the ones shown in the next section.

DATA FROM AN INDEPENDENT GROUPS (OR BETWEEN-SUBJECTS) DESIGN

As we saw in Chapter 1, in the independent groups design we are comparing the performance of two or more groups of different participants. In the example below, we have used this design to investigate the effect of a mnemonic instruction given to a group of participants before they were asked to learn a total of 20 words.

RODENTS IN SPACE: A SIMPLE MEMORY EXPERIMENT

Twenty-one first-year undergraduates participated in a simple memory experiment designed to investigate the effect of a mnemonic strategy upon memory for paired words. The participants were randomly divided into two groups. All participants were given 2 minutes to memorise a list of 20 words presented in pairs. All the participants were told to memorise the words, but those in one group, the mnemonic instruction group, were advised to try to form a mental image to link the two words in a pair (e.g., for the word pair ROCKET – HAMSTER a participant might imagine a small furry rodent being fired off into outer space). The participants in the other group, the non-mnemonic group, were not given this instruction. After learning the words for 2 minutes the participants were then required to complete some simple mental arithmetic problems for 2 minutes. Finally they were required to recall any of the words that they could remember. The number of words correctly recalled was recorded. The data are summarised below.

Memory scores (out of 20) for the mnemonic instruction group:

  20, 18, 14, 18, 17, 11, 20, 18, 20, 19, 20

Memory scores (out of 20) for the non-mnemonic group:

  10, 20, 12, 9, 14, 15, 16, 14, 19, 12

Using these data attempt to do the following:

1. Set up a data file to record this data. Give appropriate names to the variables you are using.
2. Apply value and variable labels where appropriate.
3. Enter and check the data, then save the file to floppy disk using an appropriate file name.
4. Ensure that you can re-open the file.

Now compare the data file you have constructed to the one illustrated in the next section of this chapter.

DATA FROM A REPEATED MEASURES (OR WITHIN-SUBJECTS) DESIGN

As you will remember, in the repeated measures design, every participant is exposed to each condition and thus contributes a data point from each level of the independent variable. This will be reflected in the structure of the data file, which will have a column for each level of the independent variable. In the example below we have used this design to investigate mental representation.

COMPARING MENTAL IMAGES

If you ask someone the question "How many windows are there in the front of your home?" most people will report that they attempt to answer the question by "inspecting" a mental image of their house. There has been a great deal of debate about the use of mental images, with some psychologists claiming that information is actually stored in a more abstract form and that the mental images that we feel we are inspecting are illusory (i.e., they are an "epiphenomenon"). However, several lines of evidence do support the idea that we are able to manipulate information utilising a form of representation that shares many qualities with mental images. This experiment is modelled on one such line of evidence.

Continued on the next page.

Imagine you were asked to decide whether or not a Lion was bigger than a Wolf. You could make your decision by recalling information about size that was represented in some abstract form. Alternatively, you could form a mental image of these two animals standing side-by-side and decide which was the taller. If you adopted the mental imagery approach, then you might expect the decision to take longer when the two animals were of a similar size than when they were of very different sizes. If the decision were based on a more abstract form of representation, then you would expect the relative size of the animals to have no effect on the speed of the decision. Thus, psychologists have argued that if it takes longer to compare the size of two similar sized animals than two dissimilar sized animals, this would offer some support for the idea that these decisions are based on the manipulation of image-like forms of mental representation.

In our experiment each of the 16 participants undertook 20 trials. In each trial the participant was presented with a pair of animal names and had to decide as quickly as possible which of the animals was the largest. The time taken to make this decision was recorded (in milliseconds). For half of the trials the difference in size between the two animals was large (e.g., Mosquito – Elephant) and for the other half of the trials the difference in size was small (e.g., Horse – Zebra). In the data table below we have recorded the mean decision time (in milliseconds) for the large size difference trials and for the small size difference trials.

DATA

Participant	Large diff.	Small diff.
1	936	878
2	923	1005
3	896	1010
4	1241	1365
5	1278	1422
6	871	1198
7	1360	1576
8	733	896
9	941	1573
10	1077	1261
11	1438	2237
12	1099	1325
13	1253	1591
14	1930	2742
15	1260	1357
16	1271	1963

Using the above data, attempt to do the following:

1. Set up an SPSS data file to record these data. Give appropriate names to the variables you are using.
2. Apply value and variable labels where appropriate.
3. Enter and check the data, then save the file to floppy disk using an appropriate file name.
4. Ensure that you can re-open the file.

Now compare your data file to the one shown in the next section of this chapter.

Section 7: Answers to data entry exercises

RODENTS IN SPACE: AN EXAMPLE OF THE DATA FILE FROM AN INDEPENDENT GROUPS DESIGN

Below is a screen-shot of the data file we constructed for this simple memory experiment. Your data table might not look identical, but should have the same basic characteristics. Note that there are two variables. The first is a nominal variable (or *grouping variable)* that we have used to record whether the participant was in the mnemonic or in the non-mnemonic group. The second variable is a ratio variable and has been used to record the number of words each participant recalled. If you have the **Value Labels** button (on the tool bar) depressed, then the first column will display the value labels rather than the values (i.e., mnemonic or non-mnemonic rather than 1 or 2 as shown here).

> **TIP** Remember, the data file constructed for an experiment that employed an independent groups design will always require a nominal variable that is used to indicate the condition under which each participant was tested.

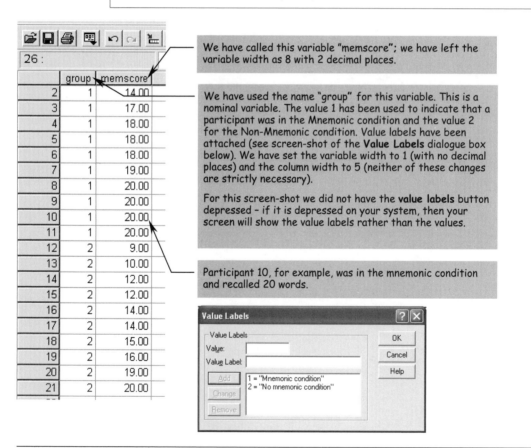

We have called this variable "memscore"; we have left the variable width as 8 with 2 decimal places.

We have used the name "group" for this variable. This is a nominal variable. The value 1 has been used to indicate that a participant was in the Mnemonic condition and the value 2 for the Non-Mnemonic condition. Value labels have been attached (see screen-shot of the **Value Labels** dialogue box below). We have set the variable width to 1 (with no decimal places) and the column width to 5 (neither of these changes are strictly necessary).

For this screen-shot we did not have the **value labels** button depressed – if it is depressed on your system, then your screen will show the value labels rather than the values.

Participant 10, for example, was in the mnemonic condition and recalled 20 words.

COMPARING MENTAL IMAGES: AN EXAMPLE OF THE DATA FILE FROM A REPEATED MEASURES DESIGN

Below is a screen-shot of the data file we constructed to record the data from our mental imagery experiment. Your data table might not look identical, but should have the same basic characteristics.

There are two variables in the file, but in contrast to the data table for the independent groups design, here each of the variables is used to record the performance of the participants. As this is a repeated measures design each participant was tested under both conditions. There is therefore no need for a nominal variable.

Compare this data file to the one on the previous page. Make sure that you understand why these two files have a different structure.

	large	small	var
1	936.00	878.00	
2	923.00	1005.00	
3	896.00	1010.00	
4	1241.00	1365.00	
5	1278.00	1422.00	
6	871.00	1198.00	
7	1360.00	1576.00	
8	733.00	896.00	
9	941.00	1573.00	
10	1077.00	1261.00	
11	1438.00	2237.00	
12	1099.00	1325.00	
13	1253.00	1591.00	
14	1930.00	2742.00	
15	1260.00	1357.00	
16	1271.00	1963.00	
17			
18			

We have called this variable "small" and are using it to record the participants' mean decision times on the small-difference trials. As this is a ratio variable, we have not assigned any value labels and have left the variable width and the column width at their default values.

We have given this variable the name "large" and are using it to record the participants' mean decision times for the large-difference trials. The settings are as for the variable "small" described above.

Section 8: Summary descriptive statistics and the Viewer window

DESCRIPTIVE STATISTICS

Summarising data

Descriptive statistics are a set of statistical tools that allow us to accurately describe a large volume of data with just a few values. Common descriptives include measures of central tendency (e.g., mean, median and mode), confidence intervals and measures of dispersion (e.g., range, minimum and maximum, interquartile range, standard deviation and variance). A research report should always include descriptive statistics. You should use them to provide the reader with some information about the sample, and to describe the data before performing an inferential statistical test.

There are several ways of obtaining descriptive statistics from SPSS. Descriptive statistics are often available as an optional output from the inferential statistics, but there are also several SPSS commands designed specifically to produce descriptives. Two of the most useful of these procedures are **Frequencies** and **Explore**.

The **Frequencies** command is very useful when you want to obtain descriptive statistics on all participants – for example if you want to find out the mean age of your participants. The major limitation of the **Frequencies** command is that unless you also use some other procedure (see Chapter 6), you cannot obtain descriptive statistics broken down by a grouping variable. For example, using the **Frequencies** command alone you cannot find easily the mean age for the male and for the female participants, or, in the case of an independent groups design, the mean memory score for participants in groups 1 and 2. In these situations, the **Explore** command should be used to produce descriptives broken down by one or more variable.

Illustrating data

Another way of describing data is to illustrate it in a graph (figure, chart). Graphs are described at appropriate points throughout the book and in Chapter 12, where we also show you how they can be pasted into a word processing document.

> **TIP**   You can produce some basic graphs with **Frequencies**. However, **Explore** has a much larger selection of summary descriptives than does **Frequencies**.

THE FREQUENCIES COMMAND

The **Frequencies** command produces frequency distribution tables showing the number of cases (participants) who have a particular score on each variable. For example, a frequency distribution table of the variable age would tell you how many of your participants were 20 year olds, how many 21 and so on for each of the ages represented in the group of participants. In addition to this important function, the **Frequencies** command will also produce a range of descriptives including measures of central tendency and measures of dispersion.

To obtain a Frequencies output:

1. Once your data are entered, checked and saved, click on the word **Analyze** at the top of the screen (see below).
2. Select (click on) **Descriptive Statistics**.
3. Select **Frequencies**.

SPSS will now present you with the **Frequencies** dialogue box shown below. This dialogue box contains two boxes. The left hand box lists all the variables in the data file. The right hand box (which will be empty when you first use the command) lists the names of the variables which will be analysed (i.e., for which a frequencies printout will be produced).

4. Select the first variable you want included in the frequency analysis by clicking on the variable name in the left hand box.

5. The arrow button between the two boxes will now be highlighted and will be pointing to the right hand box. Click on this arrow button. The selected variable will be moved to the right hand box. Repeat this procedure until the right hand box contains the names of all the variables you want included in the Frequencies analysis.

TIP   You can select more than one variable by holding down the either the <shift> key or the <ctrl> while clicking on the names of the variables. If you <shift> click the first and last variables in a list, all the variables in the list will be selected. By contrast, holding down the <ctrl> key while clicking on the names of variables will either select or deselect just that variable. By using <ctrl>click and <shift>click in combination you can quickly select just those variable you require. You can then click on the arrow key to move all the selected variables into the right hand box.

---

6.   When you have selected all the variables you are interested in, click on the **Statistics** button – Statistics (**not** the word **Statistics** on the menu bar in Version 8). This will reveal the **Frequencies: Statistics** dialogue box (shown below) which lists all the descriptive statistics available in the **Frequencies** command.

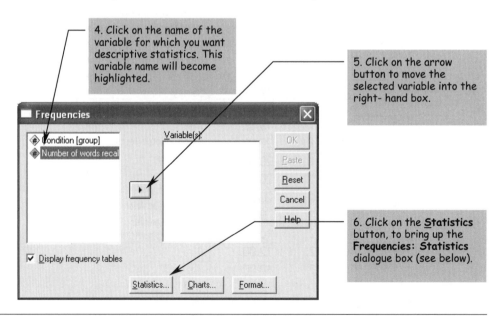

7. In the **Frequencies: Statistics** dialogue box (see below) select all the descriptive statistics you require by clicking in the boxes so that a tick appears.

8. When you have selected all the statistics you require, click on ⌷Continue⌷ (the **Continue** button) to return you to the **Frequencies** dialogue box (see below).

7. Click in the boxes next to the names of the descriptive statistics that you require. A tick in a box indicates that a descriptive has been requested. In this example, we have requested the Mean, Median, Mode, Standard deviation and Variance.

8. Once you have chosen your descriptive statistics, click on the **Continue** button to return to the **Frequencies** dialogue box.

9. Finally, click on the ⌷OK⌷ button to execute the frequencies command.

9. Click on the **OK** button to execute the Frequencies command.

The Viewer window will now become the active window. The results of the frequencies analysis will be presented in this window.

TIP Clicking on the **Format** button in the **Frequencies** dialogue box will allow you to adjust the way the output appears on the page. Experiment with these settings to discover the different ways of organising the output.

On page 63 we have annotated the Frequencies output. This output was produced using the data file for the mental imagery experiment that we entered earlier in this chapter. We requested the mean, mode, median, standard deviation and variance for both of the variables in this file. However, before we examine this output we need to learn a little about the Viewer window.

THE VIEWER WINDOW

The Viewer window is composed of two distinct parts or "panes". The left hand pane acts as a "navigator" or "outline". This is a bit like a table of contents that lists all of the components of the output that are shown in the larger pane. Clicking on an icon in the navigator pane moves you to that part of the output in the main or "display" pane.

This is the navigator pane of the Viewer window. The arrow (which is red on your screen) indicates the part of the output we are currently looking at in the main pane.

This display pane shows the output produced by SPSS. For longer outputs, a scroll bar will appear on the right which allows you to scroll up and down or you can navigate yourself by clicking on the icons in the smaller pane.

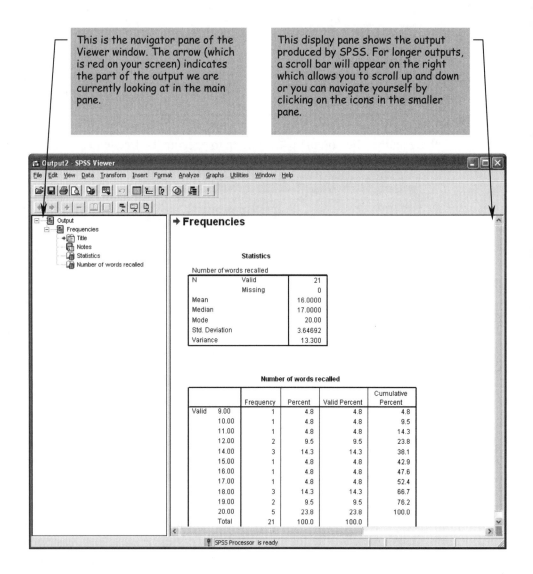

Statistics

Number of words recalled

N	Valid	21
	Missing	0
Mean		16.0000
Median		17.0000
Mode		20.00
Std. Deviation		3.64692
Variance		13.300

Number of words recalled

		Frequency	Percent	Valid Percent	Cumulative Percent
Valid	9.00	1	4.8	4.8	4.8
	10.00	1	4.8	4.8	9.5
	11.00	1	4.8	4.8	14.3
	12.00	2	9.5	9.5	23.8
	14.00	3	14.3	14.3	38.1
	15.00	1	4.8	4.8	42.9
	16.00	1	4.8	4.8	47.6
	17.00	1	4.8	4.8	52.4
	18.00	3	14.3	14.3	66.7
	19.00	2	9.5	9.5	76.2
	20.00	5	23.8	23.8	100.0
	Total	21	100.0	100.0	

Points to note about the two panes of the Viewer window

1. Output can be hidden or displayed. A closed book icon represents a hidden section of output and an open book represents a section of output that is being displayed. Double-click on a book icon to either open or close it and either display or hide the associated section of output.

2. Click on one of the minus signs to collapse and hide all of the output from a command. Click on a plus sign to expand and display all of the output from a command.

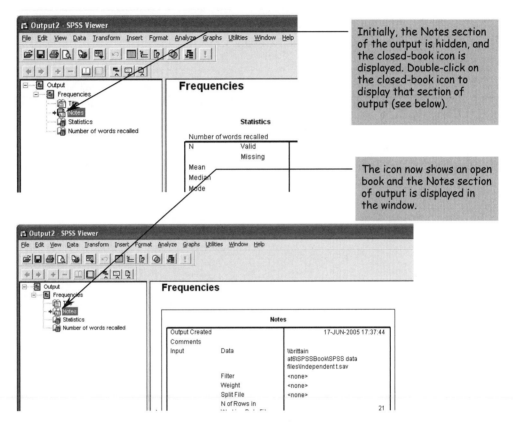

3. Most of the output produced by the SPSS commands is in the form of tables known as Pivot Tables. The "Statistics" table shown above is an example of a Pivot Table. Pivot Tables can be edited in various ways – see Chapter 12 for full details.

4. Some parts of the output are in the form of plain text. The title "Frequencies" is an example of text output.

5. You can select output either by dragging the mouse over the section in the main pane or by clicking on the appropriate icons in the navigator window. Click on the name of a command to select all the output from that command. You can select all of the output by clicking on the highest level "Output" icon. Lower level icons (e.g., "Statistics") select only that particular part of the output.

6. Selected output can be cut, copied and pasted using the relevant options on the Edit menu or can be printed using the Print command available under the File menu (see Chapter 12 for details of printing output).

> **TIP**   Sometimes you will want to delete all the output in the Viewer window. The easiest way to do this is to click on the "Output" icon in the navigator pane and then press the Delete key on your keyboard. You can now start your new analyses with a blank output window.

7. You can change the relative width of the two panes by clicking on and dragging the line that separates the two panes.

> **TIP**   If you find the icons in the navigator pane too small you can enlarge them by selecting **Outline Si̲ze** from the **V̲iew** menu. Now select **S̲mall**, **M̲edium** or **L̲arge**.

Now that we can navigate our way around the output in the Viewer window, we can look in more detail at the output produced by the Frequencies command.

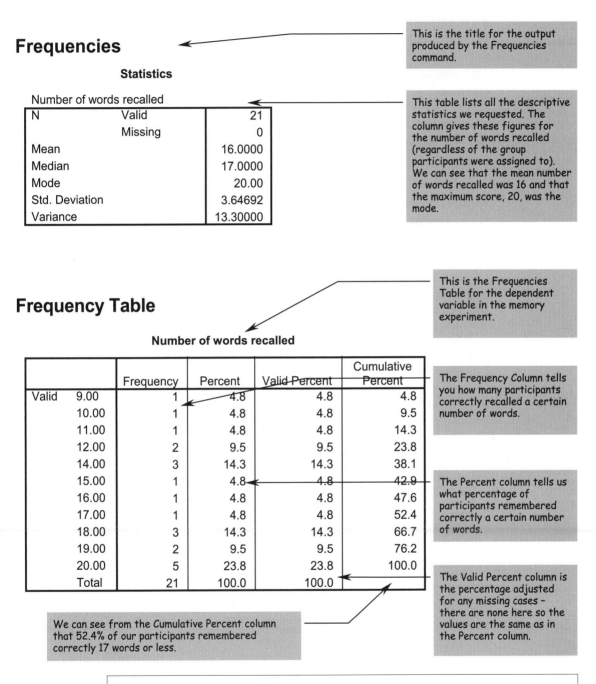

Frequencies

This is the title for the output produced by the Frequencies command.

Statistics

Number of words recalled

N	Valid	21
	Missing	0
Mean		16.0000
Median		17.0000
Mode		20.00
Std. Deviation		3.64692
Variance		13.30000

This table lists all the descriptive statistics we requested. The column gives these figures for the number of words recalled (regardless of the group participants were assigned to). We can see that the mean number of words recalled was 16 and that the maximum score, 20, was the mode.

Frequency Table

This is the Frequencies Table for the dependent variable in the memory experiment.

Number of words recalled

		Frequency	Percent	Valid Percent	Cumulative Percent
Valid	9.00	1	4.8	4.8	4.8
	10.00	1	4.8	4.8	9.5
	11.00	1	4.8	4.8	14.3
	12.00	2	9.5	9.5	23.8
	14.00	3	14.3	14.3	38.1
	15.00	1	4.8	4.8	42.9
	16.00	1	4.8	4.8	47.6
	17.00	1	4.8	4.8	52.4
	18.00	3	14.3	14.3	66.7
	19.00	2	9.5	9.5	76.2
	20.00	5	23.8	23.8	100.0
	Total	21	100.0	100.0	

The Frequency Column tells you how many participants correctly recalled a certain number of words.

The Percent column tells us what percentage of participants remembered correctly a certain number of words.

The Valid Percent column is the percentage adjusted for any missing cases – there are none here so the values are the same as in the Percent column.

We can see from the Cumulative Percent column that 52.4% of our participants remembered correctly 17 words or less.

TIP   When reporting summary descriptive statistics, you should think about how many decimal places to use. A rule-of-thumb is to round to one more decimal place than you measured.

The Explore command allows you easily to obtain descriptive statistics for separate groups of participants. For example, we can use it to display the mean and standard deviation of the memory scores separately for the participants in the Mnemonic and Non-Mnemonic groups of our simple memory experiment as well as the confidence intervals.

To obtain an Explore output:

1. Once your data are entered, checked and saved, click on the word **Analyze** at the top of the screen (see below).
2. Select (click on) **D̲escriptive Statistics**.
3. Select **Explore**.

SPSS will now present you with the **Explore** dialogue box shown on the next page. This dialogue box contains several boxes with the left hand box listing all the variables in the data file.

4. Select the variable for which the descriptives are required by clicking on the variable name (Number of words recalled) in the left hand box. The arrow buttons will now be highlighted. Click on the top arrow button and the selected variable will be moved to the top box called the **Dependent List**.

5. Select the grouping variable by clicking on the variable name (Condition) in the left hand box. Click on the middle arrow button and the selected variable will be moved to the middle box called the **Factor List**.

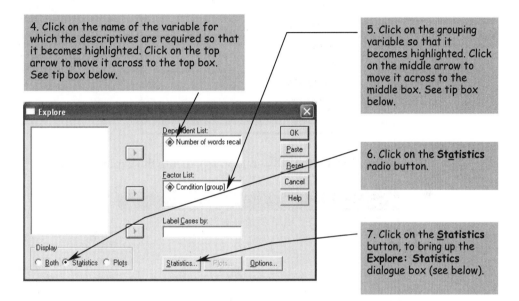

6. Check that the **Statistics** radio button is selected.

7. Click on the Statistics button – Statistics (not the word Statistics on the menu bar in Version 8). This will reveal the **Explore: Statistics** dialogue box (shown below).

> **TIP**   We have shown you here how to use the Explore command when your data are from an experiment involving an independent groups design. If your data are from an experiment involving a repeated measures design, then there will be several columns/variables for which descriptives will be required – move all of these into the **Dependent List**. There will be no grouping variable so you would miss out step 5.

8. You should find that the box for descriptive statistics is already ticked and that the confidence interval is set to 95%. If this is the case, and you don't want to change this, click on [Continue] (the **Continue** button) to return you to the **Explore** dialogue box.

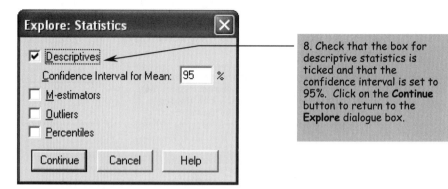

8. Check that the box for descriptive statistics is ticked and that the confidence interval is set to 95%. Click on the **Continue** button to return to the **Explore** dialogue box.

9. Finally, click on the [OK] button to execute the explore command.

9. Click on the **OK** button to execute the Explore command.

The Viewer window will now become the active window. The output of the explore analysis using the data from the memory experiment is presented on the next page.

THE OUTPUT PRODUCED BY THE EXPLORE COMMAND

Explore

These are the titles for the output produced by the Explore command.

Condition

This table provides information about the cases that were processed, listing both valid and missing cases. Check that this information is correct.

Case Processing Summary

	Condition	Cases					
		Valid		Missing		Total	
		N	Percent	N	Percent	N	Percent
Number of words recalled	Mnemonic condition	11	100.0%	0	.0%	11	100.0%
	No mnemonic condition	10	100.0%	0	.0%	10	100.0%

This table provides the descriptive statistics for each condition, including the mean, the 95% Confidence Interval, the median, variance, standard deviation as well as other information.

Descriptives

	Condition			Statistic	Std. Error
Number of words recalled	Mnemonic condition	Mean		17.7273	.86435
		95% Confidence Interval for Mean	Lower Bound	15.8014	
			Upper Bound	19.6532	
		5% Trimmed Mean		17.9747	
		Median		18.0000	
		Variance		8.218	
		Std. Deviation		2.86674	
		Minimum		11.0	
		Maximum		20.0	
		Range		9.00	
		Interquartile Range		3.00	
		Skewness		-1.595	.661
		Kurtosis		2.214	1.279
	No mnemonic condition	Mean		14.1000	1.12990
		95% Confidence Interval for Mean	Lower Bound	11.5440	
			Upper Bound	16.6560	
		5% Trimmed Mean		14.0556	
		Median		14.0000	
		Variance		12.767	
		Std. Deviation		3.57305	
		Minimum		9.00	
		Maximum		20.0	
		Range		11.00	
		Interquartile Range		5.25	
		Skewness		.337	.687
		Kurtosis		-.590	1.334

Chapter Three

Tests of difference for two sample designs

An introduction to the t-*tests*
The independent t-*test*
The paired t-*test*
An introduction to the nonparametric
     equivalents of the t-*test*
The Mann–Whitney test
The Wilcoxon test

Section 1: An introduction to the *t*-tests

The *t*-test is a parametric test used to determine whether two means are significantly different from one another. There are three types of *t*-test:

1. The single sample *t*-test
2. The independent *t*-test
3. The paired *t*-test (sometimes called the repeated, the dependent or the correlated *t*-test).

The single sample *t*-test, which is the most simple, determines whether the observed mean is different from a set value. This form of the test will not be dealt with here. The independent *t*-test is used when comparing means from two independent groups of individuals. The paired *t*-test is used when comparing the means of two sets of observations from the same individuals or from pairs of individuals (e.g., when using a matched-subjects design).

All forms of the *t*-test require that the data are of at least interval level of measurement, are normally distributed and have equal variances.

In some textbooks you might find this test referred to as the Student's *t*-test. This is because William Gossett, who devised the test, worked for the Guinness Brewing Company who did not permit him to publish under his own name. For this reason he wrote under the pseudonym of "Student".

Section 2: The independent *t*-test

This test compares the performance of the participants in group A with the performance of the participants in group B. This test should be used when the data are parametric and obtained using an independent groups design. These two groups could constitute a male and a female group because we wish to examine sex differences, or they could constitute two groups of participants who undergo different drug conditions, one a low dose drug condition and one a high dose drug condition. This type of *t*-test is often also called an *unrelated t*-test. In the example shown next, we use the data from the memory experiment used in the data entry exercise in Chapter 2. It was hypothesised that the group receiving mnemonic instructions would remember more than the group who did not receive any specific mnemonic instructions. If you use these data and follow the instructions given next, then you will be able to compare the output you produce with the annotated output that we give at the end of this section.

TO PERFORM AN INDEPENDENT *T*-TEST

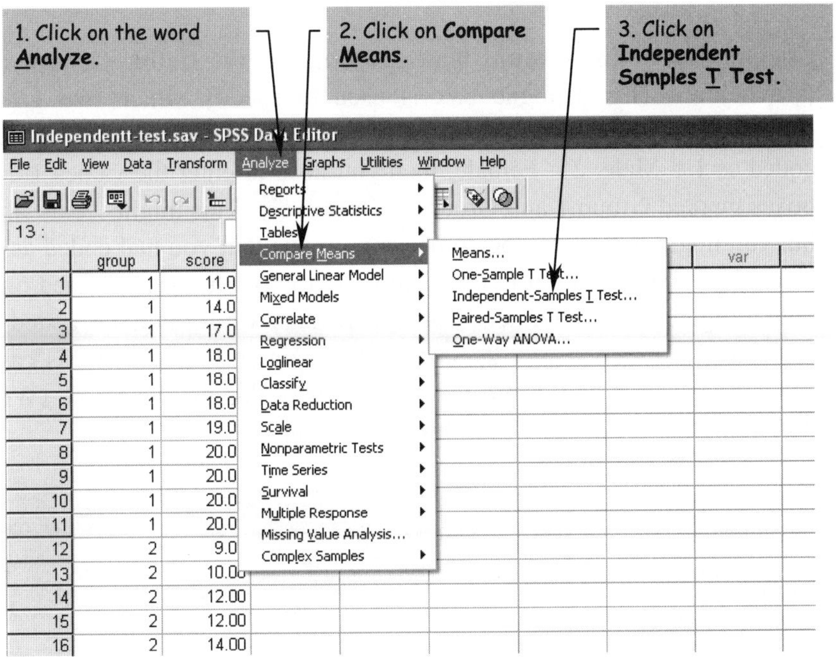

4. You will now be presented with the **Independent-Samples T Test** dialogue box (see below). As is typical in SPSS, the box on the left lists all of the variables in your data file. Click on the name of the dependent variable in your analysis and then click on the arrow button to move this variable name into the box marked **Test Variable(s)**.

5. Now click on the name of the independent variable and then click on the arrow button to move this into the box marked **Grouping Variable**.

Once you have entered the dependent and independent variables into their appropriate boxes, the dialogue box will look like this:

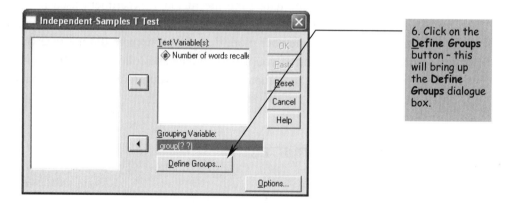

6. Click on the on the **Define Groups** button - this will bring up the **Define Groups** dialogue box.

6. Click on the **Define Groups** button to bring up the **Define Groups** dialogue box (see below). This dialogue box is used to specify which two groups you are comparing. For example, if your independent variable is SEX which you have coded as 1 = Male, 2 = Female, then you need to enter the values 1 and 2 into the boxes marked Group 1 and Group 2 respectively. This might seem rather pointless, but you might not always be comparing groups that you had coded as 1 and 2. For example, you might want to compare two groups who were defined on the basis of their religious belief (Atheists and Christians who could be coded as 0 and 2 respectively – see Chapter 2, Section 2, on Value Labels). In this case we would enter the values 0 and 2 into the two boxes in this dialogue box. (We will not be describing the use of the **Cut point** option here.)

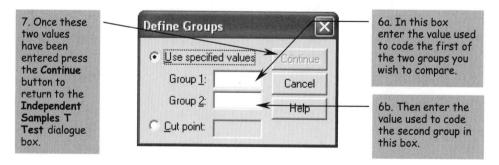

7. Once these two values have been entered press the **Continue** button to return to the **Independent Samples T Test** dialogue box.

6a. In this box enter the value used to code the first of the two groups you wish to compare.

6b. Then enter the value used to code the second group in this box.

7. Clicking on the **Continue** button in the **Define Groups** dialogue box will return you to the **Independent-Samples T Test** dialogue box. You will see that your two values have been entered into the brackets following the name of your independent variable (you may have noticed that previously there were question marks inside these brackets).

8. Finally, click on [OK] in the **Independent-Samples T Test** dialogue box. The output of the *t*-test will appear in the Output window.

The output from this independent *t*-test is shown, with annotations, on the following page. We also show you how you would describe the results of the test, were you to write a report on this experiment.

> **TIP**   When describing your results, it is normal practice to round off the values of descriptive statistics but to report all the decimal places when describing the outcome of inferential statistical tests.

Obtained Using Menu Items: Compare <u>M</u>eans > Independent-Samples <u>T</u> Test

T-Test

Useful descriptives showing that those in the mnemonic condition remembered the most words. You can calculate the effect size from these descriptives (see next page).

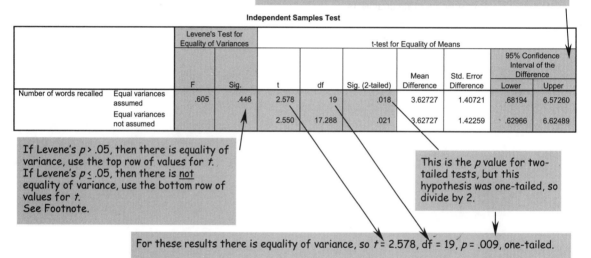

Group Statistics

	Condition	N	Mean	Std. Deviation	Std. Error Mean
Number of words recalled	Mnemonic condition	11	17.7273	2.86674	.86435
	No mnemonic condition	10	14.1000	3.57305	1.12990

These lower and upper confidence limits enclose the confidence interval. We are 95% confident that the mean difference for the population falls between 0.68 and 6.57. Note, 0 is not within those limits: remember that indicates a significant difference (Chapter 1, Section 2).

Independent Samples Test

		Levene's Test for Equality of Variances		t-test for Equality of Means					95% Confidence Interval of the Difference	
		F	Sig.	t	df	Sig. (2-tailed)	Mean Difference	Std. Error Difference	Lower	Upper
Number of words recalled	Equal variances assumed	.605	.446	2.578	19	.018	3.62727	1.40721	.68194	6.57260
	Equal variances not assumed			2.550	17.288	.021	3.62727	1.42259	.62966	6.62489

If Levene's *p* > .05, then there is equality of variance, use the top row of values for *t*.
If Levene's *p* ≤ .05, then there is <u>not</u> equality of variance, use the bottom row of values for *t*.
See Footnote.

This is the *p* value for two-tailed tests, but this hypothesis was one-tailed, so divide by 2.

For these results there is equality of variance, so *t* = 2.578, df = 19, *p* = .009, one-tailed.

TIP Equality (or at least similarity) of variance is one of the requirements for using parametric statistical tests. SPSS, however, carries out two versions of the independent groups *t*-test: the top row for when there is equality of variance and the bottom row for when the variances are unequal. If you use the latter in a report, you must note that fact.

MEASURE OF EFFECT SIZE

The output for the independent groups t-test does not include a measure of the effect and this is not an option that you can select. However, from the output you can calculate d which provides you with a measure of the extent to which two means differ in terms of standard deviations (see Chapter 1, Section 2). You use the following formula: $d = (x_1 - x_2)/\text{mean SD}$, which requires you to take the mean of one condition from the mean of the other condition (it is not important which mean to take from which, so you can ignore the sign) and divide by the mean standard deviation. To find the mean standard deviation, add the standard deviation for each condition together and divide by two: (SD of condition 1 + SD of condition 2)/2.

If you look at the output, the mean and standard deviation for each condition is provided in a table called **Group Statistics**. The mean standard deviation is $(2.9+3.6)/2 = 3.25$. Therefore the effect size, $d = (17.7–14.1)/3.25 = 1.11$. This would be considered to be a large effect size.

INFORMATION TO INCLUDE IN A REPORT

In a report you might write: More words were recalled in the mnemonic condition (mean = 17.7 words) than in the no mnemonic condition (mean = 14.1 words). The mean difference between conditions was 3.63 and the 95% confidence interval for the estimated population mean difference is between 0.68 and 6.57. The effect size was large ($d = 1.11$). An independent t-test showed that the difference between conditions was significant ($t = 2.578$, df = 19, $p = .009$, one-tailed).

It would be helpful in your report to include more than just the descriptive statistics that are provided by performing the independent t-test on SPSS. In Chapter 2, Section 8, we showed you how to use the Explore command and the output using this command with the data from the memory experiment is included at the end of that section. This output provides you with the 95% confidence interval for the mean of each condition. The sample mean for the mnemonic condition is 17.7 and we can be 95% confident that the population mean falls between 15.8 and 19.7. The sample mean for the no mnemonic condition is 14.1 and we can be 95% confident that the population mean falls between 11.5 and 16.7. A useful way of presenting this information in your report is to show it graphically using an error bar chart. On the next page, we show you how to create such a chart using SPSS.

To obtain such a chart:

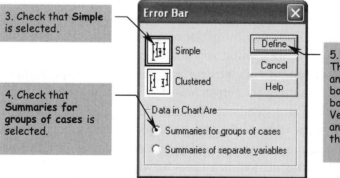

1. Click on the word **Graphs**.

2. Click on **Error Bar**. The **Error Bar** dialogue box will appear (see below).

The menu bar in Version 12 does not have as many options.

3. Check that **Simple** is selected.

4. Check that **Summaries for groups of cases** is selected.

5. Click on **Define**. This will bring up another dialogue box. This dialogue box differs between Version 12 and 13 and we show both on the next page.

TIP   Although SPSS calls it an error bar graph, it can also show confidence intervals. That is what we will demonstrate here.

Version 13

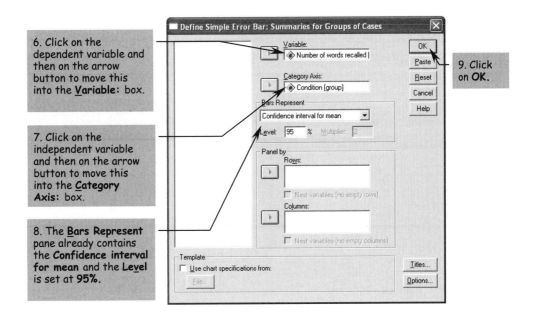

6. Click on the dependent variable and then on the arrow button to move this into the **Variable:** box.

7. Click on the independent variable and then on the arrow button to move this into the **Category Axis:** box.

8. The **Bars Represent** pane already contains the **Confidence interval for mean** and the **Level** is set at **95%**.

9. Click on **OK.**

Version 12

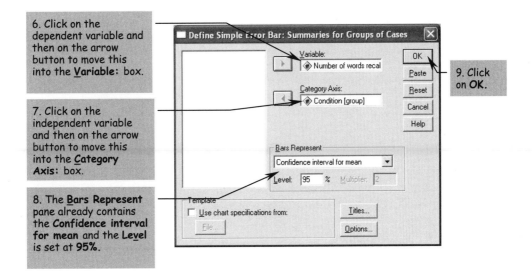

6. Click on the dependent variable and then on the arrow button to move this into the **Variable:** box.

7. Click on the independent variable and then on the arrow button to move this into the **Category Axis:** box.

8. The **Bars Represent** pane already contains the **Confidence interval for mean** and the **Level** is set at **95%**.

9. Click on **OK.**

The output is displayed next.

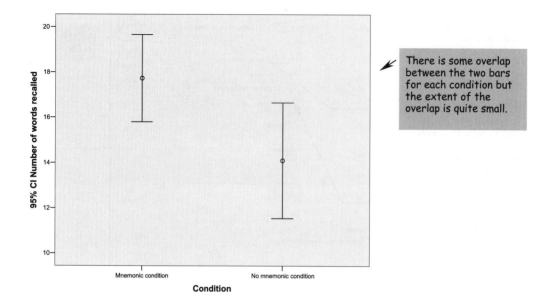

There is some overlap between the two bars for each condition but the extent of the overlap is quite small.

Section 3: The paired *t*-test

In the repeated measures design, data are collected from each participant in all levels of the independent variable. For example, we might compare participant 1's memory performance under noisy conditions with participant 1's memory performance under quiet conditions. In this situation it is likely that the data from participants will be correlated, for example if participant A has a good memory then his/her scores on a memory test will be high regardless of condition. It is for this reason that a repeated measures *t*-test is often called a *correlated* *t*-test. With a repeated measures design, it is essential that the data are kept in the correct order, so that participant 1's data on variable A is indeed compared with participant 1's data on variable B. The test itself considers pairs of data together, and for this reason this test is also known as a *paired* *t*-test.

To demonstrate the use of the paired *t*-test we are going to analyse the data from the mental imagery experiment, shown in the second data entry exercise in Chapter 2. It was hypothesised that, as participants would compare their mental images of the two animals to determine which was the larger, their decision times for the small size difference trials would be longer than for the large size difference trials. A paired *t*-test is conducted to test this hypothesis.

TO PERFORM A PAIRED *T*-TEST

4a. You will now see the **Paired-Samples T Test** dialogue box (see below). You need to choose the names of the two variables that you want to compare. As before, all of the variables in your data file are listed in the left hand box. Click on each of the **two** variables that you want to compare. These variable names will now be highlighted.

4b. Note that the names of the two variables you have highlighted will appear in the box marked **Current Selections.** This is useful when you have a large number of variables in your data file, as you may not be able to see both of the selected variables at the same time.

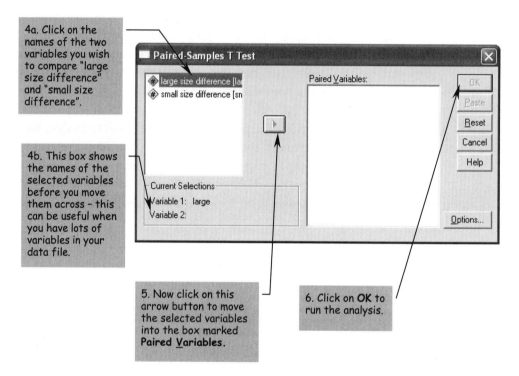

4a. Click on the names of the two variables you wish to compare "large size difference" and "small size difference".

4b. This box shows the names of the selected variables before you move them across – this can be useful when you have lots of variables in your data file.

5. Now click on this arrow button to move the selected variables into the box marked **Paired Variables.**

6. Click on **OK** to run the analysis.

SPSS will perform the paired *t*-test. The annotated output is shown on the following page.

SPSS OUTPUT FOR PAIRED (OR RELATED) *T*-TEST

Obtained Using Menu Items: > Compare <u>M</u>eans > <u>P</u>aired-Samples T Test

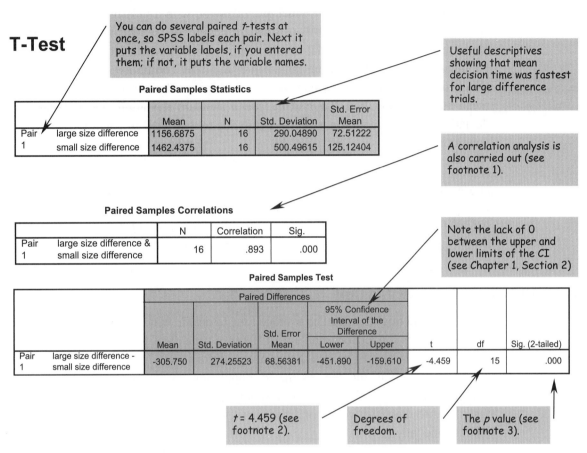

T-Test

You can do several paired *t*-tests at once, so SPSS labels each pair. Next it puts the variable labels, if you entered them; if not, it puts the variable names.

Useful descriptives showing that mean decision time was fastest for large difference trials.

Paired Samples Statistics

		Mean	N	Std. Deviation	Std. Error Mean
Pair 1	large size difference	1156.6875	16	290.04890	72.51222
	small size difference	1462.4375	16	500.49615	125.12404

A correlation analysis is also carried out (see footnote 1).

Paired Samples Correlations

		N	Correlation	Sig.
Pair 1	large size difference & small size difference	16	.893	.000

Note the lack of 0 between the upper and lower limits of the CI (see Chapter 1, Section 2)

Paired Samples Test

		Paired Differences							
					95% Confidence Interval of the Difference				
		Mean	Std. Deviation	Std. Error Mean	Lower	Upper	t	df	Sig. (2-tailed)
Pair 1	large size difference - small size difference	-305.750	274.25523	68.56381	-451.890	-159.610	-4.459	15	.000

t = 4.459 (see footnote 2).

Degrees of freedom.

The *p* value (see footnote 3).

Footnotes

1. SPSS performs a Pearson's correlation (see Chapter 4, Section 3) but you can ignore it if you only want a *t*-test. A significant correlation tells you that participants who were fast on large size difference trials were also fast on small size difference trials. It does not mean that the scores are significantly different.

2. The minus sign just means that the mean value for the first variable name in the **Paired <u>V</u>ariables** box is lower on average than the mean value for the second variable name.

3. A *p* value can never equal zero. SPSS rounds to 3 decimal places, so *p* must be less than .0005 or it would appear as .001. In a report put $p < .0005$ if the hypothesis was two-tailed. Here the hypothesis was one-tailed, so divide by 2 which gives $p < .00025$, one-tailed.

As with the independent t-test, the output for the paired t-test does not include a measure of the effect and this is not an option that you can select. However, from the output you can calculate d which provides you with a measure of the extent to which two means differ in terms of standard deviations (see Chapter 1, Section 2). You use the following formula: $d = (x_1 - x_2)/$mean SD, which requires you to take the mean of one condition from the mean of the other condition (it is not important which mean to take from which, so you can ignore the sign) and divide by the mean standard deviation. To find the mean standard deviation, add the standard deviation for each condition together and divide by two: (SD of condition 1 + SD of condition 2)/2.

If you look at the output, the mean and standard deviation for each condition is provided in a table called **Paired Samples Statistics**. The mean standard deviation is $(290.0+500.5)/2 = 395.25$. Therefore the effect size, $d = (1156.7–1462.4)/395.25 = 0.77$ (ignoring the minus sign). This would be considered to be a large effect size.

INFORMATION TO INCLUDE IN A REPORT

In a report you might write: The average time to decide which of the pair of animals was larger, was longer for small size difference trials than for large size difference trials.   The mean difference between conditions was –305.75 and the 95% confidence interval for the estimated population mean difference is between –159.61 and –451.89. The effect size was large ($d = 0.77$). A paired t-test showed that the difference between conditions was significant ($t = 4.459$, df = 15, $p <$ .00025, one-tailed).

It would be helpful in your report to include more than just the descriptive statistics that are provided by performing the paired t-test on SPSS. In Chapter 2, Section 8, we showed you how to use the Explore command and you can follow our instructions until step 4 when you would select both variables (large size difference and small size difference) to be moved to the **Dependent List** box. You would miss out step 5 but follow the remaining steps as described. The output provides you with the 95% confidence interval for the mean of each condition. Next we show you how to create an error bar chart with data from an experiment using a repeated measures design.

CREATING AN ERROR BAR CHART: REPEATED MEASURES

To obtain such a chart:

1. On the menu bar, click on **Graphs** (see Creating An Error Bar Chart: Independent Groups, above).

2. Click on **Error Bar**. This will display the **Error Bar** dialogue box (see below).

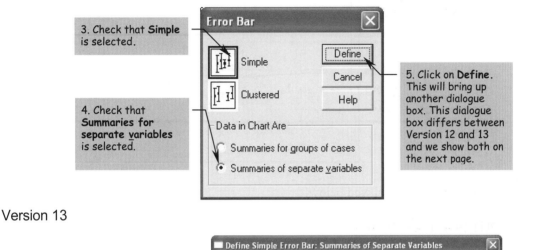

3. Check that **Simple** is selected.

4. Check that **Summaries for separate variables** is selected.

5. Click on **Define**. This will bring up another dialogue box. This dialogue box differs between Version 12 and 13 and we show both on the next page.

Version 13

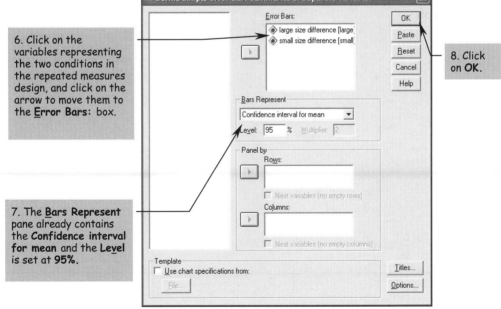

6. Click on the variables representing the two conditions in the repeated measures design, and click on the arrow to move them to the **Error Bars:** box.

7. The **Bars Represent** pane already contains the **Confidence interval for mean** and the **Level** is set at **95%**.

8. Click on **OK**.

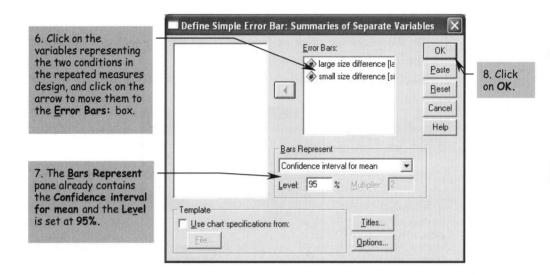

6. Click on the variables representing the two conditions in the repeated measures design, and click on the arrow to move them to the **Error Bars:** box.

7. The **Bars Represent** pane already contains the **Confidence interval for mean** and the **Level** is set at **95%**.

8. Click on **OK**.

The output is displayed below.

SPSS OUTPUT FOR BAR CHART

Graph

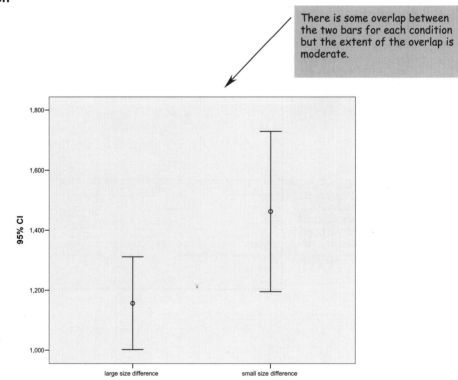

There is some overlap between the two bars for each condition but the extent of the overlap is moderate.

Section 4: An introduction to the nonparametric equivalents of the *t*-test

MANN–WHITNEY TEST AND WILCOXON MATCHED-PAIRS SIGNED-RANKS TEST

The Mann–Whitney test and the Wilcoxon matched-pairs signed-ranks test are nonparametric tests of difference and are used to explore whether two data samples are different. Both tests involve ranking the data, and the calculations are carried out on the ranks. In the annotated output pages for these tests, there is a brief explanation of how each test is performed. When reporting descriptive statistics to accompany the results of a nonparametric test of difference, such as the Mann–Whitney or Wilcoxon test, you should normally give the median and range (not the mean and standard deviation) as the measures of central tendency and dispersion. The median and range are more appropriate descriptives for nonparametric tests because these are distribution-free tests and do not assume normal distribution.

The Wilcoxon test is the nonparametric equivalent of the paired *t*-test, and is used for data from repeated measures and matched pairs designs. The Mann–Whitney test is the nonparametric equivalent of the independent *t*-test, and is used to compare data collected in an independent groups design. It is worth pointing out that there is an independent groups version of the Wilcoxon test. When you request a Mann–Whitney U test, SPSS also gives the statistic for this version of the Wilcoxon test.

These nonparametric tests should be used in preference to the equivalent *t*-tests under the following circumstances:
1. When data are only of ordinal level of measurement;
2. If the data are interval or ratio, but are abnormally distributed (e.g., are severely skewed);
3. If the data are interval or ratio, but the variances of the two samples do not meet an equality of variance test.

Section 5: The Mann–Whitney test

EXAMPLE STUDY: SEX DIFFERENCES AND EMPHASIS ON PHYSICAL ATTRACTIVENESS

To demonstrate how to perform the Mann–Whitney, we shall use the data from an experiment which was designed to determine whether males and females differ in the emphasis they place on the importance of the physical attractiveness of their partner. Previous research has reported that men are more concerned than women about the physical attractiveness of their heterosexual partner. However, current advertising trends and societal pressure may have altered the emphasis placed on physical attractiveness, and more specifically the importance they attach to "body" or physique compared with other characteristics of their ideal partner.

The hypothesis tested is two-tailed: that men and women will differ in the importance they attach to physique. The design employed was an independent groups design. The independent variable was whether the participant was male or female, operationalised by asking equal numbers of males and females to take part in the experiment (only one partner from a relationship participated). The dependent variable was the importance attached to body shape, operationalised by asking participants to rank order 10 characteristics of an ideal partner, one of these being body shape. (These data are available in Appendix I or from the web address listed there.)

HOW TO DO IT

1. Click on the word **Analyze**.

2. Click on **Nonparametric Tests**.

3. Click on **2 Independent Samples**.

The data have been entered with the variable names "sex" and "rating". Follow steps 4 to 10, shown in the shaded boxes below, then click on ⬜ OK ⬜. The SPSS output, which will appear after a short delay, is shown on the following page with explanatory comments.

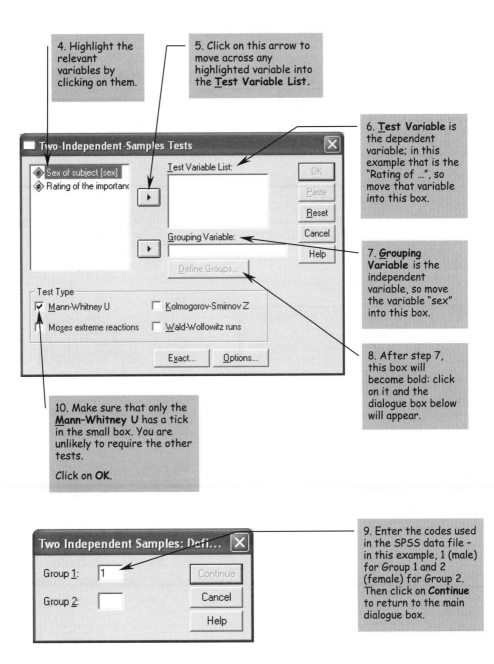

4. Highlight the relevant variables by clicking on them.

5. Click on this arrow to move across any highlighted variable into the **Test Variable List**.

6. **Test Variable** is the dependent variable; in this example that is the "Rating of ...", so move that variable into this box.

7. **Grouping Variable** is the independent variable, so move the variable "sex" into this box.

8. After step 7, this box will become bold: click on it and the dialogue box below will appear.

10. Make sure that only the **Mann–Whitney U** has a tick in the small box. You are unlikely to require the other tests.

Click on **OK**.

9. Enter the codes used in the SPSS data file – in this example, 1 (male) for Group 1 and 2 (female) for Group 2. Then click on **Continue** to return to the main dialogue box.

Obtained Using Menu Items: <u>N</u>onparametric Tests > <u>2</u> Independent Samples

NPar Tests

Mann–Whitney Test

Ranks

	Sex of subject	N	Mean Rank	Sum of Ranks
Rating of the importance of body as characteristic in a partner	Male	20	17.88	357.50
	Female	20	23.13	462.50
	Total	40		

You do not need to use this part of the output, which gives you some information about the calculations for the Mann-Whitney U test: first all the data from both groups combined are assigned ranks from the lowest to the highest; then the ranks given to one group are compared with the ranks given to the other group; the mean ranks shown here indicate whether there are more high ranks in one group than in the other.

Test Statistics[b]

	Rating of the importance of body as characteristic in a partner
Mann–Whitney U	147.500
Wilcoxon W	357.500
Z	-1.441
Asymp. Sig. (2-tailed)	.150
Exact Sig. [2*(1-tailed Sig.)]	.157[a]

The calculated value of U for the Mann-Whitney U Test.

SPSS also gives the calculated value of an independent samples version of the Wilcoxon test. You do not need to use it.

Depending on the size of your data file, the output may or may not include the Exact Sig. (NB the value shown here is not from the Exact option button, but produced automatically by SPSS.)

a. Not corrected for ties.

b. Grouping Variable: Sex of subject

In a report you would write: There was no statistically significant difference between men and women in the importance they attached to body shape in a partner ($U = 147.500$, $N_1 = 20$, $N_2 = 20$, $p = .157$, two-tailed).

> **TIP**   If you are reporting descriptive statistics, you should avoid reporting the mean rank or sum of ranks given in this SPSS output and that for the Wilcoxon test described next. Instead obtain the median and range by using the Explore command.

Section 6: The Wilcoxon test

EXAMPLE STUDY: QUALITY OF E-FIT IMAGES

The police frequently use a computerised facial composite system to help eyewitnesses recall the face of a perpetrator. One such system is E-FIT (the Electronic Facial Identification Technique). In a study by Newlands (1997), participants were shown a short video clip of a mock crime scenario depicting an instance of petty theft. Participants were then asked to generate an E-FIT composite of the perpetrator. On completion, they were asked to rate the likeness of their E-FIT image to the person they remember seeing in the video. They were then shown a photograph of the perpetrator and again asked to rate the likeness of their E-FIT to that person.

The hypothesis tested was one-tailed: that the likeness ratings of the E-FIT to the perpetrator would be more favourable when recalling the perpetrator from memory than when seeing a photograph of the perpetrator. The design employed was a repeated measures design. The independent variable was the presence or absence of a photograph of the perpetrator, operationalised by asking participants to rate the likeness of their E-FIT, first to their recall of perpetrator and then to a photograph of the perpetrator. The dependent variable was measured on an ordinal scale and was the likeness rating, operationalised by the response on a 7-point scale where point 1 was "very good likeness" and point 7 "no likeness".

For the purposes of this book, we have created a data file that will reproduce some of the findings of this study. (These data are available in Appendix I or from the web address listed there.)

HOW TO DO IT

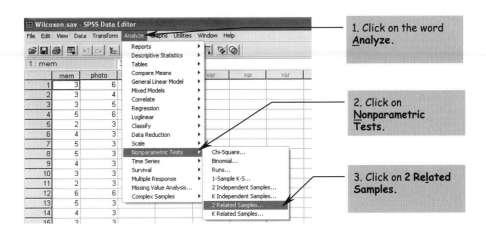

The dialogue box shown below will appear. The variable labels, and the variable names (mem and photo), used in the data file appear in the box on the left hand side. Follow steps 4 to 8, shown in the shaded boxes, then click on ⬚OK⬚. The SPSS output, which will appear after a short delay, is shown on the following page with explanatory comments.

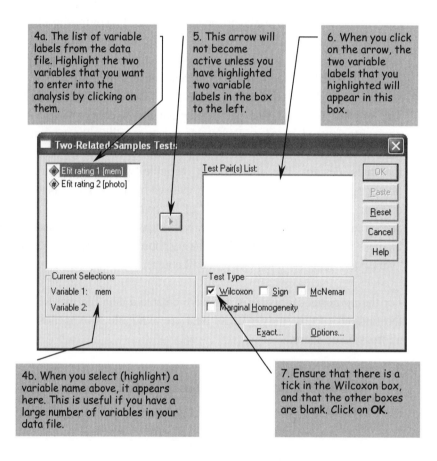

4a. The list of variable labels from the data file. Highlight the two variables that you want to enter into the analysis by clicking on them.

5. This arrow will not become active unless you have highlighted two variable labels in the box to the left.

6. When you click on the arrow, the two variable labels that you highlighted will appear in this box.

Two-Related-Samples Tests

Efit rating 1 [mem]
Efit rating 2 [photo]

Test Pair(s) List:

OK
Paste
Reset
Cancel
Help

Current Selections
Variable 1: mem
Variable 2:

Test Type
☑ Wilcoxon   ☐ Sign   ☐ McNemar
☐ Marginal Homogeneity

Exact...   Options...

4b. When you select (highlight) a variable name above, it appears here. This is useful if you have a large number of variables in your data file.

7. Ensure that there is a tick in the Wilcoxon box, and that the other boxes are blank. Click on OK.

Obtained Using Menu Items: <u>N</u>onparametric Tests > 2 Re<u>l</u>ated Samples

NPar Tests

Wilcoxon Signed Ranks Test

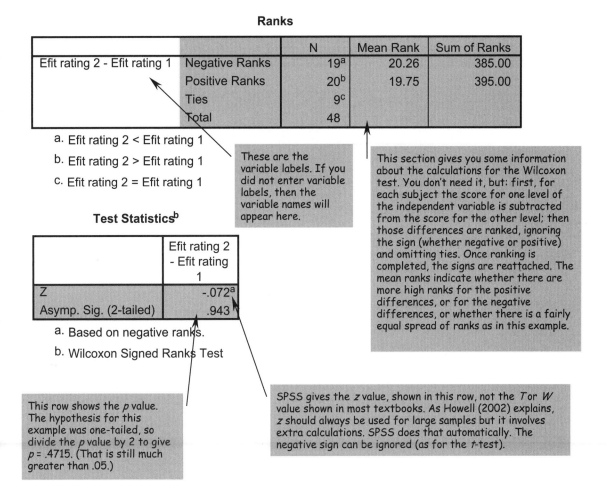

Ranks

		N	Mean Rank	Sum of Ranks
Efit rating 2 - Efit rating 1	Negative Ranks	19[a]	20.26	385.00
	Positive Ranks	20[b]	19.75	395.00
	Ties	9[c]		
	Total	48		

a. Efit rating 2 < Efit rating 1

b. Efit rating 2 > Efit rating 1

c. Efit rating 2 = Efit rating 1

These are the variable labels. If you did not enter variable labels, then the variable names will appear here.

This section gives you some information about the calculations for the Wilcoxon test. You don't need it, but: first, for each subject the score for one level of the independent variable is subtracted from the score for the other level; then those differences are ranked, ignoring the sign (whether negative or positive) and omitting ties. Once ranking is completed, the signs are reattached. The mean ranks indicate whether there are more high ranks for the positive differences, or for the negative differences, or whether there is a fairly equal spread of ranks as in this example.

Test Statistics[b]

	Efit rating 2 - Efit rating 1
Z	-.072[a]
Asymp. Sig. (2-tailed)	.943

a. Based on negative ranks.

b. Wilcoxon Signed Ranks Test

This row shows the *p* value. The hypothesis for this example was one-tailed, so divide the *p* value by 2 to give *p* = .4715. (That is still much greater than .05.)

SPSS gives the *z* value, shown in this row, not the *T* or *W* value shown in most textbooks. As Howell (2002) explains, *z* should always be used for large samples but it involves extra calculations. SPSS does that automatically. The negative sign can be ignored (as for the *t*-test).

In a report you would write: There was no significant difference between the conditions ($z = 0.072$, $N - $ Ties $= 39$, $p = .4715$, one-tailed).

Note: if you were performing this test by calculator, the N used to look up the critical value in the statistics table for Wilcoxon is the number of subjects minus the ties (those who got the same score in both conditions). In this example we would calculate from values given in the Ranks table above:

$$N - \text{Ties} = \text{Total (48)} - \text{Ties (9)} = 39.$$

Chapter Four

Tests of correlation

An introduction to tests of correlation
Descriptive statistics in correlation
Pearson's r: *parametric test of correlation*
Spearman's r_s: *nonparametric test of correlation*

Section 1: An introduction to tests of correlation

Researchers often wish to measure the degree of relationship between two variables. For example, there is likely to be a relationship between age and reading ability in children. Such an investigation is not a true experiment, for the same reason that a natural independent groups design (e.g., when age group or sex is selected as the grouping variable) is not a true experiment. In both, the experimenter does not manipulate the independent variable, and no statement about causation can be made. In a natural independent groups design, the experimenter chooses the levels of the independent variable from "natural" characteristics, and then looks for differences between the groups. In a correlation there is no independent variable: you simply measure two variables. So, if someone wished to investigate the effect of smoking on respiratory function, then, in a natural independent groups design, you could choose to measure and then compare respiratory function in smokers with that in non-smokers. A more common design, however, would be for researchers to measure both how many cigarettes people smoke and their respiratory function, and then test for a correlation.

An important point to remember is that correlation does not imply causation. In any correlation, there could be a third variable which explains the association between the two variables that you measured. For example, there may be a correlation between the number of ice creams sold and the number of people who drown. Here temperature is the third variable, which could explain the relationship between the measured variables. Even when there seems to be a clear cause and effect relationship, a correlation alone is not sufficient evidence for a causal relationship. Only if one variable has been manipulated can one draw such conclusions.

Francis Galton carried out early work on correlation, and one of his colleagues, Pearson, developed a method of calculating correlation coefficients for parametric data: Pearson's Product Moment Correlation Coefficient (Pearson's r). When one or both of the scales is **not** either interval or ratio, or if the data do not meet the other two assumptions for using parametric statistical tests, then a nonparametric test of correlation such as Spearman's r_s should be used. The s is to distinguish it from Pearson's r. This test was originally called Spearman's ρ (the Greek letter rho).

Note that for a correlation to be acceptable one should normally test at least 100 participants; otherwise a small number of participants with extreme scores could skew the data and either prevent a correlation from being revealed when it does exist or cause an apparent correlation that does not really exist. The scattergram is a useful tool for checking such eventualities.

Section 2: Descriptive statistics in correlation

One of the easiest ways to tell if two items are related and to spot trends is to plot scattergrams or scatterplots. Figure 4.1 shows a hypothetical example. Each point on the scattergram represents the age and the reading ability of one child. The line running through the data points is called a regression line. It represents the "best fit" of a straight line to the data points. The line in Figure 4.1 slopes upwards from left to right: as one variable increases in value, the other variable also increases in value and this is called a positive correlation. The closer the points are to being on the line itself, the stronger the correlation. If all the points fall along the straight line, then it is said to be a perfect correlation. The scattergram will also show you any outliers.

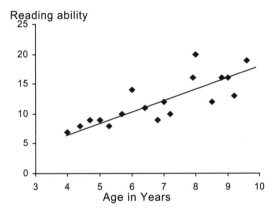

Figure 4.1. Scattergram illustrating a positive correlation: hypothetical data for the relationship between age and reading ability in children.

In the scattergram shown in Figure 4.2, the dots are scattered randomly, all over the graph. It is not possible to draw any meaningful best fit line at all, and the correlation would be close to zero: that is, there is no relationship between the two variables.

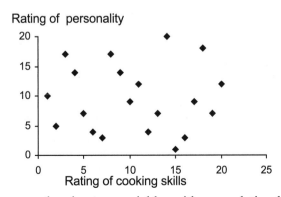

Figure 4.2. Scattergram showing two variables with zero relationship.

It is often the case that as one variable increases in value, the other variable decreases in value: this is called a negative correlation. In the following example of how to produce a scattergram with SPSS, we are going to use data that give a negative correlation.

EXAMPLE STUDY: RELATIONSHIP BETWEEN AGE AND CFF

A paper by Mason, Snelgar, Foster, Heron and Jones (1982) described an investigation of (among other things) whether the negative correlation between age and CFF (explained below) is different for people with Multiple Sclerosis than for control participants. For this example, we have created a data file that will reproduce some of the findings for the control participants. CFF can be described briefly and somewhat simplistically as follows. If a light is flickering on and off at a low frequency, then most people can detect the flicker. If the frequency of flicker is increased then eventually it looks like a steady light. The frequency at which someone can no longer perceive flicker is called his or her critical flicker frequency (CFF). (These data are available in Appendix I or from the web address listed there.)

How to obtain a scattergram

Click on **Graphs** on the menu bar, and then from the menu select **Scatter**. In the **Scatter/Dot** dialogue box, shown below, click on the **Simple Scatter** display, then click on the **Define** button. (Note: in Version 12 and earlier, the dialogue box is called **Scatterplot**.)

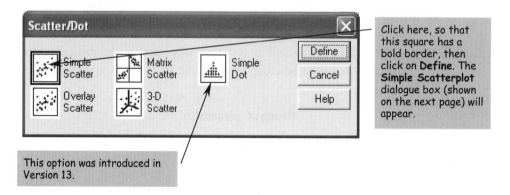

The other options in the **Scatter/Dot** (**Scatterplot**) dialogue box produce other types of graph, which you can explore in the future. We will only be describing the **Simple Scatter** command. After you have clicked on the **Define** button, the **Simple Scatterplot** dialogue box will appear.

In the **Simple Scatterplot** dialogue box, shown below, move the variable names, one into the box labelled **X Axis**, and one into the **Y Axis** box. You can use the **Titles** button and the **Options** button if you wish.

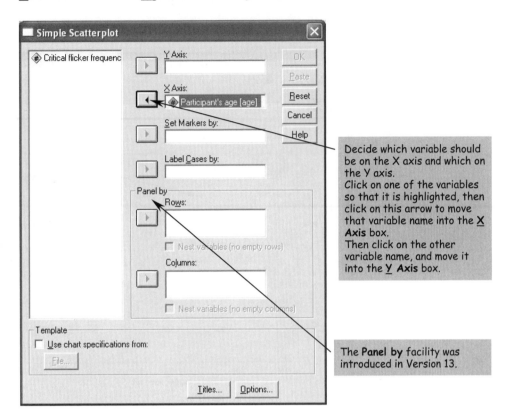

When you have finished, click on **OK**. The Output Window will open, containing the scattergram: a part of that window is shown on the next page.

> **TIP** The **Panel by** facility, introduced in Version 13, allows you to plot a scattergram for two different groups at the same time. For example, if we had recorded the gender of the participants then we could plot a scattergram for men and for women separately by moving the grouping variable name into **Columns**. A second grouping variable (e.g., patient or control participant) could be used in **Rows** to produce 4 separate scattergrams in all.

To add the regression line, you have to edit the graph: start by double-clicking in the scattergram, and the SPSS Chart Editor window, shown at the bottom of this page, will appear.

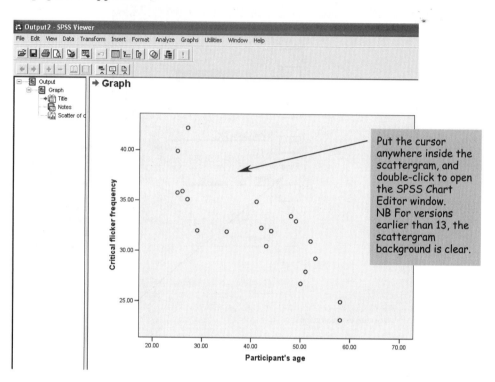

From this point in the procedure, changes were made between SPSS Versions 11 and 12, and another change between Versions 12 and 13. Here we show you how to produce the regression line for Version 12 and also for Version 13. The procedure for Version 10 or 11 is shown in Appendix III.

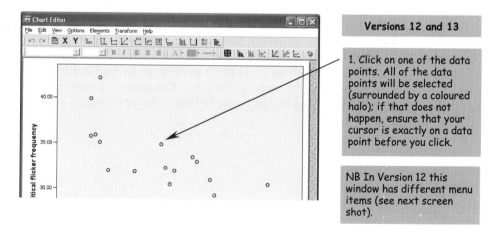

Versions 12 and 13

1. Click on one of the data points. All of the data points will be selected (surrounded by a coloured halo); if that does not happen, ensure that your cursor is exactly on a data point before you click.

NB In Version 12 this window has different menu items (see next screen shot).

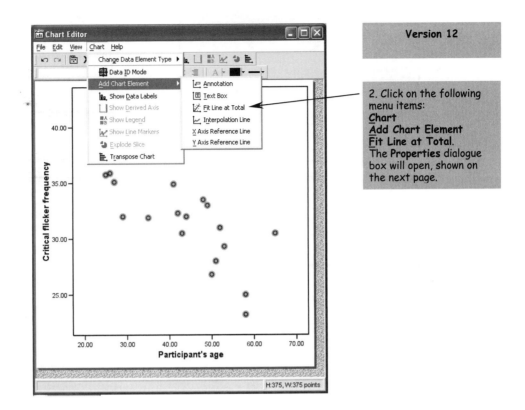

2. Click on the following menu items:
Chart
Add Chart Element
Fit Line at Total.
The **Properties** dialogue box will open, shown on the next page.

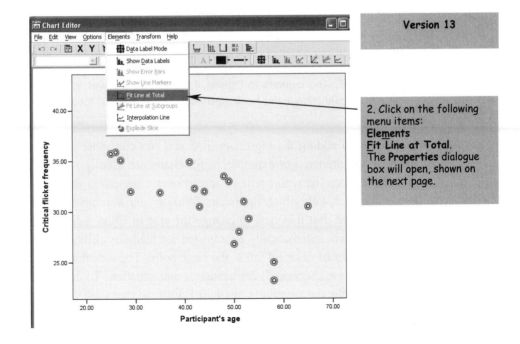

2. Click on the following menu items:
Elements
Fit Line at Total.
The **Properties** dialogue box will open, shown on the next page.

Properties ☒

Chart Size | Lines | Fit Line | Variables

☐ Display Spikes

Fit Method

☐ Mean of Y   ☐ Quadratic

● Linear   ☐ Cubic

☐ Loess

% of points to fit: 50

Kernel: Epanechnikov ▾

Confidence Intervals

● None

☐ Mean

☐ Individual

%: 95

Apply | Close | Help

Versions 12 and 13

This dialogue box will open at the Fit Line tab, which is what we want. You could explore the other tabs on another occasion, to see what they do. NB Version 12 does not have the Variables tab.

3. Check that the **Linear** option button is selected. As you can see, there are various other methods of fitting a line through data. Those other methods can be used, if appropriate for your data, in more advanced stages.

4. Close this dialogue box. You will return to the Chart Editor Window which will display the regression line in the scattergram.

5. Close the Chart Editor Window to return to the Output Window.

You can copy the scattergram and paste it into a Word document for a report, adding a suitable figure legend. For example, see Figure 4.3 on the next page.

TIP   Figure legends should be suitable for the work into which you are incorporating the figure. The legend to Figure 4.3 might be suitable for a report about the study into age and CFF. The legends to Figures 4.1 and 4.2, however, are intended to help you follow the explanation in this book, and would not be suitable for a report.

In addition to adding the regression line you can edit other elements of the chart, to improve appearance. For example, SPSS charts are usually rather large. If you leave them large, then the report will be spread over more pages than necessary which can hinder the ease with which the reader follows your argument. You can shrink charts easily in Word, but it is best to change the size in Chart Editor as then the font and symbol size will automatically be adjusted for legibility. Editing would also be useful when a number of cases all fall at the same point. The data that we use to illustrate use of Spearman's r_s (Section 4) demonstrates that situation. To clearly illustrate the data you can edit the data symbols in Chart Editor, so that they vary in size according to the number of cases at each point. Guidelines on the appearance of Figures are given in APA (2001).

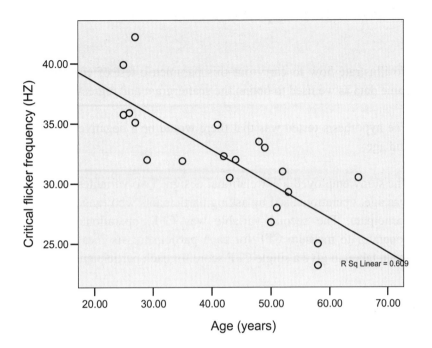

Figure 4.3. Critical flicker frequency (in Hz) plotted against participant's age (in years).

A scattergram is a descriptive statistic that illustrates the data, and can be used to check the data. For example, there may be some extreme outliers that strongly influence the regression line, or there may be a non-linear relationship. If there does appear to be a linear relationship (as Pearson's r makes the assumption that any relationship will be linear) we can find out whether or not it is significant with an inferential statistical test of correlation. A test of correlation will give both the significance value and the strength of the correlation. The strength of correlation is indicated by the value of the correlation coefficient which varies between 1 and 0. A perfect negative correlation would have a coefficient of -1, and a perfect positive correlation would have a coefficient of $+1$. In psychology perfect correlations (in which all the points fall exactly on the regression line) are extremely rare and rather suspect.

Note the R Sq Linear value that appears in the scattergram (Versions 12 and 13). This is not the correlation coefficient itself; it is the square of Pearson's r (which we demonstrate in Section 3). r^2 is itself a useful statistic that we will return to in Section 3. You can remove the R Sq legend if you wish: in the Chart Editor window double-click on the legend, so that it is selected, then press delete key.

Section 3: Pearson's *r*: parametric test of correlation

To illustrate how to carry out this parametric test of correlation, we will use the same data as we used to obtain the scattergram and regression line.

The hypothesis tested was that there would be a negative correlation between CFF and age.

The study employed a correlational design. Two variables were measured. The first was age, operationalised by asking participants who ranged in age from 25 to 66 to participate. The second variable was CFF, operationalised by using a flicker generator to measure CFF for each participant: six measures were made, and the mean taken to give a single CFF score for each participant.

HOW TO PERFORM A PEARSON'S *R*

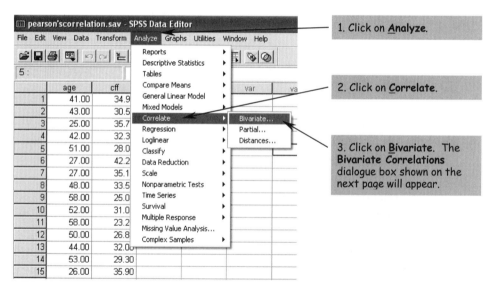

TIP SPSS will correlate each variable that you include with every other variable that you include. Thus, if you included three variables A, B and C, it will calculate the correlation coefficient for A * B, A * C and B * C. In the Pearson's *r* example we have just two variables, but in the Spearman's r_s example we include three variables so that you can see what a larger correlation matrix looks like.

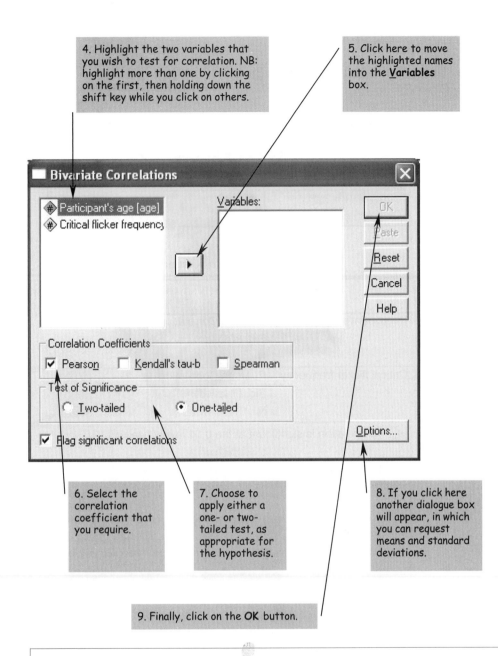

4. Highlight the two variables that you wish to test for correlation. NB: highlight more than one by clicking on the first, then holding down the shift key while you click on others.

5. Click here to move the highlighted names into the **Variables** box.

6. Select the correlation coefficient that you require.

7. Choose to apply either a one- or two-tailed test, as appropriate for the hypothesis.

8. If you click here another dialogue box will appear, in which you can request means and standard deviations.

9. Finally, click on the **OK** button.

TIP In the **Bivariate Correlations** dialogue box, you have the option of choosing either a one- or two-tailed test, and SPSS will then print the appropriate value of *p*. In the statistical tests that we have covered previously, SPSS prints the two-tailed *p* value, and if you have a one-tailed hypothesis you halve that value to give the one-tailed *p* value.

The annotated output for Pearson's *r* is shown on the next page.

Obtained Using Menu Item: <u>C</u>orrelate > <u>B</u>ivariate

Correlations

Useful descriptives obtained by using the **Options** button in the **Bivariate Correlations** dialogue box.

Descriptive Statistics

	Mean	Std. Deviation	N
Participant's age	42.4000	12.55891	20
Critical flicker frequency	32.1375	4.58249	20

Correlations

		Participant's age	Critical flicker frequency
Participant's age	Pearson Correlation	1	-.780**
	Sig. (1-tailed)		.000
	N	20	20
Critical flicker frequency	Pearson Correlation	-.780**	1
	Sig. (1-tailed)	.000	
	N	20	20

**. Correlation is significant at the 0.01 level (1-tailed).

The Pearson's correlation coefficient or Pearson's *r*.

The *p* value. (See Note 3 after Paired *t*-test)

N, the number of cases.

A complete matrix is printed.
Two of the cells are for each variable with itself (for these cells *p* is not calculated: in Version 13 the space is left blank; in earlier versions a "." is printed for Pearson's, and still is in Spearman's output – see below).
The other two cells contain the same information about the correlation between the two variables.

In addition to the *p* value/s in the matrix, SPSS prints this message. Significant correlations are flagged by asterixes; this is particularly useful if you have entered several variables and so have a large correlation matrix.

What you might write in a report is given below, after we tell you about effect sizes in correlation.

> **TIP**   For correlations, the sign of the coefficient indicates whether the correlation is positive or negative, so you must report it (unlike the sign in a *t*-test analysis).

EFFECT SIZES IN CORRELATION

The value of r indicates the strength of the correlation, and it is a measure of effect size (see Chapter 1, Section 2). As a rule of thumb, r values of 0 to .2 are generally considered weak, .3 to .6 moderate, and .7 to 1 strong. The strength of the correlation alone is not necessarily an indication of whether it is an important correlation: the significance value should normally also be considered. With small sample sizes this is crucial, as strong correlations may easily occur by chance. With large to very large sample sizes, however, even a small correlation can be highly statistically significant. To illustrate that, look at a table of the critical values of r (in the back of most statistics text books). For example, if you carry out a correlation study with a sample of 100 and obtain r of .2, it is significant at the .05 level, two-tailed. Yet .2 is only a weak correlation. In some survey studies sample sizes may be in the thousands, so significance alone cannot be used a guide. Instead the effect size and the proportion of variation explained may be more important.

The concept of proportion of variance explained is described in Chapter 7, Section 1. Briefly, a correlation coefficient allows us to estimate the proportion of variation within our data that is explained by the relationship between the two variables. (The remaining variation is down to extraneous variables, both situational and participant.) The proportion of variation explained is given by r^2. Thus, for the age and CFF example in which $r = .78$, $r^2 = .6084$ and we can say that 60% of the variation in the CFF data can be attributed to age. Note that, logically, we can just as easily say that 60% of the variation in the age data can be attributed to CFF. The latter statement should make it clear that we are not implying a causal relationship: we cannot do so with correlation. The important practical point is that the two variables have quite a lot of variation in common, and one could use a person's age to predict what their CFF might be. If their measured CFF is outside the lower confidence limit for their age, then we could investigate further.

Note that the proportion of variation explained does not have to be large to be important. How important it is may depend on the purpose of the study (see Howell, 2002, pp 304–305). Proportion of variance explained in correlational designs will be returned to in Chapter 8 on multiple regression.

Reporting the results

In a report you might write: There was a significant negative correlation between age and CFF ($r = -.780$, $N = 20$, $p < .0005$, one-tailed). It is a fairly strong correlation: 60.8% of the variation is explained. The scattergram (Figure 4.3) shows that the data points are reasonably well distributed along the regression line, in a linear relationship with no outliers.

Section 4: Spearman's r_s: nonparametric test of correlation

If either (or both) of the two variables involved in a correlational design are nonparametric (because they do not meet the assumptions for parametric data, see Chapter 1, Section 2), then we use a nonparametric measure of correlation. Here, we describe two such tests, Spearman's r_s and Kendall's tau-b.

EXAMPLE STUDY: THE RELATIONSHIPS BETWEEN ATTRACTIVENESS, BELIEVABILITY AND CONFIDENCE

Previous research using mock juries has shown that attractive defendants are less likely to be found guilty than unattractive defendants, and that attractive individuals are frequently rated more highly on other desirable traits, such as intelligence. In a study undertaken by one of our students, participants saw the testimony of a woman in a real case of alleged rape. They were asked to rate her, on a scale of 1 to 7, in terms of how much confidence they placed in her testimony, how believable she was and how attractive she was. (These data are available in Appendix I or from the web address listed there.)

The design employed was correlational; with three variables each measured on a 7 point scale. Although it often accepted that such data could be considered interval in nature (see Chapter 1, Section 2), for the purpose of this Section we will consider it as ordinal data. The hypotheses tested were that:

1. There would be a positive relationship between attractiveness and confidence placed in testimony.
2. There would be a positive relationship between attractiveness and believability.
3. There would be a positive relationship between confidence placed in testimony and believability.

> **TIP** We are using this study to illustrate use of Spearman's r_s and some other aspects of correlation. However, multiple regression (Chapter 8) would usually be more appropriate for 3 or more variables in a correlational design.

HOW TO PERFORM SPEARMAN'S R_S

Carry out steps 1 to 5 as for the Pearson's r (previous Section). At step 6 select **Spearman** instead of **Pearson** (see **Bivariate Correlations** dialogue box below).

This example also illustrates the fact that you can carry out more than one correlation at once. There are three variables, and we want to investigate the relationship between each variable with each of the other two. To do this you simply highlight all three variable names and move them all into the **Variables** box. The SPSS output for Spearman's r_s is shown below.

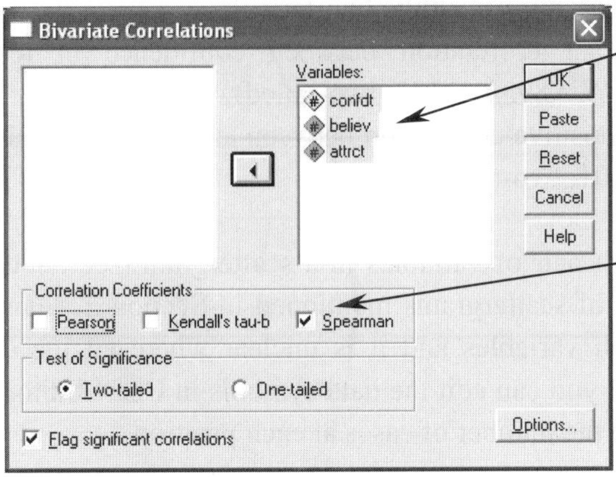

We have moved the three variables into here from the left hand box.

Pearson is the default, so unselect that, and select for **Spearman** instead.

SPSS OUTPUT FOR SPEARMAN'S R_S

Obtained Using Menu Item: Correlate > Bivariate

Nonparametric Correlations

Correlations

			confdt	believ	attrct
Spearman's rho	confdt	Correlation Coefficient	1.000	.372**	.157
		Sig. (2-tailed)	.	.000	.143
		N	89	89	89
	believ	Correlation Coefficient	.372**	1.000	.359**
		Sig. (2-tailed)	.000	.	.001
		N	89	89	89
	attrct	Correlation Coefficient	.157	.359**	1.000
		Sig. (2-tailed)	.143	.001	.
		N	89	89	89

**. Correlation is significant at the 0.01 level (2-tailed).

This cell contains the values for the correlation between variables CONFDT and BELIEV:
.372 is r_s
.000 is p
89 is number of cases.
These values would be reported as in the first statement on the next page.

As in the Pearson's output a complete matrix is printed, but this matrix is larger because 3 variables were entered.

Look for the diagonal: the output for each bivariate correlation is given twice, once below the diagonal, and once above it.

REPORTING THE RESULTS

When reporting the outcome for each correlation, you would write at the appropriate points:

There was a significant positive correlation between confidence in testimony and believability ($r_s = .372$, $N = 89$, $p < .0005$, two-tailed).

There was no significant correlation between confidence in testimony and attractiveness ($r_s = .157$, $N = 89$, $p = .143$, two-tailed).

There was a significant positive correlation between attractiveness and believability ($r_s = .359$, $N = 89$, $p = .001$, two-tailed).

You could illustrate each pair of variables in a scattergram (see Section 2). These data illustrate an aspect of scattergrams mentioned in Section 2. Many cases have the same values on both variables and it is unclear where all the cases are. To clearly illustrate the data you can edit the data symbols in Chart Editor, so that they vary in size according to the number of cases at each position.

Note that the R Sq Linear value, given in the scattergram when you add a regression line, is the square of Pearson's r (r^2) and not the square of Spearman's r_s. As described in Section 3, r^2 indicates the proportion of variation explained. You will see that it is rather small for each of these three relationships; the largest is 18.4%. As this research deals with possible influences on jury decisions, a small amount of variance explained might nonetheless be important.

HOW TO PERFORM KENDALL'S TAU-B:

Some researchers prefer to use Kendall's tau instead of Spearman's r_s. To undertake a Kendall's tau, follow the same steps as for Pearson's r, but at step 6 select **Kendall's tau-b**. The output takes the same form as that for Spearman's r_s. Kendall's tau-b takes ties into account. Kendall's tau-c, which ignores ties, is available in **Crosstabs** (see Chapter 5, Section 4).

Chapter Five

Tests for nominal data

*Nominal data and dichotomous
  variables*

*Chi-square tests versus the chi-square
  distribution*

The goodness-of-fit chi-square

The multi-dimensional chi-square

*The McNemar test for repeated
  measures*

Section 1: Nominal data and dichotomous variables

NOMINAL DATA

As stated in Chapter 1, Section 2, in nominal data the responses consist of a classification to a particular category: for example, being male or female. We can then allocate a number, for convenience when entering data into a computer. These are numbers that cannot be put into any meaningful order; if they could, then they would be ordinal data. In nominal data, the numbers only represent the category of which the participant is a member. That is why nominal data are sometimes called qualitative data and by contrast the ordinal, interval and ratio levels of measurement are called quantitative data. The use of those terms in this way is a different use than in qualitative research and quantitative research. Quantitative research can include all levels of measurement, including nominal.

The independent variable, whether in related designs or independent groups designs, and for true or natural groups experiments, can be thought of as a nominal variable. So, in the Mann–Whitney U test example we compared men and women for their rating of the importance of body shape in their partners. In the paired t-test example the IV also had two levels: large difference and small difference. In SPSS, for independent groups designs (but not for related designs) the independent variable is indicated by a column holding 1s or 2s, and that column is called the grouping variable. When we talk about the level of measurement in those types of design, we are referring to the level of measurement of the dependent variable because the choice of the test depends on the level of the measurement of the DV, and not that of the IV. It is when both variables are nominal that we must use a test devised for nominal data.

Nominal variables can have more than two values. For example, if you recorded smoking status of your participants, then you could use three categories: smoker, never smoked and ex-smoker. If you recorded nationality or culture then there may be a huge number of categories amongst your participants, in a cosmopolitan city such as London, for example. Each of those categories would be represented by a number in a package such as SPSS. Some nominal variables can only have two values however, and they are known as dichotomous variables.

DICHOTOMOUS VARIABLES

A dichotomous variable is a nominal variable that can **only** take one of two values. For example, if you classify smoking status as smoker or non-smoker, then someone who smokes only very occasionally would be classified as a smoker, whereas an ex-chain smoker would be classified as a non-smoker.

DESCRIPTIVES FOR NOMINAL DATA

An important point for you to think about is which summary descriptives are appropriate for nominal data. If you have recorded your participant's sex, then finding the mean is **meaningless**. So is the median, and so is any measure of dispersion.

The only summary descriptives suitable for nominal data are counts, or frequencies, and percentages. Thus we could say that of 20 participants, 15 (75%) are women, and 5 (25%) are men. We can display those counts and percentages in a table, as will be shown with chi-square. We can also illustrate them using a bar chart, also shown with chi-square. Note that histograms should be used for displaying data of at least ordinal level of measurement, and not for nominal data.

ENTERING NOMINAL DATA INTO SPSS

When students first consider chi-square (covered below) they think that the data entry will be more complex than it actually is. For any variable measured on a nominal scale, you simply enter the number chosen to represent the category. So, we still enter data on one row for each participant. For the participant's sex, we have a column with variable name **Sex** in which we could enter a 1 if that participant is a male or a 2 if she is female. In a **Smoking Status** column, the participants could be given a 1 for "smoker", a 2 for "never smoked", or a 3 for "ex-smoker". We can enter as many nominal variables as we like, and each one will contain numbers that are codes for the categories. Each column is independent of all the others, so you can use the same numbers to represent different things in different columns, as for the sex and smoking status examples. More examples can be seen in Sections 4 and 5, and in Chapter 6 where some nominal variables are used in the data handling exercises.

Section 2: Chi-square tests versus the chi-square distribution

Chi-square **tests** make use of the chi-square **distribution** to test for significance. The distinction is made clear by, for example, Howell (2002). In this book we cover the chi-square inferential **test**, and we will not give any detail of the chi-square distribution.

For some other statistical tests, including some for data with level of measurement other than nominal, a chi-square distribution is used to test for significance. Examples of such tests covered in this book include the Kruskal–Wallis and Friedman tests (see Chapter 7).

Also note that the chi-square distribution does not have to be used to test for significance in all inferential tests that are applied to nominal data. Thus for the McNemar test (Section 5), SPSS uses the binomial distribution.

There are two different forms of chi-square test, described in the next two sections.

Section 3: The goodness-of-fit chi-square

In this type of chi-square test – often referred to as either a one-dimensional chi or a goodness-of-fit test – we are testing whether the observed pattern of events differs significantly from what we might have expected by chance alone. For example, we might ask whether a group of smokers choose brand A cigarettes more often than brand B. Here we are effectively asking the question "Do significantly more than 50% of our smokers choose one brand over the other brand?" In practice this form of the chi-square test is not often used in psychology. The example of cigarette brands given above actually relates to one of the few times the authors have ever used this form of the test. An undergraduate student undertook a project examining the effect of cigarette advertising on cigarette choice. As part of this project she listed a series of personality characteristics that were implied by cigarette adverts. For example some cigarette advertisements might imply a sophisticated personality. These personality statements were then presented to smokers who were asked to indicate to which of 5 brands of cigarettes they thought the statement best applied. The responses for each statement were analysed using the chi-square goodness-of-fit test to compare the observed distribution against that predicted by the null hypothesis (that the 5 brands would be equally often selected). This is an interesting, but rare, example of the use of this form of the chi-square test in psychology. Much more common is the second form of this test, described in the next section, which allows us to consider whether two variables are independent of one another.

TO PERFORM THE GOODNESS-OF-FIT CHI-SQUARE TEST

Note that this version is accessed via the chi-square command that can be found under **Nonparametric tests** in the **Analyze** menu. However, as this form of the test is used infrequently in psychology we will not be demonstrating it here.

> **TIP** An error that some students make is to use the goodness-of-fit version of the test when they actually want the multi-dimensional chi-square test, accessed in a different way as explained next.

Section 4: The multi-dimensional chi-square

The multi-dimensional chi-square test can be thought of in two ways: as a test of association or as a test of differences between independent groups.

It can be thought of as a test of association because it allows us to test whether two variables are associated or whether they are independent of each other. For example, let us modify our cigarette example (Section 3) and say that 50 smokers and 50 non-smokers were asked to choose which of two cigarette adverts they preferred. The multi-dimensional chi-square test would allow us to ask the question: "Is the pattern of brand choice independent of whether the participant was a smoker or not?" Another example would be to determine whether receiving or not receiving a particular treatment was associated with living or dying. Yet another might be to see whether a person's sex was independent of their choice of favourite colour. In psychology we often need to test whether nominal variables are, or are not, independent of each other. The experimental hypothesis would be that the 2 variables are not independent of each other – for example, we could hypothesise that people receiving a particular treatment are less likely to die than those not receiving the treatment.

Note that another way of phrasing that last hypothesis is that there will be differences between the number of people who die under each treatment condition. Thus the multi-dimensional chi-square can also be thought of as a test of differences. Whichever way you think of it, the type of data and the way chi-square assesses that data are both the same.

GENERAL ISSUES FOR CHI-SQUARE

Causal relationships

If you have only measured existing variables, and not manipulated them, then you cannot claim to have shown a causal relationship. You can show an association, as in correlation, and you can show a difference between groups, as in natural independent groups designs. The smoking status and preferred cigarette advert is an example of a study from which you could not draw conclusions about causation. If, however, you have manipulated one of the variables and used the normal controls required for independent groups designs then you can draw conclusions about causation. The type of treatment and likelihood of dying is an example of such a study.

Type of data

In order to use chi-square our data must satisfy the following criteria:

1. The variables must be measured on a nominal level of measurement, giving frequency data. In other words, our data must be able to tell us the number of times some event has occurred. We can of course convert other types of data into nominal data. For example, suppose we have IQ scores – we could recode this data, scoring each participant as either "High IQ" or "Low IQ" depending on their score. We could then count to give frequency data – the *number* of high and low IQ participants we have observed. (See Chapter 6, Section 5, for information on how to recode in this way.)

2. For multi-dimensional chi-square, we must have collected data of this sort on at least two variables. For example, in addition to the high/low IQ data above, we might also know whether each of these participants is a smoker or not.

3. The categorisations of each of the variables must be mutually exclusive. In other words, each participant must be **either** a smoker **or** a non-smoker, and **either** high IQ **or** low IQ. Thus each variable is an independent groups variable. Another way of thinking about this is to say that each participant must fall into one and only one of the cells of the contingency table (see below).

4. Every observation must be independent of every other observation. This will not be the case if you have more than one observation per participant. (Nominal data from a repeated measures design can be analysed by means of the McNemar test, see Section 5.)

The N * N contingency table

When we have nominal data of this form we can best display the frequencies or counts in what is called a contingency table. If we have two variables, each with two levels (as in the example above), then we draw what is called a 2*2 (pronounced two by two) contingency table. So if we had 100 participants in our example data set, the contingency table might look like Table 5.1.

Table 5.1

An example of a 2*2 contingency table

	High IQ	Low IQ	Row Totals
Smokers	10	20	30
Non-Smokers	35	35	70
Column Totals	45	55	100 (Grand Total)

Contingency tables can be produced by SPSS from nominal data, as we explain next. The numbers in this table represent the numbers of participants who fall into each cell of the table (and remember that each participant can be in only one cell).

So we can see that of the 30 smokers in our study, 10 are high IQ and 20 are low IQ. Similarly we can see that of the low IQ group, 20 are smokers and 35 are non-smokers. Thus the contingency table is useful to describe the data. The rationale for the chi-square inferential test is explained below.

Rationale for chi-square test

If there were no association between smoking and IQ then we would expect the proportion of smokers in the high IQ group to be the same as the proportion in the total sample. That is, we would expect 45/100 or 45% of the smokers to be high IQ. As there were 30 smokers in total we would thus expect (45% of 30) = 13.5% of the smokers to be in the high IQ group. In this way we can work out the expected frequencies for each cell. The general formula is:

$$\text{expected frequency} = \frac{\text{row total} * \text{column total}}{\text{grand total}}$$

What chi-square does is to calculate the expected frequency for each cell and then compare the expected frequencies with the observed frequencies. If the observed and expected frequencies are significantly different then it would appear that the distribution of observations across the cells is not random. We can, therefore, conclude that there is a significant association between the two variables: IQ and smoking behaviour are not independent for our sample of (fictitious) participants.

Chi-square will actually allow us to calculate whether more than 2 variables are independent of each other. However, it is very difficult to interpret the results of such an analysis, so we would recommend that you resist the temptation to add extra variables unless you are sure you know what you are doing. It is, however, perfectly reasonable to have more than 2 categories of each variable – for example a 3*3 chi-square is quite acceptable.

EXAMPLE STUDY: INVESTIGATING TENDENCY TOWARDS ANOREXIA

To illustrate the use of chi-square we will use some fictitious data based on research conducted by one of our past students. Eighty young women completed an eating questionnaire which allowed them to be classified as either high or low anorexia (participants with high scores are more likely to develop anorexia). In addition, the questionnaire asked for the employment status of the women's mother (full-time, part-time or unemployed) and their cultural background (Caucasian, Asian or other) and type of school they attended (private or state comprehensive). Previous research has suggested that the incidence of anorexia is higher among girls attending private schools than state schools, and higher among girls whose mothers are not in full-time employment. In addition the incidence seems to be higher in Caucasian girls than non-Caucasian girls. We therefore hypothesised that there would be an association between these factors and the classification on the eating questionnaire. To test this hypothesis we conducted a series of chi-square analyses. (These data are available in Appendix I or from the web address listed there.)

TO PERFORM THE MULTI-DIMENSIONAL CHI-SQUARE TEST

The multi-dimensional chi-square is accessed under the **Crosstabs** command. Crosstabs draws up contingency tables and chi-square is an optional inferential statistic within this command.

1. Click on **Analyze**.

2. Select **Descriptive Statistics.**

3. Select **Crosstabs** and the dialogue box, shown on the next page, will appear.

Note: Do NOT use the chi-square command available under **Nonparametric Tests**. That is for one-dimensional, goodness-of-fit, chi-square.

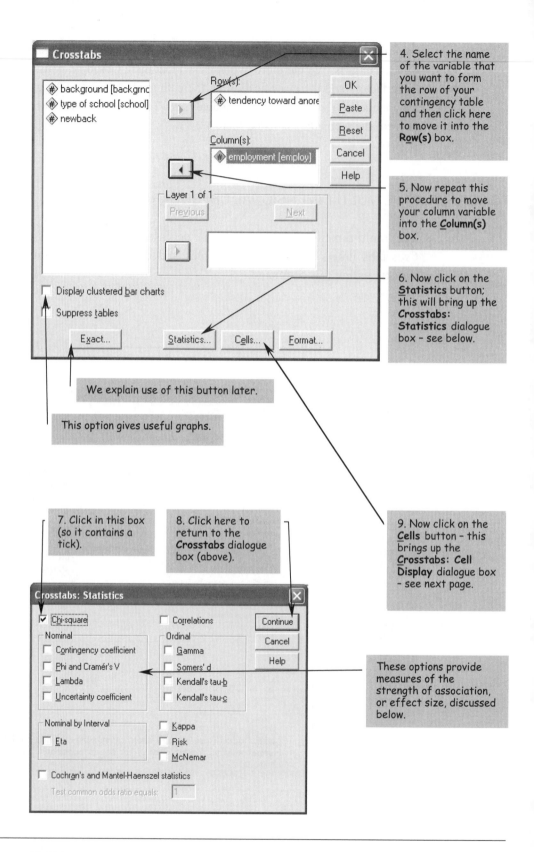

4. Select the name of the variable that you want to form the row of your contingency table and then click here to move it into the **Row(s)** box.

5. Now repeat this procedure to move your column variable into the **Column(s)** box.

6. Now click on the **Statistics** button; this will bring up the **Crosstabs: Statistics** dialogue box – see below.

We explain use of this button later.

This option gives useful graphs.

7. Click in this box (so it contains a tick).

8. Click here to return to the **Crosstabs** dialogue box (above).

9. Now click on the **Cells** button – this brings up the **Crosstabs: Cell Display** dialogue box – see next page.

These options provide measures of the strength of association, or effect size, discussed below.

Crosstabs: Cell Display

Counts
- ☑ Observed
- ☑ Expected

Percentages
- ☑ Row
- ☑ Column
- ☑ Total

Residuals
- ☐ Unstandardized
- ☐ Standardized
- ☐ Adjusted standardized

Noninteger Weights
- ⦿ Round cell counts
- ○ Truncate cell counts
- ○ No adjustments
- ○ Round case weights
- ○ Truncate case weights

Continue | Cancel | Help

10. Click on the display options you want. These options control the information included in the contingency table. We recommend you select both of the **Counts** options and all 3 **Percentages** options.

11. Click on the **Continue** button to return to the **Crosstabs** dialogue box.

These options were introduced in Version 12.

Finally, click on the ⬚ OK button in the **Crosstabs** dialogue box. SPSS will now switch to the output window and display the contingency table and the chi-square results. Two sets of annotated output are given on the next three pages. The first is from the 2*3 chi-square exploring the association between the incidence of tendency towards anorexia and mother's employment status. The second is from the 2*2 chi-square exploring the association between tendency towards anorexia and type of school attended.

Obtained Using Menu Items: Descriptive Statistics > Crosstabs

Output for first chi-square: tendency towards anorexia * employment (a variable with two levels against a variable with three levels)

Crosstabs

In this table, SPSS reminds you of the variables entered into the analysis and gives you some summary information about the cases in your data file.

Case Processing Summary

	Cases					
	Valid		Missing		Total	
	N	Percent	N	Percent	N	Percent
tendency toward anorexia * employment	80	100.0%	0	.0%	80	100.0%

This is the variable that we put into the rows of the table, and these are its two levels.

This table gives you some simple descriptive statistics: counts and percentages for the crosstabulation of the two variables.

This is the variable put into the columns, and these are its three levels.

tendency toward anorexia * employment Crosstabulation

			employment			Total
			f/t	none	p/t	
tendency toward anorexia	high	Count	14	13	11	38
		Expected Count	14.7	11.9	11.4	38.0
		% within tendency toward anorexia	36.8%	34.2%	28.9%	100.0%
		% within employment	45.2%	52.0%	45.8%	47.5%
		% of Total	17.5%	16.3%	13.8%	47.5%
	low	Count	17	12	13	42
		Expected Count	16.3	13.1	12.6	42.0
		% within tendency toward anorexia	40.5%	28.6%	31.0%	100.0%
		% within employment	54.8%	48.0%	54.2%	52.5%
		% of Total	21.3%	15.0%	16.3%	52.5%
Total		Count	31	25	24	80
		Expected Count	31.0	25.0	24.0	80.0
		% within tendency toward anorexia	38.8%	31.3%	30.0%	100.0%
		% within employment	100.0%	100.0%	100.0%	100.0%
		% of Total	38.8%	31.3%	30.0%	100.0%

If you clicked on all the Counts and Percentages that we suggested in the **Crosstabs: Cell Display** dialogue box, then all these descriptives are given in each cell. The contents of the cells are described on the Crosstabulation table for the second chi-square (see page after next).

Chi-Square Tests

	Value	df	Asymp. Sig. (2-sided)
Pearson Chi-Square	.298[a]	2	.862
Likelihood Ratio	.298	2	.862
Linear-by-Linear Association	.008	1	.930
N of Valid Cases	80		

a. 0 cells (.0%) have expected count less than 5. The minimum expected count is 11.40.

This table contains the results of chi-square tests: if either variable has more than two levels (as here), then SPSS reports these three chi-squares.

Pearson's chi-square is used most often, so report this row. (Whichever chi-square test you use, you should give its name when describing the statistical test used.)

TIP If you used the Exact option, the table above would have three extra columns: we will describe them below.

This graph is produced by selecting **Display clustered bar charts** in the **Crosstabs** dialogue box. It can usefully illustrate your results – but see next note.

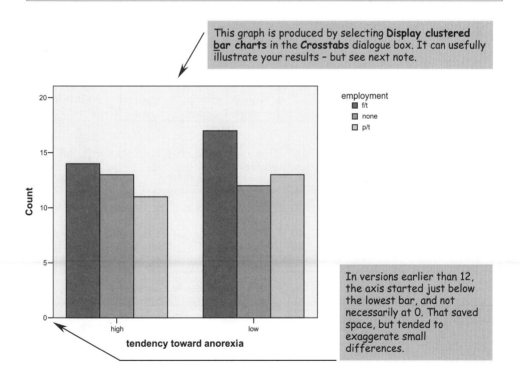

In versions earlier than 12, the axis started just below the lowest bar, and not necessarily at 0. That saved space, but tended to exaggerate small differences.

In a report you might write:
There was no relationship between tendency towards anorexia and the employment status of the mother: $\chi^2(2, N = 80) = 0.298, p = .862$.

We discuss reporting the outcome of chi-square and other issues below.

Output for second chi-square: tendency towards anorexia * education (two variables each with two levels)

> A row gives information about each level of the column variable; e.g. this row gives information for girls in the "high" group. It shows the figures for those in comprehensive education separately from those in private education. The total is for all girls in the "high" group. Here we can see that of the total of 38 "high" girls, 4 were in comprehensive education and 34 were in private education.

tendency toward anorexia * type of school Crosstabulation

			type of school comp	private	Total
tendency toward anorexia	high	Count	4	34	38
		Expected Count	15.7	22.3	38.0
		% within tendency toward anorexia	10.5%	89.5%	100.0%
		% within type of school	12.1%	72.3%	47.5%
		% of Total	5.0%	42.5%	47.5%
	low	Count	29	13	42
		Expected Count	17.3	24.7	42.0
		% within tendency toward anorexia	69.0%	31.0%	100.0%
		% within type of school	87.9%	27.7%	52.5%
		% of Total	36.3%	16.3%	52.5%
Total		Count	33	47	80
		Expected Count	33.0	47.0	80.0
		% within tendency toward anorexia	41.3%	58.8%	100.0%
		% within type of school	100.0%	100.0%	100.0%
		% of Total	41.3%	58.8%	100.0%

> Within each cell we are given:
>
> **Count** = the number of participants falling into the cell; i.e. the number of girls who are "low" and attended comprehensive education (the observed frequency)
>
> **Expected count**: the number expected for this cell assuming no association (see text)
>
> **% within tendency toward anorexia**: the cases in this cell as a % of row total; i.e. % of "low" girls who attend comprehensive school
>
> **% within type of school**: the cases in this cell as a % of the column total; i.e. the % of girls who attend comprehensive school who are "low".
>
> **% of total**: the cases in this cell as a % of the total number of participants.

> A column gives information about each level of the row variable. This column shows figures for girls in private schools. Figures are given separately for those in the "high" and "low" groups and for the total for all girls in private education. Of the total of 47 girls in private education 34 of them were "high" and 13 of them were "low".

> If each variable has only two levels (a two by two chi-square), then SPSS reports five tests as shown in this table.

Chi-Square Tests

	Value	df	Asymp. Sig. (2-sided)	Exact Sig. (2-sided)	Exact Sig. (1-sided)
Pearson Chi-Square	28.193[b]	1	.000		
Continuity Correction[a]	25.830	1	.000		
Likelihood Ratio	30.895	1	.000		
Fisher's Exact Test				.000	.000
Linear-by-Linear Association	27.840	1	.000		
N of Valid Cases	80				

a. Computed only for a 2x2 table

b. 0 cells (.0%) have expected count less than 5. The minimum expected count is 15.68.

> Continuity correction is the Yates's corrected chi-square. See text on next page.

> You can ignore Fisher's Exact Test, unless any cells have an expected count of less than five (see text below).

TIP If you used the Exact option, the table above would have one extra column: we will describe it below.

INTERPRETING AND REPORTING RESULTS FROM CHI-SQUARE

SPSS reports several different measures of p. It is probably best to use Pearson's (the chi-square test was developed by Karl Pearson). Note that for chi-square the value of df (degrees of freedom) is not related to the number of participants. It is the number of levels in each variable minus one multiplied together. So for a 2*2 chi-square, df = (2–1)(2–1), which equals 1. When reporting the outcome (see below) we also provide the value of N. That should be the number of valid cases (see Chi-Square Tests table), not necessarily the same number as originally tested.

For a 2*2 table, SPSS also calculates the result with and without the continuity correction, or Yates's correction. This is a statistical correction used in cases with relatively few participants or in which you have reason to believe that your sample is not a very good approximation to the total population. There is disagreement about whether to use it, but the Exact test, described below, can be used instead for small samples.

It is important to understand that the chi-square result on its own cannot tell you about the pattern of your results. For that you have to look at the contingency table. For example, when reporting the results of the second chi-square result (on previous page), you might write: "Within the comprehensive school a minority (only 12%) of pupils scored high on the scale, whereas in the private school the majority (72%) scored high on the scale." If you made a specific one-tailed prediction about the direction of the relationship between the two variables (here we predicted that there will be a higher tendency towards anorexia in the private school pupils) and the pattern of results revealed by the contingency is compatible with this prediction (as here), then you can use the chi-square results to assess whether this particular association is significant.

The strength of the association between the two variables can also be obtained: in the **Crosstabs: Statistics** dialogue box select for Phi and Cramér's V. The following table will appear after the Chi-Square Tests table.

Symmetric Measures

		Value	Approx. Sig.
Nominal by Nominal	Phi	-.594	.000
	Cramer's V	.594	.000
N of Valid Cases		80	

a. Not assuming the null hypothesis.

b. Using the asymptotic standard error assuming the null hypothesis.

> The value of φ (phi) indicates the magnitude of the association; it can be considered equivalent to Pearson's r (see Chapter 4, Section 3).

Just as we can square r to give an estimate of the proportion of variation that is common to the two variables, so we can square ϕ. For these data $\phi^2 = .353$, so 35.3% of the variation in the tendency towards anorexia score is accounted for by the type of school attended. Just as in the correlation examples, none of the variables in this example study were manipulated: thus the chi-square results do not imply causation. You will see that the Symmetric Measures table provides a significance value for ϕ: it can be used to assess significance of the relationship between two variables. χ^2, however, is most commonly reported for that purpose.

Thus we might write in a report:
The relationship between tendency towards anorexia and the type of school attended was significant: $\chi^2(1, N = 80) = 28.19$, $p < .0005$. The association was of moderate strength: $\phi = .594$ and thus the type of school attended accounted for 35% of the variance in the score on tendency towards anorexia scale.

You could also include a table of counts and expected frequencies, bar charts and other information as appropriate.

USE OF EXACT TESTS IN CHI-SQUARE

On page 121, and on page 122, look at the foot of the Chi-Square Tests table. There is a note that informs you of the number of cells with expected frequencies (what SPSS calls expected counts) of less than 5. It is very important that you always check this note. For both chi-square analyses above, there are no cells with this problem. However, if you do perform a chi-square analysis and SPSS reports that there are one or more cells with an expected frequency of less than 5 then you must take some action. If you are performing a 2*2 chi-square, then SPSS reports an additional statistic called Fisher's Exact test. This test can be used when cells have low expected frequencies (Siegel and Castellan, 1988, pp. 103–111). However, this test is only available for 2*2 tables. If you are performing something other than a 2*2 chi-square and encounter this problem, then you can use the **Exact** option.

To demonstrate this for you, we have undertaken a further chi-square analysis, exploring a possible association between cultural background and tendency towards anorexia. In the third SPSS output, on the next page, two cells have an expected frequency of less than 5.

Output for third chi-square: tendency towards anorexia * cultural background (a variable with two levels against a variable with three levels)

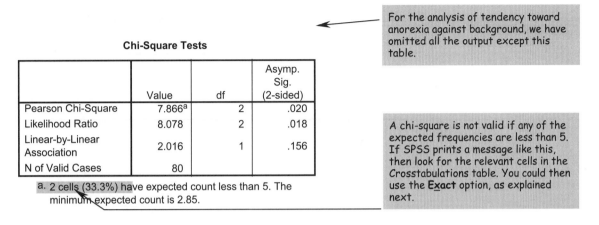

For the analysis of tendency toward anorexia against background, we have omitted all the output except this table.

Chi-Square Tests

	Value	df	Asymp. Sig. (2-sided)
Pearson Chi-Square	7.866[a]	2	.020
Likelihood Ratio	8.078	2	.018
Linear-by-Linear Association	2.016	1	.156
N of Valid Cases	80		

a. 2 cells (33.3%) have expected count less than 5. The minimum expected count is 2.85.

A chi-square is not valid if any of the expected frequencies are less than 5. If SPSS prints a message like this, then look for the relevant cells in the Crosstabulations table. You could then use the **Exact** option, as explained next.

As this was a 2*3 chi-square there is no Fisher's Exact test. Instead, we use the **Exact** button on the **Crosstabs** dialogue box. Note that in SPSS versions earlier than 12 we would use the **Recode** command (see Chapter 6, Section 5) to combine the "Asian" and "Other" groups into one "Non-Caucasian" group. That would turn our 2*3 into a 2*2 analysis and Fisher's Exact test would be reported.

Using the exact option for chi-square

If you click on the **Exact** button in the **Crosstabs** dialogue box (above), then the **Exact Tests** dialogue box, shown below will appear.

Exact Tests

- ○ Asymptotic only
- ○ Monte Carlo
  - Confidence level: 99 %
  - Number of samples: 10000
- ● Exact
  - ☑ Time limit per test: 5 minutes

[Continue] [Cancel] [Help]

Exact method will be used instead of Monte Carlo when computational limits allow.

For nonasymptotic methods, cell counts are always rounded or truncated in computing the test statistics.

Asymptotic only is the default setting: it gives the output shown above.

Click here to select **Exact** tests: you will then get the type of output shown below.

We advise that you do NOT use the Monte Carlo option unless you know what it means.

Output for third chi-square (2x3) with Exact option

Chi-Square Tests

	Value	df	Asymp. Sig. (2-sided)	Exact Sig. (2-sided)	Exact Sig. (1-sided)	Point Probability
Pearson Chi-Square	7.866[a]	2	.020	.015		
Likelihood Ratio	8.078	2	.018	.037		
Fisher's Exact Test	7.765			.017		
Linear-by-Linear Association	2.016[b]	1	.156	.191	.114	.065
N of Valid Cases	80					

a. 2 cells (33.3%) have expected count less than 5. The minimum expected count is 2.85.

b. The standardized statistic is -1.420.

You can now report the Pearson's chi-square, as we show next.

These three extra columns are printed when you select the Exact option. (We mention Point Probability below.)

In a report you would write:

The analysis showed that 2 cells had expected count less than 5, so an exact significance test was selected for Pearson's chi-square. There was a relationship between tendency towards anorexia and cultural background: $\chi^2(2, N = 80) = 7.866$, exact $p = .015$.

Output for second chi-square (2x2) with Exact option

Chi-Square Tests

	Value	df	Asymp. Sig. (2-sided)	Exact Sig. (2-sided)	Exact Sig. (1-sided)	Point Probability
Pearson Chi-Square	28.193[b]	1	.000	.000	.000	
Continuity Correction[a]	25.830	1	.000			
Likelihood Ratio	30.895	1	.000	.000	.000	
Fisher's Exact Test				.000	.000	
Linear-by-Linear Association	27.840[c]	1	.000	.000	.000	.000
N of Valid Cases	80					

a. Computed only for a 2x2 table

b. 0 cells (.0%) have expected count less than 5. The minimum expected count is 15.68.

For a 2x2 chi-square, these two columns are printed by default. However, **without** Exact option, only p value for the Fisher's Exact Test appeared in these columns, whereas **with** Exact option, p values for other tests, including Pearson's chi-square, are given.

With the Exact option, the Point Probability column appears. As in the third chi-square (2x3), the only value in this column is for Linear-by-Linear Association which is not for nominal data, so we can ignore it.

This example has no cells with expected counts less than 5: we have simply used it to illustrate the output obtained from a 2*2 chi-square with Exact option.

Section 5: The McNemar test for repeated measures

The McNemar test is used to analyse data obtained by measuring a dichotomous variable for related designs. Remember that a dichotomous variable by definition can only take one of two values (e.g., yes or no). The difference between this and the 2*2 chi-square test is that the chi-square test is for independent groups designs. Thus the McNemar test is for a situation where you measure the same thing twice – for example a "before treatment" yes/no response, and an "after treatment" yes/no response. Further, the chi-square test can be used to test for association between two variables (as described above) whereas the McNemar test cannot be used in that way. If you measure more than two values (e.g., yes/uncertain/no) SPSS will automatically apply the McNemar–Bowker test instead. We will not cover that test here.

To illustrate the use of the McNemar test, we will use an experiment that we carried out with students. It is well established that roughly two-thirds of handwriting samples can be correctly judged as being written by a man or by a woman. This is significantly above the chance level of 50% correct; the implication is that many (but not all) men and women tend to write in a gender-stereotyped manner. Very briefly, "male-handwriting" is irregular and untidy, whereas "female handwriting" is rounded and neat. If this is the case, do people have a choice in their writing style? Hartley (1991) investigated this by asking children to try to imitate the handwriting of the opposite sex. We carried out a similar study, but with first-year Psychology students.

The experimental hypothesis was that the number of correct identifications of the writer's sex, from the handwriting samples, will be different when the handwriters were mimicking the opposite sex than when they were writing normally. The independent variable was handwriting style with two levels: one level was the students' normal handwriting (before they knew the hypothesis) and the other level was their writing as if they were of the opposite sex. Each student then recruited a participant to act as judge of the handwriter's sex for both handwriting samples; the design was, therefore, repeated measures. Order of presentation of the handwriting samples was counterbalanced across participants. The dependent variable was whether the participant's judgement of the handwriter's sex was correct or incorrect: it was correct if they judged the **real** sex of the writer correctly. Hypothetical data are available in Appendix I or from the web address listed there. Note that the writer's sex is not recorded in this data; we simply recorded, for each handwriting sample, whether their sex was judged correctly or not.

The McNemar test can be accessed in two ways: via the **Descriptive Statistics** > **Crosstabs** command, or via the **Nonparametric Tests** > **2 Related Samples** command. The former command has an advantage over the latter. The **2 Related Samples** command allows you to obtain means and standard deviations as an option, but these descriptives, remember, are completely inappropriate (in fact meaningless) to use with nominal data. The **Crosstabs** command does not have that option, so you are less likely to make a mistake. Thus we will only cover the **Crosstabs** command.

Via the Crosstabs command

Crosstabs draws up contingency tables and the McNemar test is an optional inferential statistic within this command. Follow steps 1 to 6 in the instructions on performing a multi-dimensional chi-square (Section 4 above). The **Crosstabs: Statistics** dialogue box will then appear – see below. Click in the box to select McNemar, instead of chi-square, then continue.

Select the **McNemar** option. Next click on **Continue** to return to the **Crosstabs** dialogue box.

In the **Crosstabs** dialogue box, click on [OK], and the output will appear as shown on the next page.

SPSS OUTPUT FOR THE MCNEMAR TEST

Obtained Using Menu Items: <u>D</u>escriptive Statistics > <u>C</u>rosstabs

Crosstabs

Case Processing Summary

	Cases					
	Valid		Missing		Total	
	N	Percent	N	Percent	N	Percent
normal handwriting * handwriting as if opposite sex	49	100.0%	0	.0%	49	100.0%

normal handwriting * handwriting as if opposite sex Crosstabulation

Count

		handwriting as if opposite sex		Total
		correct	incorrect	
normal handwriting	correct	17	16	33
	incorrect	2	14	16
Total		19	30	49

> The table of observed counts: you can also request expected frequencies and the various percentages, as we did in chi-square above.

Chi-Square Tests

	Value	Exact Sig. (2-sided)
McNemar Test		.001[a]
N of Valid Cases	49	

a. Binomial distribution used.

> The outcome of the McNemar test: SPSS assesses its significance using the binomial distribution, and gives the value of p and N only. Notice that this is an exact p, even though we did not use the Exact option.
>
> When the Exact option is used, this table has two more columns: however, that option is not normally required because SPSS automatically uses an exact significance test for McNemar.

TIP   It would be useful to illustrate the results. For data from a related design, rather than using Clustered bar charts in the **Crosstabs** dialogue box, it is probably better to illustrate the findings with two separate bar charts obtained through the **Graphs** menu and suitably edited, as shown on the next page.

In a report you might write:

The McNemar test using binomial distribution showed a significant difference, in the number of correct judgements, between the two conditions of handwriting style ($N = 49$, exact $p = .001$).

It would also be useful to explain the pattern of results in the following way:

Of the 49 participants, 33 (67%) correctly identified the handwriter's sex for the normal handwriting. Of those 33, 17 of them correctly identified the handwriter's sex for the "opposite handwriting" and 16 of them incorrectly identified it. Of the 16 (33%) who were incorrect for the normal handwriting, 2 of them correctly identified the handwriter's sex for the "opposite handwriting" and 14 of them incorrectly identified it. In brief, there were more incorrect responses when the writer had written as if they were of the opposite sex. This pattern of results is illustrated in Figure 5.1.

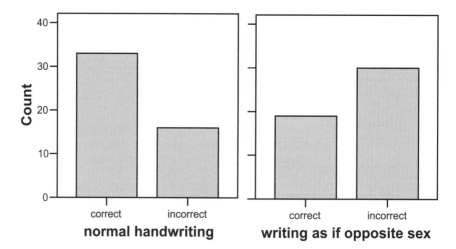

Figure 5.1 The pattern of correct and incorrect identification of handwriter's sex, when the writing was their normal handwriting and when they mimicked the writing of the opposite sex.

Note about causation:

In related designs you manipulate an independent variable and either collect data for both of its levels from the same participants (repeated measures) or collect data from matched participants (matched pairs). If you have carried out the normal controls for the design, then you can draw conclusions about causation from the McNemar test output.

Chapter Six

Data handling

An introduction to data handling
Sorting a file
Splitting a file
Selecting cases
Recoding values
Computing new variables
Counting values
Ranking cases
Other useful functions
Data file for scales or questionnaires

Section 1: An introduction to data handling

In this chapter we describe some commands which can be used to modify, manipulate, transform and correct your data file. These commands are most useful when working with complex and large data files where you have a large number of variables for each participant. Files such as these often arise from survey or questionnaire research. Large questionnaires often contain items (questions) which can be grouped into a number of sub-scores. One decision you have to make when entering data collected in this way is whether to set up a variable for every item in the questionnaire or to score the paper version of the questionnaire and enter only the totals into your data file. The advantage of this second approach is that it can be a lot quicker – especially if you have relatively few participants. However, if you adopt the approach of putting all the raw data into SPSS you gain a considerable degree of flexibility. By using the commands described in this section, you can use SPSS to calculate any sub-scale scores for you, and you can also look at, check and analyse the original data.

These commands are also very useful when you want to clean up your data. This topic is covered in great depth by Tabachnick and Fidell (2001), who describe procedures to check the accuracy of the data and to pre-process the data before engaging in further analysis. An example of this pre-processing of the data would be transforming a variable to reduce distortions such as skewness, which might otherwise invalidate some analyses. All of these techniques will require you to be familiar with the use of the commands described in this chapter.

EXAMPLE DATA

To illustrate the use of these commands, we have created a small data file (available in Appendix I or from the web address listed there) containing the results of a fictitious survey of people's attitudes to cross-racial adoption. The data file contains participant number, and demographic data such as the participant's age, sex, ethnic origin, religious belief and experience of adoption, together with their responses to 10 statements concerning aspects of adoption. These responses were made using a 5 point scale ranging from "Strongly Agree"(1) to "Strongly Disagree"(5). The response to each of these items has been recorded in variables Q1 to Q10.

> **TIP** In this chapter the screen images of the data file display variable labels rather than values. Select this option by clicking on the Value Labels button 🔲 on the toolbar.

Section 2: Sorting a file

Students who are new to SPSS sometimes worry about the order in which participants' data are entered into the SPSS data file. For example, do you have to enter all the data from participants in one condition before entering the data from the other condition? Normally the order of the cases does not matter, but there are occasions when you might want to sort a data file so that the cases are in some meaningful order perhaps to make it easier to check the accuracy of the data file. One situation when order of cases does become relevant is when you are "splitting" a file (see the Split file command in Section 3 below).

> **TIP**   If you are likely to change the order of the cases in a file by using either the **Sort Cases** or **Split File** commands then you will not be able to rely on the SPSS case numbers (the numbers on the extreme left of the data window) to identify participants. For this reason it is always best to create your own participant identification variable and record this number both in the data file and on any original paper records so that you can check the data later if necessary.

THE SORT CASES COMMAND

In this example we will sort the data by two variables, first by participants' sex, and then within sex we will sort by ethnicity.

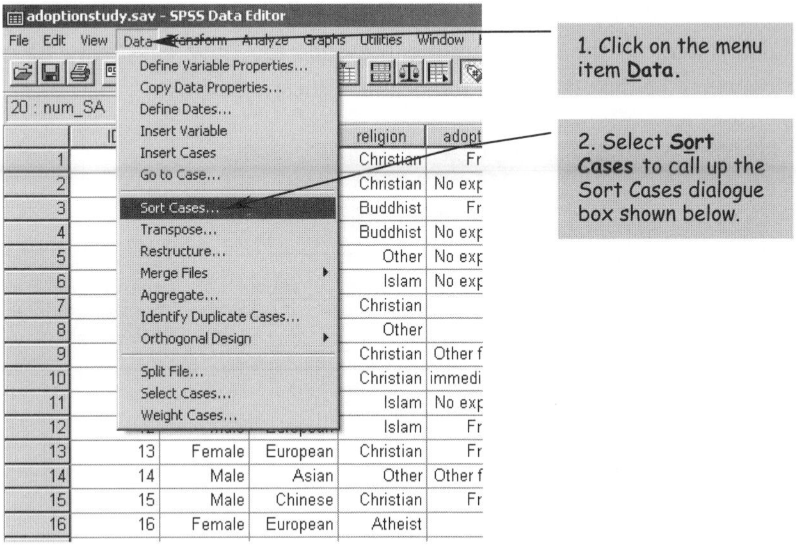

1. Click on the menu item **Data**.

2. Select **Sort Cases** to call up the Sort Cases dialogue box shown below.

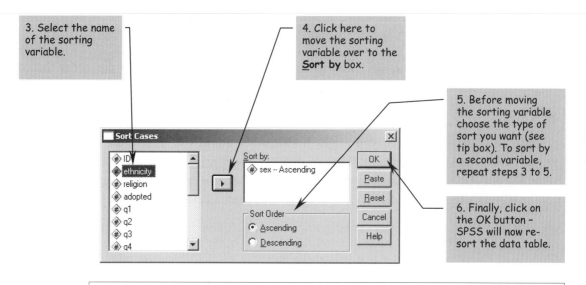

3. Select the name of the sorting variable.

4. Click here to move the sorting variable over to the **Sort by** box.

5. Before moving the sorting variable choose the type of sort you want (see tip box). To sort by a second variable, repeat steps 3 to 5.

6. Finally, click on the OK button – SPSS will now re-sort the data table.

Sort Cases

ID
ethnicity
religion
adopted
q1
q2
q3
q4

Sort by:
sex -- Ascending

Sort Order
○ Ascending
○ Descending

OK
Paste
Reset
Cancel
Help

TIP   You can sort in either ascending or descending order. **Ascending** order puts participants with a low value on the sort variable before participants with a higher value (e.g., Male before Female if we used the code Male = 1, Female = 2). **Descending** would sort in the reverse order. You will probably want **Ascending** order. If, after having made the sort, you decide you have sorted in the wrong order you will need to click on the variable name in the **Sort by** box and then click on the appropriate sort order.

It is possible to sort by string variables (variables that contain letters rather than numbers) – but we recommend that you avoid using string variables anyway.

The cases in your data file will now be sorted by sex and ethnicity. Once the file has been sorted, the data from participant 1 are not necessarily in the first row of the data table, so the "id" variable provides the only easy way of cross-referencing between the data table and the original questionnaires.

adoptionstudy.sav – SPSS Data Editor

File   Edit   View   Data   Transform   Analyze   Graphs   Utilities   Window   Help

1 : ID   8

	ID	sex	ethnicity	religion	adopted
1	8	Male	Asian	Other	Self
2	14	Male	Asian	Other	Other famil
3	18	Male	Asian	Christian	Other famil
4	2	Male	African	Christian	No experie
5	15	Male	Chinese	Christian	Friend
6	7	Male	European	Christian	Self
7	12	Male	European	Islam	Friend
8	19	Female	Asian	Buddhist	Self

Note that after a sort the id number no longer matches the case number.

Section 3: Splitting a file

The **Split File** function is a particularly useful feature of SPSS. **Split File** semi-permanently splits a data file into groups, and in subsequent analysis the output can be organised according to these groups. For example, you can request SPSS to organise all subsequent output so that statistics are presented separately for male and female participants. To split a file, follow the steps shown below.

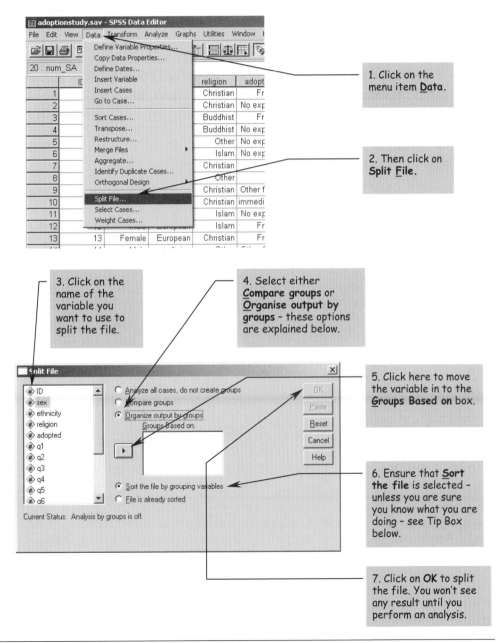

1. Click on the menu item **Data**.

2. Then click on **Split File**.

3. Click on the name of the variable you want to use to split the file.

4. Select either **Compare groups** or **Organise output by groups** – these options are explained below.

5. Click here to move the variable in to the **Groups Based on** box.

6. Ensure that **Sort the file** is selected – unless you are sure you know what you are doing – see Tip Box below.

7. Click on **OK** to split the file. You won't see any result until you perform an analysis.

The difference between the options **Compare groups** and **Organize output by groups** is worth exploring. The former contrasts the two groups within one section of output whereas the latter produces two different sections of output. Try the two options to see which you prefer.

UN-SPLITTING A FILE

Remember that **Split File** is a semi-permanent change. All the output will be broken down by the selected variable until you reverse the process. To do this, first repeat steps 1 and 2 above and then select the option **Analyze all cases, do not create groups**. Then click the OK button. From this point onwards, all the output will return to the normal format.

TIP   SPSS has to sort a file before it can split it. By default SPSS performs the sort automatically before splitting the file. If the file is already sorted then you can save time by selecting the **File is already sorted** option – but this is only worth doing if you have a very large file and you are certain you know that your file is sorted correctly. If in doubt do not select this option.

Section 4: Selecting cases

An alternative to splitting a file, is to select certain cases and use only these in subsequent analyses. For example, we might be particularly interested in the responses made by our Atheist respondents. **Select Cases** will allow us to analyse just these participants' responses. All other data will be temporarily suppressed.

COMPARING THE SELECT CASES AND SPLIT FILE COMMANDS

Select Cases is different from **Split File. Select Cases** suppresses analysis of non-selected cases, whereas **Split File** analyses all cases but arranges output by the sorting variable. Use **Select Cases** when you want to consider only some of your data. Use **Split File** when you want to analyse each of two or more groups of participants.

THE SELECT CASES COMMAND

To **Select Cases**, perform the following steps.

1. Click on the menu item **Data**.

2. Click on **Select Cases**. This will bring up the **Select Cases** dialogue box (see below).

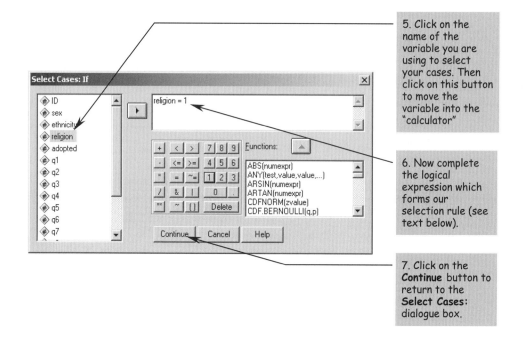

3. Select the **If condition is satisfied** option.

4. Click on the **If** button. This will bring up the **Select Cases: If** dialogue box (see below).

5. Click on the name of the variable you are using to select your cases. Then click on this button to move the variable into the "calculator"

6. Now complete the logical expression which forms our selection rule (see text below).

7. Click on the **Continue** button to return to the **Select Cases:** dialogue box.

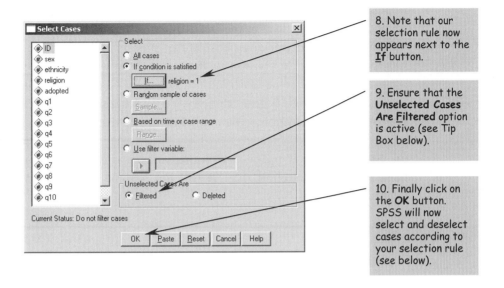

8. Note that our selection rule now appears next to the **If** button.

9. Ensure that the **Unselected Cases Are Filtered** option is active (see Tip Box below).

10. Finally click on the **OK** button. SPSS will now select and deselect cases according to your selection rule (see below).

TIP   In step 9 above, you are asked to check that the **Unselected Cases Are Filtered** option is active. The alternative is **Unselected Cases Are Deleted.** This is a dangerous option which will permanently delete the unselected cases from your data file. If you use this option make certain that you have a back-up copy of your data file.

	ID	sex	ethnicity	religion	adc		filter_$
1	1	Female	African	Christian		gree	Not Selected
2	2	Male	African	Christian	No e	ly Di	Not Selected
3	3	Female	European	Buddhist		ly A	Not Selected
4	4	Female	Chinese	Buddhist	No e	ly A	Not Selected
5	5	Female	African	Other	No e	ided	Not Selected
6	6	Female	Other	Islam	No e	ly A	Not Selected
7	7	Male	European	Christian		ly Di	Not Selected
8	8	Male	Asian	Other		ly A	Not Selected
9	9	Female	African	Christian	Othe	ly A	Not Selected
10	10	Female	Chinese	Christian	imme	gree	Not Selected
11	11	Female	European	Islam	No e	ly Di	Not Selected
12	12	Male	European	Islam		ided	Not Selected
13	13	Female	European	Christian		gree	Not Selected
14	14	Male	Asian	Other	Othe	ly Di	Not Selected
15	15	Male	Chinese	Christian		gree	Not Selected
16	16	Female	European	Atheist		gree	Selected
17	17	Female	Other	Buddhist	No e	ly Di	Not Selected
18	18	Male	Asian	Christian	Othe	gree	Not Selected
19	19	Female	Asian	Buddhist		ly A	Not Selected

adoptionstudy.sav - SPSS Data Editor
File   Edit   View   Data   Transform   Analyze   Graphs   Utilities   Window
20 : num_SA   1

11. SPSS has put a line through the case number of the deselected cases. Note that only case 16 (an atheist) has been selected.

12. SPSS has created a new variable called **filter_$**, which it uses to choose which cases are selected.

You can construct very complex selection rules by using the logical operators AND, OR and NOT. The selection rules can either be typed in from the keyboard or can be built up using the calculator keypad that appears in the dialogue box. Right click on a keypad button to confirm its meaning. If we wanted to select only Chinese Christians who had some experience of adoption we could construct the following expression: **religion = 3 and ethnicity = 3 and adopted = 0.** This is not the only way to make this selection – you might like to try others.

The **Select Cases: If** dialogue box also contains a list of functions that you can include in your selection rule. Right-click on the functions to obtain a brief description of each.

De-selecting cases

The **Select Cases** function can be very useful, but it is important to remember that it is semi-permanent. **Select Cases** will stay in force until you either make some other selection or choose the **All cases** option in the **Select Cases** dialogue box (see step 3 above).

Selection methods

The **Select Cases** dialogue box offers a total of four methods of selecting cases (see step 3 above). The **If Condition is satisfied** method is the one we use most frequently. The **Random sample of cases** method allows you to sample cases at random form your data file. SPSS offers the options of either selecting an approximate percentage of your cases or of selecting an exact number of cases. The **Based on time or case range** method allows you to select cases that fall in a particular range of cases (as defined by the SPSS case number on the extreme left of the data table), or to select cases on the basis of a time or date range (this option is outside the scope of this book). In the **Use filter variable** method, a case is selected if the value of the chosen variable is not zero (and is not missing) – this option can be useful if you have a yes/no variable coded as 1/0. Using this method you could easily select only the "yes" responses.

It is useful to note that a line of text at the bottom of the **Select Cases** dialogue box indicates the current selection rule. Finally, remember to re-select **All cases** after you have completed your analysis of the selected cases.

Section 5: Recoding values

There are many occasions when you need to recode some of your data. This might be because you made an error when entering the data, but it is more likely that you will want to recode your data in light of some preliminary data analysis or in order to allow you to undertake an additional analysis.

For example, early analysis of our adoption survey might reveal that we have very few participants who report experience of adoption through either "immediate family" or "other family". In light of this we might decide to collapse these two categories together into one new category. We could do this manually, but for a large data set it would be time consuming. SPSS provides the **Recode** command for this purpose.

SPSS offers two **Recode** options. We can either change the values in the existing ethnicity variable, or we can create a new variable in which the new ethnic groups are classified. These two options are called **Recode Into Same Variables** and **Recode Into Different Variables** respectively. It is usually safer to recode into a different (new) variable rather than overwriting the original data – that way if you make a mistake you will be able to go back to the original values and try again. To recode a variable, follow the steps outlined below.

RECODE INTO DIFFERENT VARIABLES

1. Click on the menu item **Transform**.

2. Click on **Recode**.

3. Choose which type of recode you want to perform – **Recode Into Different Variables** is the safest.

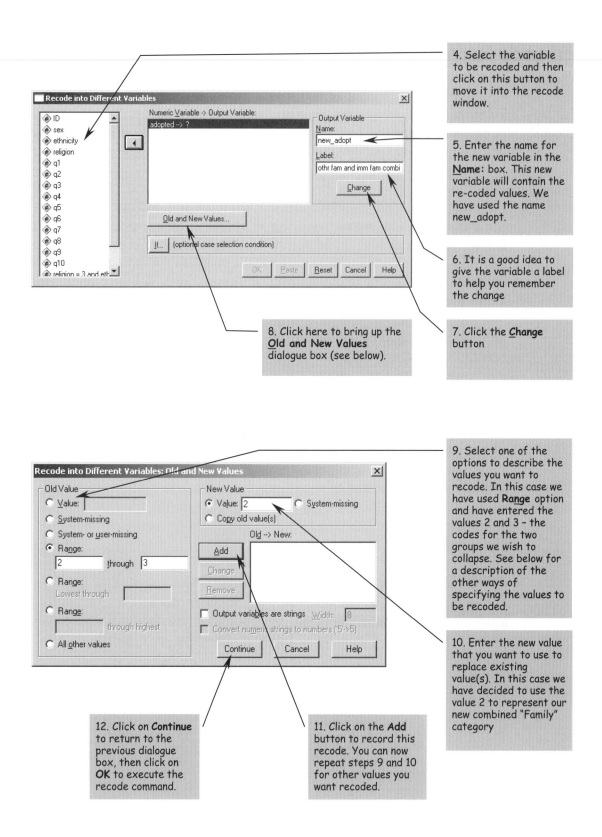

4. Select the variable to be recoded and then click on this button to move it into the recode window.

5. Enter the name for the new variable in the **Name:** box. This new variable will contain the re-coded values. We have used the name new_adopt.

6. It is a good idea to give the variable a label to help you remember the change

7. Click the **Change** button

8. Click here to bring up the **Old and New Values** dialogue box (see below).

9. Select one of the options to describe the values you want to recode. In this case we have used **Range** option and have entered the values 2 and 3 – the codes for the two groups we wish to collapse. See below for a description of the other ways of specifying the values to be recoded.

10. Enter the new value that you want to use to replace existing value(s). In this case we have decided to use the value 2 to represent our new combined "Family" category

12. Click on **Continue** to return to the previous dialogue box, then click on **OK** to execute the recode command.

11. Click on the **Add** button to record this recode. You can now repeat steps 9 and 10 for other values you want recoded.

In the **Recode Into Different Variables: Old and New Values** dialogue box (see step 7 above), you are offered a total of seven different methods of specifying the values you want to recode, and you can use a combination of these methods if required. The **Range: Lowest through** and the **Range: through highest** are often very useful – for example if you want to recode all categories 6 and above together you could use the **Range: through highest** option entering the value 6 in the box. When using these two options you should bear in mind your missing values. If, for example, you used 9 as the missing value, then recoding in this way would result in the missing observation being included in the new category which you may not want.

The **Value:** option allows you to specify a single value that you want to recode. The **All other values** option is, in effect an "and for everything I haven't yet specified" option which allows you to tell SPSS how to recode all of the values not covered by one of the previous recode instructions.

You are less likely to use the **System-missing** or the **System- or user-missing** options. System missing values are rather like user-missing values (what in Chapter 2 we simply called missing values). Both are used to indicate that there is no valid value for a variable. However, a system missing value indicates that SPSS rather than you (the "user") has declared a value non-valid – perhaps, for example, because for this participant it is not possible to calculate a valid value for the variable. These two options allow you to recode these two types of missing values but they should be used with caution. Think carefully about the implications of your actions before using these options.

Note that by entering a value into the **New Value** box which has previously been specified as a missing value (see step 8 above), you can effectively remove a range of values from an analysis by recoding valid responses into missing values. Similarly, by clicking on the **System-missing** option in the **New Value** box you can instruct SPSS to regard any value or range of values as system missing from this point onwards.

The **Copy old value(s)** option is very useful, as it allows you to specify a range of values that should remain unchanged.

TIP Remember, the big advantage of using **Recode into Different Variables** (rather than **Recode into Same Variable** described below) is that you do not lose anything. If you make an error, the original data are still available in the old variable and you can simply try again.

If you are certain that you know what you are doing, and you have a backup of your data file, you might decide that you can over-write the existing data rather than create a new variable. To do this, follow the steps 1 and 2 described above (**Transform > Recode**) but at step 3 select **Into Same Variables.** From this point onwards the procedure is very similar to that described above except that you omit steps 5 to 7 as there is no new variable to name. The results of this recode will over-write the old data in the data table.

CONDITIONAL RECODE

On some occasions you might want to recode a variable only if a particular condition is satisfied for that participant. For example, you might want to perform the recode described above, but only for the female participants. This can be achieved by using the **If** button which appears on the **Recode into Different Variables** and the **Recode into Same Variables** dialogue boxes. Follow the procedure described above up to and including step 7. Then, follow the new steps described below.

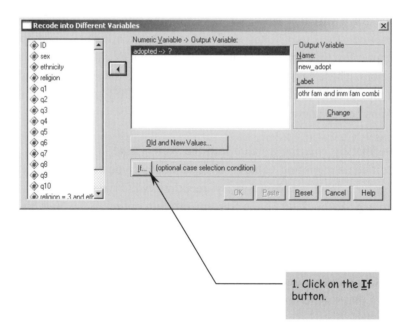

1. Click on the **If** button.

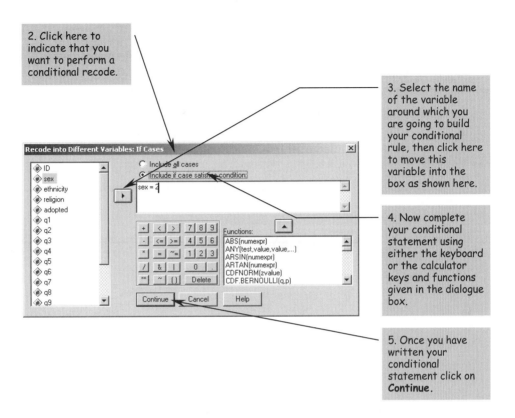

2. Click here to indicate that you want to perform a conditional recode.

3. Select the name of the variable around which you are going to build your conditional rule, then click here to move this variable into the box as shown here.

4. Now complete your conditional statement using either the keyboard or the calculator keys and functions given in the dialogue box.

5. Once you have written your conditional statement click on **Continue**.

This will then return you to the **Recode into Different Variables** dialogue box. Now click on the **Old and New Values** button and proceed as described on page 142.

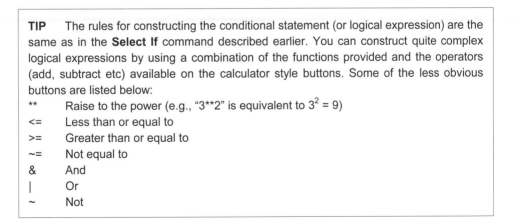

TIP   The rules for constructing the conditional statement (or logical expression) are the same as in the **Select If** command described earlier. You can construct quite complex logical expressions by using a combination of the functions provided and the operators (add, subtract etc) available on the calculator style buttons. Some of the less obvious buttons are listed below:

**	Raise to the power (e.g., "3**2" is equivalent to $3^2 = 9$)
<=	Less than or equal to
>=	Greater than or equal to
~=	Not equal to
&	And
|	Or
~	Not

Section 6: Computing new variables

On occasions we need to calculate a new variable based on the values for existing variables. For example, you may have entered the response given by each participant to each question in a questionnaire. You could now use SPSS to calculate the overall score for the questionnaire or several separate scores for the sub-scales within the questionnaire. In our fictitious survey of attitudes to adoption, we administered a 10 item questionnaire which was made up of two sub-scales. We therefore need to sum the responses to all the items that contribute to each of the sub-scales. SPSS can do this for us using the **Compute** command.

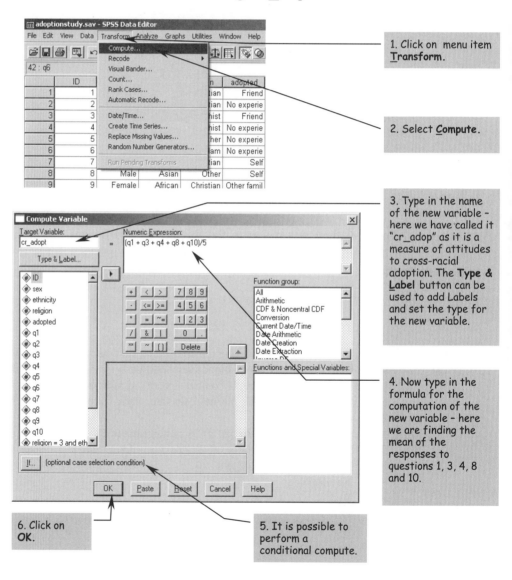

1. Click on menu item **Transform**.

2. Select **Compute**.

3. Type in the name of the new variable – here we have called it "cr_adop" as it is a measure of attitudes to cross-racial adoption. The **Type & Label** button can be used to add Labels and set the type for the new variable.

4. Now type in the formula for the computation of the new variable – here we are finding the mean of the responses to questions 1, 3, 4, 8 and 10.

5. It is possible to perform a conditional compute.

6. Click on OK.

TIP   When entering the name of the new variable (see step 3 above) it is possible to enter a variable label to act as a reminder of what the new variable means. Do this by clicking on the **Type&Label** button. You can then either type in a text label, or by selecting the **Use expression as label** option, you can ask SPSS to use your numeric expression as the variable label. In this case the label would be "(q1+q3+q4+q8+q10)/5".

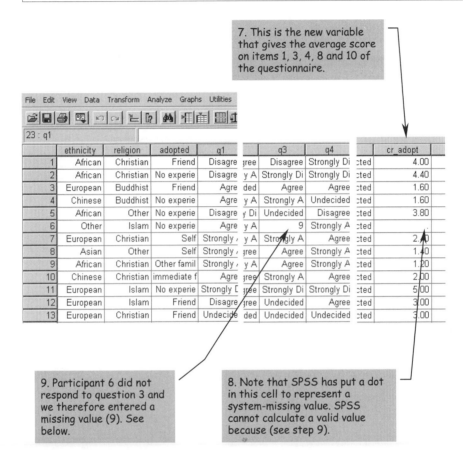

7. This is the new variable that gives the average score on items 1, 3, 4, 8 and 10 of the questionnaire.

9. Participant 6 did not respond to question 3 and we therefore entered a missing value (9). See below.

8. Note that SPSS has put a dot in this cell to represent a system-missing value. SPSS cannot calculate a valid value because (see step 9).

COMPUTE AND MISSING VALUES

When using **Compute** you must think carefully about missing values. SPSS will not be able to compute the value of the new variable if **any** of the values for the variables involved in the compute statement are missing. In the example above, participant 6 had not answered question 3 and we had entered a missing value (9) in this cell of the data table. As SPSS knows that this is not a valid response it refuses to compute a value for the new variable "cr_adopt" for this participant. With more complex compute statements involving lots of variables this can be a major problem. One way round this problem is to make use of the functions such as Mean which make allowances for missing values.

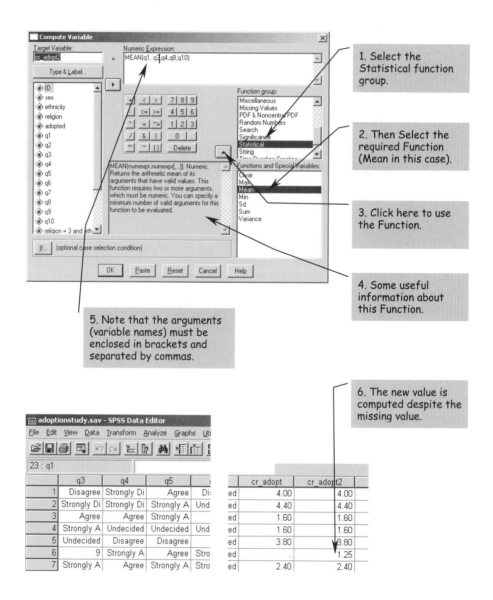

1. Select the Statistical function group.

2. Then Select the required Function (Mean in this case).

3. Click here to use the Function.

4. Some useful information about this Function.

5. Note that the arguments (variable names) must be enclosed in brackets and separated by commas.

6. The new value is computed despite the missing value.

TIP   It is important to consider whether the new values computed using Functions in this way are legitimate. Remember one or more of the scores contributing to the new variable was missing. This is especially important for Functions such as Sum.

Section 7: Counting values

Sometimes it is useful to be able to count for each participant how many times a particular value occurs over a range of variables. If, as in our example data set, you have a series of variables which represent the responses to questionnaire items, you might want to find out how many times each participant has answered "Strongly Agree". You could do this by asking SPSS to count the number of times the value 1 (the value used to code the response "Strongly Agree") has occurred in variables Q1 to Q10. Using **Count**, SPSS will create a new variable that will contain a value representing the number of times the value 1 occurs in variable Q1 to Q10.

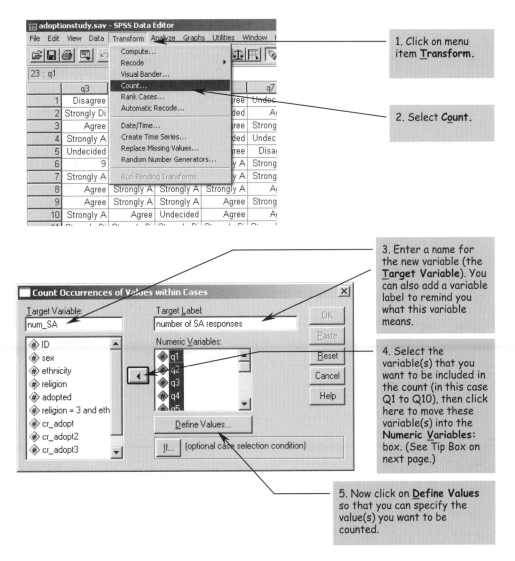

1. Click on menu item **Transform**.

2. Select **Count**.

3. Enter a name for the new variable (the **Target Variable**). You can also add a variable label to remind you what this variable means.

4. Select the variable(s) that you want to be included in the count (in this case Q1 to Q10), then click here to move these variable(s) into the **Numeric Variables:** box. (See Tip Box on next page.)

5. Now click on **Define Values** so that you can specify the value(s) you want to be counted.

TIP When selecting more than one variable – as in step 4 above – you can select them all in one go by holding down the shift Key and clicking on the first and then the last of the variables. You can then click on the 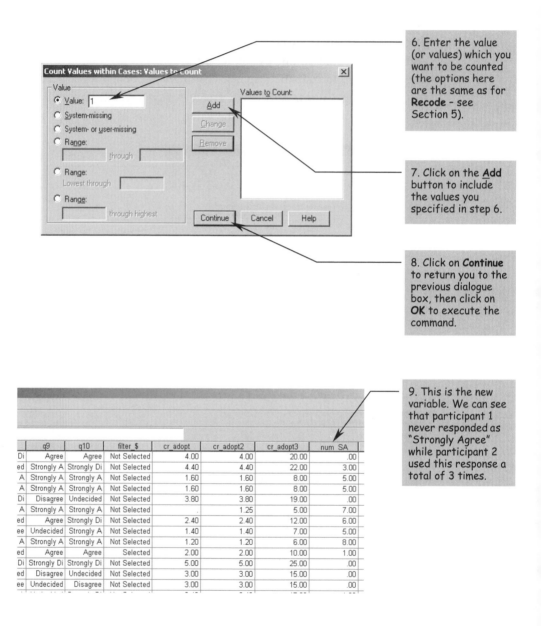 button to move them all together.

6. Enter the value (or values) which you want to be counted (the options here are the same as for **Recode** – see Section 5).

7. Click on the **Add** button to include the values you specified in step 6.

8. Click on **Continue** to return you to the previous dialogue box, then click on **OK** to execute the command.

9. This is the new variable. We can see that participant 1 never responded as "Strongly Agree" while participant 2 used this response a total of 3 times.

	q9	q10	filter_$	cr_adopt	cr_adopt2	cr_adopt3	num_SA
Di	Agree	Agree	Not Selected	4.00	4.00	20.00	.00
ed	Strongly A	Strongly Di	Not Selected	4.40	4.40	22.00	3.00
A	Strongly A	Strongly A	Not Selected	1.60	1.60	8.00	5.00
A	Strongly A	Strongly A	Not Selected	1.60	1.60	8.00	5.00
Di	Disagree	Undecided	Not Selected	3.80	3.80	19.00	.00
A	Strongly A	Strongly A	Not Selected		1.25	5.00	7.00
ed	Agree	Strongly Di	Not Selected	2.40	2.40	12.00	6.00
ee	Undecided	Strongly A	Not Selected	1.40	1.40	7.00	5.00
A	Strongly A	Strongly A	Not Selected	1.20	1.20	6.00	8.00
ed	Agree	Agree	Selected	2.00	2.00	10.00	1.00
Di	Strongly Di	Strongly Di	Not Selected	5.00	5.00	25.00	.00
ed	Disagree	Undecided	Not Selected	3.00	3.00	15.00	.00
ee	Undecided	Disagree	Not Selected	3.00	3.00	15.00	.00

CONDITIONAL COUNT

It is possible to perform a conditional count – which is to only count the occurrences of a value(s) for participants who satisfy some particular criterion. This is done by clicking on the **If** button either before or after you have specified the values to be counted (see step 5 above). This will bring up a dialogue box almost identical to the one we used for the conditional recode described in Section 5. You can now specify your conditional rule and then click on the **Continue** button.

Section 8: Ranking cases

Sometimes it is useful to convert interval or ratio scores (scale data) into ordinal scores. We might, for example, want to convert the variable "cr_adopt" which we calculated using **Compute** in Section 6, into a rank score. That is, we might want to rank all of our participants on the basis of their score on this variable. The participant who had the highest overall raceadop score would be given a rank of 1, the next highest a rank of 2 and so on. The **Rank Cases** command calculates the ranks for us and generates a new variable to contain the ranks. We can rank in either ascending or descending order, and can even rank on the basis of more than one variable.

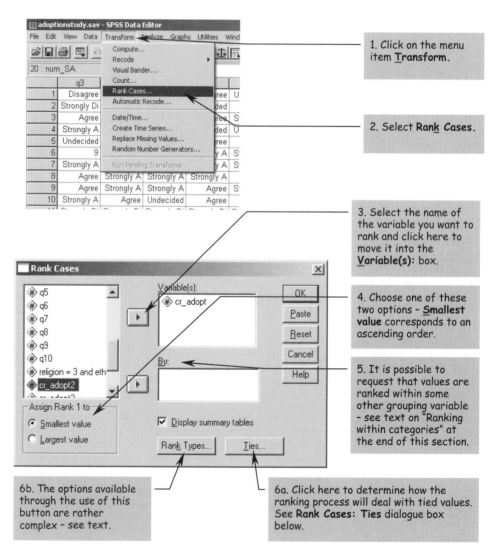

1. Click on the menu item **Transform**.

2. Select **Rank Cases**.

3. Select the name of the variable you want to rank and click here to move it into the **Variable(s):** box.

4. Choose one of these two options – **Smallest value** corresponds to an ascending order.

5. It is possible to request that values are ranked within some other grouping variable – see text on "Ranking within categories" at the end of this section.

6b. The options available through the use of this button are rather complex – see text.

6a. Click here to determine how the ranking process will deal with tied values. See **Rank Cases: Ties** dialogue box below.

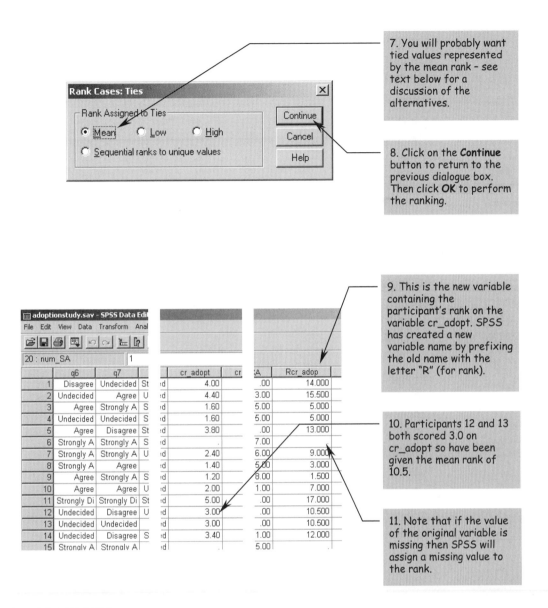

7. You will probably want tied values represented by the mean rank – see text below for a discussion of the alternatives.

8. Click on the **Continue** button to return to the previous dialogue box. Then click **OK** to perform the ranking.

9. This is the new variable containing the participant's rank on the variable cr_adopt. SPSS has created a new variable name by prefixing the old name with the letter "R" (for rank).

10. Participants 12 and 13 both scored 3.0 on cr_adopt so have been given the mean rank of 10.5.

11. Note that if the value of the original variable is missing then SPSS will assign a missing value to the rank.

RANKING TIED VALUES

SPSS provides four alternative methods of handling tied values. The default, **Mean** method, gives the tied values the mean of the available ranks. You can see this option in operation above where participants 12 and 13 both scored 3.0 on cr_adopt and were given a rank of 10.5 – the mean of ranks 10 and 11. This is the ranking method described in most introductory statistics books. The **Low** option assigns the tied participants the lowest of the available ranks – so in this case both would have been ranked 10. The **Highest** option would award both participants the highest of the available ranks – 11 in this case. The **Sequential ranks to unique values** option would assign a rank of 10 to both participants 12 and 13, but would then assign a rank of 11 to the next highest scoring participant, thus ensuring that all the sequential ranks are awarded – this means that the highest rank will **not** be equal to the number of valid cases (as it would for the other three methods).

Try these options for yourself and compare the results.

TYPES OF RANKING

SPSS provides a wide range of different ranking methods. These are available by clicking on the **Ran<u>k</u> Types** button (see step 6b above). These options are rather complex and are beyond the scope of this book. Right-click on each of the options to obtain a brief description of their function. If in doubt leave the **<u>M</u>ean** option selected.

RANKING WITHIN CATEGORIES

By specifying a second variable in the **<u>B</u>y** box (see step 5 above) it is possible to request SPSS to rank the scores on the first variable within categories formed by the second variable. For example, if we specified the variable sex in this box, then SPSS would first rank all the male participants and then rank all the female participants. Thus, in this case we would have two participants (one male and one female) with a rank of 1.

Section 9: Other useful functions

Under the **Transform** and **Data** menu items you will find several other useful commands. These are described briefly here. In explaining these commands, we have not made use of the annotated screen images used above. Instead, to save space we have described the actions required to execute a command in words only. We describe a series of actions using a simple shorthand notation. So, clicking on the menu item **Transform** then selecting **Compute** would be written as:

Transform ⇒ **Compute**

This notation will also be used in some of the later sections of this book.

AUTOMATIC RECODE

Automatic Recode converts string variables into numeric variables. For example, if you had coded sex as a string variable, using the strings "M" and "F" to code male and female, you may discover that some commands will not work with string variables. **Automatic Recode** will resolve this problem by recoding string variables into numeric variables. The old string variables are recoded in alphabetical order, so in the case above "F" would be recoded as 1 and "M" as 2. Any value or variable labels are transferred. If there were no value labels then the old strings are used as the labels (therefore, in the case above the value label "F" would be attached to the value 1).

The commands needed are:

Transform ⇒ **Automatic Recode**

Now select the name of the variable to be recoded and move it into the **Variable ->** **New Name** box. Next specify a new name for the variable, click on **New Name** and finally click on ` OK `.

CATEGORIZE VARIABLES

The **Categorize variables** command is a relatively new introduction to SPSS. It is really an automatic recode function, in that it allows you to recode a continuous variable (e.g., age) into a categorical variable. For example, we might recode age so that we had five different age categories rather than the actual age of the participants recorded. Note that **Categorize variable** recodes on the basis of the value of the input variable, not the frequency of the values. Thus, the above example will create five categories covering an equal age range, but probably not an equal number of participants in each age category. You can choose the number of categories that your input variable is recoded into.

This command is accessed by:

Transform ⇒ **Categorize variables**

CREATE TIME SERIES AND REPLACE MISSING VALUES

Time series are special types of data in which measurements are made repeatedly over a period of time. Time series data in SPSS are unusual in that each row of the data file becomes a sampling time rather than a participant. The analysis of time series data is beyond the scope of this book, but the **Create Time Series** and **Replace Missing Values** commands allow you to create new variables based on time series data, and estimate values to replace missing observations respectively.

Section 10: Data file for scales or questionnaires

In this section, we demonstrate how SPSS can be used to help you handle data obtained using scales or questionnaires. We describe a simple data check, and how to recode responses from reversed items. Checking the reliability and dimensionality of a scale are covered in Chapter 11, Sections 4 and 5.

We have entered data obtained with Larsen's (1995) Attitudes to Recycling (ATR) scale, used for a Research Methods exercise with first-year Psychology students at University of Westminster. There are 20 items, used in the order that they are printed in Larsen (1995, Table 1). Two changes were made, as Larsen developed his scale in USA: "styrofoam" was replaced with "polystyrene"; "sorting garbage" was replaced with "sorting rubbish into different containers". We used a Likert-type scale with responses from 1 (strongly agree) to 5 (strongly disagree). The data file "ScaleV1.sav" (see Appendix I or from the web address listed there) holds fifty cases, which we will use to demonstrate some issues around use of scales in Psychology. Normally one would need many more cases.

If you open the data file from the web, then in Variable View note that:
1. "Qnum" holds a number that was written on each questionnaire as the data were entered. In this data file it is the same number as the SPSS case number, but if we subsequently modify the order of cases in the data file (see Section 2) then "Qnum" will allow identification of the questionnaire for a particular case.
2. The responses to each item have been entered separately: "q_a" to "q_t". Students often wish to obtain total or mean score by hand from scales or questionnaires, and enter those totals only. It is much better practice to enter the responses to each item: various checks can then be carried out on data, as we explain in this section and in Chapter 11. **Compute** can be used to accurately calculate the total or mean response for each participant.
3. We defined 9 as missing value for all scale items in advance; there were only two missing values but defining them in advance speeds up data entry.

A SIMPLE CHECK ON DATA ENTRY

Click on menu items **Analyze** ⇒ **Descriptive Statistics** ⇒ **Descriptives**. Select all the item variable names for analysis, then click on OK. That gives the default output, which is all that we need at this stage. A section of the output is shown on the next page. Inspect the minimum and maximum values of all items: for "q_c" the maximum value is 6, yet the responses were from 1 to 5. Note any such oddities.

Descriptive Statistics

	N	Minimum	Maximum	Mean	Std. Deviation
q_a	50	2	5	3.96	.832
q_b	50	1	5	2.06	.913
q_c	50	2	6	3.94	1.058
q_d	50	2	5	4.34	.688

This error in data entry can be found and corrected in the following way:

1. In Data View, click on the "q_c" variable name.
2. Click on menu items **Edit** ⇒ **Find**.
3. In the **Find Data in Variable ...** dialogue box, type 6, and click on the **Find Next** button. (Note: the "..." above will actually be the variable name of the column you are in.)
4. A cell containing a 6 will be found. It is from questionnaire number 2.
5. Click on **Find Next** again, in case there are others. Note questionnaire numbers.
6. Go back to the questionnaires, and check the actual response/s.

In this data file only one error was found. The response on questionnaire 2 to item c was actually 5. Correct that response, and save the data file as ScaleV2.sav, so that you can use it in the next exercise.

REVERSALS

Good scales or questionnaires have some items that are reversed to avoid participant response bias. Some scales are printed with the code for each response to assist data entry; however, others don't as the numbers may distract or lead the respondent. We can use SPSS to reverse the entered scores. First, consider which direction you want a high score to indicate. For example, consider these two items from a library satisfaction questionnaire:

1. The University library is an excellent place to make notes for coursework.
2. I find it very difficult to study in the University library.

   With responses on a scale of 1 (strongly agree) to 5 (strongly disagree), then any individual with strong views should respond in opposite directions to those two items. Do you want your final score to represent overall *satisfaction* with the library or overall *dissatisfaction*? That will determine which items you reverse.

> **TIP** This type of data can be scored in either direction. It is crucial that you keep track of the scale on the original items, and what the final score represents.

You need data file ScaleV2.sav, that you saved in the previous exercise. If we want high scores from these data to mean that the participant thinks that recycling and related environmental issues are important, then the following items should be reversed: b, g, h, i, k, l, m, p, q, r. We can do this using the Recode command in the following way. This procedure is illustrated above in Section 5.

1. Click on menu items **Transform** ⇒ **Recode** ⇒ **Into Different Variables**.
2. In the **Recode into Different Variables** dialogue box:
   move across, one after the other, the variables that hold responses for items that need to be reversed.
3. Select the first (q_b) and enter the name for the output variable: we suggest q_bR (the R to indicate that the scores within it have been reversed from the original variable). Click on the **Change** button.
4. Repeat in turn for all the items that need to be reversed.
5. Click on the **Old and New Values** button.
6. In the **Recode into Different Variables: Old and New Values** dialogue box, enter the old and new values one at a time. It will then look as shown below. Remember to recode all the values: in the example data file we have some missing values.

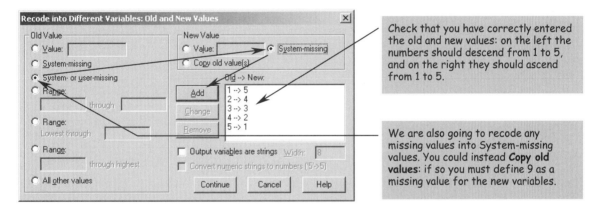

Check that you have correctly entered the old and new values: on the left the numbers should descend from 1 to 5, and on the right they should ascend from 1 to 5.

We are also going to recode any missing values into System-missing values. You could instead **Copy old values**: if so you must define 9 as a missing value for the new variables.

7. Click on **Continue**, then on **OK**. The new variables will be at the right hand end of the data file.
8. You can delete the original variables for those items that you have reversed. This has the advantage that you then cannot use the original variable by mistake in future analyses. You should be careful, however, that you do not delete any of the original variables that you still need! If you save versions of your data file as you proceed, you will always have original variables if you need them again.
9. Save the data file as ScaleV3.sav. The variables and the first case should be as shown below. The file is now ready to use in other exercises on assessing the reliability and dimensionality of the scale (Chapter 11, Sections 4 and 5).

Qnum	q_a	q_c	q_d	q_e	q_f	q_j	q_n	q_o	q_s	q_t	q_bR	q_gR	q_hR	q_iR	q_kR	q_lR	q_mR	q_pR	q_qR	q_rR
1	4	3	4	4	4	4	5	4	3	5	4	4	4	4	4	4	3	3	1	3

Chapter Seven

Analysis of Variance

*An introduction to Analysis of
    Variance (ANOVA)*
One-way between-subjects ANOVA
Two-way between-subjects ANOVA
One-way within-subjects ANOVA
Two-way within-subjects ANOVA
Mixed ANOVA
Some additional points
Planned and unplanned comparisons
*Nonparametric equivalents to
    ANOVA: Kruskal–Wallis and
    Friedman*

Section 1: An introduction to Analysis of Variance (ANOVA)

WHAT IS ANOVA?

ANOVA is an enormously useful statistical procedure that is very widely used in psychological research. The popularity of this statistical procedure is based on two important characteristics:

1. ANOVA will allow us to handle the data from experiments that have designs involving more than two conditions. You will remember that the *t*-test allowed us to compare the means of two sets of scores (either from two groups of participants – an independent *t*-test – or from a repeated measures design involving two conditions – a dependent or paired *t*-test). However, in practice, we may wish to design experiments involving more than two conditions and in these situations, rather than using several *t*-tests to compare all possible differences, we can use a single ANOVA. This single test will tell us whether the change in the independent variable has affected the scores – that is, whether the different conditions have resulted in significantly different scores. It should be noted that ANOVA cannot tell us precisely which pairs of conditions are significantly different. For example, if the independent variable has three conditions, ANOVA will tell us whether the scores significantly vary across those conditions. However, it will not tell us whether condition 1 is significantly different from condition 2, whether condition 2 is significantly different from condition 3, or whether condition 1 is significantly different from condition 3. Such comparisons of specific means require some additional statistical procedures called planned and unplanned comparisons, which we will cover later in this chapter.

2. ANOVA also allows us to investigate the effect of more than one independent variable. All the experimental designs that we have considered so far have involved investigating the effect of just one IV on one DV. ANOVA will allow us to design experiments involving more than one IV. For example, we could examine the effect of participants' sex as well as their age on their memory for a list of words. Here we have two IVs (sex and age) and one DV (memory score). A single ANOVA test will allow us simultaneously to examine the effect of these two IVs. In fact ANOVA can handle any number of IVs in a single experiment – but in practice we rarely include more than three or four for reasons that will become apparent shortly.

This ability to include more than one IV in an experimental design not only saves time but also allows us to investigate how these IVs combine to affect the DV. For example, we might know that two new drugs are each quite safe when administered on their own. However, it could be that when administered together they are lethal. This is an example of a drug interaction. In statistics we are interested in how independent variables interact. That is, we can ask questions about how the sex **and** the age of a participant **combine** to affect memory score – it might be that male participants' performances decline with age but that female participants' performances improve with age. Such an *interaction* between these two variables is clearly of enormous theoretical importance, but it is only by manipulating both variables in one design that we can discover this interaction. A major advantage of ANOVA over the procedures we have looked at so far is that it can reveal such interactions.

WHEN CAN WE USE ANOVA?

In order to legitimately use ANOVA, the following conditions must be met:
1. The dependent variable comprises of interval or ratio data.
2. The populations are normally distributed.
3. The population variances are all equal.
4. In the case of independent groups designs, independent random samples must have been taken from each population.

HOW DOES IT WORK?

We all know that humans vary in performance, both between individuals and within individuals over time. For these reasons, if we conduct a simple experiment comparing, say, the time it takes to learn a list of short words, medium length words and long words, we would not expect all the participants within a condition to take the same amount of time. We naturally accept that some participants will be faster than others (i.e., there will be variation between individuals). We also know that any one participant might take less or more time on one occasion than on other occasions (i.e., there will be variation within individuals). Remember that we can measure the amount of variation within a set of scores with measures of dispersion, such as the standard deviation or the *variance.*

Now let us imagine for a moment that we were RobotoPsychologists – that is, we were interested in the psychology of robots (rather than robots interested in psychology!). If we repeated our learning experiment with a group of R2D2 robots, we would expect all of the robots in one condition to react at exactly the same speed. That is, robots would not vary either between or within individuals. Table 6.1 shows some hypothetical data for robots and for humans.

Table 6.1: Time (in seconds) taken to learn three different lists of words for a group of human and robot participants. The robots show no individual differences and so the variance within each condition is zero.

ROBOTS			
LIST A	*LIST B*	*LIST C*	
10	20	30	
10	20	30	
10	20	30	
10	20	30	
10	20	30	
10	20	30	
10	20	30	
10	20	30	
Mean = 10	*Mean = 20*	*Mean = 30*	***Grand Mean = 20***

HUMANS			
LIST A	*LIST B*	*LIST C*	
30	54	68	
40	58	75	
35	45	80	
45	60	75	
38	52	85	
42	56	90	
36	65	75	
25	52	88	
Mean = 36.375	*Mean = 55.25*	*Mean = 79.50*	***Grand Mean = 57.04***

Let us just consider the data from the humans for the moment. If we asked you to "eye-ball" the raw data and guess whether there was a difference in learning times for the three lists, you would probably have no problem saying that the difference did appear to be significant. In making this judgement you are actually doing something quite sophisticated. What you are doing is deciding whether the natural variation between individuals within the conditions is large or small compared to the variation between individuals across the different conditions. That is, you are asking "OK, so not all the participants in the List A condition took the same time, and OK not all the participants in the List B or List C condition took the same time, but is this natural variation (or noise) large or small compared to the difference in times between the three conditions?" In this case participants within each condition might vary from each other by several seconds, but this is small compared to the larger differences between the times produced under the three different list conditions.

Let us look at the robots' data again. Robots perform identically under identical conditions (or at least our robots do), so within each condition every robot has exactly the same learning time. Thus the variance within each condition is zero. But if we compare the performance between the three conditions, it is clear that all the robots were fastest at learning the short words and all took longest to learn the long words. You might conclude that you want to switch from Psychology to RobotoPsychology, but there is also a more important point here. What we want to do is make our human participants' data more like the robots' data – that is, we want to reduce the variance down towards zero. In fact all the practices of good experimental design, such as giving all participants the same instructions and testing under identical conditions, are designed to do just this – to reduce the variance within each condition. This good experimental practice will reduce the variance but will not eliminate it – our participants will never behave exactly like the robots. So, if we cannot eliminate the variance perhaps we can account for it. What we need is a statistical procedure that takes account of the variance within the conditions and compares this to the variance between conditions. If the variance between conditions is much larger than the variance within conditions then surely we can say that the IV is having a larger effect on the scores than the individual differences are. Clearly, for the robots the variance within the conditions is zero and the variance between the conditions is quite large. For our humans, the situation is not quite so clear cut, but if we calculate the variances we will find the same basic pattern applies:

Variance between conditions > variance within conditions

This concept of calculating the variance due to nuisance factors such as individual differences and comparing it to the variance due to our manipulation of the IV is central to ANOVA. Exactly how we calculate these variances can get rather complex for some designs, but this does not alter the basic principle that we simply want to ask whether or not the variance in the data brought about by our manipulation of the IV is larger than that brought about by the other nuisance factors such as individual differences. The variance brought about by these nuisance variables is usually referred to as the *error variance*, so we ask whether the error variance is less than the variance due to the manipulation of the IV.

A convenient way of expressing this is to calculate the ratio of the variance due to our manipulation of the IV and the error variance. This ratio is known as the *F*-ratio (named after Fisher). The *F*-ratio is:

F = Variance due to manipulation of IV/Error variance

If the error variance is small compared to the variance due to the IV (as in the case of our robots where the error variance is zero), then the F-ratio will be a number greater than 1 (a large number divided by a smaller number always gives rise to a number greater than 1). If, on the other hand, the effect of the IV is small, and/or the error variance is large (perhaps because our participants varied considerably or because we did not adequately control the experiment) then the F-ratio will be a number less than 1 (a small number divided by larger number will always result in a number less than 1). Thus, we can now say that the effect of the IV is definitely not significant if the F-ratio is less than 1. This is because the error variance is actually larger than the variance caused by our manipulation of the IV.

So, the F-ratio is simply the ratio of these two estimates of variance. The larger the F-ratio, the greater the effect of the IV compared to the "noise" (error variance) in the data. An F-ratio equal to or less than 1 indicates a non-significant result as it shows that the scores were equally affected or more affected by the nuisance variables (such as individual differences) as they were by the manipulation of the IV.

HOW DO WE FIND OUT IF THE F-RATIO IS SIGNIFICANT?

Once we have calculated the value of the F-ratio and found it is larger than 1, we need to determine whether it is large enough to be regarded as significant. That is, we ask whether the effect of the IV is sufficiently larger than the effect of the nuisance variables to regard the result as significant. When calculating the F-ratio with a calculator, we consult F tables to discover, given the number of observations we made, what value F had to exceed to be considered as significant. When using SPSS to perform ANOVA, the output reports the exact p value for that particular F-ratio. This p value is the probability of getting this F-ratio by chance alone and it needs to be less than 0.05 for the F-ratio to be regarded as significant.

WHAT ABOUT DEGREES OF FREEDOM?

You will remember from performing a t-test, another test of difference, that we need to calculate and report the degrees of freedom associated with our analysis. One complication with ANOVA is that for each F value we must report two sets of degrees of freedom. This is because we need to remember how many observations went into our calculation of the error variance and also how many went into our calculation of the variance due to the manipulation of the IV. As these are the bottom and top halves of the F-ratio equation, these are sometimes referred to as the denominator and numerator degrees of freedom respectively. A good statistics text will explain the calculation of degrees of freedom in detail, but as SPSS calculates and reports these for you, all you need know is to expect two values for each *F*-ratio. We will look at how to report these degrees of freedom and the *F*-ratio in more detail later.

WHAT TERMS ARE USED WITH ANOVA?

Different textbooks tend to use slightly different terminologies to describe ANOVA. To avoid the problems this can create we are going to use what we consider to be the simplest terminology.

Factors

These are really independent variables, but as there may well be more than one of them per study, it makes sense to call them factors from now on.

Levels of factors

These are similar to conditions. In the experiments we considered earlier, we had a single IV which was manipulated to create two conditions. We would now describe this as a single factor with two levels. In ANOVA designs a factor can have as many levels as we like. For example, we might have a factor of Drug Dosage which might be manipulated to create four levels of 0mg, 10mg, 20mg and 30mg.

Between-subjects factors

These are factors whose levels vary between participants, so that each participant will experience only one level of a factor. For example, a participant can be administered 0mg, 10mg, 20mg or 30mg. This is a factor that is manipulated using an independent groups design, which we will now refer to as a "between-subjects design".

Within-subjects factors

These are factors whose levels vary within a participant, so that each participant will experience two or more levels of a factor. For example, a participant might be administered all four different drug dosages. This is a factor that is manipulated using a repeated measures design, which we will now refer to as a "within-subjects design".

Mixed ANOVA designs

The term "mixed ANOVA design" is used when a design includes one or more within-subjects factors and one or more between-subjects factors.

HOW DO WE DESCRIBE ANOVA DESIGNS?

When describing an ANOVA design we need to specify three things:
1. How many factors are involved in the design.
2. How many levels there are of each factor.
3. Whether each factor is a within- or a between-subjects factor.

The number of factors is described by talking about a one-way ANOVA (where there is one factor), a two-way ANOVA (two factors) and so on (e.g., a six-way ANOVA would have six factors). What this does not tell you is how many levels each factor has. You could describe this in long hand, but there is an easier convention. For example, a three-way ANOVA in which the first factor, Sex, had two levels, the second factor, Age, had three levels and the third factor, Drug Dosage, had five levels could be described more simply as a 2*3*5 ANOVA design. Note that in this terminology the number of numerals (three in this case) describes the number of factors, and the values of the numerals indicate the number of levels of each of these factors. Using this terminology we just need to make it clear whether the factors were within- or between-subjects factors. We could do this by writing:

*"A 2*3*5 (Sex*Age*Drug dose) mixed ANOVA design was employed where Sex and Age were between-subjects factors and Drug dose was a within-subjects factor."*

MAIN EFFECTS AND INTERACTIONS

Using ANOVA we can analyse data from studies that incorporate more than one factor. We can assess both the effect of each of these factors on their own and the interaction between the factors. The term "main effect" is used to describe the independent effect of a factor. For example, in the 2*3*5 ANOVA described above, three main effects will be reported. The main effect of Sex will tell us whether men performed significantly differently from women, irrespective of their age or drug dosage. The main effect of Age will tell us whether age affects performance, irrespective of sex or drug dose. Finally, the main effect of Drug dose will tell us whether drug dosage affects performance, irrespective of the sex or age of the participants. These main effects simply compare the mean for one level of a factor with the mean of the other level(s) of that factor – for example, comparing mean male performance levels to mean female performance levels. Interactions on the other hand assess the combined effect of the factors. An interaction that assesses how two factors combine to affect performance is called a two-way interaction. When three factors are involved, the interaction is known as a three-way interaction.

When attempting to understand the output from the ANOVA command in SPSS, it is very helpful if you know in advance how many results you are looking for.

1. A one-way ANOVA, where the single factor is called A, will give rise to just a single main effect of A.
2. A two-way ANOVA, where the factors are called A and B, will give rise to two main effects (main effect of A and main effect of B), and a single two-way interaction (A*B). This is a total of three results (3 *F*-ratios).
3. A three-way ANOVA, where the factors are called A, B and C, will give rise to three main effects (main effect of A, main effect of B and main effect of C), three two-way interactions (A*B, A*C and B*C) and a single three-way interaction (A*B*C). This is a total of six results.
4. A four-way ANOVA, where the factors are called A, B, C, and D, will give rise to four main effects (main effect of A, main effect of B, main effect of C and main effect of D), six two-way interactions (A*B, A*C, A*D, B*C, B*D and C*D), four three-way interactions (A*B*C, A*B*D, A*C*D and B*C*D), and a single four-way interaction (A*B*C*D). This is a total of 15 results.

You can now see why it is unusual to include more than four factors in a design. The number of possible interactions rises steeply as the number of factors increases. Furthermore, it is unlikely that you hypothesised about the shape of these higher level interactions and if they are significant they can be very hard to describe and/or explain. Using SPSS it is very easy to undertake a four- or even five-way ANOVA, but rather more difficult to explain the results. Our advice is to try to limit yourself to a maximum of three factors.

HOW DO WE CALCULATE THE *F*-RATIO?

You do not need to know how to calculate the *F*-ratio, as SPSS will do this for you. However, to fully appreciate the output that SPSS generates, it would be helpful to read this section and to realise why the calculation is dependent on the type of factor manipulated. We show this below with reference to a one-way design.

Let us go back to our learning experiment, and imagine that there are different humans taking part in each condition; that 8 participants were asked to learn list A, another 8 to learn list B and another 8 to learn list C.

Table 6.2: Time (in seconds) taken to learn three different lists of words for the group of human participants in a between-subjects design.

HUMANS		
LIST A	*LIST B*	*LIST C*
30	54	68
40	58	75
35	45	80
45	60	75
38	52	85
42	56	90
36	65	75
25	52	88
Mean = 36.375	*Mean = 55.25*	*Mean = 79.50*	*Grand Mean = 57.04*

There are two sources of variance of interest here.

1. How do the scores in one group vary from those in the other groups? We can look at how the mean of each column deviates from the grand mean. This provides us with a measure of the variance due to the factor.

2. How do the scores vary within each group? We can look at how each score within a column deviates from the mean for that condition. This provides us with a measure of noise.

Together these two sources of variance must add up to the total variance (the variance between each single score and the grand mean). That is:

$$\text{Var}_{(Total)} = \text{Var}_{(Between\ Groups)} + \text{Var}_{(Within\ Groups)}$$

The box below and overleaf shows the steps involved in calculating both sources of variance. Although you will probably never use a calculator to work out the *F*-ratio, you may find it helpful to look at the box and familiarise yourself with the procedure.

STEP A

We first calculate the **Sum of Squares (Within groups)**: this is the sum of all the squared differences between each individual data point and the mean for that group.

$SS_{(within\ groups)} = (30-36.375)^2 + (40-36.375)^2 + (35-36.375)^2 + (45-36.375)^2 + (38-36.375)^2 + (42-36.375)^2 + (36-36.375)^2 + (25-36.375)^2 + (54-55.25)^2 + (58-55.25)^2 + (45-55.25)^2 + (60-55.25)^2 + (52-55.25)^2 + (56-55.25)^2 + (65-55.25)^2 + (52-55.25)^2 + (68-79.5)^2 + (75-79.5)^2 + (80-79.5)^2 + (75-79.5)^2 + (85-79.5)^2 + (90-79.5)^2 + (75-79.5)^2 + (88-79.5)^2$

$SS_{(within\ groups)} = 953.375$

Then we calculate the **Sum of Squares (Between Groups)**: this is the sum of all the squared differences between the means for each condition and the grand mean, multiplied by the number of observations per group.

$SS_{(between\ groups)} = [(36.375-57.04)^2 + (55.25-57.04)^2 + (79.5-57.04)^2]*8 = 7477.583$

Then we calculate the **Sum of Squares (Total)**: this is the sum of the squared differences between each individual data point and the grand mean.

Alternatively (more easily) this can be calculated by summing the $SS_{(between\ groups)}$ and the $SS_{(within\ groups)}$.

$SS_{(total)} = 7477.583 + 953.375 = 8430.958$

(If you want to check this you can calculate it the long way: $(30-57.04)^2 + (40-57.04)^2 +$ etc. until $+ (88-57.04)^2 = 8430.958$).

STEP B

We need to figure out the degrees of freedom for each **Sum of Squares**.

For the Sum of Squares (Within Groups):
There are 3 groups and 8 participants per group. We lose one df for each group mean. Thus the df (within) is 24–3 = 21. You could express this, when you have n observations in each of the k groups as: df (within) = k(n–1).

For the Sum of Squares (Between Groups):
There are three groups but we lose one df, so the df (between) is 3–1 = 2. You could express this as: df (between) = k–1.

For Sum of Squares (Total):
The total df is based on 24 scores, we lose one df, so the df (total) is 24–1 = 23. You could express this as: df (total) = nk–1.

continues on next page

STEP C

Now we can calculate the Mean Square by dividing each Sum of Squares by its df. This provides us with a measure of the average deviation of individual values from their respective mean.

Mean Square (Within groups) (The average variation within the groups)

$MS_{(within\ groups)} = 953.375/21 = 45.399$

Mean Square (Between groups) (The average variation between groups)

$MS_{(Between\ groups)} = 7477.583/2 = 3736.792$

STEP D

We now have the two Mean Squares for **the *F*-ratio**:

$F = 3736.792/45.399 = 82.354$

If you calculate *F* with a calculator, you next look in Tables of *F* to determine whether your calculated *F*-ratio is significant.

Imagine that in our learning experiment, eight participants took part and each performed in each level of the factor. We would be able to calculate both a mean score for each list and a mean score for each participant; see below.

Table 6.3: Time (in seconds) taken to learn three different lists of words for the group of human participants in a within-subjects design.

HUMANS			
LIST A	LIST B	LIST C	Participant Mean
35	42	64	*47*
48	60	90	*66*
36	65	75	*58.67*
40	55	70	*55*
38	52	85	*58.33*
25	42	58	*41.67*
30	42	60	*44*
42	60	90	*64*
Mean = 36.755	*Mean = 52.25*	*Mean = 74.0*	***Grand Mean = 54.33***

The calculation of F for the within-subjects design is more complicated. Again, we want to determine the sources of variance. However, with this design we have repeated observations of each participant as every person performs in every level of the factor. This allows us to separate out participant variance from error variance; we can distinguish between variation caused by individual differences and variation caused by different participants performing differently in the different conditions – the error variance. So, we have three sources of variance and we can ask:

1. How do the scores in one condition vary from those in the other condition? We can compare overall differences between the three lists. As before, we can look at how the mean of each column deviates from the grand mean. This provides us with a measure of the variance due to our manipulation of the factor.
2. How do participants vary in their average scores? We can get an indication of how much individuals differ from each other by looking at how much each participant's average score deviates from the grand mean. This provides us with a measure of participant variance.
3. How much error variance is there? We can work this out by looking at the extent to which each score is not what we would predict from the row and column means. You can also think of this as the variance resulting from different participants responding differently to the change in the factor.

For example, with regard to the score for participant one in list A – we know that his/her mean time is 47 seconds. Participant one is on average 7.33 seconds faster compared with the overall grand mean of 54.33 seconds. The mean for the list A column is 36.75 seconds, so participants are on average 17.58 seconds faster at learning list A than the overall grand mean of 54.22 seconds. So, altogether we would expect participant one to be 17.58+7.33 seconds faster than the grand mean of 54.33 seconds at leaning list A, giving an expected time of 29.42 seconds. The observed score is 35 seconds, which is slower than we would expect. (Looking at participant one's scores, we can see that s/he is relatively faster with lists B and C compared with list A.)

With regard to participant two's score in list A condition – we know that his/her row mean is 66 seconds which is 11.67 seconds slower than the grand mean of 54.33 seconds. So, we would expect participant two to be 17.58 seconds faster at learning list A, but 11.67 seconds slower because this participant is slower on average. Thus, we expect a time of 54.33–17.58+11.67 and this is 48.42 seconds. The observed score is 48 seconds which is close to what we would expect.

The extent to which the observed scores vary from the expected scores reflects the extent to which participants are inconsistent and, as illustrated above, provides us with a measure of error variance.

Using SPSS to calculate the *F*-ratio

The calculation of the *F*-ratio for a within-subjects factor is tricky and as you will see the SPSS output is quite complex. SPSS will give you much more information than just the *F*-ratio statistic, because for some time it has been using the General Linear Model (GLM) procedure. ANOVA has many similarities to a different statistical test called multiple regression (see Chapter 8). ANOVA can be considered to be a special case of multiple linear regression, which itself is a special case of the general linear model. This is why you will see both ANOVA and multiple regression statistics in the SPSS output.

Now let us see how to perform the various different types of ANOVA using SPSS.

Section 2: One-way between-subjects ANOVA

EXAMPLE STUDY: THE EFFECTS OF WITNESS MASKING

To practise the use of the one-way between-subjects ANOVA we shall consider an applied experiment, which looked at the effects of masking the face of a witness. There is growing awareness that the identity of witnesses in sensitive cases should be protected, especially in light of the move towards televising live court cases. The technology to mask a witness's face is available and has been used in America. Towell, Kemp and Pike (1996) reported the results of a study investigating the effect that masking might have on jurors' memory for a witness's testimony and on jurors' perceptions of the witness's credibility. The testimony of an alleged victim of rape presented in a televised trial in America was shown to participants.

The design employed was a one-way between-subjects ANOVA design. The between-subjects factor, presentation condition, had four levels: unmasked, grey blob, pixelation and negation. These were operationalised by showing some participants the witness unmasked, so that her face was fully visible; some with her face masked by a grey blob, some with her face masked by pixelation and some with her face negated (white and black were reversed). One of the dependent variables was the percentage of facts from the testimony correctly remembered by the participants. The hypothesis was that there would be a negative effect of masking on memory. Results revealed that participants' memory for the victim's testimony was affected by presentation condition; whilst negating the face did not lower memory compared to the unmasked condition, both masking with a grey blob and pixelation impaired memory. For the purposes of this book, we have created a data file that will reproduce some of these findings. (These data are available in Appendix I or from the web address listed there.)

SPSS provides two ways of carrying out a one-way, between-subjects ANOVA, one using the **General linear model** command and one using the **One-Way ANOVA** command. The first command can also be used to perform a multi-between-subjects ANOVA. The second command will only permit analysis of a one-way ANOVA design, but does have the advantage of a much simpler output. Both methods allow you to do planned and unplanned comparisons to evaluate the differences between pairs of group means (these are covered in Section 8 of this chapter).

We will now describe both methods.

1. Click on the word **Analyze**.

2. Click on **General Linear Model**.

3. Click on **Univariate**. The **Univariate** dialogue box will appear – see below.

4. Select the dependent variable "memory" and move it into the **Dependent Variable** box.

5. Select the grouping variable (i.e. the between-subjects factor) "presentation condition" and move it into the **Fixed Factor(s)** box.

6. Click on the **Options** button to obtain descriptive statistics. The **Univariate Options** dialogue box will appear (see next page).

TIP   As explained in the SPSS help files, the levels of a fixed factor include all the levels about which conclusions are desired. It is rare in psychological research to choose the levels of a factor by a random procedure; however, were we to do so, then this could be thought to increase the generalisability of our findings as we would have chosen the levels in an unbiased way.

This is the variable name rather than the variable label that appeared in the previous dialogue box. See tip box below.

7. Click here to obtain mean and standard deviation for each level of the factor.

8. Click here to obtain partial eta squared, a measure of effect size, which tells you the proportion of total variance accounted for by the factor.

9. Click on **Continue** to return to the **Univariate** dialogue box.

> **TIP**   Means, standard errors and 95% confidence intervals for each level of a factor can also be obtained by clicking on the factor/variable name in the **Estimated Marginal Means** box and then clicking on ▶️. You should only use this option if the number of participants in each level is the same. Check whether the estimated means are correct if you have an unequal sample size.

Finally, click on the 🔲 button and SPSS will calculate the test for you. See the next two pages for an example of the output using the **Univariate** command, which includes the means, standard deviations and N (number of scores) obtained by clicking on **Descriptive statistics**.

Obtained Using Menu Items: General Linear Model > Univariate

Univariate Analysis of Variance

Between-Subjects Factors

		Value Label	N
presentation condition	1	unmasked	10
	2	greyblob	10
	3	pixelated	10
	4	negated	10

SPSS reminds you of the factor that you are analysing, what the levels of that factor are, and the number of participants in each level.

Descriptive Statistics

This table will appear if you requested **Descriptive statistics** in the **General linear model: Options** dialogue box.

Dependent Variable: MEMORY

presentation condition	Mean	Std. Deviation	N
unmasked	66.7000	5.3344	10
greyblob	55.7000	3.8020	10
pixelated	57.7000	5.4171	10
negated	67.2000	4.5898	10
Total	61.8250	7.0014	40

The mean and the standard deviation (SD) for each level of the factor.

The Total mean and SD: that is, for all participants regardless of which condition they were in.

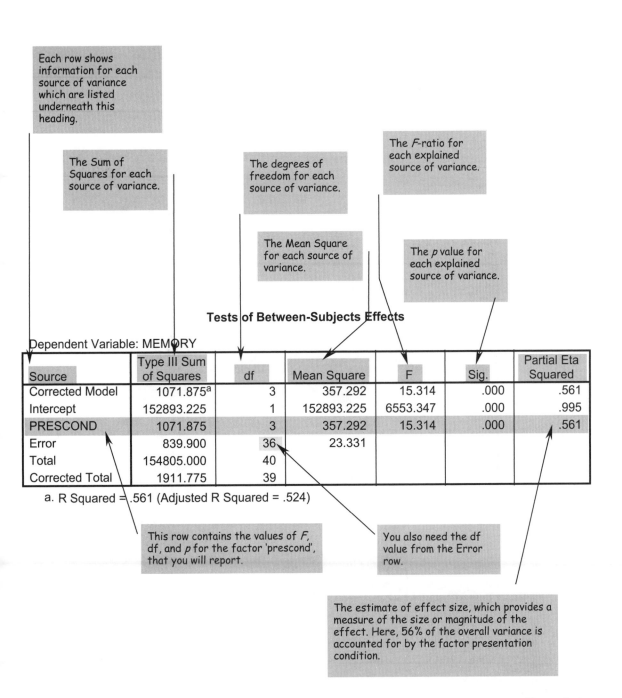

Each row shows information for each source of variance which are listed underneath this heading.

The Sum of Squares for each source of variance.

The degrees of freedom for each source of variance.

The *F*-ratio for each explained source of variance.

The Mean Square for each source of variance.

The *p* value for each explained source of variance.

Tests of Between-Subjects Effects

Dependent Variable: MEMORY

Source	Type III Sum of Squares	df	Mean Square	F	Sig.	Partial Eta Squared
Corrected Model	1071.875[a]	3	357.292	15.314	.000	.561
Intercept	152893.225	1	152893.225	6553.347	.000	.995
PRESCOND	1071.875	3	357.292	15.314	.000	.561
Error	839.900	36	23.331			
Total	154805.000	40				
Corrected Total	1911.775	39				

a. R Squared = .561 (Adjusted R Squared = .524)

This row contains the values of *F*, *df*, and *p* for the factor 'prescond', that you will report.

You also need the df value from the Error row.

The estimate of effect size, which provides a measure of the size or magnitude of the effect. Here, 56% of the overall variance is accounted for by the factor presentation condition.

In a report you would write: There was a statistically significant effect of the presentation condition ($F(3,36) = 15.314$, $p < .0005$, partial $\eta^2 = .56$).

To identify which pair(s) of conditions significantly differed, you would carry out planned or unplanned comparisons as appropriate (see Section 8).

As stated earlier, one-way between-subjects ANOVA can be carried out in two different ways in SPSS. This is the second way.

1. Click on the word **Analyze**.

2. Click on **Compare Means**.

3. Click on the words **One-Way ANOVA**. The **One-Way ANOVA** dialogue box will appear – see below.

4. Select the dependent variable "memory" and move it into the **Dependent List:** box.

5. Select the grouping variable (i.e. the between-subjects factor) "presentation condition" and move it into the **Factor:** box.

6. Click on **Options**. The **One-Way ANOVA: Options** dialogue box will appear (see below).

7. Select **Descriptive**. This will give you a number of additional statistics, including 95% confidence intervals for each condition, but no measure of effect size.

8. Click on **Continue** to return to the **One-Way ANOVA** dialogue box.

Finally, click on the ⬚ᵒᵏ button. See the next page annotated output.

SPSS OUTPUT FOR ONE-WAY BETWEEN-SUBJECTS ANALYSIS OF VARIANCE

Obtained Using Menu Items: Compare <u>M</u>eans > <u>O</u>ne-Way ANOVA

Oneway

This table is produced by selecting **Descriptive** in the **One-Way ANOVA: Options** dialogue box.

Descriptives

MEMORY

	N	Mean	Std. Deviation	Std. Error	95% Confidence Interval for Mean		Minimum	Maximum
					Lower Bound	Upper Bound		
unmasked	10	66.7000	5.33437	1.68688	62.8840	70.5160	58.00	75.00
greyblob	10	55.7000	3.80205	1.20231	52.9802	58.4198	48.00	61.00
pixelated	10	57.7000	5.41705	1.71302	53.8249	61.5751	51.00	68.00
negated	10	67.2000	4.58984	1.45144	63.9166	70.4834	58.00	74.00
Total	40	61.8250	7.00142	1.10702	59.5858	64.0642	48.00	75.00

This table shows the outcome of the analysis of variance. Each row shows information for a source of variance.

ANOVA

MEMORY

	Sum of Squares	df	Mean Square	F	Sig.
Between Groups	1071.875	3	357.292	15.314	.000
Within Groups	839.900	36	23.331		
Total	1911.775	39			

This row contains the values of *F*, df, and *p* for the factor "prescond", that you will report.

You also need the df value from the Error row.

In a report you would write: There was a statistically significant effect of presentation condition (*F*(3,36) = 15.314, *p* < .0005).

> **TIP** You could include in your results section information regarding the confidence intervals for each condition – see Chapter 3 for guidance on how to obtain an error bar chart.

Section 3: Two-way between-subjects ANOVA

EXAMPLE STUDY: THE EFFECT OF DEFENDANT'S ATTRACTIVENESS AND SEX ON SENTENCING

To practise how to analyse data from the two-way between-subjects ANOVA design, we will consider the possible effects of both attractiveness and also the gender of the defendant in a mock trial. In the study described here, the testimony of a hypothetical defendant describing a murder and admitting guilt was presented as written text to 60 participants. 20 participants simply received the written text with no photograph attached, 20 participants received the text and a photograph of an attractive defendant and 20 participants received the text and a photograph of an unattractive defendant. The photograph was of either a man or a woman. Participants were asked to indicate how many years in jail the defendant should receive as punishment.

The design employed was a 3*2 between-subjects ANOVA design. The first between-subjects factor was the knowledge about attractiveness which had three levels; the factor is operationalised as showing either no photograph of defendant (so no knowledge about attractiveness), a photograph of an attractive defendant and a photograph of an unattractive defendant. The second between-subjects factor was same or different sex, operationalised by showing a photograph of the defendant of the same or opposite sex as the participant. Sex of the defendant was also given in the written text, for the participants who received no photograph. The dependent variable was the sentence given, operationalised as how many years the defendant should spend in prison, ranging from a minimum of 3 to a maximum of 25. The hypothesis tested was that the unattractive defendant would be sentenced more harshly and that the length of sentence given might also depend on the sex of the participant. (These data are available in Appendix I or from the web address listed there.)

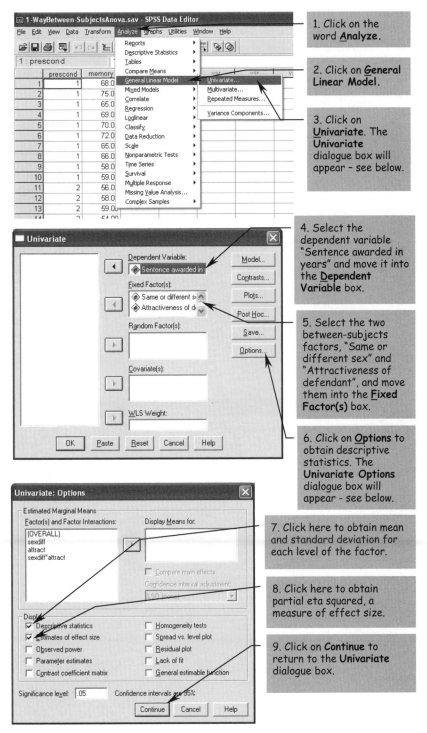

1. Click on the word **Analyze**.

2. Click on **General Linear Model**.

3. Click on **Univariate**. The **Univariate** dialogue box will appear – see below.

4. Select the dependent variable "Sentence awarded in years" and move it into the **Dependent Variable** box.

5. Select the two between-subjects factors, "Same or different sex" and "Attractiveness of defendant", and move them into the **Fixed Factor(s)** box.

6. Click on **Options** to obtain descriptive statistics. The **Univariate Options** dialogue box will appear - see below.

7. Click here to obtain mean and standard deviation for each level of the factor.

8. Click here to obtain partial eta squared, a measure of effect size.

9. Click on **Continue** to return to the **Univariate** dialogue box.

Finally, click on the [OK] button. The annotated output is shown on pages 186–187.

As the analysis will reveal a statistically significant effect of attractiveness of defendant, we show you here how to display the means for this variable as a graph.

1. Select **Graphs** on the menu bar.
2. Select **Bar** to get the following dialogue box.

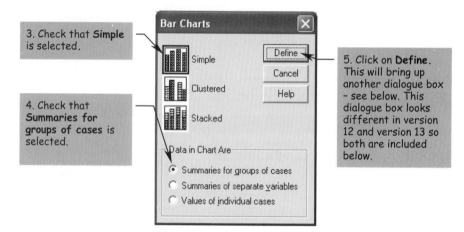

3. Check that **Simple** is selected.

4. Check that **Summaries for groups of cases** is selected.

5. Click on **Define**. This will bring up another dialogue box – see below. This dialogue box looks different in version 12 and version 13 so both are included below.

Version 13

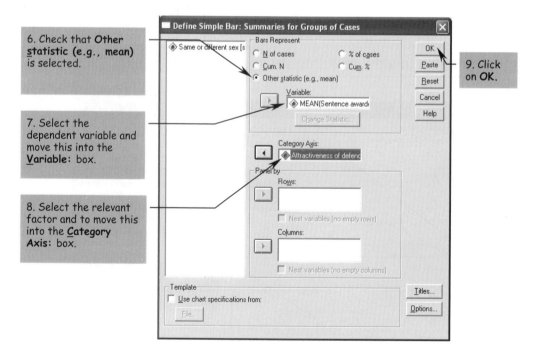

6. Check that **Other statistic (e.g., mean)** is selected.

7. Select the dependent variable and move this into the **Variable:** box.

8. Select the relevant factor and to move this into the **Category Axis:** box.

9. Click on **OK**.

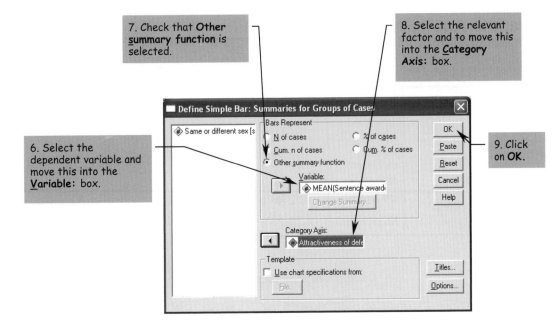

7. Check that Other summary function is selected.

8. Select the relevant factor and to move this into the Category Axis: box.

6. Select the dependent variable and move this into the Variable: box.

9. Click on OK.

All of the two-way between-subjects ANOVA output and the chart are shown on the next two pages.

Obtained Using Menu Items: General Linear Model > Univariate

Univariate Analysis of Variance

SPSS reminds you of the factors that you are analysing, what the levels of each factor are, and the number of participants in each level.

Between-Subjects Factors

		Value Label	N
Same or different sex	1	Same sex as defendant	30
	2	Opposite sex to defendant	30
Attractiveness of defendant	1	Attractive	20
	2	Unattractive	20
	3	No picture	20

This table was produced by requesting **Descriptive statistics** in the **Univariate: Options** dialogue box.

Descriptive Statistics

Dependent Variable: Sentence awarded in years

Same or different sex	Attractiveness	Mean	Std. Deviation	N
Same sex as defendant	Attractive	7.50	1.780	10
	Unattractive	11.20	2.300	10
	No picture	14.50	1.269	10
	Total	11.07	3.403	30
Opposite sex to defendant	Attractive	7.50	2.415	10
	Unattractive	10.30	2.058	10
	No picture	13.50	1.650	10
	Total	10.43	3.191	30
Total	Attractive	7.50	2.065	20
	Unattractive	10.75	2.173	20
	No picture	14.00	1.522	20
	Total	10.75	3.286	60

These rows show descriptives for each level of the factor "attract", collapsing across the levels of the other factor, "sexdiff".

Each of these six rows shows the descriptives for one of the conditions of the study. Thus, the first row is for participants who were given a photo of an attractive defendant and who were the same sex as that defendant.

These two rows show descriptives for each level of the factor "sexdiff", collapsing across the levels of the other factor, "attract".

This table shows the outcome of the analysis of variance. Each row shows information for a source of variance.

Tests of Between-Subjects Effects

Dependent Variable: Sentence awarded in years

Source	Type III Sum of Squares	df	Mean Square	F	Sig.	Partial Eta Squared
Corrected Model	431.550[a]	5	86.310	22.658	.000	.677
Intercept	6933.750	1	6933.750	1820.236	.000	.971
sexdiff	6.017	1	6.017	1.579	.214	.028
attract	422.500	2	211.250	55.457	.000	.673
sexdiff * attract	3.033	2	1.517	.398	.674	.015
Error	205.700	54	3.809			
Total	7571.000	60				
Corrected Total	637.250	59				

a. R Squared = .677 (Adjusted R Squared = .647)

This row shows information about the main effect of the factor "sexdiff".

This row shows information about the main effect of the factor "attract".

This row shows information about the interaction between the factors "sexdiff" and "attract".

In a report you would write, at appropriate points:

The main effect of whether the sex of the defendant was the same as or different from the sex of the participant was not significant ($F(1,54) = 1.579$, $p = .214$, partial $\eta^2 = .03$).

There was a significant main effect of knowledge about attractiveness ($F(2,54) = 55.457$, $p < .0005$, partial $\eta^2 = .67$), see graph below.

There was no significant interaction between the factor of knowledge about attractiveness and the factor of same or different sex ($F(2,54) = 0.398$, $p = .674$, partial $\eta^2 = .02$).

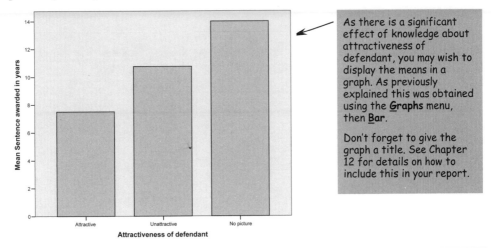

As there is a significant effect of knowledge about attractiveness of defendant, you may wish to display the means in a graph. As previously explained this was obtained using the **Graphs** menu, then **Bar**.

Don't forget to give the graph a title. See Chapter 12 for details on how to include this in your report.

Section 4: One-way within-subjects ANOVA

EXAMPLE STUDY: THE STROOP EFFECT

Many experiments have been conducted to investigate the Stroop effect. The most common way of demonstrating this effect is to show participants the names of colours printed in an incongruous colour (e.g., the word "red" written in green ink) and ask them to name the colour of the ink. Results show that this is not an easy task because of our tendency to read the word, which then interferes with the task of naming the colour of the ink. In one experiment with undergraduate students, we devised three lists. One list was incongruent and contained four words with strong colour associations (grass, coal, blood, sky) repeated three times in a random order, each time in a different incongruent colour ink (e.g., "grass" printed in black, red and blue ink). The second list was congruent and contained the same four words repeated three times in a random order, each time in their congruent colour ink (e.g. "grass" printed in green ink). The third list was neutral and contained four new words, matched in word length to the original words, and repeated three times. These words were not associated with any particular colour and were printed in one of the four different colour inks (e.g. "table" written in green). These three lists constituted the different experimental conditions, and all participants completed all three lists. The order of the lists was counterbalanced across subjects.

The design employed was a one-way within-subjects ANOVA design. The within-subjects factor, the type of list, had three levels: incongruent, congruent and neutral. The dependent variable was the total time taken in seconds to name the colour of the ink of the 12 words in the list. The hypothesis was that there would be an effect of list on performance. (These data are available in Appendix I or from the web address listed there.)

HOW TO DO IT

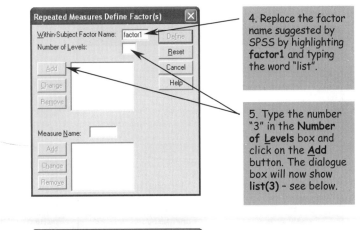

1-WayWithin-SubjectsAnova.sav - SPSS Data Editor

	incong	cong
1	13.00	9.0
2	13.00	10.0
3	16.00	9.0
4	13.00	8.0
5	14.00	9.0
6	15.00	10.0
7	14.00	8.0
8	13.00	9.0
9	16.00	8.0
10	17.00	9.0

1. Click on the word **Analyze**.

2. Click on **General Linear Model**.

3. Click on **Repeated Measures**. The **Repeated Measures Define Factor(s)** dialogue box will appear – see below.

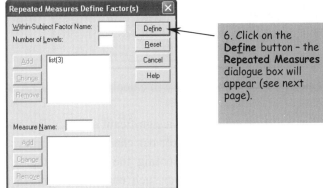

Repeated Measures Define Factor(s)

Within-Subject Factor Name: factor1

Number of Levels:

4. Replace the factor name suggested by SPSS by highlighting **factor1** and typing the word "list".

5. Type the number "3" in the **Number of Levels** box and click on the **Add** button. The dialogue box will now show **list(3)** – see below.

Repeated Measures Define Factor(s)

Within-Subject Factor Name:

Number of Levels:

list(3)

6. Click on the **Define** button – the **Repeated Measures** dialogue box will appear (see next page).

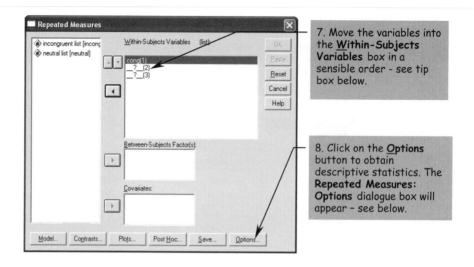

7. Move the variables into the **Within-Subjects Variables** box in a sensible order - see tip box below.

8. Click on the **Options** button to obtain descriptive statistics. The **Repeated Measures: Options** dialogue box will appear - see below.

TIP As SPSS does a trend test, it makes sense to enter the variables in line with the hypothesis. Here, we would expect the time taken to name the ink colour to be shortest for the congruent list, longer for the neutral list and longest for the incongruent list.

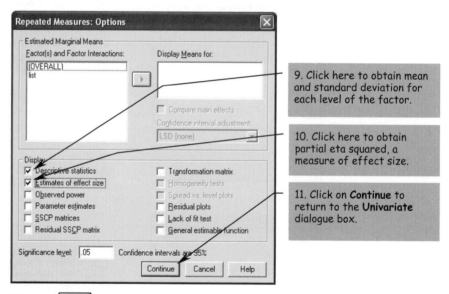

9. Click here to obtain mean and standard deviation for each level of the factor.

10. Click here to obtain partial eta squared, a measure of effect size.

11. Click on **Continue** to return to the **Univariate** dialogue box.

Click on [OK] and SPSS will calculate the ANOVA.

You will find that there is a significant effect of list, and you may wish to include in your results section an error bar chart, which displays the mean for each condition and a vertical bar representing the 95% confidence intervals of the mean. We showed you how to obtain such chart in Chapter 3 and Section 3 illustrates the necessary steps when the manipulation involves a within-subjects factor.

SPSS OUTPUT FOR ONE-WAY WITHIN-SUBJECTS ANALYSIS OF VARIANCE

Obtained Using Menu Items: General Linear Model > Repeated Measures

Within-Subjects Factors

Measure: MEASURE_1

list	Dependent Variable
1	cong
2	neutral
3	incong

On this page we show all of the output, reduced to fit the page. The shaded tables are the parts of the output that are normally required in an undergraduate course: these tables appear full size and annotated on the following two pages.
See Section 7 for information about the other tables.

Descriptive Statistics

	Mean	Std. Deviation	N
congruent list	8.9000	.73786	10
neutral list	11.1000	1.19722	10
incongruent list	14.4000	1.50555	10

Multivariate Tests[b]

Effect		Value	F	Hypothesis df	Error df	Sig.	Partial Eta Squared
list	Pillai's Trace	.920	45.993[a]	2.000	8.000	.000	.920
	Wilks' Lambda	.080	45.993[a]	2.000	8.000	.000	.920
	Hotelling's Trace	11.498	45.993[a]	2.000	8.000	.000	.920
	Roy's Largest Root	11.498	45.993[a]	2.000	8.000	.000	.920

a. Exact statistic

b.
   Design: Intercept
   Within Subjects Design: list

Mauchly's Test of Sphericity[b]

Measure: MEASURE_1

					Epsilon[a]		
Within Subjects Effect	Mauchly's W	Approx. Chi-Square	df	Sig.	Greenhouse-Geisser	Huynh-Feldt	Lower-bound
list	.892	.914	2	.633	.903	1.000	.500

Tests the null hypothesis that the error covariance matrix of the orthonormalized transformed dependent variables is proportional to an identity matrix.

a. May be used to adjust the degrees of freedom for the averaged tests of significance. Corrected tests are displayed in the Tests of Within-Subjects Effects table.

b.
   Design: Intercept
   Within Subjects Design: list

These tables appear in the Output Viewer as shown here. When you print, however, large tables may split into two separate tables. See Chapter 12 for information on how to format tables for printing.

Tests of Within-Subjects Effects

Measure: MEASURE_1

Source		Type III Sum of Squares	df	Mean Square	F	Sig.	Partial Eta Squared
list	Sphericity Assumed	153.267	2	76.633	68.741	.000	.884
	Greenhouse-Geisser	153.267	1.805	84.906	68.741	.000	.884
	Huynh-Feldt	153.267	2.000	76.633	68.741	.000	.884
	Lower-bound	153.267	1.000	153.267	68.741	.000	.884
Error(list)	Sphericity Assumed	20.067	18	1.115			
	Greenhouse-Geisser	20.067	16.246	1.235			
	Huynh-Feldt	20.067	18.000	1.115			
	Lower-bound	20.067	9.000	2.230			

Tests of Within-Subjects Contrasts

Measure: MEASURE_1

Source	list	Type III Sum of Squares	df	Mean Square	F	Sig.	Partial Eta Squared
list	Linear	151.250	1	151.250	102.736	.000	.919
	Quadratic	2.017	1	2.017	2.663	.137	.228
Error(list)	Linear	13.250	9	1.472			
	Quadratic	6.817	9	.757			

Tests of Between-Subjects Effects

Measure: MEASURE_1
Transformed Variable: Average

Source	Type III Sum of Squares	df	Mean Square	F	Sig.	Partial Eta Squared
Intercept	3944.533	1	3944.533	1957.765	.000	.995
Error	18.133	9	2.015			

Within-Subjects Factors

Measure: MEASURE_1

list	Dependent Variable
1	cong
2	neutral
3	incong

These are the names for each level of the factor "LIST". If there is a meaningful order by which you entered them into the **Repeated Measures** dialogue box, then the table Tests of Within-Subjects Contrasts, shown on the next page, will also be relevant.

Descriptive Statistics

	Mean	Std. Deviation	N
congruent list	8.9000	.73786	10
neutral list	11.1000	1.19722	10
incongruent list	14.4000	1.50555	10

Useful descriptives that you can incorporate into your report, obtained by ticking **Descriptive statistics** in the **Repeated Measures: Options** dialogue box.

This table shows the outcome of the analysis of variance.

For information about the non-highlighted rows see Section 7.

Tests of Within-Subjects Effects

Measure: MEASURE_1

Source		Type III Sum of Squares	df	Mean Square	F	Sig.	Partial Eta Squared
list	Sphericity Assumed	153.267	2	76.633	68.741	.000	.884
	Greenhouse-Geisser	153.267	1.805	84.906	68.741	.000	.884
	Huynh-Feldt	153.267	2.000	76.633	68.741	.000	.884
	Lower-bound	153.267	1.000	153.267	68.741	.000	.884
Error(list)	Sphericity Assumed	20.067	18	1.115			
	Greenhouse-Geisser	20.067	16.246	1.235			
	Huynh-Feldt	20.067	18.000	1.115			
	Lower-bound	20.067	9.000	2.230			

This row is the one you will normally use. It gives the values for the factor "LIST" which was a within-subjects factor with three levels (the three types of list).

You also need the df for the Error term.

In a report you would write: There was a significant effect of the type of list, $F(2,18) = 68.741$, $p < .0005$, partial $\eta^2 = .88$.

Tests of Within-Subjects Contrasts

Measure: MEASURE_1

Source	list	Type III Sum of Squares	df	Mean Square	F	Sig.	Partial Eta Squared
list	Linear	151.250	1	151.250	102.736	.000	.919
	Quadratic	2.017	1	2.017	2.663	.137	.228
Error(list)	Linear	13.250	9	1.472			
	Quadratic	6.817	9	.757			

For these data there is a significant linear trend, $F(1,9) = 102.736$, $p < .0005$, partial $\eta^2 = .92$, over the mean values for each level of the factor, illustrated in the figure below. For the congruent list, the participants take the shortest time to name the ink colour of the 12 words; for the neutral list they take a longer time; and for the incongruent list they take the longest time. Note that the Tests of Within-Subjects Contrasts table shows only whether a trend is significant or not. It is not a test of whether the individual conditions significantly differ from one another; for that you need planned or unplanned comparisons (see Section 8).

For these data there is no significant quadratic trend, $F(1,9) = 2.663$, $p = .137$, partial $\eta^2 = .23$. A linear trend test is used to see if the points tend to fall onto a straight line (as here). A quadratic trend test looks for a "U" shaped or inverted "U" shaped trend. If you entered the three levels in the order "cong", "incong" and "neutral", then the quadratic trend would be significant. You might like to try this.

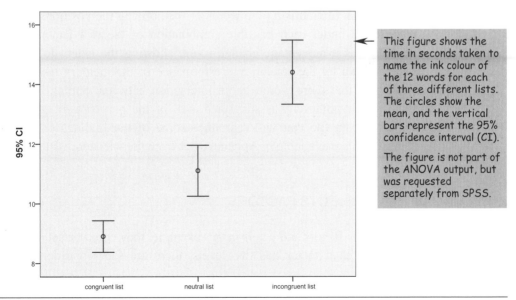

Section 5: Two-way within-subjects ANOVA

EXAMPLE STUDY: THE EFFECTS OF TWO MEMORY TASKS ON FINGER TAPPING PERFORMANCE

To practise a two-way within-subjects ANOVA, we shall look at an experiment carried out to examine the effects of two memory tasks on tapping performance. Research has identified that right index finger tapping is largely controlled by the left hemisphere, and left index finger tapping by the right hemisphere. If a cognitive task is performed at the same time as this finger tapping task, then the way in which the cognitive task interferes with such tapping could reflect the extent to which either hemisphere is involved in controlling the cognitive task. Many studies that required participants to tap as fast as possible with their index finger whilst also performing a verbal task, found that right hand tapping was disrupted more than left hand tapping. This result is compatible with the notion that the left side of the brain controls both right hand tapping and many verbal tasks. In a study published by Towell, Burton and Burton (1994), participants were asked to tap with each hand whilst memorising either the words presented to them on a screen (a verbal memory task) or the position of the words on the screen (a visuo-spatial memory task). Memorising the words should disrupt right hand tapping more than left hand tapping whereas, because the right side of the brain controls many visuospatial tasks, memorising the positions of words should disrupt left hand tapping more than right hand tapping.

The design employed was a 2*2 within-subjects ANOVA. Each factor had two levels; the first was tapping hand (left or right hand) and the second was the memory task (memorising the words or memorising the positions). All participants were tested under each possible combination of the two factors. The dependent variable was a percentage change score, showing the extent to which tapping is slowed down by the concurrent performance of the memory task. The hypothesis tested was that there would be an interaction between tapping hand and memory task. This hypothesis was supported and for the purposes of this book, we have created a data file that will reproduce some of the findings of the above paper. (These data are available in Appendix I or from the web address listed there.)

LABELLING WITHIN-SUBJECTS FACTORS

Consider the factors and levels in this example; they could be set out as in Table 6.4 below. As each factor has two levels, there are four conditions, each with one level of one factor and one level for the other factor. The name that will be given, in the SPSS data file, to each column containing the data for each condition can then incorporate a number for each level of each factor, as shown in the bottom row of Table 6.4. In these column names:

"h1s1" means tapping hand 1 (right) and stimulus for task 1 (memorising words)
"h2s2" means tapping hand 2 (left) and stimulus for task 2 (memorising positions)

Table 6.4: An illustration of the numbering system for within-subjects factors.

Factor 1	Tapping Hand			
Levels	Right		Left	
Factor 2	Memory Task		Memory Task	
Levels	Words	Position	Words	Position
Column name, SPSS data file, for conditions	h1s1	h1s2	h2s1	h2s2

You should jot down a rough table such as this before entering the data for any design with two or more within-subjects factors. This will help you when you define the within-subjects factors, because you will find that the numbers that you have used for the column names will match with the numbers that SPSS uses when requesting variable selection.

HOW TO DO IT

1. Click on the word **Analyze**.

2. Click on **General Linear Model**.

3. Click on **Repeated Measures**. The **Repeated Measures Define Factor(s)** dialogue box will appear – see next page.

Repeated Measures Define Factor(s)

Within-Subject Factor Name: factor1

Number of Levels:

Add
Change
Remove

Measure Name:

Add
Change
Remove

Define
Reset
Cancel
Help

4. Change the factor name suggested by SPSS by highlighting **factor1** and typing the word that represents the first factor, "hand".

5. Type the number "2" in the **Number of Levels** box and click on the **Add** button. **hand(2)** will appear in the box next to **Add** (see below).

Repeated Measures Define Factor(s)

Within-Subject Factor Name: task

Number of Levels: 2

Add — hand(2)
Change
Remove

Measure Name:

Add
Change
Remove

Define
Reset
Cancel
Help

6. Repeat steps 4 and 5 for the second factor, i.e. type in the name that represents the second factor "task" in the **Within-Subject Factor Name:** box and type "2" in the **Number of Levels** box and click on the **Add** button.

7. Click the **Define** button – the **Repeated Measures** dialogue box will appear (see below).

This key helps explain the numbers in the brackets below; "hand" refers to the first number and "task" to the second number. This will help you enter the variables in the correct order into the **Within-Subjects Variables** box.

The variable names are given in brackets after the variable labels.

Repeated Measures

Rt hand and position [
Rt hand and word [h1s
Left hand and position
Left hand and word [h2

Within-Subjects Variables   (hand,task):

__?__(1,1)
__?__(1,2)
__?__(2,1)
__?__(2,2)

OK
Paste
Reset
Cancel
Help

Between-Subjects Factor(s):

Covariates:

Model...   Contrasts...   Plots...   Post Hoc...   Save...   Options...

8. Select **Rt hand and word [h1s1]** which is the condition where the level "hand 1" (the right hand) is combined with the level "stimulus 1" (memorising words).

9. Click on the arrow button to add it to the list in the **Within-Subjects Variables** box, where **Rt hand and word [h1s1]** should appear next to the slot **(1,1)**.

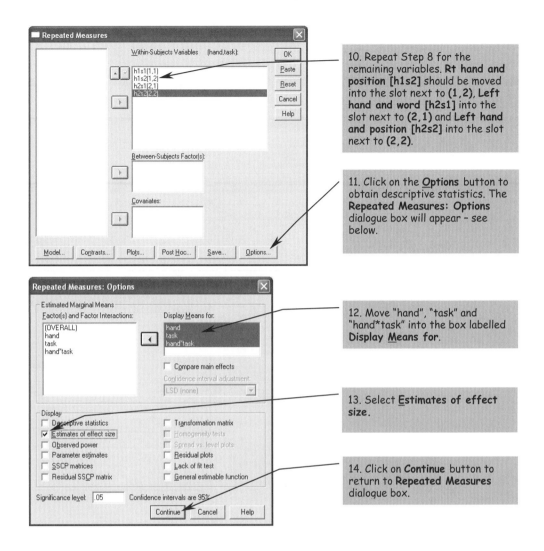

10. Repeat Step 8 for the remaining variables. **Rt hand and position [h1s2]** should be moved into the slot next to **(1,2)**, **Left hand and word [h2s1]** into the slot next to **(2,1)** and **Left hand and position [h2s2]** into the slot next to **(2,2)**.

11. Click on the **Options** button to obtain descriptive statistics. The **Repeated Measures: Options** dialogue box will appear – see below.

12. Move "hand", "task" and "hand*task" into the box labelled **Display Means for**.

13. Select **Estimates of effect size**.

14. Click on **Continue** button to return to **Repeated Measures** dialogue box.

Click on OK. SPSS will perform the calculations. You may wish to obtain an interaction graph should the analysis reveal a statistically significant interaction – this is an option available on the **Repeated Measures** dialogue box – see the steps outlined on the next page.

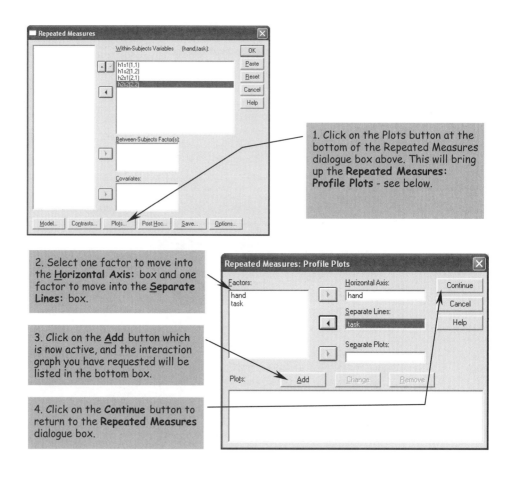

1. Click on the Plots button at the bottom of the Repeated Measures dialogue box above. This will bring up the **Repeated Measures: Profile Plots** - see below.

2. Select one factor to move into the **Horizontal Axis:** box and one factor to move into the **Separate Lines:** box.

3. Click on the **Add** button which is now active, and the interaction graph you have requested will be listed in the bottom box.

4. Click on the **Continue** button to return to the **Repeated Measures** dialogue box.

Click on [OK] to obtain the ANOVA output, shown over the next five pages with the interaction graph at the end of the output.

SPSS OUTPUT FOR TWO-WAY WITHIN-SUBJECTS ANALYSIS OF VARIANCE

Obtained Using Menu Items: General Linear Model > Repeated Measures

General Linear Model

Within-Subjects Factors

Measure: MEASURE_1

hand	task	Dependent Variable
1	1	h1s1
	2	h1s2
2	1	h2s1
	2	h2s2

On this page and the next page we show all of the output, reduced to fit the page. The shaded tables are the parts of the output that you would normally require: these tables appear full size after we show you the complete output.

For information about other tables see Section 7.

Multivariate Tests[b]

Effect		Value	F	Hypothesis df	Error df	Sig.	Partial Eta Squared
hand	Pillai's Trace	.006	.133[a]	1.000	23.000	.719	.006
	Wilks' Lambda	.994	.133[a]	1.000	23.000	.719	.006
	Hotelling's Trace	.006	.133[a]	1.000	23.000	.719	.006
	Roy's Largest Root	.006	.133[a]	1.000	23.000	.719	.006
task	Pillai's Trace	.078	1.955[a]	1.000	23.000	.175	.078
	Wilks' Lambda	.922	1.955[a]	1.000	23.000	.175	.078
	Hotelling's Trace	.085	1.955[a]	1.000	23.000	.175	.078
	Roy's Largest Root	.085	1.955[a]	1.000	23.000	.175	.078
hand * task	Pillai's Trace	.173	4.807[a]	1.000	23.000	.039	.173
	Wilks' Lambda	.827	4.807[a]	1.000	23.000	.039	.173
	Hotelling's Trace	.209	4.807[a]	1.000	23.000	.039	.173
	Roy's Largest Root	.209	4.807[a]	1.000	23.000	.039	.173

a. Exact statistic

b.
Design: Intercept
Within Subjects Design: hand+task+hand*task

Mauchly's Test of Sphericity[b]

Measure: MEASURE_1

Within Subjects Effect	Mauchly's W	Approx. Chi-Square	df	Sig.	Epsilon[a] Greenhouse-Geisser	Huynh-Feldt	Lower-bound
hand	1.000	.000	0	.	1.000	1.000	1.000
task	1.000	.000	0	.	1.000	1.000	1.000
hand * task	1.000	.000	0	.	1.000	1.000	1.000

Tests the null hypothesis that the error covariance matrix of the orthonormalized transformed dependent variables is proportional to an identity matrix.

a. May be used to adjust the degrees of freedom for the averaged tests of significance. Corrected tests are displayed in the Tests of Within-Subjects Effects table.

b.
Design: Intercept
Within Subjects Design: hand+task+hand*task

Tests of Within-Subjects Effects

Measure: MEASURE_1

Source		Type III Sum of Squares	df	Mean Square	F	Sig.	Partial Eta Squared
hand	Sphericity Assumed	2.295	1	2.295	.133	.719	.006
	Greenhouse-Geisser	2.295	1.000	2.295	.133	.719	.006
	Huynh-Feldt	2.295	1.000	2.295	.133	.719	.006
	Lower-bound	2.295	1.000	2.295	.133	.719	.006
Error(hand)	Sphericity Assumed	398.267	23	17.316			
	Greenhouse-Geisser	398.267	23.000	17.316			
	Huynh-Feldt	398.267	23.000	17.316			
	Lower-bound	398.267	23.000	17.316			
task	Sphericity Assumed	70.906	1	70.906	1.955	.175	.078
	Greenhouse-Geisser	70.906	1.000	70.906	1.955	.175	.078
	Huynh-Feldt	70.906	1.000	70.906	1.955	.175	.078
	Lower-bound	70.906	1.000	70.906	1.955	.175	.078
Error(task)	Sphericity Assumed	834.213	23	36.270			
	Greenhouse-Geisser	834.213	23.000	36.270			
	Huynh-Feldt	834.213	23.000	36.270			
	Lower-bound	834.213	23.000	36.270			
hand * task	Sphericity Assumed	21.441	1	21.441	4.807	.039	.173
	Greenhouse-Geisser	21.441	1.000	21.441	4.807	.039	.173
	Huynh-Feldt	21.441	1.000	21.441	4.807	.039	.173
	Lower-bound	21.441	1.000	21.441	4.807	.039	.173
Error(hand*task)	Sphericity Assumed	102.585	23	4.460			
	Greenhouse-Geisser	102.585	23.000	4.460			
	Huynh-Feldt	102.585	23.000	4.460			
	Lower-bound	102.585	23.000	4.460			

Tests of Within-Subjects Contrasts

Measure: MEASURE_1

Source	hand	task	Type III Sum of Squares	df	Mean Square	F	Sig.	Partial Eta Squared
hand	Linear		2.295	1	2.295	.133	.719	.006
Error(hand)	Linear		398.267	23	17.316			
task		Linear	70.906	1	70.906	1.955	.175	.078
Error(task)		Linear	834.213	23	36.270			
hand * task	Linear	Linear	21.441	1	21.441	4.807	.039	.173
Error(hand*task)	Linear	Linear	102.585	23	4.460			

Tests of Between-Subjects Effects

Measure: MEASURE_1

Transformed Variable: Average

Source	Type III Sum of Squares	df	Mean Square	F	Sig.	Partial Eta Squared
Intercept	2544.862	1	2544.862	33.553	.000	.593
Error	1744.438	23	75.845			

Estimated Marginal Means

1. hand

Measure: MEASURE_1

hand	Mean	Std. Error	95% Confidence Interval	
			Lower Bound	Upper Bound
1	4.994	1.017	2.890	7.098
2	5.303	.952	3.334	7.273

2. task

Measure: MEASURE_1

task	Mean	Std. Error	95% Confidence Interval	
			Lower Bound	Upper Bound
1	6.008	1.137	3.655	8.361
2	4.289	1.021	2.178	6.401

3. hand * task

Measure: MEASURE_1

hand	task	Mean	Std. Error	95% Confidence Interval	
				Lower Bound	Upper Bound
1	1	6.326	1.352	3.530	9.123
	2	3.662	.967	1.662	5.662
2	1	5.690	1.122	3.369	8.011
	2	4.916	1.248	2.334	7.499

Tests of Within-Subjects Effects

Measure: MEASURE_1

Source		Type III Sum of Squares	df	Mean Square	F	Sig.	Partial Eta Squared
hand	Sphericity Assumed	2.295	1	2.295	.133	.719	.006
	Greenhouse-Geisser	2.295	1.000	2.295	.133	.719	.006
	Huynh-Feldt	2.295	1.000	2.295	.133	.719	.006
	Lower-bound	2.295	1.000	2.295	.133	.719	.006
Error(hand)	Sphericity Assumed	398.267	23	17.316			
	Greenhouse-Geisser	398.267	23.000	17.316			
	Huynh-Feldt	398.267	23.000	17.316			
	Lower-bound	398.267	23.000	17.316			
task	Sphericity Assumed	70.906	1	70.906	1.955	.175	.078
	Greenhouse-Geisser	70.906	1.000	70.906	1.955	.175	.078
	Huynh-Feldt	70.906	1.000	70.906	1.955	.175	.078
	Lower-bound	70.906	1.000	70.906	1.955	.175	.078
Error(task)	Sphericity Assumed	834.213	23	36.270			
	Greenhouse-Geisser	834.213	23.000	36.270			
	Huynh-Feldt	834.213	23.000	36.270			
	Lower-bound	834.213	23.000	36.270			
hand * task	Sphericity Assumed	21.441	1	21.441	4.807	.039	.173
	Greenhouse-Geisser	21.441	1.000	21.441	4.807	.039	.173
	Huynh-Feldt	21.441	1.000	21.441	4.807	.039	.173
	Lower-bound	21.441	1.000	21.441	4.807	.039	.173
Error(hand*task)	Sphericity Assumed	102.585	23	4.460			
	Greenhouse-Geisser	102.585	23.000	4.460			
	Huynh-Feldt	102.585	23.000	4.460			
	Lower-bound	102.585	23.000	4.460			

This table shows the outcome of trend tests. Each factor only has two levels, and so:
1. only linear tests can be carried out, and not quadratic;
2. the values are simply those for the analysis of variance.
If, however, you have at least one factor with three or more levels, then this table would be useful as shown in the one-way within ANOVA example.

Tests of Within-Subjects Contrasts

Measure: MEASURE_1

Source	hand	task	Type III Sum of Squares	df	Mean Square	F	Sig.	Partial Eta Squared
hand	Linear		2.295	1	2.295	.133	.719	.006
Error(hand)	Linear		398.267	23	17.316			
task		Linear	70.906	1	70.906	1.955	.175	.078
Error(task)		Linear	834.213	23	36.270			
hand * task	Linear	Linear	21.441	1	21.441	4.807	.039	.173
Error(hand*task)	Linear	Linear	102.585	23	4.460			

Estimated Marginal Means

These three tables give the descriptives requested in the **Repeated Measures: Options** dialogue box: "hand", "task", and "hand*task" were moved into the box labelled **Display Means for**.

1. hand

Measure: MEASURE_1

hand	Mean	Std. Error	95% Confidence Interval	
			Lower Bound	Upper Bound
1	4.994	1.017	2.890	7.098
2	5.303	.952	3.334	7.273

This table shows descriptives for each level of the factor "hand", collapsed across the other factor "task". We used the code 1 = right and 2 = left, so the first row is for the right hand, and the second row is for the left hand.

2. task

Measure: MEASURE_1

task	Mean	Std. Error	95% Confidence Interval	
			Lower Bound	Upper Bound
1	6.008	1.137	3.655	8.361
2	4.289	1.021	2.178	6.401

This table shows descriptives for each level of the factor "task" collapsed across the two levels of the factor "hand".

3. hand * task

Measure: MEASURE_1

hand	task	Mean	Std. Error	95% Confidence Interval	
				Lower Bound	Upper Bound
1	1	6.326	1.352	3.530	9.123
	2	3.662	.967	1.662	5.662
2	1	5.690	1.122	3.369	8.011
	2	4.916	1.248	2.334	7.499

This table shows descriptives for each of the conditions of the study. Thus, the first row gives details of performance when participants were tapping with their right hand while memorising words. The bottom row gives details of performance when participants were tapping with their left hand while memorising the positions of the words.

> The interaction graph shown below was obtained by clicking on the **Plots** button at the bottom of the **Repeated Measures** dialogue box.
>
> The labels and title are not helpful so double click on the graph to change them. For more information see Chapter 12.

Estimated Marginal Means of MEASURE_1

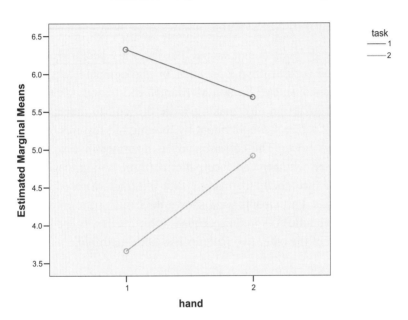

In a report you would write, at appropriate points:

The main effect of tapping hand was not significant: $F(1,23) = 0.133$, $p = .719$, partial $\eta^2 = .01$.

The main effect of type of task was not significant: $F(1,23) = 1.955$, $p = .175$, partial $\eta^2 = .08$.

There was a significant interaction between tapping hand and type of task: $F(1,23) = 4.807$, $p = .039$, partial $\eta^2 = .17$. This interaction is displayed in the graph above, showing that right hand tapping was disrupted more by memorising words than memorising positions, and that this effect of type of task was reduced for left hand tapping.

Section 6: Mixed ANOVA

In this section, we show you how to perform an ANOVA that involves both between- and within-subjects factors in the same experiment. We shall do so by referring to a study employing a three-way mixed design.

EXAMPLE STUDY: THE EFFECTS OF INVERSION, NEGATION AND PRIMING ON THE PERCEPTION OF FACE-LIKE PATTERNS

It has previously been demonstrated that faces are peculiarly difficult to recognise when inverted (upside-down) or when in photographic negative (negated). In an earlier published study, Kemp, McManus and Pigott (1990) demonstrated that negation and inversion also make it more difficult to detect minor changes to the appearance of a face, brought about by moving the features (the eyes being moved up, down, in or out). The current study is a further investigation of these effects, designed to see whether non-face patterns (three dots arranged in the positions of the eyes and the mouth to make a face-like pattern) are also affected by these transformations. Participants were shown three such patterns at a time. One of these patterns showed the dots in their original location. The participants were required to decide which of the other two patterns had been modified.

The design employed was a 2*2*2 mixed ANOVA design. The first factor was the within-subjects factor of negation, with two levels, operationalised by showing face-like dot patterns as normal images or in photographic negative. The second factor was the within-subjects factor of orientation, with two levels, operationalised by showing the face-like dot patterns upright or inverted. The third factor was the between-subjects factor of priming where some participants were primed by being asked to perform this task on faces before taking part in the experiment whereas others were not.

The dependent variable was the percentage of correct judgements made by the participants. The hypothesis tested was that the effects of negation and inversion would only be apparent in the group that was primed.

For the purposes of this book, we have created a data file that will reproduce some of the findings of this later study. In the data file, the columns holding the data for the combination of levels of the two within-subjects factors have been named using the numbering systems that we described in Section 5. (These data are available in Appendix I or from the web address listed there.)

HOW TO DO IT

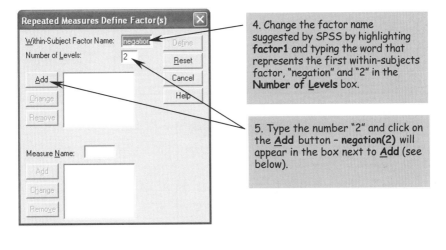

1. Click on the word **Analyze**.

2. Click on **General Linear Model**.

3. Click on **Repeated Measures**. The **Repeated Measures Define Factor(s)** dialogue box will appear – see next page.

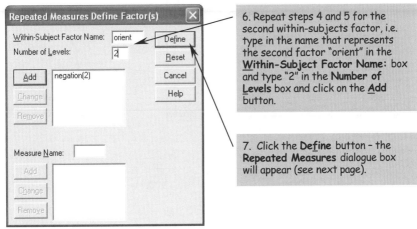

4. Change the factor name suggested by SPSS by highlighting **factor1** and typing the word that represents the first within-subjects factor, "negation" and "2" in the **Number of Levels** box.

5. Type the number "2" and click on the **Add** button – **negation(2)** will appear in the box next to **Add** (see below).

6. Repeat steps 4 and 5 for the second within-subjects factor, i.e. type in the name that represents the second factor "orient" in the **Within-Subject Factor Name:** box and type "2" in the **Number of Levels** box and click on the **Add** button.

7. Click the **Define** button – the **Repeated Measures** dialogue box will appear (see next page).

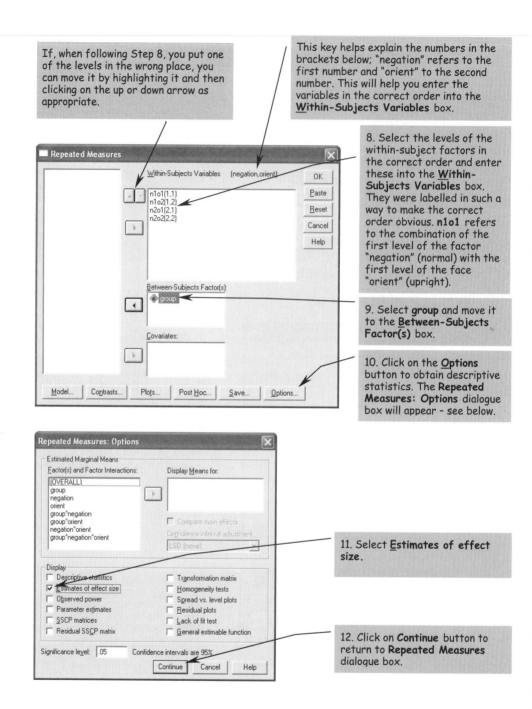

If, when following Step 8, you put one of the levels in the wrong place, you can move it by highlighting it and then clicking on the up or down arrow as appropriate.

This key helps explain the numbers in the brackets below; "negation" refers to the first number and "orient" to the second number. This will help you enter the variables in the correct order into the **Within-Subjects Variables** box.

8. Select the levels of the within-subject factors in the correct order and enter these into the **Within-Subjects Variables** box. They were labelled in such a way to make the correct order obvious. **n1o1** refers to the combination of the first level of the factor "negation" (normal) with the first level of the face "orient" (upright).

9. Select **group** and move it to the **Between-Subjects Factor(s)** box.

10. Click on the **Options** button to obtain descriptive statistics. The **Repeated Measures: Options** dialogue box will appear – see below.

11. Select **Estimates of effect size**.

12. Click on **Continue** button to return to **Repeated Measures** dialogue box.

Click on OK. SPSS will calculate the ANOVA and produce the output that is explained on the next three pages.

SPSS OUTPUT FOR THREE-WAY MIXED ANALYSIS OF VARIANCE

Obtained Using Menu Items: General Linear Model > Repeated Measures

General Linear Model

Within-Subjects Factors

Measure: MEASURE_1

negation	orient	Dependent Variable
1	1	n1o1
	2	n1o2
2	1	n2o1
	2	n2o2

On this page we show the first four tables, reduced to fit the page. On the following two pages we show the remaining three tables: they hold the information that you are most likely to need.

Between-Subjects Factors

		Value Label	N
group	1.00	unprimed	38
	2.00	primed	23

If you requested **Descriptive statistics** in the **Repeated Measures: Options** dialogue box, the Descriptive Statistics table would appear here.

Multivariate Tests[b]

Effect		Value	F	Hypothesis df	Error df	Sig.	Partial Eta Squared
negation	Pillai's Trace	.002	.137[a]	1.000	59.000	.713	.002
	Wilks' Lambda	.998	.137[a]	1.000	59.000	.713	.002
	Hotelling's Trace	.002	.137[a]	1.000	59.000	.713	.002
	Roy's Largest Root	.002	.137[a]	1.000	59.000	.713	.002
negation * group	Pillai's Trace	.006	.384[a]	1.000	59.000	.538	.006
	Wilks' Lambda	.994	.384[a]	1.000	59.000	.538	.006
	Hotelling's Trace	.007	.384[a]	1.000	59.000	.538	.006
	Roy's Largest Root	.007	.384[a]	1.000	59.000	.538	.006
orient	Pillai's Trace	.009	.539[a]	1.000	59.000	.466	.009
	Wilks' Lambda	.991	.539[a]	1.000	59.000	.466	.009
	Hotelling's Trace	.009	.539[a]	1.000	59.000	.466	.009
	Roy's Largest Root	.009	.539[a]	1.000	59.000	.466	.009
orient * group	Pillai's Trace	.038	2.319[a]	1.000	59.000	.133	.038
	Wilks' Lambda	.962	2.319[a]	1.000	59.000	.133	.038
	Hotelling's Trace	.039	2.319[a]	1.000	59.000	.133	.038
	Roy's Largest Root	.039	2.319[a]	1.000	59.000	.133	.038
negation * orient	Pillai's Trace	.048	3.006[a]	1.000	59.000	.088	.048
	Wilks' Lambda	.952	3.006[a]	1.000	59.000	.088	.048
	Hotelling's Trace	.051	3.006[a]	1.000	59.000	.088	.048
	Roy's Largest Root	.051	3.006[a]	1.000	59.000	.088	.048
negation * orient * group	Pillai's Trace	.051	3.185[a]	1.000	59.000	.079	.051
	Wilks' Lambda	.949	3.185[a]	1.000	59.000	.079	.051
	Hotelling's Trace	.054	3.185[a]	1.000	59.000	.079	.051
	Roy's Largest Root	.054	3.185[a]	1.000	59.000	.079	.051

a. Exact statistic

b.
  Design: Intercept+group
  Within Subjects Design: negation+orient+negation*orient

For information about these two tables see Section 7.

Mauchly's Test of Sphericity[b]

Measure: MEASURE_1

Within Subjects Effect	Mauchly's W	Approx. Chi-Square	df	Sig.	Epsilon[a] Greenhouse-Geisser	Huynh-Feldt	Lower-bound
negation	1.000	.000	0	.	1.000	1.000	1.000
orient	1.000	.000	0	.	1.000	1.000	1.000
negation * orient	1.000	.000	0	.	1.000	1.000	1.000

Tests the null hypothesis that the error covariance matrix of the orthonormalized transformed dependent variables is proportional to an identity matrix.

a. May be used to adjust the degrees of freedom for the averaged tests of significance. Corrected tests are displayed in the Tests of Within-Subjects Effects table.

b.
  Design: Intercept+group
  Within Subjects Design: negation+orient+negation*orient

This table shows the outcome of any part of the mixed ANOVA that incorporates a within-subjects factor. See Section 7 for an explanation of the 2nd-4th rows of each cell.

Measure: MEASURE_1

Source		Type III Sum of Squares	df	Mean Square	F	Sig.	Partial Eta Squared
negation	Sphericity Assumed	9.470	1	9.470	.137	.713	.002
	Greenhouse-Geisser	9.470	1.000	9.470	.137	.713	.002
	Huynh-Feldt	9.470	1.000	9.470	.137	.713	.002
	Lower-bound	9.470	1.000	9.470	.137	.713	.002
negation * group	Sphericity Assumed	26.587	1	26.587	.384	.538	.006
	Greenhouse-Geisser	26.587	1.000	26.587	.384	.538	.006
	Huynh-Feldt	26.587	1.000	26.587	.384	.538	.006
	Lower-bound	26.587	1.000	26.587	.384	.538	.006
Error(negation)	Sphericity Assumed	4079.831	59	69.150			
	Greenhouse-Geisser	4079.831	59.000	69.150			
	Huynh-Feldt	4079.831	59.000	69.150			
	Lower-bound	4079.831	59.000	69.150			
orient	Sphericity Assumed	33.631	1	33.631	.539	.466	.009
	Greenhouse-Geisser	33.631	1.000	33.631	.539	.466	.009
	Huynh-Feldt	33.631	1.000	33.631	.539	.466	.009
	Lower-bound	33.631	1.000	33.631	.539	.466	.009
orient * group	Sphericity Assumed	144.622	1	144.622	2.319	.133	.038
	Greenhouse-Geisser	144.622	1.000	144.622	2.319	.133	.038
	Huynh-Feldt	144.622	1.000	144.622	2.319	.133	.038
	Lower-bound	144.622	1.000	144.622	2.319	.133	.038
Error(orient)	Sphericity Assumed	3678.712	59	62.351			
	Greenhouse-Geisser	3678.712	59.000	62.351			
	Huynh-Feldt	3678.712	59.000	62.351			
	Lower-bound	3678.712	59.000	62.351			
negation * orient	Sphericity Assumed	201.313	1	201.313	3.006	.088	.048
	Greenhouse-Geisser	201.313	1.000	201.313	3.006	.088	.048
	Huynh-Feldt	201.313	1.000	201.313	3.006	.088	.048
	Lower-bound	201.313	1.000	201.313	3.006	.088	.048
negation * orient * group	Sphericity Assumed	213.273	1	213.273	3.185	.079	.051
	Greenhouse-Geisser	213.273	1.000	213.273	3.185	.079	.051
	Huynh-Feldt	213.273	1.000	213.273	3.185	.079	.051
	Lower-bound	213.273	1.000	213.273	3.185	.079	.051
Error(negation*orient)	Sphericity Assumed	3950.946	59	66.965			
	Greenhouse-Geisser	3950.946	59.000	66.965			
	Huynh-Feldt	3950.946	59.000	66.965			
	Lower-bound	3950.946	59.000	66.965			

From the highlighted rows, and associated error dfs, you can report the following:

The main effect of negation was not significant: $F(1,59) = 0.137$, $p = .713$, partial $\eta^2 = .00$.

The group by negation interaction was not significant: $F(1,59) = 0.384$, $p = .538$, partial $\eta^2 = .01$.

The main effect of orientation was not significant: $F(1,59) = 0.539$, $p = .466$, partial $\eta^2 = .01$.

The orientation by group interaction was not significant: $F(1,59) = 2.319$, $p = .133$, partial $\eta^2 = .04$.

The negation by orientation interaction was not significant: $F(1,59 = 3.006$, $p = .088$, partial $\eta^2 = .05)$.

The three-way interaction between negation, orientation and group was not significant: $F(1,59) = 3.185$, $p = .079$, partial $\eta^2 = .05$.

This table shows the outcome of trend tests. Each factor only has two levels, and so this output has the same drawbacks as previously described for the example two-way within-subjects ANOVA (and only tests for linear trends).

Tests of Within-Subjects Contrasts

Measure: MEASURE_1

Source	negation	orient	Type III Sum of Squares	df	Mean Square	F	Sig.	Partial Eta Squared
negation	Linear		9.470	1	9.470	.137	.713	.002
negation * group	Linear		26.587	1	26.587	.384	.538	.006
Error(negation)	Linear		4079.831	59	69.150			
orient		Linear	33.631	1	33.631	.539	.466	.009
orient * group		Linear	144.622	1	144.622	2.319	.133	.038
Error(orient)		Linear	3678.712	59	62.351			
negation * orient	Linear	Linear	201.313	1	201.313	3.006	.088	.048
negation * orient * group	Linear	Linear	213.273	1	213.273	3.185	.079	.051
Error(negation*orient)	Linear	Linear	3950.946	59	66.965			

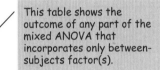

This table shows the outcome of any part of the mixed ANOVA that incorporates only between-subjects factor(s).

Tests of Between-Subjects Effects

Measure: MEASURE_1

Transformed Variable: Average

Source	Type III Sum of Squares	df	Mean Square	F	Sig.	Partial Eta Squared
Intercept	990995.857	1	990995.857	5833.883	.000	.990
group	193.383	1	193.383	1.138	.290	.019
Error	10022.271	59	169.869			

In this example there is only one between-subjects factor. If there had been two, then each main effect and the two-way interaction between the factors would appear in this table. From the highlighted row, and the error df, you can report:

The main effect of priming was not significant: $F(1,59) = 1.138$, $p = .290$, partial $\eta^2 = .02$.

TIP   If you requested **Display Means for** using the **Repeated Measures: Options** dialogue box, then the tables of Estimated Marginal Means will appear here, at the end of the output. For this example, there would be seven tables of descriptives:

three tables: one for each of the three factors, showing descriptives for each level of a factor ignoring the other factors;

three tables: one for each of the three two-way interactions, showing descriptives for each combination of levels of two of the factors ignoring the third factor;

and one table for the three-way interaction, showing descriptives for each of the eight conditions.

These means are very useful to help you interpret the results of the ANOVA.

Section 7: Some additional points

The within-subjects Analysis of Variance output contains several sections that describe statistical concepts that are beyond those normally covered in an undergraduate psychology degree. However, for those readers who want to understand the entire output these sections are described below.

TEST OF BETWEEN-SUBJECTS EFFECTS

The fact that the output for a within-subjects (repeated measures) ANOVA contains details of between-subjects effects often confuses students. In fact this part of the output can usually be ignored. In effect what SPSS is doing is assuming that **participant** is an additional, between-subjects factor in the analysis. Hence for a 2*2 within-subjects analysis SPSS actually reports an N*2*2 analysis where N is the number of participants. One way to think of this is to say that the part of the output reporting between-subjects effects is asking "Did all participants perform the same?" It is in the nature of Psychology that participants are very variable in almost all tasks and hence you will find that the F-ratio is invariably very high and highly significant. As we are not normally interested in this question of whether the participants are all performing in the same way (we usually want to know about general trends across groups of participants) we can ignore this section of the output. Indeed, you will very rarely see this result reported in psychological papers.

MAUCHLY'S TEST OF SPHERICITY

If you have two or more levels of a within-subjects factor, SPSS will print a test called the Mauchly's test of Sphericity. For ANOVAs with only two levels, the contents of the table showing this test (see page 207) are not useful, but with more than two levels they can be valuable. The Mauchly's test of Sphericity is a statistical test to determine whether the data entered into the ANOVA meet certain assumptions. This is rather like the Levene's equality of variance test that we described when looking at the independent t-test. With the within-subjects ANOVA, the assumption being tested is effectively that the correlations between all the variables are roughly the same. A chi value is estimated to test the significance of the Mauchly's test of Sphericity procedure (hence the output reports "Approx. Chi-square"). The significance of this value of chi is reported. If it is significant (i.e., less than .05) then the assumptions behind the normal within-subjects ANOVA have been violated. When this does occur there are two things you can do: corrections using Epsilon, or Multivariate Tests.

Corrections using Epsilon

SPSS provides three estimates of a statistic called **Epsilon** that can be used to correct for a violation of these assumptions (see page 208). The greater the violation the smaller will be the value of Epsilon. To adjust the F-ratio, both numerator and denominator degrees of freedom must be multiplied by Epsilon before the p value is calculated. However, SPSS computed the correction for you and report the corrected values of p in the "Tests of Within-Subjects Effects" table.

All you need to do is decide which of the three estimates of Epsilon you need to use. Greenhouse–Geisser Epsilon is probably the most appropriate value to use, but if you have relatively few participants this can tend to be rather too conservative (i.e., its use will decrease the chances of finding a significant result) – in these cases the Huynh–Feldt Epsilon may be preferable. The third estimate (called the "Lower-bound Epsilon") is a minimum value for Epsilon that will give the most conservative correction. SPSS gives corrected values in the table. When reporting any result, make it clear which you have used.

> **TIP**   When, as in the example on page 207, the Mauchly's test of Sphericity is not significant, the Epsilon will be zero and all the entries in the Tests of Within-Subjects Effects table will be identical.

Multivariate Tests

A second solution is to use what is called the **multivariate approach** (as opposed to the normal procedure that we have been describing up to now which is known as the univariate approach). The multivariate approach makes fewer assumptions about the data and hence is more appropriate when the Mauchly's test of Sphericity is significant. In the Multivariate Tests table, SPSS reports four different multivariate statistics: Pilliai's Trace, Wilks' Lambda, Hotelling's Trace and Roy's Largest Root (see page 207). Each of these tests reports a value of F with associated degrees of freedom and a significance value. You will probably find that there is little difference between the significance of F reported by these four procedures – pick one of them and report it! The multivariate values of F are always lower than the univariate values, and hence if a result is not significant by the univariate method it cannot be significant for the multivariate method. For this reason SPSS does not report the multivariate estimates when the univariate test is non-significant.

> **TIP** Remember, if your within-subjects factor has only two levels, then the multivariate estimates and the Epsilon corrected values in the Tests of Within-Subjects Effects table are all identical to the Sphericity Assumed values. This is because with only two levels of a factor there is only one correlation that can be calculated and hence you cannot be violating the assumptions described above.

IN SUMMARY

1. If the Mauchly's test of Sphericity is reported, look to see if it is significant.
2. If not significant (i.e., $p > .05$) then report the univariate results as described in the main text.
3. If the Mauchly's test of Sphericity is significant then either:
   a. Use the values for your chosen Epsilon from the Tests of Within-subjects Effects table

   or:

   b. Adopt a multivariate approach and report one of the four statistics given in the Multivariate Tests table.
4. Either way, when reporting the result, make it clear which solution you have adopted.

Section 8: Planned and unplanned comparisons

You have by now gathered that a significant F-ratio in ANOVA tells us that the dependent variable varies with the levels of the factor. However, unless the factor has only two levels, ANOVA does not tell us which means are different from which other means. If there are only two levels and there is a significant main effect of that factor, then the mean for one level must be significantly different from the mean for the other level. For a factor with more than two levels, a significant F-ratio tells us that the dependent variable varies with the levels of the factor, but we need to turn to other devices to analyse the data in more detail. These can allow us to compare means or groups of means in a variety of ways and help us understand and interpret the results. When deciding on which tests to use to make these comparisons, we need to be clear whether they are:

1. Planned (*a priori*) comparisons. These are decided upon before the data was collected. The researcher has predicted which means will differ significantly from each other.
2. Unplanned (*a posteriori* or *post-hoc*) comparisons. Here differences among means are explored after the data has been collected.

Why should this matter? We need to use different tests for these two kinds of comparisons because the probability of a Type I error is smaller when the comparisons are planned in advance. Type I error involves **incorrectly** rejecting a null hypothesis, thus concluding that there is a significant effect when in fact the means differ due to chance. When making multiple comparisons, we run the risk of Type I errors. Howell (1987) gives the following example: assume that we give a group of males and a group of females 50 words and ask them to give us as many associations to these words as possible in 1 minute. For each word, we then test whether there is a significant difference in the number of associations given by male and female participants. We could run 50 more or less independent t tests, but we would run the risk that 2.5 of these (50*0.05) will be declared "significant" by chance.

Why is there a greater risk of making a Type I error when carrying out unplanned comparisons? Consider the following. Imagine an experiment to look at the effect of five different levels of noise on memory that employed a one-way ANOVA design. You will have five means (one for each condition) and could do a total of ten comparisons (you could compare mean 1 to mean 2; mean 1 to mean 3; mean 1 to mean 4 etc.). Assume that the null hypothesis is true, and that noise does not affect memory, but that by chance two of the means are far enough apart to lead us erroneously to reject the null hypothesis, thus the data contain one Type I error. If you had planned your single comparison in advance, you would have a probability of 0.1 of hitting on the one comparison out of 10 that involves the Type I error. But if you first look at the data, you are certain to make a Type I error since you are likely to test the largest difference you can observe.

UNPLANNED COMPARISONS IN SPSS

Unplanned or *post-hoc* comparisons are easy to perform in SPSS and you can do as many as you like, with two restrictions: firstly, if any factor has two levels, SPSS will not perform the post-hoc tests because the main effect is sufficient; secondly, they can only be used to compare levels from between-subjects factors. There is a range of post-hoc tests to choose from. They can be used in conjunction with the **One-Way ANOVA** or the **General Linear Model** command. To obtain the dialogue box to perform such comparisons, simply click on the **Post Hoc** button in either dialogue box. We show you here how to perform such comparisons using the one-way between-subjects ANOVA data from Section 2; however, the procedure is the same for more than one-way between-subjects factorial designs using the **General Linear Model** command.

One-Way ANOVA

1. Select **Analyze** on the menu bar
2. Select **Compare Means**
3. Select **One-Way ANOVA** and the dialogue box below appears.

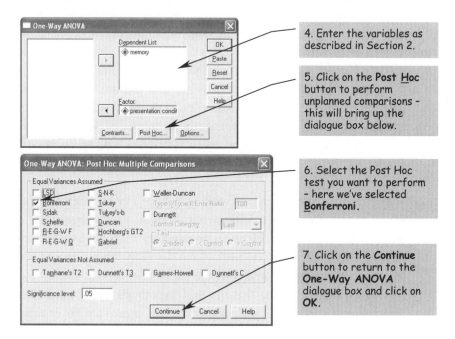

4. Enter the variables as described in Section 2.

5. Click on the **Post Hoc** button to perform unplanned comparisons – this will bring up the dialogue box below.

6. Select the Post Hoc test you want to perform – here we've selected **Bonferroni**.

7. Click on the **Continue** button to return to the **One-Way ANOVA** dialogue box and click on **OK**.

General Linear Model

1. Select **Analyze** on the menu bar
2. Select **General Linear Model**
3. Select **Univariate** and the dialogue box below appears.

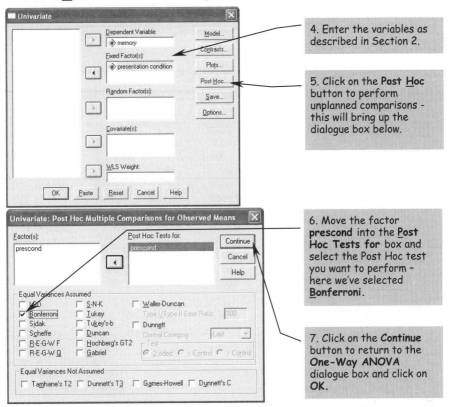

4. Enter the variables as described in Section 2.

5. Click on the **Post Hoc** button to perform unplanned comparisons - this will bring up the dialogue box below.

6. Move the factor **prescond** into the **Post Hoc Tests for** box and select the Post Hoc test you want to perform – here we've selected **Bonferroni**.

7. Click on the **Continue** button to return to the **One-Way ANOVA** dialogue box and click on **OK**.

You can also do unplanned comparisons on any between-subjects factor (with three or more levels) in a mixed design. There is a post-hoc button in the **Repeated Measures** dialogue box. In a mixed design, the post-hoc output can only be applied to the between-subjects factor(s).

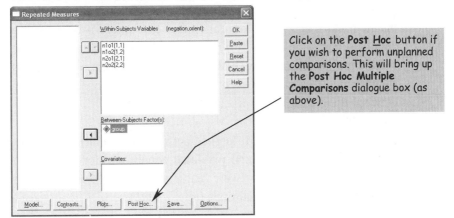

Click on the **Post Hoc** button if you wish to perform unplanned comparisons. This will bring up the **Post Hoc Multiple Comparisons** dialogue box (as above).

Post Hoc Tests

presentation condition

Multiple Comparisons

This heading and the **Multiple Comparisons** table will appear after all the other tables in the ANOVA output.

Dependent Variable: memory
Bonferroni

(I) presentation condition	(J) presentation condition	Mean Difference (I-J)	Std. Error	Sig.	95% Confidence Interval	
					Lower Bound	Upper Bound
unmasked	greyblob	11.0000*	2.16012	.000	4.9690	17.0310
	pixelated	9.0000*	2.16012	.001	2.9690	15.0310
	negated	-.5000	2.16012	1.000	-6.5310	5.5310
greyblob	unmasked	-11.0000*	2.16012	.000	-17.0310	-4.9690
	pixelated	-2.0000	2.16012	1.000	-8.0310	4.0310
	negated	-11.5000*	2.16012	.000	-17.5310	-5.4690
pixelated	unmasked	-9.0000*	2.16012	.001	-15.0310	-2.9690
	greyblob	2.0000	2.16012	1.000	-4.0310	8.0310
	negated	-9.5000*	2.16012	.001	-15.5310	-3.4690
negated	unmasked	.5000	2.16012	1.000	-5.5310	6.5310
	greyblob	11.5000*	2.16012	.000	5.4690	17.5310
	pixelated	9.5000*	2.16012	.001	3.4690	15.5310

Based on observed means.
*. The mean difference is significant at the .05 level.

SPSS prints a complete matrix (as it does for correlations). You have to pick out the comparisons required, and ignore the repetitions.

As our factor had four levels there are six possible comparisons. Their *p* values are highlighted here.

> **TIP** If you had requested post hoc tests for two factors using the **General Linear Model** command, then two tables would be printed, one for each factor.

In a report you would write:

Employing the Bonferroni post-hoc test, significant differences were found between the unmasked and greyblob conditions ($p < .0005$), between the unmasked and pixelated conditions ($p = .001$), between the greyblob and negated conditions ($p < .0005$), and between the pixelated and negated conditions ($p = .001$). There was no significant difference between the unmasked and negated conditions ($p = 1$), or between the greyblob and pixelated conditions ($p = 1$).

Or, to abbreviate:

There was no significant difference between the unmasked and negated conditions, or between the greyblob and pixelated conditions (for both, $p = 1$). The greyblob and pixelated conditions were each significantly different from each of the unmasked and negated conditions (all $p = .001$).

Generally, for planned comparisons the technique of linear contrasts is used, which allows us to compare one level, or set of levels, with another level or set of levels. The simplest way of doing this is to assign weights to each. These weights are known as coefficients. This technique is available on SPSS which uses the t-statistic to test specific contrasts. Indeed, the print-out will give you two t-values, one for "assume equal variances" and one for "does not assume equal". Since the variances of the groups being compared should be broadly similar (otherwise you should not be using ANOVA), you can "assume equal variances", but check both values and their significance. A point to note here is that the overall main effect does not have to be significant for you to test for specific differences using planned comparisons.

By assigning weights (or coefficients) we can make three sorts of comparisons:
1. We can compare one condition with one other condition.
2. We can compare one condition with the mean of two or more other conditions.
3. We can compare the mean of one set of conditions with the mean of another set of conditions.

In all three of these cases we assign a weight of zero to a condition (or conditions) that we do not want to be included in the comparison. Conditions (or groups of conditions) that are to be compared with each other are assigned opposite signs (positive or negative). In all cases the sum of the weights must be zero.

So, suppose you had four conditions, C1, C2, C3 and C4. If you wanted to compare only conditions 1 and 3 you could assign the weights: **1, 0, –1, 0.**

If you wanted to compare the average of the first 2 conditions with the third condition you could assign the weights: **1, 1, –2, 0.**

If you wanted to compare the mean of the first two groups with the mean of the last two groups you could use the weights: **1, 1, –1, –1.**

TIP   If you wish to perform more than one planned comparison on the same set of data, then you need to check that the comparisons are independent of one another, that they are non-overlapping – these are called **orthogonal** comparisons. You can do this by taking each pair of comparisons and checking that the products of the coefficients assigned to each level sum to zero (see any good statistics text, for example Howell, 2002).

If you perform a planned comparison using the **One-Way ANOVA** command, then you have to design your own contrasts as shown above, and enter the weights (coefficients) into a dialogue box. We show you how to do this next.

HOW TO DO IT USING THE ONE-WAY ANOVA COMMAND

1. Select **Analyze** on the menu bar
2. Select **Compare Means**
3. Select **One-Way ANOVA** and the dialogue box below appears.

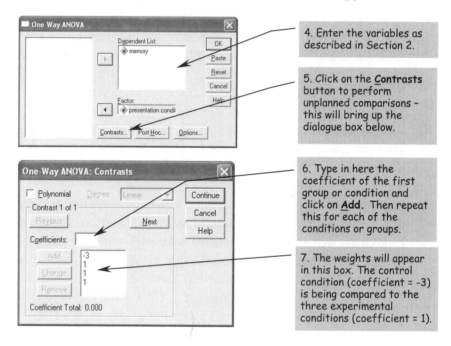

4. Enter the variables as described in Section 2.

5. Click on the **Contrasts** button to perform unplanned comparisons – this will bring up the dialogue box below.

6. Type in here the coefficient of the first group or condition and click on **Add**. Then repeat this for each of the conditions or groups.

7. The weights will appear in this box. The control condition (coefficient = -3) is being compared to the three experimental conditions (coefficient = 1).

The dialogue box above shows a planned comparison for the data from the one-way between-subjects ANOVA experiment, where the control group (who were shown the witness giving evidence with her face visible) is compared with the three experimental groups (who were all shown the witness giving evidence with her face masked). A linear contrast is requested and the coefficients have been entered, first for group 1, then groups 2, 3 and 4. (These data are available in Appendix I or from the web address listed there.) The output overleaf shows that this comparison is significant.

SPSS OUTPUT FOR CONTRASTS

Obtained Using Menu Items: Compare <u>M</u>eans > <u>O</u>ne-Way ANOVA

These tables will appear after all the other tables in the ANOVA output.

Contrast Coefficients

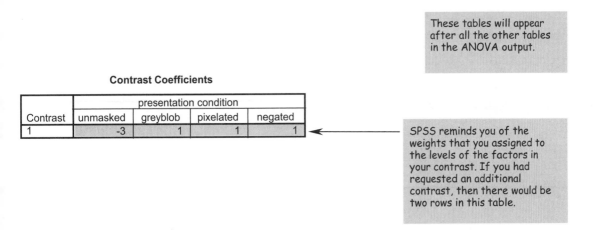

Contrast	presentation condition			
	unmasked	greyblob	pixelated	negated
1	-3	1	1	1

SPSS reminds you of the weights that you assigned to the levels of the factors in your contrast. If you had requested an additional contrast, then there would be two rows in this table.

Contrast Tests

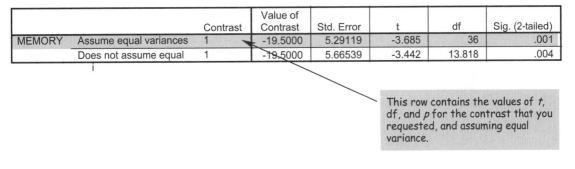

		Contrast	Value of Contrast	Std. Error	t	df	Sig. (2-tailed)
MEMORY	Assume equal variances	1	-19.5000	5.29119	-3.685	36	.001
	Does not assume equal	1	-19.5000	5.66539	-3.442	13.818	.004

This row contains the values of *t*, df, and *p* for the contrast that you requested, and assuming equal variance.

In a report you would write:

A planned comparison revealed that participants who saw the witness's face unmasked remembered significantly more of her testimony than the participants in the three masking conditions ($t = 3.685$, df = 36, $p = .001$).

Note that the contrast test can tell you whether the conditions that you compared are significantly different or not, but nothing about the **direction** of the difference/s. In order to fully interpret the result, you will need to obtain descriptive statistics for the conditions or groups compared.

The other ANOVA commands allow you to choose between a range of pre-set contrasts, as shown in the dialogue box below:

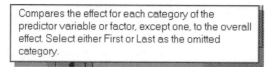

Click on the arrow to view the list of contrasts available on most ANOVA commands. Select the one appropriate one for your planned comparison.

Above, four different pre-set contrasts are visible: **Deviation**, **Simple**, **Difference** and **Helmert**. If you scroll down, then two others appear and these are **Repeated** and **Polynomial**. If you click on one and then right click on the mouse, SPSS Help provides an explanation of what that specific contrast does. So, for example for Deviation, the following SPSS help box appears:

> Compares the effect for each category of the predictor variable or factor, except one, to the overall effect. Select either First or Last as the omitted category.

With **Deviation**, if there are three levels of the factor, two comparisons will be carried out. If you select the last to be omitted, then levels 1 and 2 will be compared to the overall effect (of levels 1, 2 and 3 combined). If you select the first to be omitted, then levels 2 and 3 will be compared to the overall effect of all three.

For **Helmert**, SPSS Help provides the following description:

> In a Helmert contrast, the effect for each category of the predictor variable or factor (except the last) is compared to the mean effect of subsequent categories.

With Helmert, if there are three levels of the factor, two comparisons will be performed. Level 1 is compared to levels 2 and 3 combined, and level 2 is compared to level 3.

The Polynomial contrast should be used to look for trends in the data, for example it can be used to look for a linear trend.

Section 9: Nonparametric equivalents to ANOVA: Kruskal–Wallis and Friedman

EXAMPLE STUDY: THE COGNITIVE INTERVIEW

To explore the use of the nonparametric equivalents of the one-way ANOVA, we shall look at a study investigating the use of the Cognitive Interview. One application of memory research has been the adoption of the use of the Cognitive Interview (CI) by many police forces in Britain. This provides the police officer with a toolkit of mnemonic techniques to assist recall by a witness or victim, so that as full and accurate account as possible of a crime incident can be recorded. Research has demonstrated that the CI elicits more information than the standard police interview. Newlands (1997) investigated the effect the CI has on perpetrator identification, and examined whether the CI affected the confidence with which a participant made an identification. There is evidence to suggest that the more one talks about a facial image, the harder it is to maintain that image in one's mind's eye. A mock crime scenario was seen by 60 participants, 20 of whom were then interviewed using the CI, 20 using the standard police interview (SI) and 20 participants were simply asked to visualise the face of the perpetrator. Participants were then asked to identify the perpetrator from a photo array. Three confidence ratings were provided by participants: confidence in decision after viewing the video, after being interviewed or visualising the face and finally after making an identification.

Two hypotheses were tested: that CI and SI interviews affect a participant's confidence at making an identification compared with a visualisation condition, and that confidence levels decline after attempting to make an identification. The design employed had two factors; the between-subjects factor of condition (CI, SI or visualisation) and the within-subjects factor of time of confidence rating (before and after interview/visualisation and after identification). The dependent variable was measured on an ordinal scale and is the confidence rating, operationalised as the response on a 7 point scale where point 1 was "complete confidence" and point 7 "complete guess".

For the purposes of this book, we have created a data file that will reproduce some of the findings from this study. We have used this same data file to demonstrate both of the nonparametric equivalents of ANOVA. (These data are available in Appendix I or from the web address listed there.)

THE KRUSKAL–WALLIS TEST

The Kruskal–Wallis test is a nonparametric equivalent of the one-way between-subjects analysis of variance. It was employed here to test the hypothesis that the CI and SI interviews affect a participant's confidence at making an identification compared with the visualisation condition. The second confidence rating was therefore the dependent variable, and condition was the between-subjects factor.

How to perform the Kruskal–Wallis

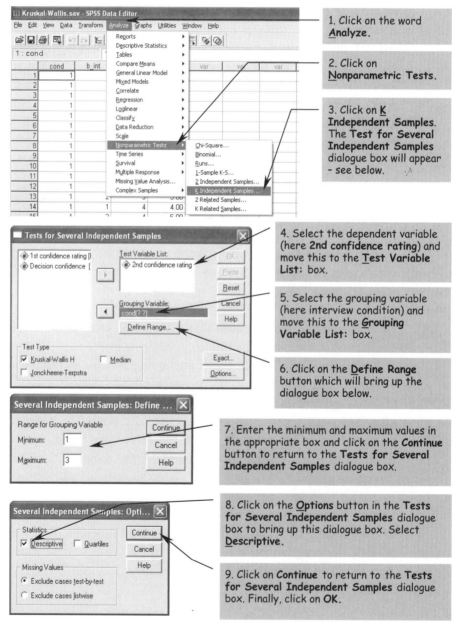

1. Click on the word **Analyze**.

2. Click on **Nonparametric Tests**.

3. Click on **K Independent Samples**. The **Test for Several Independent Samples** dialogue box will appear – see below.

4. Select the dependent variable (here **2nd confidence rating**) and move this to the **Test Variable List:** box.

5. Select the grouping variable (here interview condition) and move this to the **Grouping Variable List:** box.

6. Click on the **Define Range** button which will bring up the dialogue box below.

7. Enter the minimum and maximum values in the appropriate box and click on the **Continue** button to return to the **Tests for Several Independent Samples** dialogue box.

8. Click on the **Options** button in the **Tests for Several Independent Samples** dialogue box to bring up this dialogue box. Select **Descriptive**.

9. Click on **Continue** to return to the **Tests for Several Independent Samples** dialogue box. Finally, click on **OK**.

Obtained by Using Menu Items: <u>N</u>onparametric Tests > <u>K</u> Independent Samples

Descriptives, from the **Options** button in the dialogue box. The first row is for the confidence rating; however, it is for all 60 participants regardless of the between-subjects condition they were in.
For a report, descriptives for each group separately, obtained using **Custom Tables**, would be much more useful (see Chapter 2).

NPar Tests

Descriptive Statistics

	N	Mean	Std. Deviation	Minimum	Maximum
2nd confidence rating	60	2.98	1.282	1	6
Condition	60	2.00	.823	1	3

Kruskal–Wallis Test

Ranks

	Condition	N	Mean Rank
2nd confidence rating	CI	20	41.72
	Visualisation	20	12.45
	SI	20	37.33
	Total	60	

Information about the calculations for the Kruskal–Wallis: it can be considered as an extension of the Mann–Whitney U test. See the annotated output of that test for an explanation of this part.

Test Statistics^{a,b}

The calculated value for the Kruskal-Wallis, which is assessed for significance using χ^2 distribution.

	2nd confidence rating
Chi-Square	34.622
df	2
Asymp. Sig.	.000

The degrees of freedom = k-1, where k is the number of levels of the factor.

The *p* value.

a. Kruskal Wallis Test

b. Grouping Variable: Condition

In a report you would write:

For the second confidence rating there was a significant effect of interview condition: $\chi^2(2, N = 60) = 34.622, p < .0005$.

The Friedman test is the nonparametric equivalent of the one-way within-subjects analysis of variance. Confusingly, the Friedman test is sometimes referred to as the Friedman two-way ANOVA (this is because for a within-subjects analysis of variance, the participants are also considered to be a factor). The Friedman test was employed here to test the hypothesis that participants' confidence levels declined after attempting to make an identification, regardless of the condition in which they participated.

How to perform the Friedman test

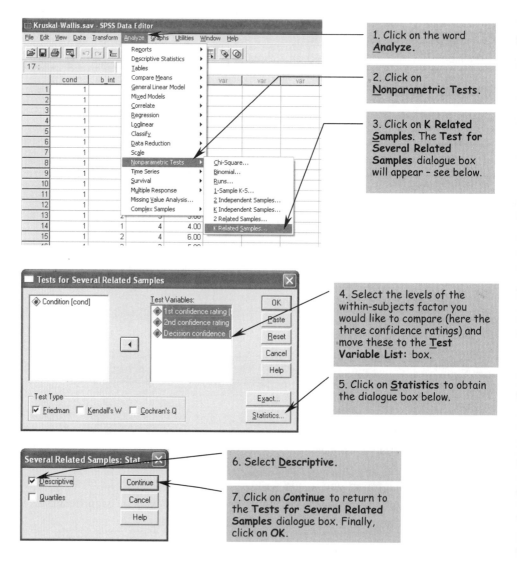

SPSS OUTPUT FOR FRIEDMAN ONE-WAY WITHIN-SUBJECTS

Obtained by Using Menu Items: <u>N</u>onparametric Tests > K Related <u>S</u>amples

Descriptives for each level of the within-subjects factor, time of confidence rating, were obtained using the **Statistics** button in the dialogue box.

NPar Tests

Descriptive Statistics

	N	Mean	Std. Deviation	Minimum	Maximum
1st confidence rating	60	1.78	.72	1	3
2nd confidence rating	60	2.98	1.28	1	6
Decision confidence	60	3.9500	1.3952	1.00	7.00

Friedman Test

Ranks

	Mean Rank
1st confidence rating	1.32
2nd confidence rating	2.07
Decision confidence	2.62

In Friedman's test, for each participant the scores for each level of the factor are put into rank order. SPSS has calculated the mean rank for each level of the factor.

The calculated value for Friedman's test, which is assessed for significance using χ^2 distribution.

Test Statistics^a

N	60
Chi-Square	60.414
df	2
Asymp. Sig.	.000

a. Friedman Test

The degrees of freedom = k-1, where k is the number of levels of the factor.

The *p* value.

In a report you would write:
Confidence varied significantly across the three assessment points: $\chi^2(2, N = 60) = 60.414, p < .0005$.

Chapter Eight

Multiple regression

An introduction to multiple regression
Performing a multiple regression on
SPSS

Section 1: An introduction to multiple regression

WHAT IS MULTIPLE REGRESSION?

Multiple regression is a statistical technique that allows us to predict someone's score on one variable on the basis of their scores on several other variables. An example might help. Suppose we were interested in predicting how much an individual enjoys their job. Variables such as salary, extent of academic qualifications, age, sex, number of years in full-time employment and socio-economic status might all contribute towards job satisfaction. If we collected data on all of these variables, perhaps by surveying a few hundred members of the public, we would be able to see how many and which of these variables gave rise to the most accurate prediction of job satisfaction. We might find that job satisfaction is most accurately predicted by type of occupation, salary and years in full-time employment, with the other variables not helping us to predict job satisfaction. As with bivariate correlation, multiple regression does not imply causal relationships.

When using multiple regression in psychology, many researchers use the term "independent variables" to identify those variables that they think will influence some other "dependent variable". We prefer the terminology of "predictor variables" for those variables that may be useful in predicting the scores on another variable, the "criterion variable". Thus, in our example above, type of occupation, salary and years in full-time employment would emerge as significant predictor variables, which allow us to estimate the criterion variable – how satisfied someone is likely to be with their job. As we have pointed out before, human behaviour is inherently noisy and therefore it is not possible to produce totally accurate predictions, but multiple regression allows us to identify a set of predictor variables which together provide a useful estimate of a participant's likely score on a criterion variable.

HOW DOES MULTIPLE REGRESSION RELATE TO CORRELATION AND ANALYSIS OF VARIANCE?

In Chapter 4 we introduced you to correlation and the regression line. If two variables are correlated, then knowing the score on one variable will allow you to predict the score on the other variable. The stronger the correlation, the closer the scores will fall to the regression line and therefore the more accurate the prediction. Multiple regression is simply an extension of this principle, in which we predict one variable on the basis of two or more other variables. Having more than one predictor variable is useful when predicting human behaviour, as our actions, thoughts and emotions are all likely to be influenced by some combination of several factors. The advantage of applying multiple regression instead of several bivariate correlations (between the criterion variable and each of the predictor variables) is that multiple regression corrects for the correlations among the predictor variables. The bivariate correlation between a particular variable (X_1) and the criterion variable may be partly, or only, due to the correlation between X_1 and another predictor variable (X_2) (see ice cream and temperature example in Chapter 4, Section 1). Using multiple regression we can test theories (or models) about precisely which set of variables allow us to predict behaviour.

As we discussed in Chapter 7, Section 1, on Analysis of Variance, human behaviour is rather variable and therefore difficult to predict. What we are doing in both ANOVA and multiple regression is seeking to account for the variance in the scores we observe. Thus, in the example above, people might vary greatly in their levels of job satisfaction. Some of this variance will be accounted for by the variables we have identified. For example, we might be able to say that salary accounts for a fairly large percentage of the variance in job satisfaction, and hence it is very useful to know someone's salary when trying to predict their job satisfaction. You might now be able to see that the ideas here are rather similar to those underlying ANOVA. In ANOVA we are trying to determine how much of the variance is accounted for by the IVs (relative to the percentage of the variance we cannot account for). In multiple regression we are not restricted to a few levels of the IVs: instead we measure the variables and test how well they predict the score on the dependent variable (or criterion variable). Thus, ANOVA is actually a rather specific and restricted example of the general approach adopted in multiple regression.

A current trend in statistics is to emphasise the similarity between multiple regression and ANOVA, and between bivariate correlation and the *t*-test. All of these statistical techniques are basically seeking to do the same thing – explain the variance in the level of one variable on the basis of the level of one or more other variables. These other variables might be manipulated directly in the case of controlled experiments (allowing causal relationships to be tested), or be observed in the case of surveys or observational studies, but the underlying principle is the same. Thus, although we have given separate chapters to each of these procedures they are fundamentally all the same procedure. This underlying single approach is called the General Linear Model – a term you first encountered when we were undertaking ANOVA in Chapter 7, Section 1.

Causation

Whether we can draw conclusions about cause and effect relationships, of course, depends on whether variables were manipulated or simply measured. In ANOVA we often directly manipulate the factors and measure the resulting change in the dependent variable. Sometimes, however, the levels of the factors are chosen from existing groups (such as educated to degree level or not) and then causal relationships cannot be assumed. In multiple regression we normally measure the naturally occurring scores on a number of predictor variables and try to establish which set of the observed variables gives rise to the best prediction of the criterion variable. In such studies, a significant outcome does not imply causation. If one can, however, manipulate a predictor variable used in a multiple regression then conclusions about causation could be drawn (provided all the normal controls for experimental research are applied).

WHEN SHOULD I USE MULTIPLE REGRESSION?

1. You can use this statistical technique when exploring linear relationships between the predictor and criterion variables – that is, when the relationship follows a straight line. (To examine non-linear relationships, special techniques can be used.)
2. The criterion variable that you are seeking to predict should be measured on a continuous scale (such as interval or ratio scale). There are separate methods for predicting values on a nominal criterion/dependent variable (see Chapter 10).
3. The predictor variables that you select should be measured on a ratio, interval or ordinal scale. A nominal predictor variable is legitimate but only if it is dichotomous, that is there are no more than two categories (see Chapter 5, Section 1). For example, sex is acceptable (where male is coded as 1 and female as 0) but gender identity (masculine, feminine and androgynous) could not be coded as a single variable. Instead, you would create three different variables each with two categories (masculine/not masculine; feminine/not feminine and androgynous/not androgynous). The term dummy variable is used to describe this type of dichotomous variable.
4. Multiple regression requires a large number of observations. The estimate of R (the multiple correlation, see below) depends on the number of predictor variables as well as the number of participants (N). One rule of thumb is to have at least ten times as many participants as predictor variables. Tabachnick & Fidell (2001) suggest that N should equal the greater of the following: either the number of predictors times 8, plus 50; or the number of predictors plus 104. Of course you could instead calculate N for the power that you require.
5. You should screen your data for outliers, normality and homoscedasticity of residuals (see Tabachnick & Fidell, 2001 for guidelines).

TERMINOLOGY

There are certain terms we need to clarify to allow you to understand the results of this statistical technique.

Beta (standardised regression coefficient)

Beta (β) is a measure of how strongly each predictor variable influences the criterion variable. β is measured in units of standard deviation. For example, if β = 2.5, a change of one standard deviation in the predictor variable will result in a change of 2.5 standard deviations in the criterion variable. Thus, a higher β value indicates a greater impact of the predictor variable on the criterion variable. The unstandardised equivalent, B, is also provided by SPSS.

With only one predictor variable in your model, then β is equivalent to the correlation coefficient between the predictor and the criterion variable. This equivalence makes sense, as this situation is a correlation between two variables. When you have more than one predictor variable, however, you cannot compare the contribution of each predictor variable by simply comparing the bivariate correlation coefficients. β is computed to allow you to make such comparisons and to assess the strength of the relationship between each predictor variable and the criterion variable.

R, R Square, Adjusted R Square

R is a measure of the correlation between the observed values of the criterion variable and its predicted values. In our example this would be the correlation between the levels of job satisfaction reported by the participants and the levels predicted for them by the predictor variables. Note that, unlike r or r_s, R can only take positive values even if all the individual correlations or the βs are negative. R Square (R^2) is the square of this measure of correlation and indicates the proportion of the variance in the criterion variable which is accounted for by the model – in our example the proportion of the variance in the job satisfaction scores accounted for by the set of predictor variables (salary, etc.). In essence, this is a measure of how good a prediction of the criterion variable we can make by knowing the predictor variables. However, R^2 tends to somewhat over-estimate the success of the model when applied to the real world, so an Adjusted R^2 value is calculated which takes into account the number of predictor variables in the model and the number of observations (participants) that the model is based on. This Adjusted R^2 value gives the most useful measure of the success of the model. If, for example, we have an Adjusted R^2 value of .75 we can say that our model has accounted for 75% of the variance in the criterion variable.

Multicollinearity

When choosing a predictor variable you should select one that might be correlated with the criterion variable, but that is not strongly correlated with the other predictor variables. However, correlations amongst the predictor variables are not unusual. The term multicollinearity (or collinearity) is used to describe the situation when a high correlation is detected between two or more predictor variables. Such high correlations cause problems when trying to draw inferences about the relative contribution of each predictor variable to the success of the model. SPSS provides you with a means of checking for this and we describe this below.

Selection methods

There are different ways that the relative contribution of each predictor variable can be assessed. In the "simultaneous" method (which SPSS calls the **Enter** method), the researcher specifies the set of predictor variables that make up the model. The success of this model in predicting the criterion variable is then assessed.

In contrast, "hierarchical" methods enter the variables into the model in a specified order. The order specified should reflect some theoretical consideration or previous findings. If you have no reason to believe that one variable is likely to be more important than another you should not use this method. As each variable is entered into the model its contribution is assessed. If adding the variable does not significantly increase the predictive power of the model then the variable is dropped.

In "statistical" methods, the order in which the predictor variables are entered into (or taken out of) the model is determined according to the strength of their correlation with the criterion variable. There are several statistical methods, called forward selection, backward selection and stepwise selection. In **Forward** selection, SPSS enters the variables into the model one at a time in an order determined by the strength of their correlation with the criterion variable. The effect of adding each is assessed as it is entered, and variables that do not significantly add to the success of the model are excluded.

In **Backward** selection, SPSS enters all the predictor variables into the model. The weakest predictor variable is then removed and the regression re-calculated. If this significantly weakens the model then the predictor variable is re-entered – otherwise it is deleted. This procedure is then repeated until only useful predictor variables remain in the model.

Stepwise is the most sophisticated of these statistical methods. Each variable is entered in sequence and its value assessed. If adding the variable contributes to the model then it is retained, but all other variables in the model are then re-tested to see if they are still contributing to the success of the model. If they no longer contribute significantly they are removed. Thus, this method should ensure that you end up with the smallest possible set of predictor variables included in your model.

In addition to the **Enter**, **Stepwise**, **Forward** and **Backward** methods, SPSS also offers the **Remove** method in which variables are removed from the model in a block – the use of this method will not be described here.

If you have no theoretical model in mind, and/or you have relatively low numbers of cases, then it is probably safest to use **Enter**, the simultaneous method. Statistical procedures should be used with caution and only when you have a large number of cases. This is because minor variations in the data due to sampling errors can have a large effect on the order in which variables are entered and therefore the likelihood of them being retained. However, one advantage of the **Stepwise** method is that it should always result in the most parsimonious model. This could be important if you wanted to know the minimum number of variables you would need to measure to predict the criterion variable. If, for this or some other reason, you decide to select a statistical method, then you should really validate your results with a second independent set of data. This can be done either by conducting a second study, or if you have sufficient data by randomly splitting your data set into two halves. Use **Select Cases** with **Random sample of cases** method (see Chapter 6, Section 4) and set sample size at 50%. A variable called filter_$ will be added to your data file. To ensure that you run a separate analysis on each randomly selected half, proceed as follows. First, reset **Select Cases** to **All cases**. Second, use **Select Cases** with **If Condition is satisfied** method to select those cases for which filter_$ = 0, and run your analysis on the selected cases. Third, use **Select Cases** with **If Condition is satisfied** method to select those cases for which filter_$ = 1, and run your analysis on those cases. Only results that are common to both analyses should be reported.

Section 2: Performing a multiple regression on SPSS

EXAMPLE STUDY

In an investigation of children's spelling, a colleague of ours, Corriene Reed, decided to look at the importance of several psycholinguistic variables on spelling performance. Previous research has shown that age of acquisition has an effect on children's reading and also on object naming. A total of 64 children, aged between 7 and 9 years, completed standardised reading and spelling tests and were then asked to spell 48 words that varied systematically according to certain features such as age of acquisition, word frequency, word length and imageability. Word length and age of acquisition emerged as significant predictors of whether the word was likely to be spelt correctly.

Further analysis was conducted on the data to determine whether the spelling performance on this list of 48 words accurately reflected the children's spelling ability as estimated by a standardised spelling test. Children's chronological age, their reading age, their standardised reading score and their standardised spelling score were chosen as the predictor variables. The criterion variable was the percentage correct spelling score attained by each child using the list of 48 words.

For the purposes of this book, we have created a data file that will reproduce some of the findings from this second analysis. As you will see, the standardised spelling score derived from a validated test emerged as a strong predictor of the spelling score achieved on the word list. The data file contains only a sub-set of the data collected and is used here to demonstrate multiple regression. (These data are available in Appendix I or from the web address listed there.)

HOW TO PERFORM THE TEST

Click on **Analyze** ⇒ **Regression** ⇒ **Linear**

You will be presented with the **Linear Regression** dialogue box shown below. You now select the criterion (dependent) and the predictor (independent) variables.

The percentage correct spelling score ("spelperc") is the criterion variable. As the predictor variables, we have used chronological age ("age"), reading age ("readage"), standardised reading score ("standsc") and standardised spelling score ("spellsc").

As we have a relatively small number of cases and do not have any strong theoretical predictions, we recommend you select **Enter** (the simultaneous method). This is usually the safest to adopt.

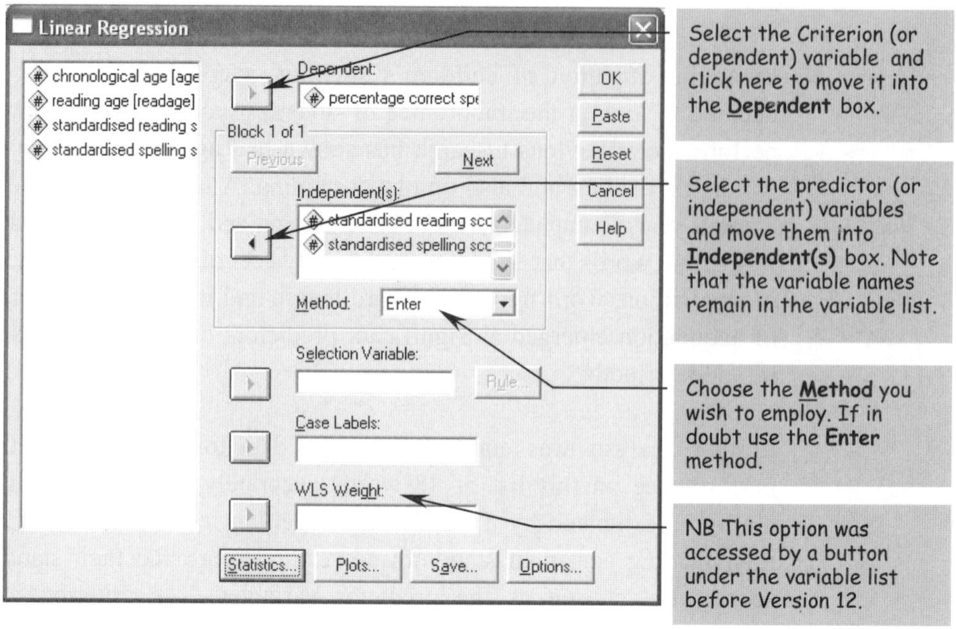
Linear Regression
chronological age [age
reading age [readage]
standardised reading s
standardised spelling s
Dependent:
percentage correct spe
Block 1 of 1
Previous
Next
Independent(s):
standardised reading scc
standardised spelling scc
Method:
Enter
Selection Variable:
Rule...
Case Labels:
WLS Weight:
Statistics...
Plots...
Save...
Options...
OK
Paste
Reset
Cancel
Help
Select the Criterion (or dependent) variable and click here to move it into the Dependent box.
Select the predictor (or independent) variables and move them into Independent(s) box. Note that the variable names remain in the variable list.
Choose the Method you wish to employ. If in doubt use the Enter method.
NB This option was accessed by a button under the variable list before Version 12.

Now click on the Statistics... button. This will bring up the **Linear Regression: Statistics** dialogue box shown below.

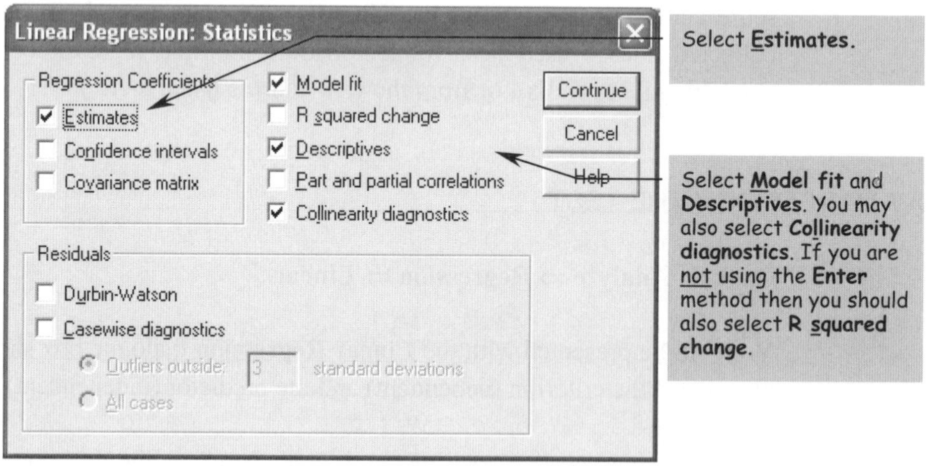
Linear Regression: Statistics
Regression Coefficients
Estimates
Confidence intervals
Covariance matrix
Model fit
R squared change
Descriptives
Part and partial correlations
Collinearity diagnostics
Continue
Cancel
Help
Residuals
Durbin-Watson
Casewise diagnostics
Outliers outside:
3
standard deviations
All cases
Select Estimates.
Select Model fit and Descriptives. You may also select Collinearity diagnostics. If you are not using the Enter method then you should also select R squared change.

In the **Linear Regression: Statistics** dialogue box shown on the previous page, there are various options that you can choose. The **Collinearity diagnostics** option gives some useful additional output that allows you to assess whether you have a problem with collinearity in your data. The **R squared change** option is useful if you have selected a statistical method such as stepwise as it makes clear how the power of the model changes with the addition or removal of a predictor variable from the model.

When you have selected the statistics options you require, click on the **Continue** button. This will return you to the **Linear Regression** dialogue box. Now click on the ☐ OK ☐ button. The output that will be produced is illustrated on the following pages.

TIP   The SPSS multiple regression default (under Options button) is to **Exclude cases listwise**. Hence, although the researcher collected data from 52 participants, SPSS analysed the data from only the 47 participants who had no missing values.

Obtained Using Menu Items: **Regression** > **Linear** (Method = Enter)

Descriptive Statistics

	Mean	Std. Deviation	N
percentage correct spelling	59.7660	23.93307	47
chronological age	93.4043	7.49104	47
reading age	89.0213	21.36483	47
standardised reading score	95.5745	17.78341	47
standardised spelling score	107.0851	14.98815	47

This first table is produced by the **Descriptives** option.

This second table gives details of the correlation between each pair of variables. We do not want strong correlations between the predictor variables. The values here are acceptable.

Correlations

		percentage correct spelling	chronological age	reading age	standardised reading score	standardised spelling score
Pearson Correlation	percentage correct spelling	1.000	-.074	.623	.778	.847
	chronological age	-.074	1.000	.124	-.344	-.416
	reading age	.623	.124	1.000	.683	.570
	standardised reading score	.778	-.344	.683	1.000	.793
	standardised spelling score	.847	-.416	.570	.793	1.000
Sig. (1-tailed)	percentage correct spelling	.	.311	.000	.000	.000
	chronological age	.311	.	.203	.009	.002
	reading age	.000	.203	.	.000	.000
	standardised reading score	.000	.009	.000	.	.000
	standardised spelling score	.000	.002	.000	.000	.
N	percentage correct spelling	47	47	47	47	47
	chronological age	47	47	47	47	47
	reading age	47	47	47	47	47
	standardised reading score	47	47	47	47	47
	standardised spelling score	47	47	47	47	47

Variables Entered/Removed[b]

Model	Variables Entered	Variables Removed	Method
1	standardised spelling score, chronological age, reading age, standardised reading score[a]	.	Enter

a. All requested variables entered.

b. Dependent Variable: percentage correct spelling

This third table tells us about the predictor variables and the method used. Here we can see that all of our predictor variables were entered simultaneously (because we selected the Enter method).

Model Summary

Model	R	R Square	Adjusted R Square	Std. Error of the Estimate
1	.923[a]	.852	.838	9.63766

a. Predictors: (Constant), standardised spelling score, chronological age, reading age, standardised reading score

This table is important. The Adjusted R Square value tells us that our model accounts for 83.8% of variance in the spelling scores – a very good model!

ANOVA[b]

Model		Sum of Squares	df	Mean Square	F	Sig.
1	Regression	22447.277	4	5611.819	60.417	.000[a]
	Residual	3901.149	42	92.884		
	Total	26348.426	46			

a. Predictors: (Constant), standardised spelling score, chronological age, reading age, standardised reading score

b. Dependent Variable: percentage correct spelling

This table reports an ANOVA, which assesses the overall significance of our model. As $p < .05$ the model is significant.

B, or the unstandardised coefficient, for each predictor variable shows the predicted increase in the value of the criterion variable for a 1 unit increase in that predictor (while controlling for the other predictors). The next column gives the standard error of B.

Coefficients[a]

Model		Unstandardized Coefficients		Standardized Coefficients		
		B	Std. Error	Beta	t	Sig.
1	(Constant)	-232.079	30.500		-7.609	.000
	chronological age	1.298	.252	.406	5.159	.000
	reading age	-.162	.110	-.144	-1.469	.149
	standardised reading score	.530	.156	.394	3.393	.002
	standardised spelling score	1.254	.165	.786	7.584	.000

a. Dependent Variable: percentage correct spelling

The Standardized Beta (β) Coefficients give a measure of the contribution of each variable to the model in terms of standard deviations. β is the predicted change in SD of the criterion variable, for a change of 1SD in the predictor (while controlling for the other predictors). Thus, if chronological age increases by 1 SD, then we can predict that percentage correct spelling will increase by .406 SD.

The t and Sig (p) values give a rough indication of the impact of each predictor variable – a big absolute t value and small p value suggests that a predictor variable is having a large impact on the criterion variable.

If you requested **Collinearity diagnostics** they will be included in this table – see next page.

Collinearity diagnostics

If you requested the optional **Collinearity diagnostics** from the **Statistics** button, these will be shown in an additional two columns of the Coefficients table (the last table shown above) and a further table (titled Collinearity diagnostics) that is not shown here. You can simply look at the two new columns, shown below. If you wish to explore collinearity issues further, use Results Coach (Chapter 12, Section 3) with the Collinearity diagnostics table.

Coefficients[a]

Model		Unstandardized Coefficients		Standardized Coefficients	t	Sig.	Collinearity Statistics	
		B	Std. Error	Beta			Tolerance	VIF
1	(Constant)	-232.079	30.500		-7.609	.000		
	chronological age	1.298	.252	.406	5.159	.000	.568	1.759
	reading age	-.162	.110	-.144	-1.469	.149	.365	2.737
	standardised reading score	.530	.156	.394	3.393	.002	.262	3.820
	standardised spelling score	1.254	.165	.786	7.584	.000	.329	3.044

a. Dependent Variable: percentage correct spelling

See text below.

The tolerance values are a measure of the correlation between the predictor variables and can vary between 0 and 1. The closer to zero the tolerance value is for a variable, the stronger the relationship between this and the other predictor variables. You should worry about variables that have a very low tolerance. SPSS will not include a predictor variable in a model if it has a tolerance of less than .0001. However, you may want to set your own criteria rather higher – perhaps excluding any variable that has a tolerance level of less than .01. VIF is an alternative measure of collinearity (in fact it is the reciprocal of tolerance) in which a large value indicates a strong relationship between predictor variables.

On the next page, we suggest how you might report the outcome of a multiple regression analysis.

REPORTING THE RESULTS

When reporting the results of a multiple regression analysis, you should inform the reader about the proportion of the variance accounted for by the model, the significance of the model and the significance of the predictor variables.

In the results section, we could write:

Using the enter method, a significant model emerged: $F(4,42) = 60.417$, $p < .0005$. The model explains 83.8% of the variance (Adjusted $R^2 = .838$). Table 8.1 gives information for the predictor variables entered into the model. Reading age was not a significant predictor, but the other three variables were.

Table 8.1

The unstandardised and standardised regression coefficients for the variables entered into the model.

Variable	B	SE B	β
Standardised spelling score	1.25	0.17	0.79**
Chronological age	1.30	0.25	0.41**
Standardised reading score	0.53	0.16	0.39*
Reading age	-0.16	0.11	-0.14

$*p = .002.$ $**p < .0005.$

You would also include other information, such as summary descriptives for all variables, and the correlation matrix for all the variables that you included in the multiple regression analysis.

OUTPUT FROM MULTIPLE REGRESSION USING STEPWISE METHOD

Obtained Using Menu Items: **Regression** > **Linear** (Method = Stepwise)

Reproduced below are the key parts of the output produced when the **Stepwise** method is selected. For this method you should also select the **R squared change** option in the **Linear Regression: Statistics** dialogue box (shown above). The first two tables are the same as for the Enter method, so we have omitted them here.

Variables Entered/Removed[a]

Model	Variables Entered	Variables Removed	Method
1	standardised spelling score		Stepwise (Criteria: Probability-of-F-to-enter <= .050, Probability-of-F-to-remove >= .100).
2	chronological age		Stepwise (Criteria: Probability-of-F-to-enter <= .050, Probability-of-F-to-remove >= .100).
3	standardised reading score		Stepwise (Criteria: Probability-of-F-to-enter <= .050, Probability-of-F-to-remove >= .100).

This table shows us the order in which the variables were entered and removed. We can see that in this case three variables were added and none were removed.

Each time a variable is added SPSS defines a new model, indicated by the model number in the leftmost column.

a. Dependent Variable: percentage correct spelling

Here we can see that model 1, which included only standardised spelling score, accounted for 71% of the variance (Adjusted R^2 = .711). The inclusion of chronological age into model 2 resulted in an additional 9% of the variance being explained (R^2 change = .094). The final model 3 also included standardised reading score which resulted in an additional 3% of variance explained (R^2 change = .034). This final model accounted for 83% of the variance (Adjusted R^2 = .833).

Model Summary

Model	R	R Square	Adjusted R Square	Std. Error of the Estimate	R Square Change	F Change	df1	df2	Sig. F Change
1	.847[a]	.717	.711	12.8708	.717	114.055	1	45	.000
2	.900[b]	.811	.802	10.6481	.094	21.747	1	44	.000
3	.919[c]	.844	.833	9.7665	.034	9.302	1	43	.004

a. Predictors: (Constant), standardised spelling score

b. Predictors: (Constant), standardised spelling score, chronological age

c. Predictors: (Constant), standardised spelling score, chronological age, standardised reading score

ANOVA[d]

Model		Sum of Squares	df	Mean Square	F	Sig.
1	Regression	18893.882	1	18893.882	114.055	.000[a]
	Residual	7454.543	45	165.657		
	Total	26348.426	46			
2	Regression	21359.610	2	10679.805	94.193	.000[b]
	Residual	4988.815	44	113.382		
	Total	26348.426	46			
3	Regression	22246.870	3	7415.623	77.744	.000[c]
	Residual	4101.556	43	95.385		
	Total	26348.426	46			

a. Predictors: (Constant), standardised spelling score

b. Predictors: (Constant), standardised spelling score, chronological age

c. Predictors: (Constant), standardised spelling score, chronological age, standardised reading score

d. Dependent Variable: percentage correct spelling

> This table reports the ANOVA result for the three models. They are all significant.

> Here SPSS reports B, β, *t* and sig (*p*) values, and the Collinearity Statistics, for each of the models. These were explained in the output from the **Enter** method.

Coefficients[a]

Model		Unstandardized Coefficients		Standardized Coefficients			Collinearity Statistics	
		B	Std. Error	Beta	t	Sig.	Tolerance	VIF
1	(Constant)	-85.032	13.688		-6.212	.000		
	standardised spelling score	1.352	.127	.847	10.680	.000	1.000	1.000
2	(Constant)	-209.328	28.959		-7.228	.000		
	standardised spelling score	1.576	.115	.987	13.679	.000	.827	1.209
	chronological age	1.075	.230	.336	4.663	.000	.827	1.209
3	(Constant)	-209.171	26.562		-7.875	.000		
	standardised spelling score	1.197	.163	.750	7.349	.000	.348	2.875
	chronological age	1.092	.211	.342	5.162	.000	.827	1.210
	standardised reading score	.406	.133	.301	3.050	.004	.371	2.698

a. Dependent Variable: percentage correct spelling

> This table gives statistics for the variables that were excluded from each model.

Excluded Variables[d]

Model		Beta In	t	Sig.	Partial Correlation	Collinearity Statistics		
						Tolerance	VIF	Minimum Tolerance
1	chronological age	.336[a]	4.663	.000	.575	.827	1.209	.827
	reading age	.208[a]	2.249	.030	.321	.675	1.481	.675
	standardised reading score	.288[a]	2.317	.025	.330	.371	2.696	.371
2	reading age	.036[b]	.395	.695	.060	.517	1.933	.435
	standardised reading score	.301[b]	3.050	.004	.422	.371	2.698	.348
3	reading age	-.144[c]	-1.469	.149	-.221	.365	2.737	.262

a. Predictors in the Model: (Constant), standardised spelling score

b. Predictors in the Model: (Constant), standardised spelling score, chronological age

c. Predictors in the Model: (Constant), standardised spelling score, chronological age, standardised reading score

d. Dependent Variable: percentage correct spelling

Thus, the final model to emerge from the **Stepwise** analysis contains only three predictor variables. The predictor variable reading age, which was not significant in the **Enter** analysis, was not included in the **Stepwise** analysis as it did not significantly strengthen the model.

REPORTING THE RESULTS

In your results section, you would report the significance of the model by citing F and the associated p value, along with the Adjusted R square, which indicates the strength of the model. So, for the final model (Model 3) reported above, we could write:

Using the stepwise method, a significant model emerged: $F(3,43) = 77.74$, $p < .0005$. The model explains 83.3% of the variance (Adjusted $R^2 = .833$). Table 8.2 gives information for the predictor variables that are included in the model. Reading age was excluded.

Table 8.2
The unstandardised and standardised regression coefficients for the variables included in the model.

Variable	B	SE B	β
Standardised spelling score	1.20	0.16	0.75**
Chronological age	1.09	0.21	0.34**
Standardised reading score	0.41	0.13	0.3*

$*p = .004.$ $**p < .0005.$

Include other information as necessary for your report.

Chapter Nine

Analysis of covariance and multivariate analysis of variance

An introduction to analysis of covariance

Performing analysis of covariance on SPSS

An introduction to multivariate analysis of variance

Performing multivariate analysis of variance on SPSS

Section 1: An introduction to analysis of covariance

WHAT IS ANALYSIS OF COVARIANCE?

Analysis of covariance (ANCOVA) is a statistical technique that allows us to look at the effect of an independent variable on a dependent variable, whilst partialling out or removing the effect of another variable. Imagine, for example, you were interested in the speed with which students could learn how to use different computerised statistical packages (SPSS is not the only one available!). You might choose three different packages and give these to three different groups of first-year students who have no prior knowledge of any statistical package. However, you are aware that the dependent variable here, speed of learning, might be influenced by other factors, such as familiarity with computer software. If you measured familiarity with computer software before exposing students to one of the statistical packages, you could then control for and remove its effect on the dependent variable so that you can obtain a clearer insight into the differences in learning speed for the different packages.

We have previously explained that ANOVA is a rather specific and restricted example of the general approach adopted in multiple regression. With ANOVA, we manipulate the independent variable(s) to examine their effect on the dependent variable. With multiple regression, we measure the naturally occurring levels of the predictor variables to see if this allows us to predict the score on the dependent variable and the predictor variables could be continuous variables (i.e., measured on an interval or ratio scale). With ANCOVA, we look at the effect of an independent variable on a dependent variable (as does ANOVA) but in addition we acknowledge the influence of another variable – a covariate – and ANCOVA partials out (or removes) the effect of the covariate by using the regression equation to measure its influence (as in multiple regression).

WHAT DOES ANCOVA DO?

You may have already realised from your own experience with research that it is not always possible to control for all possible confounding variables and where you can identify and measure a variable that you know will influence the dependent variable, then ANCOVA will allow you to get rid of the effects of this variable. The effect of this is to reduce error variance. Remember, we talked about how ANOVA compares the amount of variance brought about by our manipulation of the IV against the amount of error variance, that is, the variance brought about by other "nuisance variables" such as individual differences. By getting rid of the effects due to a covariate, we can reduce the error variance, which in turn leads to a larger F-value.

If we return to our example of looking at the influence of type of statistical package on speed of learning, we may expect the group that was given SPSS to learn the fastest. However, we would also expect to see variability in the performance of students within each group, and because speed of learning is also related to familiarity with computer software, some of this variability will be directly attributable to differences in familiarity. If we ran a test of correlation, we would probably find that there is a positive correlation so that as familiarity increases so does speed of learning. ANCOVA examines the association between familiarity and speed and removes the variance due to this association.

You might be thinking that had we randomly assigned our participants to the three groups, then probably there would be no systematic differences in familiarity across each of the three groups. Therefore, the means on this covariate would not differ too much. This is the ideal situation in which to use ANCOVA, because it will get rid of the effects of the covariate, reduce error variance and hence result in a larger F-value. However, it is also possible to use ANCOVA when the means on the covariate differ significantly. For example, imagine that in one group, either due to bad luck or poor experimental control, there were more individuals with greater familiarity with computer software. ANCOVA is now useful because it will adjust the means on our dependent variable, speed of learning, to an estimate of what they would have been if the groups had not differed in level of familiarity. In other words, these adjusted means are our best guess as to what the means would have been had our three groups not differed on the covariate.

So, by performing an ANCOVA, we may either:
1. Reduce error variance, or
2. Reduce error variance and adjust the means on the dependent variable.

WHEN SHOULD I USE ANCOVA?

We have described how ANCOVA can be used when you have one between-subjects factor (IV); however, it can also be used when you have more than one between-subjects factor. It is also possible to have more than one covariate although interpreting the output from such an analysis would be difficult. We have already said that it is best to use ANCOVA when participants are randomly assigned to one of the levels of the independent variable and the covariate should be measured beforehand rather than afterwards, as exposure to the independent variable may affect the covariate.

ANCOVA is commonly used when there is a pretest–posttest design, where a test is given before participants are allocated to the experimental condition and then the same test is given after the experimental condition. Here, the pretest scores are used as the covariate. Richard's research student, Helen Paterson, used such a design to study witness memory for a crime scenario. She was interested in the effect on a participant's memory of information obtained through discussion with fellow witnesses. She showed participants a video and then gave them a pretest questionnaire. Participants were allocated to one of three groups: a discussion and a misinformation group, a discussion and no misinformation group and a control group where there was no discussion. The participants were then given a posttest questionnaire. Performance on the pretest recognition questionnaire was the covariate in her analysis.

You might be wondering why Helen did not work out the difference between the pretest and posttest scores, that is the extent to which performance changed, and then perform a one-way ANOVA. However, calculating difference scores does not eliminate the variation present in the pretest scores – these scores vary because participants differ in their ability to remember the information from the video, caused by such things as differences in attention directed to the video. This variation will not be removed by calculating difference scores (the pretest scores will normally be correlated with the difference scores). Helen is not interested in this variation and by partialling out or removing it she can focus on the effect of participating in one of the three groups.

Check for the following when choosing one or more covariates:

1. A covariate should be chosen on the basis of existing theory and research.
2. A covariate should not be a continuous or discrete variable.
3. A covariate should be measured before the experimental manipulation takes place.
4. A covariate should be measured reliably, that is if it were measured several times across a time period, there would be a high correlation between the scores.
5. The relationship between a covariate and the dependent variable must be linear (straight-line). You can check this by looking at the scatterplots for each group and if there is more than one covariate then they should not be strongly correlated with each other.
6. There should be *homogeneity of regression*. The relationship between the dependent variable and the covariate should be similar for all experimental groups, so that the regression lines are parallel. So, using our first example, the relationship

between learning speed of statistical package and familiarity with computer software should be similar for each of the three groups tested.

7. In addition, ANCOVA makes the same assumptions as ANOVA (see Chapter 7, Section 1).

Section 2: Performing analysis of covariance on SPSS

EXAMPLE STUDY: THE EFFECTS OF CO-WITNESSES

Let us consider a hypothetical study, like the one described above, that investigated the influence of co-witnesses on memory accuracy for a crime video.

In this hypothetical study, an independent groups design was used, with one between-subjects factor. The factor was the group that participants were allocated to (called "group") and had three levels:

1. Group 1 involved a discussion of the video with a group of co-witnesses that included a confederate (a stooge) who inserted misinformation into the discussion.
2. Group 2 involved a discussion of the video with a group of co-witnesses that did not include a confederate so no misinformation was supplied.
3. Group 3 was a control group and there was no discussion or misinformation and instead participants sat quietly and wrote down what they remembered.

The covariate was participants' performance on a pretest recognition questionnaire (called "time1") and the dependent variable was participants' performance on a posttest recognition questionnaire (called "time2"). The hypothesis was that there would be an effect of group on recognition memory.

Analysis (of fictitious data) using ANCOVA revealed a significant effect of the group that participants were allocated to. (These data are available in Appendix I or from the web address listed there.)

We have chosen to show you the ANCOVA procedure with a one-way between-subjects design, so that we can also show you how to check for homogeneity of regression statistically. It is much harder to check for this assumption statistically with more complex designs, so we shall also show you how you can look for this graphically and at the same time check that there is a linear relationship between your covariate and dependent variable. We do this first and after that we show you how to perform the ANCOVA test itself.

> **TIP**   If you have read Chapter 7 or performed ANOVA on SPSS, then you will have already seen the dialogue boxes that appear next. This is because SPSS has incorporated ANCOVA as an option in the ANOVA dialogue box.

HOW TO CHECK FOR HOMOGENEITY OF REGRESSION

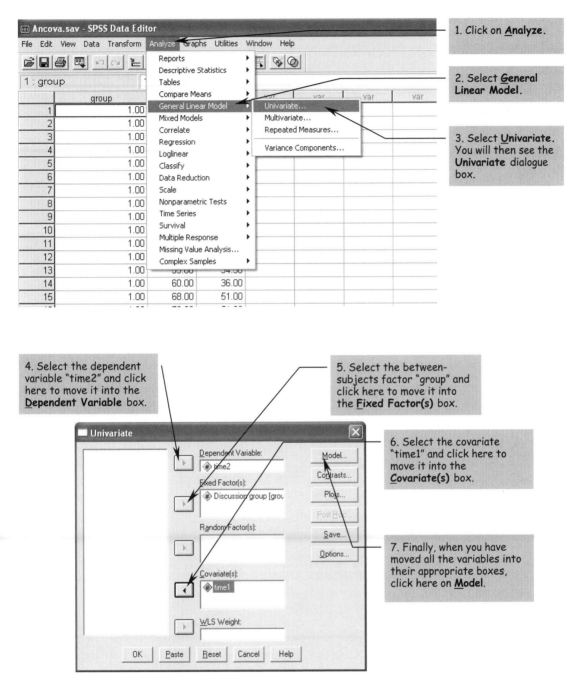

1. Click on **Analyze**.

2. Select **General Linear Model**.

3. Select **Univariate**. You will then see the **Univariate** dialogue box.

4. Select the dependent variable "time2" and click here to move it into the **Dependent Variable** box.

5. Select the between-subjects factor "group" and click here to move it into the **Fixed Factor(s)** box.

6. Select the covariate "time1" and click here to move it into the **Covariate(s)** box.

7. Finally, when you have moved all the variables into their appropriate boxes, click here on **Model**.

When you click on the **Model** button, the following **Univariate: Model** dialogue box will appear.

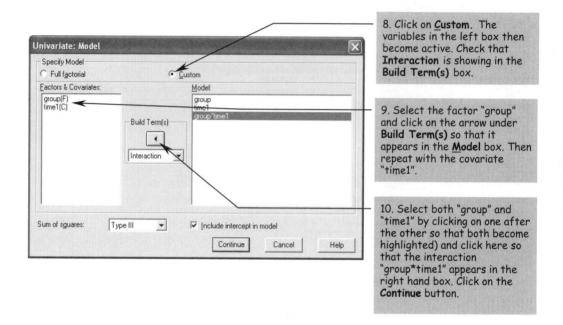

8. Click on **Custom**. The variables in the left box then become active. Check that **Interaction** is showing in the **Build Term(s)** box.

9. Select the factor "group" and click on the arrow under **Build Term(s)** so that it appears in the **Model** box. Then repeat with the covariate "time1".

10. Select both "group" and "time1" by clicking on one after the other so that both become highlighted) and click here so that the interaction "group*time1" appears in the right hand box. Click on the **Continue** button.

Once you click on the **Continue** button you will return to the **Univariate** dialogue box. Now click on the ☐ OK ☐ button. The output is shown on the following pages.

SPSS OUTPUT FROM PROCEDURE TO CHECK FOR HOMOGENEITY OF REGRESSION

Univariate Analysis of Variance

Between-Subjects Factors

		Value Label	N
Discussion group	1.00	discussion with stooge	24
	2.00	discussion without stooge	24
	3.00	no discussion-- writing	24

SPSS reminds you that TIME2 is the dependent variable. Here, you are interested in looking to see if there is an interaction between the covariate, TIME1, and the independent variable.

Tests of Between-Subjects Effects

Dependent Variable: TIME2

Source	Type III Sum of Squares	df	Mean Square	F	Sig.
Corrected Model	3416.612[a]	5	683.322	17.800	.000
Intercept	131.446	1	131.446	3.424	.069
GROUP	94.590	2	47.295	1.232	.298
TIME1	2656.160	1	2656.160	69.193	.000
GROUP * TIME1	47.377	2	23.689	.617	.543
Error	2533.598	66	38.388		
Total	185960.210	72			
Corrected Total	5950.210	71			

a. R Squared = .574 (Adjusted R Squared = .542)

This is the only row that you are interested in. If this interaction is statistically significant, then the data violate the assumption of homogeneity of regression slopes. Here SPSS reports the interaction to be non-significant so this assumption has **not** been violated.

TIP Now that we have checked for homogeneity of regression slopes, we can perform the ANCOVA test. First, however, we show you how to inspect the relationship between the covariate and the dependent variable graphically, using scatterplots. This procedure can be used to check that there is a linear relationship between the covariate and the dependent variable, and also that there is homogeneity of regression.

HOW TO CHECK FOR LINEAR RELATIONSHIP BETWEEN COVARIATE AND DEPENDENT VARIABLE

There are differences between Version 12 and Version 13 in how this procedure is carried out. We describe both here. (If you are using versions earlier than 12, the procedure is given in Appendix III.)

1. Click on **Graphs** ⇒ **Scatter**. You will then see the dialogue box called **Scatter/Dot** (Version 13) or **Scatterplot** (Version 12).

For Version 13

2. Select **Simple Scatter** and then click on the **Define** button.

3. Select the dependent variable "time2" and move it across into the **Y Axis** box. Select the covariate "time1" and move it across into the **X Axis** box. Finally, select your factor "group" and move it across into the **Set Markers by:** box. Then click on the **OK** button.

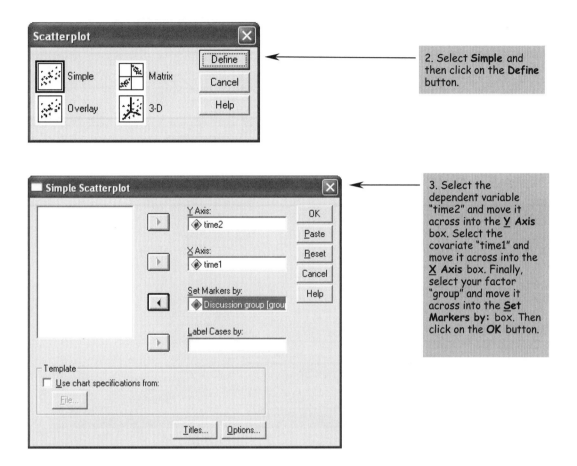

2. Select **Simple** and then click on the **Define** button.

3. Select the dependent variable "time2" and move it across into the **Y Axis** box. Select the covariate "time1" and move it across into the **X Axis** box. Finally, select your factor "group" and move it across into the **Set Markers by:** box. Then click on the **OK** button.

TIP The **Set Markers by** option in the **Simple Scatterplot** dialogue box can have other uses. For example, you may have carried out a correlational study with participants who are from different backgrounds and you might wish to separate out those from urban and those from rural backgrounds.

A graph will appear in the Viewer window, but this will not include the regression lines. To obtain these, double click on the graph itself in the output window. This will bring up the **SPSS Chart Editor** window shown next. Again there are differences between Versions 12 and 13: both are described.

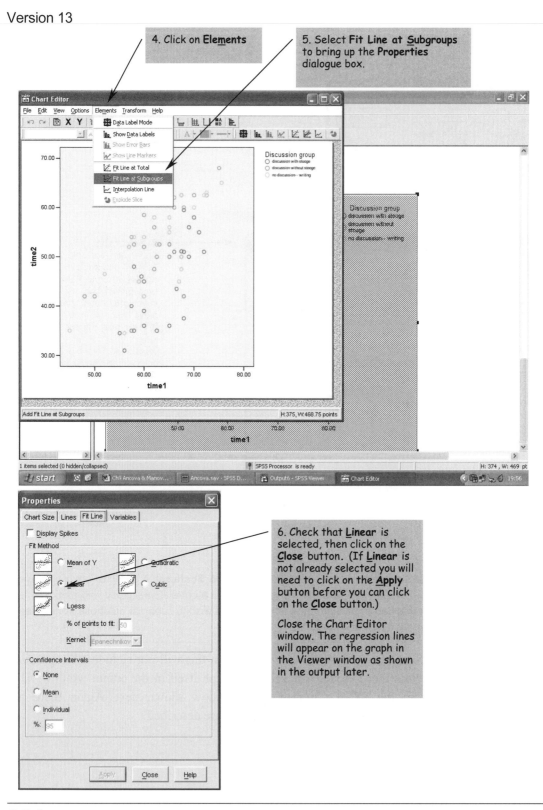

4. Click on **Elements**

5. Select **Fit Line at Subgroups** to bring up the **Properties** dialogue box.

6. Check that **Linear** is selected, then click on the **Close** button. (If **Linear** is not already selected you will need to click on the **Apply** button before you can click on the **Close** button.)

Close the Chart Editor window. The regression lines will appear on the graph in the Viewer window as shown in the output later.

Version 12

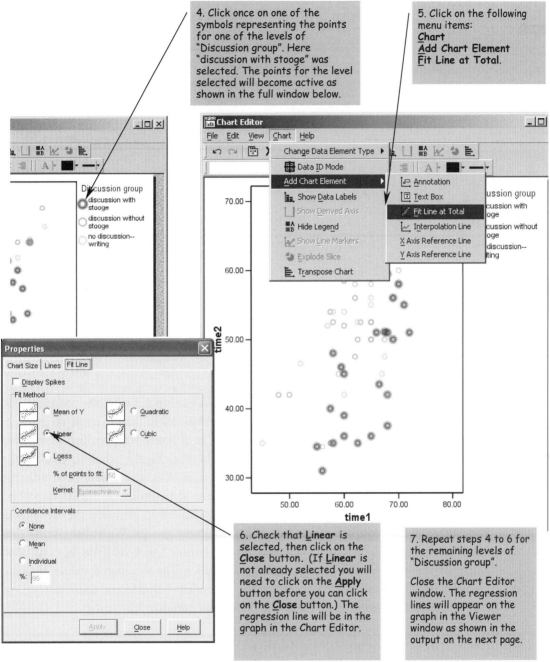

4. Click once on one of the symbols representing the points for one of the levels of "Discussion group". Here "discussion with stooge" was selected. The points for the level selected will become active as shown in the full window below.

5. Click on the following menu items:
Chart
Add Chart Element
Fit Line at Total.

6. Check that **Linear** is selected, then click on the **Close** button. (If **Linear** is not already selected you will need to click on the **Apply** button before you can click on the **Close** button.) The regression line will be in the graph in the Chart Editor.

7. Repeat steps 4 to 6 for the remaining levels of "Discussion group".

Close the Chart Editor window. The regression lines will appear on the graph in the Viewer window as shown in the output on the next page.

TIP In both versions 12 and 13, double clicking on the symbols will bring up a different **Properties** dialogue box that allows you to change the appearance of the symbols and lines.

Graph

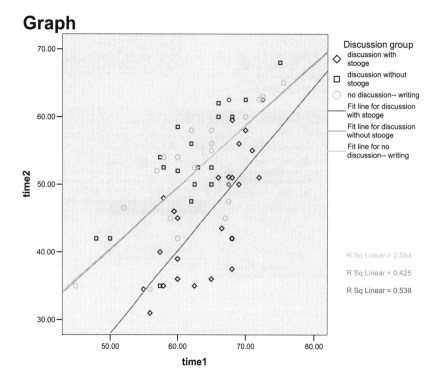

Inspect your graph to see if there is a linear relationship between the covariate and the dependent variable – if there is no linear relationship then there is no point in performing ANCOVA. Here, there appears to be a linear relationship. Remember that the slopes of the regression lines should be roughly parallel, that is the relationship between the covariate and the dependent variable should be similar for all three groups (the assumption of homogeneity of regression). This is important because ANCOVA assumes that the overall relationship between the dependent variable and the covariate is true for each of the three groups. We already know that this assumption has not been violated by our earlier check and this is confirmed here by the fact that the slopes are almost parallel. The R squared values indicate how strong the relationship is between the dependent variable and the covariate – a covariate should be correlated with the dependent variable.

Now that we have checked that there is a linear relationship between the covariate and the dependent variable and that there is homogeneity of regression, we can perform the ANCOVA test.

1. Click on **Analyze** ⇒ **General Linear Model** ⇒ **Univariate**.
    You will then see the **Univariate** dialogue box. You will find that you have already performed the actions shown for this dialogue box when checking for homogeneity of regression.

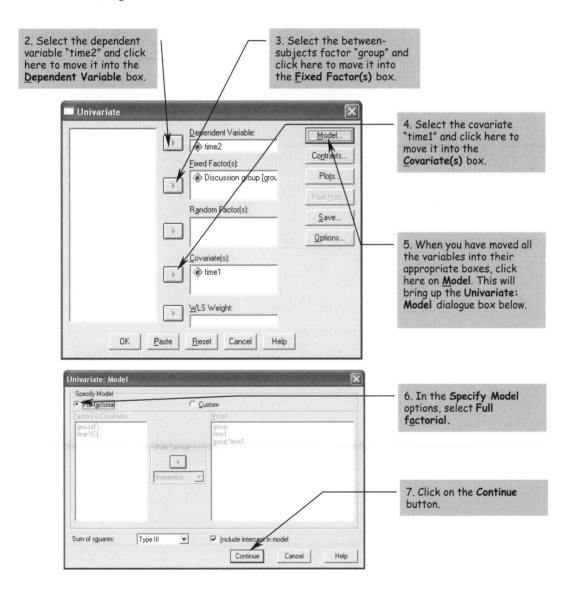

2. Select the dependent variable "time2" and click here to move it into the **Dependent Variable** box.

3. Select the between-subjects factor "group" and click here to move it into the **Fixed Factor(s)** box.

4. Select the covariate "time1" and click here to move it into the **Covariate(s)** box.

5. When you have moved all the variables into their appropriate boxes, click here on **Model**. This will bring up the **Univariate: Model** dialogue box below.

6. In the **Specify Model** options, select **Full factorial**.

7. Click on the **Continue** button.

You will return to the **Univariate** dialogue box where you can click on the Options button. This will bring up the **Univariate: Options** dialogue box, shown next.

8. Move "group" into the **Display Means for:** box to obtain means for the levels of group.

9. Click here to check for assumption of homogeneity of variance–covariance matrices.

10. Click here to obtain an indication of the size or magnitude of the effect. In the SPSS output, this appears as partial eta squared.

11. Click on the **Continue** button. You will return to the **Univariate** dialogue box.

Click on [OK] and SPSS will calculate the ANCOVA.

SPSS OUTPUT FOR ANCOVA

Univariate Analysis of Variance

Between-Subjects Factors

		Value Label	N
Discussion group	1.00	discussion with stooge	24
	2.00	discussion without stooge	24
	3.00	no discussion- - writing	24

Levene's Test of Equality of Error Variances[a]

Dependent Variable: time2

F	df1	df2	Sig.
.584	2	69	.560

Tests the null hypothesis that the error variance of the dependent variable is equal across groups.

a. Design: Intercept+time1+group

To check that the assumption of equality of variance was not violated, we clicked on **Homogeneity tests** in the **Univariate: Options** dialogue box. A significance level greater than 0.05, as here, shows that the data do not violate the assumption of equality of error variances.

The first line highlighted shows that the covariate is significantly related to the dependent variable. The next line shows the main effect of group.

Tests of Between-Subjects Effects

Dependent Variable: time2

Source	Type III Sum of Squares	df	Mean Square	F	Sig.	Partial Eta Squared
Corrected Model	3369.234[a]	3	1123.078	29.589	.000	.566
Intercept	107.412	1	107.412	2.830	.097	.040
time1	2659.726	1	2659.726	70.075	.000	.508
group	1052.041	2	526.021	13.859	.000	.290
Error	2580.976	68	37.956			
Total	185960.210	72				
Corrected Total	5950.210	71				

a. R Squared = .566 (Adjusted R Squared = .547)

Estimated Marginal Means ←

These are the adjusted means, i.e. the effect of the covariate has been statistically removed. To obtain these, we clicked on **Display Means for** in the **Univariate: Options** dialogue box.

Discussion group

Dependent Variable: time2

Discussion group	Mean	Std. Error	95% Confidence Interval	
			Lower Bound	Upper Bound
discussion with stooge	44.558[a]	1.263	42.038	47.079
discussion without stooge	52.721[a]	1.260	50.206	55.235
no discussion-- writing	52.725[a]	1.258	50.214	55.236

a. Covariates appearing in the model are evaluated at the following values:
time1 = 63.4375.

HOW TO REPORT YOUR RESULTS

In a report you would write, at appropriate points:

After adjusting for pretest scores, there was a significant effect of the between-subjects factor group, $F(2,68) = 13.86$, $p < .0005$, partial $\eta^2 = .29$. Adjusted mean recognition scores suggest that discussion with confederate, who introduced misinformation, lowered recognition memory compared with discussion without confederate or a writing-only control group.

Section 3: An introduction to multivariate analysis of variance

WHAT IS MULTIVARIATE ANALYSIS OF VARIANCE?

Another technique that is also similar to ANOVA is called multivariate analysis of variance (MANOVA) and is used when the design involves more than one dependent variable. Imagine you wanted to look at the effects of different factors on a psychological construct that is complex to operationalise, such as fear of crime. You may find it difficult to think of a single dependent variable that captures all the elements that a complex variable like this involves, and instead you may decide to measure several different variables, each of which measures a different aspect of the more complex dependent variable. This type of design is quite common in clinical research when evaluating the impact of an intervention program, as several different outcome measures would be explored, for example cognitive and behavioural measures. Like ANOVA, MANOVA can be used to explore the effects of one or more independent variables and interactions between independent variables. However, whereas ANOVA can only be used when there is one dependent variable (and is hence described as a univariate test), MANOVA can handle several dependent variables all together (and is hence described as a multivariate test).

If you were conducting a study to see if being a victim of crime influences fear of crime, you may wish to compare those who have been a victim several times, those who have been a victim once and those who have never been a victim. You may then want to measure a number of different aspects of fear of crime, including objective measures such as the number of security measures implemented in the home, the number of times per week participants go out on their own, as well as using a self report measure. You could perform one-way ANOVAs on each of the different dependent variables but, as you may remember from Section 8 in Chapter 7, by performing multiple tests we run an increased risk of making a Type 1 error, that is incorrectly rejecting a null-hypothesis. In the same way that we use ANOVA rather than conducting multiple t-tests, we use MANOVA rather than conducting multiple ANOVAs.

WHAT DOES MANOVA DO?

MANOVA allows you to not only look at the effect of different independent variables and see if these interact, it also tells you if there is any relationship between the different dependent variables. Because all of these are analysed simultaneously, MANOVA can check whether the different levels of the factors not only differ from one another on one dependent variable but whether they differ along a combination of several dependent variables. It does this by creating a new dependent variable which is the linear combination of each of the original dependent variables. MANOVA will tell you if the mean differences among groups on the combined dependent variable are larger than expected by chance.

It might be helpful to compare MANOVA with other tests that also combine variables. In the chapter on multiple regression, a model containing a combination of predictor variables sought to predict the scores on a criterion variable. Here, MANOVA does the opposite by seeking to predict an independent variable from a combination of dependent variables. In the next chapter you will read about how variables are combined together to predict category membership in a type of analysis called Discriminant Analysis.

You may remember that in ANOVA the statistic calculated is the F-ratio, which is the ratio of the variance due to the manipulation of the IV and the error variance. Conceptually, MANOVA does something similar but this is statistically far more complicated and it will provide you with a choice of four different statistics to choose from, all of which indicate whether there are statistically significant differences among the levels of the independent variable on the linear combination of the dependent variables:

Pillai's Trace
Hotelling's Trace
Wilks' Lambda
Roy's Largest Root

SPSS will report a value for each of these, along with the F tests for each. If your factor has only two levels, then the F tests reported will be identical. This is because when the factor has only two levels, and hence one degree of freedom, there is only one way of combining the different dependent variables to separate the levels or the groups. However, when your factor has more than two levels, then the F tests reported for the four test statistics are usually different and it is possible that some may be significant and some not. Most researchers report the values for the Wilks' Lambda, so we suggest you report these too. However, Pillai's is considered to be the most robust (although all four are reasonably robust), so you might consider reporting the values for Pillai's when your sample size is small.

If you find a significant result, you will then want to follow it up. One possibility is to look at the univariate ANOVAs that are included in the SPSS printout, after the section that presents the MANOVA test statistics. This will tell you which of the individual dependent variables are contributing to the significant overall result. If you do this then you need to consider something we mentioned earlier, the possibility of committing a Type I error, and one way of avoiding this is to apply a Bonferroni correction. Normally, a result is regarded as "significant" if the p value is less than .05. If our design involves two dependent variables and we want to look at the two ANOVAs performed on these, then we apply the following correction: $.05 \div 2 = .025$, and for our result to be significant p now has to be less than .025. If our design involves three dependent variables and we want to look at the three ANOVAs performed on these, then we apply the following correction: $.05 \div 3 = .017$, and for our result to be significant p now has to be less than .017. So .05 is divided by the number of dependent variables in the study. Another possibility is to explore a significant MANOVA result by conducting Discriminant Analysis and this test is described in the next chapter.

WHEN SHOULD I USE MANOVA?

MANOVA can be used when your design is a simple one-way design or with more complex designs where you have more than one independent variable or factor. There should be some conceptual reason for considering several dependent variables together in the same analysis. Adding dependent variables may decrease the power of the test, so MANOVA should only be used when there is a reason to measure several dependent variables.

There is some controversy over the extent to which the dependent variables can or should be correlated. Multicollinearity should be avoided (see Chapter 8, Section 1) so check that the correlation coefficients for any pair of dependent variables do not exceed 0.90. Tabachnick and Fidell (2001) suggest that the dependent variables should not be correlated with each other and that each should measure different aspects of the construct you are interested in. Certainly, if the dependent variables are correlated, and MANOVA shows a significant result, then it is difficult to tease apart the contribution of each of the individual dependent variables to this overall effect. Rather than looking at the univariate ANOVAs, you would need to explore your data using Discriminant Analysis as this will allow you to explore the relationship between the dependent variables. We recommend that you perform tests of correlation to check the strength of the correlations between your dependent variables to help you decide how best to follow up any significant MANOVA result.

Also check for the following:

1. The dependent variables should not be continuous or discrete and any relationship between them should be linear (straight-line). You can check this by looking at the

scatterplots between pairs of dependent variables for each level of your factor. (If you are not sure how to generate scatterplots on SPSS, then see earlier in this chapter on how to check for linear relationships between covariate and dependent variables.)

2. You must ensure that the number of cases in each cell is greater than the number of dependent variables.

3. There should be *homogeneity of variance–covariance matrices* and this is similar to the assumption of homogeneity of variance that we've mentioned previously in relation to parametric tests. SPSS can check this assumption for you and we will show you how to do this below.

4. There should be both univariate and multivariate *normality of distributions*. Assessment of multivariate normality is difficult in practice, however you should at least check that each dependent variable is normally distributed, that is that univariate normality holds, as this is likely to reflect multivariate normality. Giles (2002) points to two ways in which normality may be violated. The first is *platykurtosis* and this is evident when the distribution curve looks like a low plateau. You can check for this by generating histograms of each dependent variable. The second is the present of *outliers;* these are data points far outside the area covered by the normal distribution (see Tabachnick and Fidell, 2001, for advice on screening for outliers).

Generally, if you have equal sample sizes and a reasonable number of participants in each group, and you've checked for outliers before conducting your analysis, then MANOVA will still be a valid test even with modest violations of these assumptions.

Section 4: Performing multivariate analysis of variance on SPSS

EXAMPLE STUDY: FEAR OF CRIME

Let us return to the example we mentioned above, a study looking at fear of crime. This hypothetical study involved one between-subjects factor with three levels:

1. Group 1: those who have been a victim several times.
2. Group 2: those who have been a victim once.
3. Group 3: those who have never been a victim.

The dependent variables were:

1. The number of security measures implemented to the front door, and to selected windows in living room, bedroom and kitchen.
2. The number of times per week participants go out on their own.
3. A self report measure scored out of 20, with a higher score reflecting a higher subjective report of anxiety about crime.

The hypothesis was that there would be a difference between the groups in their overall fear of crime score. Analysis (of this fictitious data set) revealed a difference between groups in their overall fear of crime. These data are available in Appendix I or from the web address listed there.

Before conducting the MANOVA procedure, we first check to see whether our dependent variables are correlated.

To obtain such correlations, click on **Analyze** $\Rightarrow$ **Correlate** $\Rightarrow$ **Bivariate** and then select your dependent variables (see Chapter 4 for more detail on obtaining correlations). Below is the SPSS output.

Correlations

		security	outings	report
security	Pearson Correlation	1	-.023	-.029
	Sig. (2-tailed)		.902	.877
	N	30	30	30
outings	Pearson Correlation	-.023	1	-.323
	Sig. (2-tailed)	.902		.082
	N	30	30	30
report	Pearson Correlation	-.029	-.323	1
	Sig. (2-tailed)	.877	.082	
	N	30	30	30

This correlation matrix suggests that there are no significant correlations between the different dependent variables.

HOW TO PERFORM MANOVA

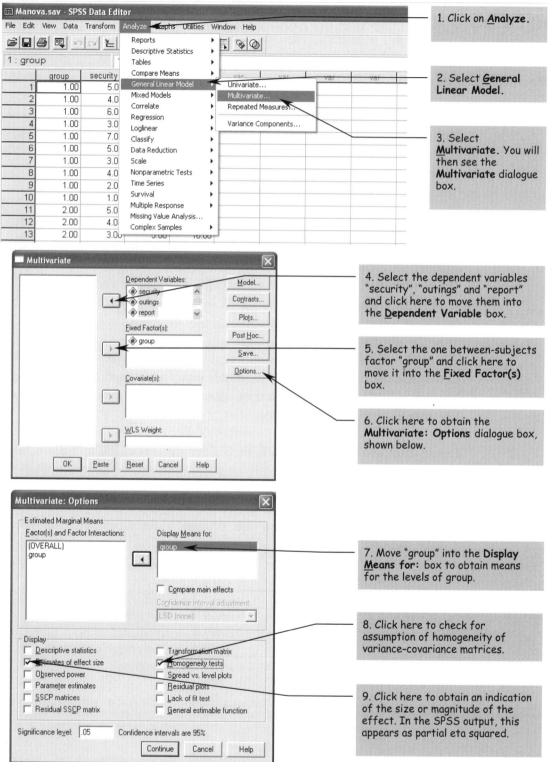

1. Click on **Analyze**.

2. Select **General Linear Model**.

3. Select **Multivariate**. You will then see the **Multivariate** dialogue box.

4. Select the dependent variables "security", "outings" and "report" and click here to move them into the **Dependent Variable** box.

5. Select the one between-subjects factor "group" and click here to move it into the **Fixed Factor(s)** box.

6. Click here to obtain the **Multivariate: Options** dialogue box, shown below.

7. Move "group" into the **Display Means for:** box to obtain means for the levels of group.

8. Click here to check for assumption of homogeneity of variance-covariance matrices.

9. Click here to obtain an indication of the size or magnitude of the effect. In the SPSS output, this appears as partial eta squared.

SPSS OUTPUT FOR MANOVA

General Linear Model

Between-Subjects Factors

		Value Label	N
group	1.00	victim several times	10
	2.00	victim once	10
	3.00	never been victim	10

Box's Test of Equality of Covariance Matrices[a]

Box's M	9.965
F	.694
df1	12
df2	3532.846
Sig.	.759

Box's Test checks whether your data violate the assumption of homogeneity of variance-covariance matrices and was obtained by clicking on **Homogeneity tests** in the **Multivariate: Options** dialogue box. If this is significant, then you have violated this assumption. As this test is very sensitive, it is most useful when your sample size is small and unequal.

Tests the null hypothesis that the observed covariance matrices of the dependent variables are equal across groups.

a. Design: Intercept+group

Partial eta squared values were obtained by selecting **Estimates of effect size.** These provide you with an indication of the proportion of variance in the new combined dependent variable that can be accounted for by the factor 'group'. A rule of thumb is that values larger than .14 (or 14%) indicate a large effect.

Multivariate Tests[c]

Effect		Value	F	Hypothesis df	Error df	Sig.	Partial Eta Squared
Intercept	Pillai's Trace	.984	513.563[a]	3.000	25.000	.000	.984
	Wilks' Lambda	.016	513.563[a]	3.000	25.000	.000	.984
	Hotelling's Trace	61.628	513.563[a]	3.000	25.000	.000	.984
	Roy's Largest Root	61.628	513.563[a]	3.000	25.000	.000	.984
group	Pillai's Trace	.919	7.375	6.000	52.000	.000	.460
	Wilks' Lambda	.101	17.906[a]	6.000	50.000	.000	.682
	Hotelling's Trace	8.713	34.852	6.000	48.000	.000	.813
	Roy's Largest Root	8.690	75.312[b]	3.000	26.000	.000	.897

a. Exact statistic

b. The statistic is an upper bound on F that yields a lower bound on the significance level.

c. Design: Intercept+group

In the table above, we are only interested in the results for the variable 'group', and we ignore those reported for the Intercept. Here we find the four MANOVA test statistics that tell us whether the new combined dependent variable, fear of crime, is different across the three groups of participants. Here, p is smaller than .05 for each test statistic so all are significant. We are going to report the values for Wilks' Lambda.

Levene's Test of Equality of Error Variances[a]

	F	df1	df2	Sig.
security	.678	2	27	.516
outings	.369	2	27	.695
report	.456	2	27	.638

Tests the null hypothesis that the error variance of the dependent variable is equal across groups.

a. Design: Intercept+group

These statistics were obtained by clicking on **Homogeneity tests** in the **Multivariate: Options** dialogue box. If Levene's p > .05, then there is equality of variance, and this is important both in terms of the reliability of the results below and in supporting the robustness of the multivariate statistics.

Tests of Between-Subjects Effects

Source	Dependent Variable	Type III Sum of Squares	df	Mean Square	F	Sig.	Partial Eta Squared
Corrected Model	security	1.800[a]	2	.900	.224	.801	.016
	outings	58.400[b]	2	29.200	7.860	.002	.368
	report	305.267[c]	2	152.633	49.002	.000	.784
Intercept	security	554.700	1	554.700	138.036	.000	.836
	outings	456.300	1	456.300	122.833	.000	.820
	report	4489.633	1	4489.633	1441.380	.000	.982
group	security	1.800	2	.900	.224	.801	.016
	outings	58.400	2	29.200	7.860	.002	.368
	report	305.267	2	152.633	49.002	.000	.784
Error	security	108.500	27	4.019			
	outings	100.300	27	3.715			
	report	84.100	27	3.115			
Total	security	665.000	30				
	outings	615.000	30				
	report	4879.000	30				
Corrected Total	security	110.300	29				
	outings	158.700	29				
	report	389.367	29				

a. R Squared = .016 (Adjusted R Squared = -.057)

b. R Squared = .368 (Adjusted R Squared = .321)

c. R Squared = .784 (Adjusted R Squared = .768)

These are the three univariate ANOVA test statistics. As there are three dependent variables, we apply Bonferroni correction by dividing .05 by 3, so sig. values need to be smaller than .017 for results to be significant. This is the case for two of the three dependent variables, "outings" and "report". Again, partial eta squared values are reported showing the amount of variance in the dependent variable. Approximately 78% of the variance in "report" is accounted for by 'group'.

Estimated Marginal Means

group

Dependent Variable	group	Mean	Std. Error	95% Confidence Interval	
				Lower Bound	Upper Bound
security	victim several times	4.000	.634	2.699	5.301
	victim once	4.600	.634	3.299	5.901
	never been victim	4.300	.634	2.999	5.601
outings	victim several times	2.100	.609	.849	3.351
	victim once	4.100	.609	2.849	5.351
	never been victim	5.500	.609	4.249	6.751
report	victim several times	16.000	.558	14.855	17.145
	victim once	12.500	.558	11.355	13.645
	never been victim	8.200	.558	7.055	9.345

These descriptive statistics were obtained by clicking on **Display Means for** in the **Multivariate: Options** dialogue box.

HOW TO REPORT YOUR RESULTS

In a report you would write:

There was a significant effect of the level of experienced crime (none, one or multiple experiences) on the combined dependent variable fear of crime, $F(6,50) = 17.91$, $p < .0005$; Wilks' Lambda = .1; partial $\eta^2 = .68$. Analysis of each individual dependent variable, using a Bonferroni adjusted alpha level of .017, showed that there was no contribution of the number of security measures installed, $F(2,27) = .22$, $p = .801$, partial $\eta^2 = .02$. The three groups differed in terms of the number of times they went out on their own per week, $F(2,27) = 7.86$, $p = .002$, partial $\eta^2 = .37$ and in terms of the self report measure, $F(2,27) = 49.00$, $p < .0005$, partial $\eta^2 = .78$.

A NOTE ON WITHIN SUBJECTS DESIGNS

Imagine our design involved a within-subjects factor, before and after being a victim of crime, and three dependent variables. We would analyse the data in the following way:

1. Click on **Analyze** ⇒ **General Linear Model** ⇒ **Repeated Measures**

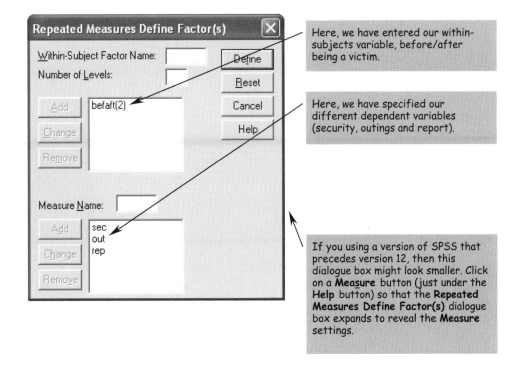

Here, we have entered our within-subjects variable, before/after being a victim.

Here, we have specified our different dependent variables (security, outings and report).

If you using a version of SPSS that precedes version 12, then this dialogue box might look smaller. Click on a **Measure** button (just under the **Help** button) so that the **Repeated Measures Define Factor(s)** dialogue box expands to reveal the **Measure** settings.

Chapter Ten

Discriminant analysis and logistic regression

Discriminant analysis and logistic regression

An introduction to discriminant analysis

Performing discriminant analysis on SPSS

An introduction to logistic regression

Performing logistic regression on SPSS

Section 1: Discriminant analysis and logistic regression

Discriminant analysis and logistic regression are statistical procedures that can be used to predict category membership. In Chapter 8 we showed how multiple regression can be used to predict a score on a criterion variable on the basis of a number of predictor variables. Discriminant analysis and logistic regression are two statistical procedures that can be used to predict category membership rather than a score. For example, in Chapter 8 multiple regression was used to predict children's spelling test score on the basis of a number of other measures. Suppose, however, we wanted to predict not the spelling score, but whether each child would be classified as a "good reader" or a "poor reader". The two procedures discussed in this chapter are designed for use in this situation when we want to predict which of several categories a participant will belong to on the basis of their scores on a set of variables.

To give another example, consider a forensic psychologist working with prison inmates. The psychologist might be interested in identifying factors that predicted whether or not a particular inmate would be reconvicted after release from prison. To undertake this analysis s/he would first need to collect data from the records of past prisoners. The data recorded will include the outcome (whether or not the prisoner was reconvicted after release) in addition to a number of other variables that s/he thinks influence the chances of reconviction. For example s/he might record the length of the sentence served, a measure of the behaviour of the prisoner when in custody (such as the number of days "on report"), a measure of the level of drug use and a measure of social support (such as number of hours of prison visits per month). The psychologist could use either discriminant analysis or logistic regression to analyse this data. Although these procedures are technically very different, their outcomes are similar in that each allows the psychologist to identify which combination of these variables is useful in predicting reconviction. The psychologist could then apply this knowledge to all new prisoners entering the jail in order to identify which are most likely to be reconvicted after their release and to target resources towards these high-risk prisoners in an attempt to reduce recidivism.

SIMILARITIES AND DIFFERENCES BETWEEN DISCRIMINANT ANALYSIS AND LOGISTIC REGRESSION

Both discriminant analysis and logistic regression allow us to predict a categorical dependent variable on the basis of a number of predictor or independent variables.

These independent variables are normally continuous variables, but logistic regression can handle categorical independent variables. In general, logistic regression can be used in a wider range of situations than discriminant analysis. For example, discriminant analysis makes various assumptions about the predictor variables, including that they should be normally distributed. Logistic regression makes no such assumptions about the distribution of the predictor variables.

In earlier versions of SPSS, one difference was that logistic regression could only be employed in situations where the dependent variable was dichotomous (i.e., had only two categories). However, more recent versions of SPSS include multinomial logistic regression, which can be used in situations where the dependent variable has more than two categories. The multinomial logistic regression command is not described in this book, but is broadly similar to the standard, or binary logistic regression command.

Another important distinction lies in the interpretation of the output. The output of the discriminant analysis is rather more difficult to interpret than that of logistic regression. Discriminant analysis results in the calculation of a discriminant function – a formula that combines the predictor variables to calculate a value that is then used to predict category membership. The value of the discriminant function is somewhat arbitrary and tells us relatively little about the basis on which the prediction is being made. Although logistic regression is a more complex procedure, the output is rather easier to interpret. Logistic regression computes the probability (actually the log odds – see below for more details) that a case will belong to a particular category.

As a result of these advantages, many researchers now recommend the use of logistic regression over discriminant analysis. However, we have chosen to include discriminant analysis because it is still commonly employed in some fields of psychology.

Section 2: An introduction to discriminant analysis

Tabachnick and Fidell (2001) note that discriminant analysis is rather like reverse MANOVA. Indeed, discriminant analysis could be described as a cross between backwards analysis of variance and multiple regression. In ANOVA designs we are manipulating membership of some group or category (the levels of the IV or factor) and investigating the effect on the DV. If we find a significant effect of one of our IVs, then we could say that we can partially predict a participant's DV score if we know which category s/he belongs to. At the heart of discriminant analysis is the attempt to predict category membership.

Discriminant analysis is similar to multiple regression in that both techniques allow us to make predictions on the basis of several predictor variables. The difference is that, while multiple regression is used to predict a participant's score on the DV, discriminant analysis is used to predict which of a number of categories or groups the participant will belong to.

In discriminant analysis the dependent variable is sometimes also referred to as the category variable, the criterion variable or the grouping variable. The other variables are independent variables or predictor variables.

AN EXAMPLE

Imagine you were a forensic psychologist working with prison inmates. It would be very useful to predict which of these individuals were most at risk of being reconvicted following their release. This might allow you to target treatment towards these high-risk individuals and produce a cost-effective program to reduce reconviction rates. First you will need to collect data on a number of likely variables for each of our prisoners. For example, if you measure the age, the number of previous convictions, and the level of drug use, then you might find that some weighted combination of these variables reliably discriminates between the group of prisoners who are reconvicted following release, and those who are not reconvicted. This combination of the predictor variables is called a discriminant function (it is a mathematical function that discriminates between the categories). You could now apply this discriminant function to all new inmates entering the prison. On the basis of the new prisoners' scores on each of the predictor variables you would make a prediction regarding their reconviction following release. You might then go on to develop a treatment program that seeks to reduce reconviction by directly tackling some of the variables you have shown to significantly predict reconviction. For example, if drug use was a variable that predicted reconviction, then you might consider pursuing a policy that concentrated on reducing dependency on drugs.

TWO STEPS IN DISCRIMINANT ANALYSIS

As the above example shows, there are often two distinct steps involved in discriminant analysis:

1. Use cases where category membership is already known, to develop a discriminant function that can reliably predict category membership in these cases.
2. Use this discriminant function to predict category membership for a new group of cases for whom category membership is not known.

> **TIP**   A discriminant function is a mathematical formula that combines a set of predictor variables to discriminate between different categories. For example, in the output given below, the discriminant function that is derived has a negative value for prisoners who were not reconvicted and a positive value for prisoners who were reconvicted. Once the discriminant function has been derived, then the value of the function can be calculated for new cases who have not yet been released, allowing us to predict their behaviour after the end of their prison sentence.

ASSUMPTIONS

The category variable can have two or more distinct levels. Category membership must be mutually exclusive (each case must be classified into no more than one category) and collectively exhaustive (every case must be a member of a category). The requirements for predictor or independent variables are similar to those for dependent variables in MANOVA, but some violation of the rules regarding the distribution of these variables may be acceptable, especially if the analysis results in accurate classification. If the rate of prediction of classification is not acceptable, this might be due to the violation of some of these assumptions, especially those regarding outliers and homogeneity of variance (see Tabachnick and Fidell, 2001).

METHODS IN DISCRIMINANT ANALYSIS

As in multiple regression, there are different methods that can be adopted. SPSS allows you to adopt either the standard (also called simultaneous or enter) method or the stepwise method (also called statistical).

Choosing a method to adopt

1. Unless you have some very good reason to do otherwise, you should use the standard or enter method.
2. The stepwise (statistical) method can be used to produce a discriminant function that includes the minimum number of predictor variables.

What does each method tell us?

Suppose we were seeking to predict reconviction based on age, previous convictions and drug use. The two types of analysis would give us slightly different information about the data. The standard or enter method would tell us how good a prediction we can make on the basis of all three predictor variables together. In addition, we would be able to see how much each of the predictor variables contributes to the discriminant function (and hence the accuracy of our prediction). Stepwise or statistical methods would allow us to identify the best combination of predictor variables to use to predict category membership.

How does each method work?

1. **Standard or enter**: In the standard method all the variables are entered simultaneously and the predictive power of the combination of all of the variables is considered.

2. **Stepwise** or **statistical**: If there are no theoretical grounds for predicting the relative importance of the variables, then stepwise can be used to determine the smallest set of predictor variables. In stepwise, the variables are entered and/or removed based on statistical assessments of their importance. However, just like stepwise multiple regression, this approach can be dangerous. The variables adopted, and hence the predictions made, can be prone to the effect of minor variation in the predictor variables. Just as with multiple regression, if you choose to adopt a statistical method in discriminant analysis, then you should double check the validity of your discriminant function by using cross-validation procedures. Discriminant analysis (especially when you use statistical methods) tends to overestimate the success of the discriminant function. Cross-validation reduces this overestimation by checking the validity of the discriminant function derived. There are two basic approaches cross-validation:

   a. We can calculate a discriminant function based on one half of our data and test it out on the other half (a little like split-half reliability).
   b. We can test the ability of the discriminant function to classify the same cases measured at some second time interval. This is little like test-retest reliability.

Within the statistical methods, there are a variety of statistical criteria to adopt. These are the criteria by which SPSS decides which predictor variables to enter and/or remove from the discriminant function. This is a complex subject area that is covered in some detail by Tabachnick and Fidell (2001). If in doubt, we would advise you to use the default settings in SPSS.

Section 3: Performing discriminant analysis on SPSS

EXAMPLE STUDY

In a recent research project, Clive Hollin and Emma Palmer of the University of Leicester, UK, collected data on 221 inmates in an attempt to identify the variables that predict reconviction in a group of offenders (Hollin, Palmer and Clark, 200*). The data file in Appendix I contains just a few of the variables Clive and Emma measured. The variable "age" records the prisoner's age in years, and "precons" the number of previous convictions held. The variable "recon" is a categorical variable that records whether the prisoner was reconvicted after release. The value 1 indicates reconviction, while 0 indicates that the prisoner was not reconvicted. The variables "crimhist2" and "educemp2" are derived from a scale called the LSI-R (Level of Service Inventory – Revised), which is used by psychologists working in prisons. The LSI-R measures several aspects of an offender's life, including previous offending, drug use, behaviour in prison, family history and education and employment. In the data file we will be using here, we have only included the measures of criminal history (crimhist2) and of education and employment history (educemp2). We will use discriminant analysis to determine whether age, previous convictions, criminal history, and education and employment history can be used to predict reconviction.

TO PERFORM A SIMULTANEOUS (ENTER METHOD) DISCRIMINANT ANALYSIS

4. Select the DV or category variable from the list on the left and click on this button to move it into the **Grouping Variable** box.

5. Click on the **Define Range** button and enter the minimum and maximum category values (0 and 1 in this case).

6. Move all the independent (or predictor) variables into the **Independents** box.

7. Choose the **Enter** method.

8. It is possible to limit the analysis to cases chosen on the basis of a categorical section variable, but the same outcome could more easily be achieved using the **Select Cases** command described in chapter 6.

9. Click on the **Statistics** button to bring up the **Discriminant Analysis: Statistics** dialogue box (see below).

10. Select the **Means** option to obtain useful descriptive statistics and the **Univariate ANOVAs** option to request a one-way ANOVA across the levels of the category variable.

11. Click on the Continue button to return to the **Discriminant Analysis** dialogue box (shown again, below).

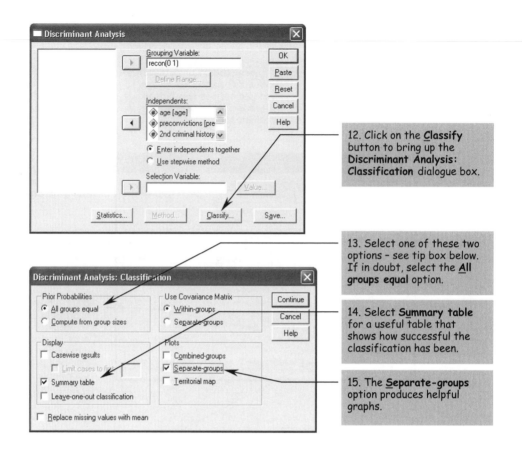

12. Click on the **Classify** button to bring up the **Discriminant Analysis: Classification** dialogue box.

13. Select one of these two options – see tip box below. If in doubt, select the **All groups equal** option.

14. Select **Summary table** for a useful table that shows how successful the classification has been.

15. The **Separate-groups** option produces helpful graphs.

Finally, click on the [Continue] button, and then on the [OK] button.

The annotated output is shown below.

TIP   In the **Discriminant Analysis: Classification** dialogue box you can set the **Prior Probabilities** to either **All groups equal** or **Compute from group sizes**. The default setting is all groups equal. In this case the analysis assumes that, all other things being equal, the probability of a case falling into any of the groups is equal. Thus, if you have two groups it assumes that the prior probability is 0.5. For three groups it would be 0.333, and so on. There may be occasions when the basic probability of each outcome might not be the same. For example, you might decide that it is rather more likely that a patient will live rather than die regardless of the treatment you offer. In cases like this it might be more appropriate to ask SPSS to compute the prior probabilities on the basis of the number of cases that fall into each group. Thus if you have 100 cases with 60 falling into one category and 40 into another, then the prior probabilities would be set at 0.6 and 0.4 respectively. If in doubt, it is safer to leave this option at the default setting of **All groups equal**.

Obtained Using Menu Items: **Classify > Discriminant** (Enter independents together)

Discriminant

Analysis Case Processing

Unweighted Cases		N	Percent
Valid		221	100.0
Excluded	Missing or out-of-range group codes	0	.0
	At least one missing discriminating variable	0	.0
	Both missing or out-of-range group codes and at least one missing discriminating variable	0	.0
	Total	0	.0
Total		221	100.0

This table tells you that 100% of the 221 cases in the data file have been included in the analysis.

If any case had a missing value for one of the IVs (the predictor variables) then the case would have been dropped from the analysis and this would have been reported in this table.

Group Statistics

reconvicted		Mean	Std. Deviation	Valid N (listwise) Unweighted	Valid N (listwise) Weighted
no	age	31.9873	12.86966	157	157.000
	preconvictions	4.9809	6.44451	157	157.000
	2nd criminal history	5.5796	3.17063	157	157.000
	2nd education and employment	4.6115	2.86144	157	157.000
yes	age	26.0000	8.32285	64	64.000
	preconvictions	7.7656	6.55802	64	64.000
	2nd criminal history	7.5313	2.88383	64	64.000
	2nd education and employment	6.0938	2.58026	64	64.000
Total	age	30.2534	12.02872	221	221.000
	preconvictions	5.7873	6.58545	221	221.000
	2nd criminal history	6.1448	3.20891	221	221.000
	2nd education and employment	5.0407	2.85771	221	221.000

This is the table of Means that we requested in the **Discriminant Analysis: Statistics** dialogue box. It gives the mean and SD for each of our IVs broken down by category membership.

For example, in this case we can see that while the overall mean age was 30.25, the individuals who were reconvicted had a mean age of only 26.0 compared to a mean of 31.99 for those who were not reconvicted.

Tests of Equality of Group Means

	Wilks' Lambda	F	df1	df2	Sig.
age	.949	11.818	1	219	.001
preconvictions	.963	8.403	1	219	.004
2nd criminal history	.924	18.127	1	219	.000
2nd education and employment	.944	12.894	1	219	.000

This table was produced because we requested Univariate ANOVAs in the **Discriminant Analysis: Statistics** dialogue box. It shows whether there is a significant effect of category for each of the predictor variables. For example, here we can see that there is a significant difference in the age of those reconvicted and not reconvicted (F = 11.818; df = 1,219; p = 0.001). In addition, SPSS gives Wilks' Lambda, a multivariate test of significance. It varies between 0 and 1; values <u>very</u> close to 1 indicate that the differences are not significant.

Analysis 1
Summary of Canonical Discriminant Functions

Canonical functions are used to discriminate between pairs of categories, or groups. For each possible orthogonal (independent) contrast, a discriminant function is calculated that best discriminates between the categories. The number of canonical functions is either one less than the number of categories, or equal to the number of predictor variables, whichever is the smaller. The following tables give details of each of the discriminant functions calculated. In this example there are only two categories so only one function is calculated.

Eigenvalues

Function	Eigenvalue	% of Variance	Cumulative %	Canonical Correlation
1	.150[a]	100.0	100.0	.362

a. First 1 canonical discriminant functions were used in the analysis.

The eigenvalue is a measure of how well the discriminant function discriminates between the categories (the larger the value the better the discrimination).

The % of Variance column allows you to compare the relative success of the functions. When there is only 1 function (as here) this column and the Cumulative % column tell us nothing useful. Where there are several functions you will probably find that only the first few usefully discriminate among groups.

Wilks' Lambda

Test of Function(s)	Wilks' Lambda	Chi-square	df	Sig.
1	.869	30.421	4	.000

This table provides a test of the null hypothesis that the value of the discriminant function is the same for the reconvicted and non-reconvicted cases. As p is less than 0.05, we can reject the null hypothesis

Standardized Canonical Discriminant Function Coefficients

	Function
	1
age	-.601
preconvictions	.249
2nd criminal history	.547
2nd education and employment	.174

This table allows you to see the extent to which each of the predictor variables is contributing to the ability to discriminate between the categories. The coefficients have been standardised so that you can compare the contribution of each regardless of the units in which it was measured. Rather like correlation coefficients, the values range from –1 to +1. In this case "age" and "2nd criminal history" are making a larger contribution than the other predictor variables.

Structure Matrix

	Function
	1
2nd criminal history	.742
2nd education and employment	.625
age	-.599
preconvictions	.505

Pooled within-groups correlations between discriminating variables and standardized canonical discriminant functions
Variables ordered by absolute size of correlation within function.

The structure matrix table gives a different measure of the contribution that each variable is making to the discriminant function. In this table the variables are ordered by the magnitude of their contribution. The negative value for the variable age tells us that age correlates negatively with the value of the function whereas criminal history correlates positively. This is because older prisoners are less likely to be reconvicted whereas prisoners with a higher criminal history score are more likely to be reconvicted.

If you have more than 2 categories, and hence more than 1 Function calculated, this table also allows you to see which of the Functions each variable is contributing most to (e.g., is a particular variable helping you predict between membership of category a and b or between b and c).

Functions at Group Centroids

	Function
reconvicted	1
no	-.247
yes	.605

Unstandardized canonical discriminant functions evaluated at group means

This table gives the mean value of the discriminant function for each of the categories. Note that in this example the mean value of the function is positive for reconvicted prisoners but negative for non-reconvicted prisoners. In this way the function is discriminating between the two categories of prisoners.

Classification Statistics

Classification Processing Summary

Processed		221
Excluded	Missing or out-of-range group codes	0
	At least one missing discriminating variable	0
Used in Output		221

This table informs you of the total number of cases processed, the number excluded and the number used in the output.

Prior Probabilities for Groups

reconvicted	Prior	Cases Used in Analysis	
		Unweighted	Weighted
no	.500	157	157.000
yes	.500	64	64.000
Total	1.000	221	221.000

The "Prior Probability" is the assumed probability that a particular case will belong to a particular category. In this case we set the Prior Probability to "All groups equal" in the **Discriminant Analysis: Classification** dialogue box, so the probability is equal for all groups – i.e. 0.5 or 50% in this example.

Separate-Groups Graphs

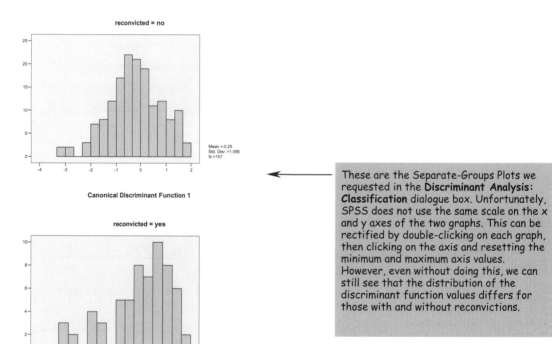

Canonical Discriminant Function 1

reconvicted = no

Mean =-0.25
Std. Dev. =1.056
N =157

Canonical Discriminant Function 1

reconvicted = yes

Mean =0.6
Std. Dev. =0.845
N =64

These are the Separate-Groups Plots we requested in the **Discriminant Analysis: Classification** dialogue box. Unfortunately, SPSS does not use the same scale on the x and y axes of the two graphs. This can be rectified by double-clicking on each graph, then clicking on the axis and resetting the minimum and maximum axis values. However, even without doing this, we can still see that the distribution of the discriminant function values differs for those with and without reconvictions.

Classification Results[a]

		reconvicted	Predicted Group Membership		Total
			no	yes	
Original	Count	no	104	53	157
		yes	16	48	64
	%	no	66.2	33.8	100.0
		yes	25.0	75.0	100.0

a. 68.8% of original grouped cases correctly classified.

This last table in the output is the Summary Table that we requested in the **Discriminant Analysis: Classification** dialogue box. It provides a particularly useful summary of the success (or otherwise) of our discriminant function. It shows a cross-tabulation of the category membership (reconvicted or not) against that we would have predicted using our discriminant function.

In this case we can see that in 104 cases the discriminant function correctly predicted that the offender would not be reconvicted, and in 48 cases it correctly predicted that they would be reconvicted. Thus 152 (104+48) of our 221 cases were correctly classified – a success rate of 68.8% (as noted in the footnote to the table). However, the table also shows us that 25% of the prisoners predicted not to be reconvicted were reconvicted, and that 33.8% of the cases predicted to be reconvicted were not. It is up to you to interpret these failures of prediction – in some cases it may be more important to avoid one type of error than another. For example in this case you may feel that it is more important to avoid erroneously predicting that someone will not be reconvicted than erroneously predicting that they will.

In a report you might write:

A discriminant analysis was performed with reconviction as the DV and age, number of previous convictions, and the criminal history and education and employment sub-scales of the LSI-R as predictor variables. A total of 221 cases were analysed. Univariate ANOVAs revealed that the reconvicted and non-reconvicted prisoners differed significantly on each of the four predictor variables. A single discriminant function was calculated. The value of this function was significantly different for reconvicted and non-reconvicted prisoners (chi-square = 30.42, df = 4, $p < 0.0005$). The correlations between predictor variables and the discriminant function suggested that age and criminal history were the best predictors of future convictions. Age was negatively correlated with the discriminant function value, suggesting that older prisoners were less likely to be reconvicted. Criminal history was positively correlated with the discriminant function value, suggesting that prisoners with higher numbers of previous convictions were more likely to be reconvicted. Overall the discriminant function successfully predicted outcome for 68.8% of cases, with accurate predictions being made for 66.2% of the prisoners who did not go on to be reconvicted and 75% of the prisoners who were reconvicted.

To perform a stepwise Discriminant analysis follow the procedure outlined for the simultaneous method except that at step 7 select **Use stepwise method** then click on the **Method** button to bring up the **Discriminant Analysis: Stepwise Method** dialogue box (see below).

Select one of these methods. These control the statistical rules used to determine when a variable is entered into the equation. If in doubt select Wilks' Lambda, the default setting.

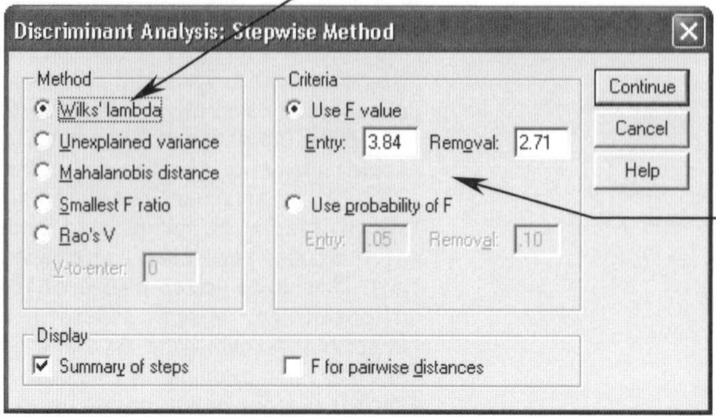

The criteria for entry and removal from the equation can be based on either F values or probability values and the values for both can be adjusted. Tabachnick and Fidell (1996) suggest that the Entry probability value could be changed from 0.05 to 0.15. This is a more liberal rule that will ensure that any important variable gets entered into the equation.

If in doubt, leave the default settings of Method at **Wilks' lambda** and of Criteria with **F** Value Entry and Removal values of 3.84 and 2.71 respectively (as shown in the **Discriminant Analysis: Stepwise Method** dialogue box above). Then click on the **Continue** button and complete steps 8–16.

The output produced by the Stepwise Discriminant analysis is similar to that for the Simultaneous, and so only tables that differ are shown below.

Analysis 1

Stepwise Statistics

Variables Entered/Removed[a,b,c,d]

		Wilks' Lambda				Exact F			
Step	Entered	Statistic	df1	df2	df3	Statistic	df1	df2	Sig.
1	2nd criminal history	.924	1	1	219.000	18.127	1	219.000	.000
2	age	.878	2	1	219.000	15.139	2	218.000	.000

At each step, the variable that minimizes the overall Wilks' Lambda is entered.

a. Maximum number of steps is 8.

b. Minimum partial F to enter is 3.84.

c. Maximum partial F to remove is 2.71.

d. F level, tolerance, or VIN insufficient for further computation.

> This table shows that two variables have been entered. In the first step the variable 2nd criminal history was entered. In the second step age was also entered. No variables were removed in this example. Wilks' Lambda is a measure of the discrimination between the categories. A smaller value indicates better discrimination. The value of Lambda falls as the second variable, age, is entered.

Variables in the Analysis

Step		Tolerance	F to Remove	Wilks' Lambda
1	2nd criminal history	1.000	18.127	
2	2nd criminal history	1.000	17.566	.949
	age	1.000	11.299	.924

> This table shows variables included in the analysis at each step. In this simple example there are only two steps.

Variables Not in the Analysis

Step		Tolerance	Min. Tolerance	F to Enter	Wilks' Lambda
0	age	1.000	1.000	11.818	.949
	preconvictions	1.000	1.000	8.403	.963
	2nd criminal history	1.000	1.000	18.127	.924
	2nd education and employment	1.000	1.000	12.894	.944
1	age	1.000	1.000	11.299	.878
	preconvictions	.794	.794	1.080	.919
	2nd education and employment	.724	.724	2.326	.914
2	preconvictions	.789	.789	1.609	.872
	2nd education and employment	.700	.700	.826	.875

> This table lists all the variables not included in the equation at each step.

> This table indicates how successful the discriminant function is at each step. A smaller value of Lambda indicates a better discrimination between categories. Here the function significantly distinguishes between the two categories at both steps 1 and 2.

Wilks' Lambda

Step	Number of Variables	Lambda	df1	df2	df3	Exact F			
						Statistic	df1	df2	Sig.
1	1	.924	1	1	219	18.127	1	219.000	.000
2	2	.878	2	1	219	15.139	2	218.000	.000

Classification Results[a]

		reconvicted	Predicted Group Membership		Total
			no	yes	
Original	Count	no	102	55	157
		yes	19	45	64
	%	no	65.0	35.0	100.0
		yes	29.7	70.3	100.0

a. 66.5% of original grouped cases correctly classified.

This is the Classification Results table for the stepwise Discriminant Analysis. It is interesting to compare this to the equivalent table produced using the simultaneous method (reproduced above). Which method results in the most successful prediction?

So far we have been trying to develop discriminant functions that can predict category membership with a reasonable level of accuracy. Having produced these functions the next step is to use them to try to make real predictions. For example, if we obtain data from another group of prisoners before they are released, we can apply our discriminant function to predict which of these prisoners will be reconvicted following release.

To do this we need to compute the discriminant function for the new cases. The easiest way to do this is to add the new cases to the existing data file. Because we do not know whether these individuals will be reconvicted we will have to enter a missing value for the variable "recon". As a result, these new cases will not be included when the discriminant function is calculated and, therefore, the result will be identical to that found before these cases were added.

Follow steps 1–16 listed previously (see pages 255–257), but then click on the **Save** button in the **Discriminant Analysis** dialogue box. The **Discriminant Analysis: Save** dialogue box will be revealed (see below).

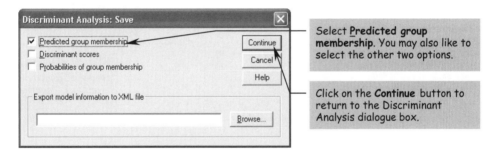

Now click on the ⸺OK⸺ button. In addition to the output described above, several new variables will be computed and added to your data file (see below).

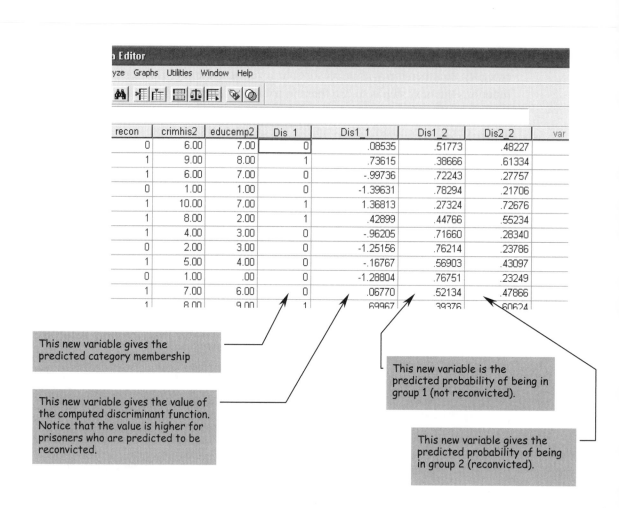

This new variable gives the predicted category membership

This new variable gives the value of the computed discriminant function. Notice that the value is higher for prisoners who are predicted to be reconvicted.

This new variable is the predicted probability of being in group 1 (not reconvicted).

This new variable gives the predicted probability of being in group 2 (reconvicted).

Thus, we can first compute the best discriminant function and then use this to make real predictions.

Section 4: An introduction to logistic regression

Logistic regression differs from discriminant analysis in that whereas discriminant analysis computes a function that best discriminates between two categories, logistic regression computes the log odds that a particular outcome will occur. For example, we can use logistic regression to compute the odds that a particular prisoner will be reconvicted after release.

The odds of an event occurring are given by the ratio of the probability of it occurring to the probability of it not occurring. For example, if four horses are running in a race and we pick one of them at random, the odds of our horse winning will be $0.25 / (1 - 0.25) = 0.333$. You will be able to see that the odds for any event lie between the values of 0 and +infinity. This is problematic for the mathematics involved in logistic regression, and to overcome this problem the log of the odds are calculated (natural log or $\log_e$). The log odds of an event will vary between −infinity and +infinity, with a high value indicating an increased probability of occurrence. A positive value indicates that the event is more likely to occur than not (odds are in favour) while a negative value indicates that the event is more likely not to occur (odds are against). To illustrate the difference between odds and log odds, consider the example of the four horse race. We have already seen that the odds of us picking the correct horse are 0.333. The odds of us picking the wrong horse are given by $0.75 / (1 - 0.75) = 3$. If we now take the log of each of these values we will see that the log odds of us picking the correct horse are $\log_e(0.333) = -1.1$ and the log odds of us picking the wrong horse are $\log_e(3) = 1.1$. The advantage of log odds over odds is clear from this example: unlike odds, log odds are symmetric about zero. The term "logistic" in the name logistic regression derives from this use of log odds.

It is possible to use logistic regression in situations when there are two or more categories of the grouping variable. In cases where there are just two categories of the grouping variable the SPSS binary logistic regression command should be employed. Where there are more than two categories the multinomial logistic regression command should be used. The multinomial command is not described here, but is similar to the binary logistic regression command.

As for discriminant analysis, we will show how the analysis can be used to predict category membership for cases where it is not known.

Section 5: Performing logistic regression on SPSS

EXAMPLE STUDY

We will demonstrate binary logistic regression using the prisoner data set used to demonstrate discriminant analysis (see Section 3 of this chapter). This will allow us to compare the output of these two commands.

TO PERFORM A BINARY LOGISTIC REGRESSION

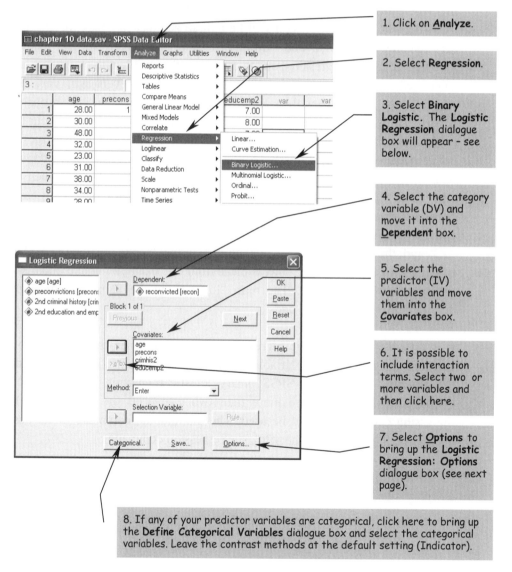

1. Click on **Analyze**.

2. Select **Regression**.

3. Select **Binary Logistic**. The **Logistic Regression** dialogue box will appear – see below.

4. Select the category variable (DV) and move it into the **Dependent** box.

5. Select the predictor (IV) variables and move them into the **Covariates** box.

6. It is possible to include interaction terms. Select two or more variables and then click here.

7. Select **Options** to bring up the **Logistic Regression: Options** dialogue box (see next page).

8. If any of your predictor variables are categorical, click here to bring up the **Define Categorical Variables** dialogue box and select the categorical variables. Leave the contrast methods at the default setting (Indicator).

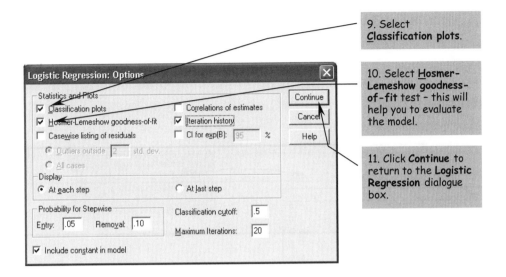

9. Select **Classification plots.**

10. Select **Hosmer-Lemeshow goodness-of-fit** test – this will help you to evaluate the model.

11. Click **Continue** to return to the **Logistic Regression** dialogue box.

Finally, click on the OK button. The annotated output is shown below.

Obtained Using Menu Items: **Regression > Binary Logistic**

Logistic Regression

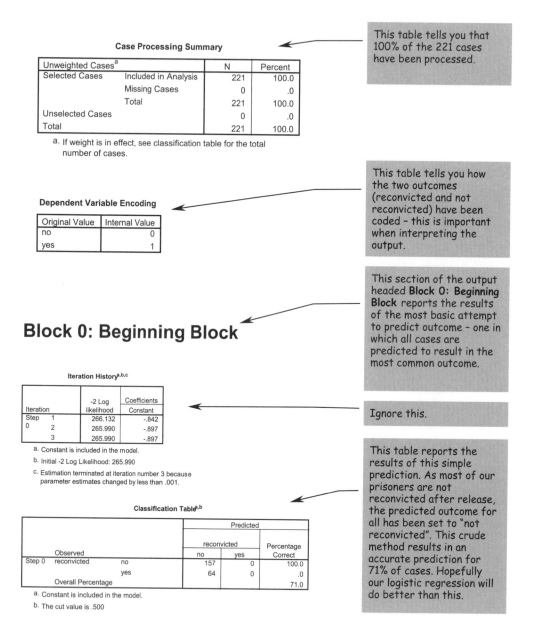

Case Processing Summary

Unweighted Cases[a]		N	Percent
Selected Cases	Included in Analysis	221	100.0
	Missing Cases	0	.0
	Total	221	100.0
Unselected Cases		0	.0
Total		221	100.0

a. If weight is in effect, see classification table for the total number of cases.

This table tells you that 100% of the 221 cases have been processed.

Dependent Variable Encoding

Original Value	Internal Value
no	0
yes	1

This table tells you how the two outcomes (reconvicted and not reconvicted) have been coded – this is important when interpreting the output.

Block 0: Beginning Block

This section of the output headed **Block 0: Beginning Block** reports the results of the most basic attempt to predict outcome – one in which all cases are predicted to result in the most common outcome.

Iteration History[a,b,c]

Iteration		-2 Log likelihood	Coefficients Constant
Step 0	1	266.132	-.842
	2	265.990	-.897
	3	265.990	-.897

a. Constant is included in the model.

b. Initial -2 Log Likelihood: 265.990

c. Estimation terminated at iteration number 3 because parameter estimates changed by less than .001.

Ignore this.

Classification Table[a,b]

			Predicted		
			reconvicted		Percentage Correct
Observed			no	yes	
Step 0	reconvicted	no	157	0	100.0
		yes	64	0	.0
	Overall Percentage				71.0

a. Constant is included in the model.

b. The cut value is .500

This table reports the results of this simple prediction. As most of our prisoners are not reconvicted after release, the predicted outcome for all has been set to "not reconvicted". This crude method results in an accurate prediction for 71% of cases. Hopefully our logistic regression will do better than this.

Variables in the Equation

		B	S.E.	Wald	df	Sig.	Exp(B)
Step 0	Constant	-.897	.148	36.612	1	.000	.408

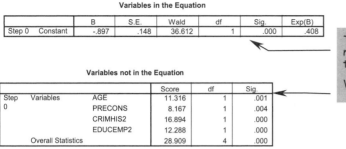

These two tables tell us that so far no variables have been entered into the equation.

We can ignore both these tables

Variables not in the Equation

			Score	df	Sig.
Step 0	Variables	AGE	11.316	1	.001
		PRECONS	8.167	1	.004
		CRIMHIS2	16.894	1	.000
		EDUCEMP2	12.288	1	.000
	Overall Statistics		28.909	4	.000

Block 1: Method = Enter

This block of output reports the results of the logistic regression analysis. This analysis should result in a more accurate prediction than that reported in **Block 0**.

Iteration History[a,b,c,d]

		-2 Log	Coefficients				
Iteration		likelihood	Constant	AGE	PRECONS	CRIMHIS2	EDUCEMP2
Step 1	1	237.530	-.888	-.031	.024	.109	.038
	2	233.181	-.797	-.052	.033	.155	.033
	3	233.002	-.727	-.058	.036	.165	.029
	4	233.001	-.722	-.058	.036	.166	.029

a. Method: Enter

b. Constant is included in the model.

c. Initial -2 Log Likelihood: 265.990

d. Estimation terminated at iteration number 4 because log-likelihood decreased by less than .010 percent.

Logistic regression employs a process known as *iteration*. In an iterative process we attempt to arrive at the best answer to a problem through a series of approximations. Each iteration results in a slightly more accurate approximation. This table reports this iterative process. The statistic **-2 log likelihood** is used in logistic regression to measure the success of the model. A high value indicates that the model poorly predicts the outcome. With each iteration we can see the value falling; however, the benefit derived at each iteration decreases until after 4 iterations SPSS terminates this process. You can also see how the coefficients of each of the predictor variables are adjusted at each iteration.

Omnibus Tests of Model Coefficients

		Chi-square	df	Sig.
Step 1	Step	32.988	4	.000
	Block	32.988	4	.000
	Model	32.988	4	.000

Omnibus tests are general tests of how well the model performs. In a report we can use either this or the Hosmer-Lemeshow test shown on the next page. When the Enter method has been employed (as here) there is only one step and so the Step, Block and Model rows in this table will be identical.

Model Summary

Step	-2 Log likelihood	Cox & Snell R Square	Nagelkerke R Square
1	233.001	.139	.198

This table give useful statistics that are equivalent to R^2 in multiple regression. It is not possible to compute an exact R^2 in logistic regression, but these two statistics are useful approximations. Here we can see that our model accounts for between 13.9% and 19.8% of the variance.

Hosmer and Lemeshow Test

Step	Chi-square	df	Sig.
1	5.876	8	.661

This table gives the results of the Hosmer-Lemeshow test that we requested. This test gives a measure of the agreement between the observed outcomes and the predicted outcomes. This statistic is a test of the null hypothesis that the model is good, hence a good model is indicated by a <u>high</u> p value: as in this example where $p = 0.661$. If the p value is less than 0.05 then the model does not adequately fit the data.

Contingency Table for Hosmer and Lemeshow Test

		reconvicted = no		reconvicted = yes		
		Observed	Expected	Observed	Expected	Total
Step 1	1	21	20.940	1	1.060	22
	2	18	19.824	4	2.176	22
	3	20	18.573	2	3.427	22
	4	19	17.698	3	4.302	22
	5	18	16.845	4	5.155	22
	6	17	15.747	5	6.253	22
	7	12	14.333	10	7.667	22
	8	12	12.867	10	9.133	22
	9	9	10.798	13	11.202	22
	10	11	9.376	12	13.624	23

This table is used in the calculation of the Hosmer-Lemeshow statistic reported in the previous table. The cases are ranked by estimated probability on the criterion variable and then divided into 10 "deciles of risk". Within each decile the numbers of observed and expected positive (reconviction) and negative (no reconviction) outcomes are calculated. The Hosmer-Lemeshow statistic (above) is then calculated from this 10*2 contingency table. Note that a high proportion of the participants in decile 1 are not reconvicted, whereas the majority of those in decile 10 are reconvicted. This pattern indicates that our model is good.

Classification Table[a]

			Predicted		
			reconvicted		Percentage Correct
	Observed		no	yes	
Step 1	reconvicted	no	138	19	87.9
		yes	44	20	31.3
	Overall Percentage				71.5

a. The cut value is .500

This table summarises the results of our prediction and should be compared to the equivalent table in **Block 0**. Our model correctly predicts the outcome for 71.5%. Although this is not much better than the situation reported in **Block 0**, we are now correctly predicting 31.3% of the prisoners who are reconvicted.

Compare this to the outcome of the discriminant analysis reported previously in this chapter.

Variables in the Equation

		B	S.E.	Wald	df	Sig.	Exp(B)	95.0% C.I.for EXP(B) Lower	Upper
Step 1a	age	-.058	.018	10.221	1	.001	.944	.911	.978
	precons	.036	.026	1.871	1	.171	1.037	.984	1.092
	crimhis2	.166	.068	5.860	1	.015	1.180	1.032	1.349
	educemp2	.029	.070	.166	1	.684	1.029	.897	1.181
	Constant	-.722	.642	1.267	1	.260	.486		

a. Variable(s) entered on step 1: age, precons, crimhis2, educemp2.

This table contains some of the most critical information.

The first column gives the coefficients for each predictor variable in the mode. The negative coefficient for AGE indicates that the odds of reconviction declines with increasing age.

The Wald statistic and associated Sig. values indicate how useful each predictor variable is. In this case only AGE and CRIMHIS2 are significant – the analysis could be rerun with only these variables included.

The Exp(B) column gives an indication of the change in the predicted odds of reconviction for each unit change in the predictor variable. Values less than 1 indicate that an increase in the value of the predictor variable is associated with a decrease in the odds of the event. Thus for every extra year of age, the odds of the prisoner being reconvicted on release decrease by a factor of 0.944. The 95% CI values indicate that the magnitude of this decrease is likely to be in the range .911 to .978

In a report you might write:

A logistic regression analysis was performed with reconviction as the DV and age, number of previous convictions, and criminal history and education and employment sub-scales of the LSI-R as predictor variables. A total of 221 cases were analysed and the full model significantly predicted reconviction status (omnibus chi-square = 32.99, df = 4, $p < 0.0005$). The model accounted for between 13.9% and 19.8% of the variance in reconviction status, with 87.9% of the non-reconvicted prisoners successfully predicted. However only 31.3% of predictions for the reconvicted group were accurate. Overall 71.5% of predictions were accurate. Table 10.1 gives coefficients and the Wald statistic and associated degrees of freedom and probability values for each of the predictor variables. This shows that only age and criminal history reliably predicted reconviction. The values of the coefficients reveal that an increase of one year of age is associated with a decrease in the odds of conviction by a factor of 0.94 (95% CI 0.91 and 0.98), and that each unit increase in criminal history score is associated with an increase in the odds of reconviction by a factor of 1.18 (95%CI 1.03–1.35).

Note: Table 10.1 is not shown here but would hold the information mentioned, extracted from the last table in the SPSS output.

We can now use the results of our logistic regression analysis to calculate the level of risk of reconviction for each new inmate who enters the prison. To do this, we need to add to the data file the data from each new prisoner as they arrive to start their sentence. For each of these new cases enter a missing value for the category variable (recon). Now repeat the analysis as before, but in the **Logistic Regression** dialogue box click on the Save button. This will bring up the **Logistic Regression: Save New Variables** dialogue box (see below).

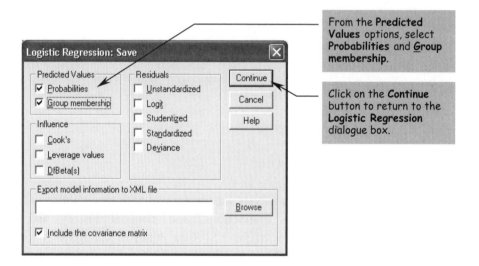

From the **Predicted Values** options, select **Probabilities** and **Group** membership.

Click on the **Continue** button to return to the **Logistic Regression** dialogue box.

Now click on the ⎣OK⎦ button. In addition to the output described above, two new variables will be added to the data file. The first of these gives the predicted probability of reconviction for each case, and the second gives the predicted group (reconvicted or not). You can use these values for the new cases to make real predictions.

Chapter Eleven

Factor analysis, and reliability and dimensionality of scales

An introduction to factor analysis

Performing a basic factor analysis on SPSS

Other aspects of factor analysis

Reliability analysis for scales and questionnaires

Dimensionality of scales and questionnaires

Section 1: An introduction to factor analysis

HOW THIS CHAPTER IS ORGANISED

This chapter is organised somewhat differently from other chapters, in that later in this first Section we will be using tables produced by SPSS in order to explain some aspects of factor analysis. We will not at that point explain how to produce those tables: instead we just use them to talk about factor analysis. We will also explain how these tables can give an indication of whether a factor analysis is likely to be useful with the variables that you have measured. For this Section, the tables are **not** derived from data suitable for a real factor analysis. Instead the data are simply convenient for the purpose. If you are already familiar with factor analysis then you could omit this Section. If you are going to use factor analysis in real research, then you should understand more about factor analysis than can be explained in any book on how to use SPSS. We recommend the following: Cooper (2002, Chapters 6 and 8); Giles (2002); Kline (1994, who introduces the calculations for factor analysis in detail); Tabachnick and Fidell (2001).

Section 2 returns to our normal style, showing firstly how to perform a factor analysis and then how to interpret the output. This is for basic aspects of factor analysis. Section 3 is a short section about other aspects of factor analysis. Finally in Sections 4 and 5 we provide some guidelines on using SPSS to check the reliability and dimensionality of scales/questionnaires. First though, we continue this section with an introduction to factor analysis.

WHAT IS FACTOR ANALYSIS?

A very simple way to start explaining factor analysis is to remind you that correlation does not imply causation: there could always be a third variable that explains the relationship between two variables. In factor analysis, you could say that we are actually looking for that "third" variable, which could now be called the factor underlying the correlations between two or more variables. This simple explanation, however, does not mean that all correlations are explained by factors. Factor analysis is the way in which you investigate whether factors might exist; it is said to *extract* the factors from the variables.

A common example used to introduce factor analysis is that of human abilities and aptitudes (e.g., see Kline, 1994). If a group of people undertake a large number of ability and aptitude tests, then each test will be correlated with at least some of the other tests. There will be groupings of tests within which all are correlated with each other, whereas for tests from two different groupings the correlation will be lower or absent. It is well established that different dimensions (such as verbal ability and spatial ability) underlie these groupings. One individual could have relatively high spatial ability, and their scores on tests that all require aspects of spatial ability will be relatively high; the same individual could have relatively low verbal ability, and their scores on tests that all require aspects of verbal ability will be relatively low. Thus across a large number of people, the tests that all require aspects of spatial ability will be highly correlated, and also the tests that all require aspects of verbal ability will be highly correlated, but there will be only moderate or low correlations between a test that taps spatial ability and another test that taps verbal ability.

To generalise, we can say that if we measure a large number of variables, then we can investigate whether those variables represent a smaller number of dimensions. If these dimensions are psychological then they can be called *psychological constructs*, but the more general term is factors. One use of factor analysis is to establish whether one or more factors do underlie a large number of variables; if so, the analysis identifies the number of factors and it also identifies which of the variables make up which factor. This use, called *exploratory factor analysis*, is available in SPSS. Typically, unless otherwise specified, "factor analysis" is used to mean "exploratory factor analysis" and that is its meaning in this book. Exploratory factor analysis is sometimes called a data reduction technique, because you could use the outcome to choose a smaller set of variables than those initially measured, for use in future studies. There are a number of different methods of carrying out factor analysis; we will mention them in Section 3.

Note that exploratory factor analysis does not test hypotheses by means of a formal test of significance. Instead we could say that it explores the possibility of a factor structure underlying the variables. The analysis provides a large amount of information, which the researcher can then use to specify factors. So exploratory factor analysis allows us to make informal inferences, instead of carrying out formal inferential tests of significance.

For hypothesis testing a somewhat different analysis, confirmatory factor analysis, has been developed. Hypotheses about the number of factors can be tested in SPSS; this will be briefly mentioned in Section 3. Otherwise you would normally need to use structural equation modelling packages (e.g., AMOS or LISREL).

Correlation and Covariance

Bivariate correlation identifies the level of linear relationship between two variables. The covariance of two variables, the extent to which they vary together, is the unstandardised equivalent. Factor analysis identifies variables that all relate to a single factor by exploring the relationships between the variables. It does so by carrying out calculations based on the matrix of correlation coefficients, or the matrix of covariances, between each variable with each of the other variables. As default, SPSS uses the correlation matrix in factor analysis.

Multiple Regression

In multiple regression we are interested in which of a number of variables (predictor variables) may be useful in predicting scores on another variable (criterion variable). Factor analysis could be used in predicting what score someone might get on a variable: for example, if you find out that a new test can be accounted for by the factor verbal ability, then someone who scores highly on other tests that tap verbal ability should also score highly on the new test.

In multiple regression, there should not be high correlations (multicollinearity) between the predictor variables: if there are, then those predictor variables may actually be measuring the same thing and so do not add to our understanding of what predicts the criterion variable. By contrast, in factor analysis we are actually interested in high correlations, because we want to investigate which variables are measuring aspects of the same thing (the same dimension, factor, or psychological construct). See Tabachnick and Fidell (2001), however, for limitations on multicollinearity in factor analysis.

Analysis of Variance

Factor analysis and ANOVA are similar in that both are methods of accounting for the variance in data. They differ, however, in that factor analysis is a method of investigating what underlies patterns of associations between variables, whereas ANOVA tests for differences between conditions.

It is important that you recognise the difference between the meaning of the term "factor" in ANOVA and its meaning in factor analysis. In a true experimental ANOVA design, the experimenter manipulates the levels of each factor in order to explore cause and effect relationships between the factors and the dependent variable. In an ANOVA design incorporating one or more natural groups factors, the levels are not manipulated but instead they are chosen or measured from existing groups such as male and female, or high extroversion and low extroversion, and so causal relationships cannot be assumed. In either case, in ANOVA terminology the word factor is simply a more convenient name for an independent variable, whereas the word factor in factor analysis means a dimension (or a psychological construct) that underlies several measured variables. So, in factor analysis the term has a more profound, but less concrete, meaning than it does in ANOVA. Of course, in any specific experiment in which an ANOVA design is used, one or more of the factors may actually represent a psychological construct.

Discriminant Analysis and Logistic Regression

These are methods for determining which variables will predict membership of, or discriminate between, different categories of another variable. The example given in Chapter 10 was an investigation of which variables would discriminate between those offenders who had been reconvicted and those who had not. In factor analysis, by contrast, we are usually not really interested in the scores of any individual participant. Instead we want to explain the pattern of correlations between variables, and identify factors (dimensions) underlying those variables.

CORRELATION MATRIX AND OTHER MATRICES IN FACTOR ANALYSIS

In this section we will consider certain aspects of factor analysis including how it makes use of the matrix of correlations. For our explanations we will use the data previously used for Spearman's r_s correlation coefficient (Chapter 4, Section 4). Those data were for only three variables, and thus are **not** appropriate for a factor analysis. Three variables, however, give rise to small matrices that will be much more useful for illustration than the large matrices produced by the number of variables typically entered into a real factor analysis.

One point to note is that factor analysis in SPSS makes use of Pearson's, not Spearman's, correlation coefficients. This is acceptable for our data because factor analysis can be used for continuous and discrete data.

To start with, we will show the Pearson's r output itself for comparison purposes. Next we will show various matrices that can be produced by means of the factor analysis command. Details of how to obtain these tables are given in Section 2 of this chapter: for now we simply use them to explain aspects of factor analysis. They can also help to indicate whether our variables have *factorability* (Tabachnick and Fidell, 2001, p. 589): that is, whether it is likely that there are any factors underlying the variables that we measured.

The three variables "confdt" (confidence in the woman's testimony), "believ" (how believable the woman was), and "attrct" (how attractive the woman was) were all entered into a Pearson's r analysis. The table below is the SPSS output. Details of the study are in Chapter 4, Section 4, and how to obtain and interpret the output for Pearson's correlation coefficient is described in Chapter 4, Section 3.

Pearson's r output

Correlations

		confdt	believ	attrct
confdt	Pearson Correlation	1	.278 **	.073
	Sig. (1-tailed)		.004	.249
	N	89	89	89
believ	Pearson Correlation	.278 **	1	.429 **
	Sig. (1-tailed)	.004		.000
	N	89	89	89
attrct	Pearson Correlation	.073	.429 **	1
	Sig. (1-tailed)	.249	.000	
	N	89	89	89

**. Correlation is significant at the 0.01 level (1-tailed).

In Pearson's *r* output, each cell of the matrix contains the values of *r*, *p*, and *N*, allowing a quick assessment of both the strength and significance of each individual bivariate correlation. In the equivalent table produced by factor analysis, shown next, the matrix of coefficients is in the upper part of the table, and the matrix of *p* values, if you request it, is in the lower part of the table. This separation reflects the fact that the coefficients are used in factor analysis calculations whereas the *p* values are just for information. These coefficient values are also known as the observed correlations. In a matrix there is usually a distinction between the on-diagonal values and the off-diagonal values: see annotations below.

Correlation matrix from factor analysis output

1(a). The upper part of this table is a complete matrix of the correlation coefficients for each variable with each of the other variables and with itself.

1(b). The diagonal of a matrix is usually worth noting in factor analysis. The diagonal in this matrix holds the correlation coefficient for each variable with itself (and, therefore, these on-diagonal values are all equal to 1.0).

Correlation Matrix

		confdt	believ	attrct
Correlation	confdt	1.000	.278	.073
	believ	.278	1.000	.429
	attrct	.073	.429	1.000
Sig. (1-tailed)	confdt		.004	.249
	believ	.004		.000
	attrct	.249	.000	

1(c). These off-diagonal values are the three possible correlation coefficients between the different pairs of variables. They are mirrored below left of the diagonal. These values are called the *observed correlations*.

2. The lower part of the table is a matrix of the p values corresponding to the correlation coefficients. The diagonal is left blank in this matrix.

> **TIP**   For an indication of factorability, look at the sizes of the correlation coefficients between the different variables. If the coefficients are mostly small (less than .3), then there is little likelihood that a factor structure underlies the variables.

Partial correlations from factor analysis output

The anti-image table (shown below) contains two matrices. The upper matrix is automatically printed if yoxu request the anti-image matrices, but for now we are most interested in the lower matrix.

In the lower matrix the values off the diagonal are the *partial correlations* with the signs reversed, known as the *negative partial correlations*. (This term does not mean that the value has to be negative; simply that the original sign is reversed.) A partial correlation is the correlation between two variables when the effects of any other variables are controlled for or 'partialled out'. Thus in Chapter 4 we said that if there is a correlation between the number of ice creams sold and the number of drownings that occur, then it is likely that the relationship is explained by a third variable, temperature. To investigate this possibility, one could partial out the effect of temperature from both variables and then find the partial correlation between them: it is likely to be small in that example.

Anti-image Matrices

		confdt	believ	attrct
Anti-image Covariance	confdt	.920	-.228	.046
	believ	-.228	.755	-.335
	attrct	.046	-.335	.813
Anti-image Correlation	confdt	.515[a]	-.273	.053
	believ	-.273	.504[a]	-.427
	attrct	.053	-.427	.506[a]

a. Measures of Sampling Adequacy(MSA)

The diagonal holds the values of the Kaiser-Meyer-Olkin (KMO) measure of sampling adequacy for each variable. The KMO will be discussed in Section 2.

The off-diagonal values are the *negative partial correlations* (see text above): these values indicate whether there is a factor structure underlying the variables (see text).

As stated above, if the correlation coefficients are mostly small then the variables are unlikely to have factorability. However, if the correlation coefficients are mostly large, then we cannot conclude that the variables definitely do have factorability. The partial correlations provide the next check, as explained here. If there is a factor structure underlying a number of variables then they should all be fairly well correlated with each other. So, we would expect the correlation between any two variables to become weaker once the effects of the other variables have been partialled out. If the partial correlation between two variables is not weaker than the correlation between them, then those two variables have a strong relationship to each other and little relationship to any of the other variables that we measured.

TIP Use of the partial correlations as an indication of factorability depends on their absolute size: thus the fact that SPSS reverses their sign and prints the negative partial correlations is irrelevant. If the partial correlations are mostly large, then there is little likelihood of a factor structure underlying the variables.

Reproduced correlations and residuals from factor analysis output

The *reproduced correlations* (the off-diagonal values in the upper matrix of the table below) are the values predicted for the correlations between the variables under the assumption that the factor analysis is correct. So, if the solution to the factor analysis represents the actual state of things, then these are the correlations that would be expected. Factor analysis then compares these predicted correlations with those that were actually obtained (the observed correlations): each *residual* value, in the lower matrix, is equal to the reproduced correlation subtracted from the observed correlation.

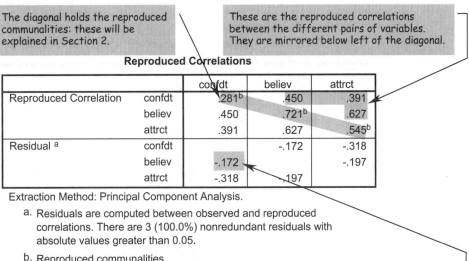

The diagonal holds the reproduced communalities: these will be explained in Section 2.

These are the reproduced correlations between the different pairs of variables. They are mirrored below left of the diagonal.

Reproduced Correlations

		confdt	believ	attrct
Reproduced Correlation	confdt	.281[b]	.450	.391
	believ	.450	.721[b]	.627
	attrct	.391	.627	.545[b]
Residual [a]	confdt		-.172	-.318
	believ	-.172		-.197
	attrct	-.318	-.197	

Extraction Method: Principal Component Analysis.

a. Residuals are computed between observed and reproduced correlations. There are 3 (100.0%) nonredundant residuals with absolute values greater than 0.05.

b. Reproduced communalities

The observed correlation (see first table in this Section) minus the reproduced correlation equals the residual: .278 - .450 = -.172

TIP Factorability: the smaller the residuals are (unlike here!), the more likely it is that the factor analysis gives a good explanation of the data. That is, the more likely it is that the identified factors do explain the actual state of things in the real world.

So far we have introduced you to some concepts that will be useful in understanding factor analysis. For that purpose we used data that were simply convenient. In Section 2 we will show you how to carry out and interpret a real factor analysis. First, though, some issues about when factor analysis can be used and more terminology.

WHEN SHOULD I USE FACTOR ANALYSIS?

The following criteria for data and number of participants are usually suggested:

1. The variables should be of at least ordinal level of measurement;
2. The variables should be normally distributed: if they do not meet criteria for normal distribution then you should consider a transformation (see Tabachnick and Fidell, 2001);
3. The relationships between variables should be reasonably linear;
4. Number of participants: it is usually considered that for a successful factor analysis, at least 100 participants should have provided data, and some say 200 or more. Two pointers are:
   a. There should be more participants than variables. Kline (1994) suggests a minimum ratio of 2:1, but the more the better. Thus if you wish to explore the factor structure underlying a questionnaire that contains 60 items, then you should test a minimum of 120 participants.
   b. There should be more participants than extracted factors. Kline suggests a minimum ratio of 20:1. In truly exploratory factor analysis, however, we do not know how many factors there will be.

   In general, the more participants you test the more likely it is that any factors that do underlie the measured variables will be revealed, and thus a sample size of 200 is a sensible minimum target.

Usefulness/validity of factor analysis

It is possible to put any data set containing a number of variables into a factor analysis, but the outcome may be invalid or simply useless. A number of methods for assessing whether the variables entered have factorability have already been described. Other pointers to factorability, and pointers to whether the extracted factors are a good solution to explaining the variables, will be described below. These pointers should be inspected before considering the factors that may have been extracted. One should then consider whether the solution provided by the factor analysis makes sense.

TERMINOLOGY

In addition to the terms introduced above, the following terms are required to follow the output from even a fairly basic factor analysis.

Component and factor

Kline (1994, p. 36) states "components are real factors because they are derived directly from the correlation matrix. Common factors of factor analysis are hypothetical because they are estimated from the data." Common factors are therefore an example of what Skinner referred to as explanatory fictions. That does not, however, mean that they are not useful, but it is important that you use caution when interpreting any factors that you derive from a factor analysis. The simplest type of factor analysis, principal component analysis, extracts components as its name suggests, whereas other types extract common factors. Thus principal component analysis and factor analysis are somewhat different things: we give more detail in Section 3.

In this book, in common with many others, the terms factor and component are used interchangeably when we discuss this simple type of factor analysis, principal component analysis, but the distinction between them should be borne in mind throughout.

Extraction

This is the name for the process by which the important factors are identified: those factors are then said to have been *extracted*. In this book we only illustrate the principal component method of extraction, and mention other methods in Section 3. Extraction is not an exact process, as should become clear as you work through Section 2.

Communality

This is a measure of how much variance in the data from a particular **variable** is explained by the analysis. Initially, **all** of the factors (or components) in the analysis (equal to the number of variables entered) are used to calculate the communalities and all of the variance is accounted for. Thus, in principal component analysis the *initial* communalities are all equal to 1 (indicating that all of the variance is explained). After the factor or component extraction, *extraction* communalities for each variable are calculated based on the extracted factors only. The higher the value of the extraction communality is for a particular variable, the more of its variance has been explained by the extracted factors. The communality is calculated from factor loadings (see below).

Eigenvalue

This is a measure of how much variance in the data is explained by a single **factor**. Remember that the analysis initially considers all the possible factors (the same number of factors as of the number of variables). The higher the value, the more of the variance is explained by that factor. The magnitude of the eigenvalue can be used to determine whether the factor explains sufficient variance for it to be a useful factor. The default value in SPSS is 1.0; you can request SPSS to extract factors with an eigenvalue of less than 1.0, as will be explained in Section 3.

Scree Plot

The scree plot is a useful graph of the eigenvalues of all of the factors initially considered. It can be used to decide on the number of factors that should be extracted. An annotated example is shown in the SPSS output below.

Factor Loadings

A factor loading is calculated for each combination of variable and extracted factor. These values are useful for seeing the pattern of which variables are likely to be explained by which factor. The factor loading can be thought of as the coefficient of the correlation between the component (or factor) and the variable: thus the larger the number, the more likely it is that the component underlies that variable. Loadings may be positive or negative: this issue is considered further in Section 3.

The initial factor loadings can be inspected for patterns. Almost always, however, a rotation will be used (see below) and then the pattern becomes more useful. SPSS uses the before-rotation factor loadings to calculate the extraction communalities; we calculate an example in our annotations of the SPSS output in Section 2.

Rotation

A factor analysis prior to rotation provides an explanation of how many factors underlie the variables; for some purposes this is sufficient. In psychology, however, we normally wish to understand what it all means: so we want to establish whether any psychological **constructs** might underlie the variables. Rotation is a mathematical technique available in factor analysis that arrives at the simplest pattern of factor loadings.

Section 2: Performing a basic factor analysis on SPSS

HYPOTHETICAL STUDY

To illustrate the use of this analysis, we shall suggest a hypothetical survey. Suppose that a psychologist who is interested in aesthetic values wanted to investigate people's appreciation of different types of plants. For example, he wished to study whether there were any underlying dimensions to liking for plants typically found in different places, such as "wild" English countryside, cottage gardens, and formal gardens. He might construct a questionnaire listing various plants to which people are asked to give a score from 1 (extreme dislike) to 7 (extreme liking). The plants could be wild flowers (e.g., celandine, primrose, bluebell, buttercup, daisy, speedwell), cottage garden type flowers (such as cornflower, poppy, sweetpea, lavender, aster), and formal garden type plants (e.g., rose, wisteria, delphinium, hellebore). A data set of 50 cases only was used, but, as explained above, many more participants are required for the results of a factor analysis to be valid. The data are shown in Appendix I or from the web address listed there. Note that these hypothetical data are skewed, which might be problematic for a real factor analysis (see Tabachnick and Fidell, 2001). The data file includes the sex of the participants, with 23 men and 27 women, so that you can try the option of selecting members of a group, if you wish. Remember that the survey described is hypothetical; we do not know what you would find if you tried this study yourself.

HOW TO PERFORM THE ANALYSIS

In this section we show you how to carry out and interpret a principal component analysis; other extraction methods are described in Section 3.

Click on **Analyze** $\Rightarrow$ **Data Reduction** $\Rightarrow$ **Factor...**

The **Factor Analysis** dialogue box, shown on the next page, will then appear. Select all the variables that you want to enter into the factor analysis, and move them across into the **Variables** box.

TIP   The first time we run a factor analysis, we can include all the variables (of ordinal, interval or ratio level of measurement) that we have measured. We should then inspect the indicators of factorability in the factor analysis output and decide on:
1. whether there is any factor structure at all – if not, then give up;
2. whether all the variables are useful – if any are not, then run a new factor analysis in which you only include the useful variables.

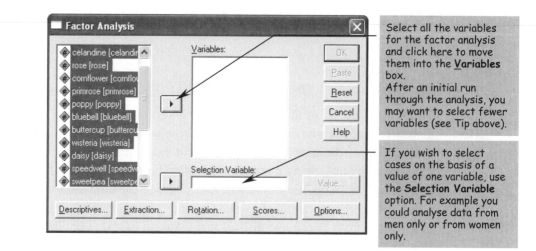

Select all the variables for the factor analysis and click here to move them into the **Variables** box.
After an initial run through the analysis, you may want to select fewer variables (see Tip above).

If you wish to select cases on the basis of a value of one variable, use the **Selection Variable** option. For example you could analyse data from men only or from women only.

Next click on the Descriptives... button, and the **Factor Analysis: Descriptives** dialogue box will appear, as shown below.

If you select **Univariate descriptives**, SPSS will print the mean, standard deviation and number of cases for each of the variables that you enter into the factor analysis.

The **Initial solution** option is normally preselected.

Select the options as shown here. Don't select **Inverse** or **Determinant** for now; we will explain those in Section 3.

Output from some of the **Correlation Matrix** options were described in Section 1. All those we have selected here will be described below. We will cover the **Inverse** and **Determinant** options in Section 3. When you have selected all of the options that you require, click on the **Continue** button to return to the **Factor Analysis** dialogue box. Now click on the Extraction... button: the **Factor Analysis: Extraction** dialogue box, shown on the next page, will appear.

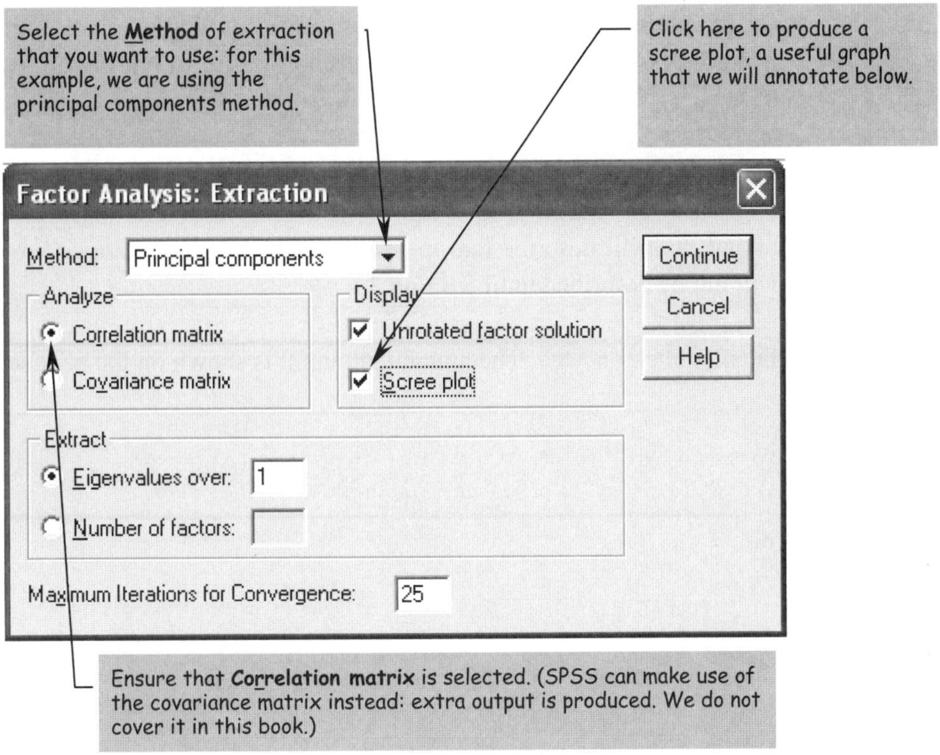

Factor Analysis: Extraction

Method: Principal components

Analyze
- ⦿ Correlation matrix
- ○ Covariance matrix

Display
- ☑ Unrotated factor solution
- ☑ Scree plot

Extract
- ⦿ Eigenvalues over: 1
- ○ Number of factors:

Maximum Iterations for Convergence: 25

Continue

Cancel

Help

Other options in the **Factor Analysis: Extraction** dialogue box will be described in Section 3. When you have selected all of the options that you require, click on the **Continue** button to return to the **Factor Analysis** dialogue box. Now click on the Rotation... button: the **Factor Analysis: Rotation** dialogue box, shown below, will appear.

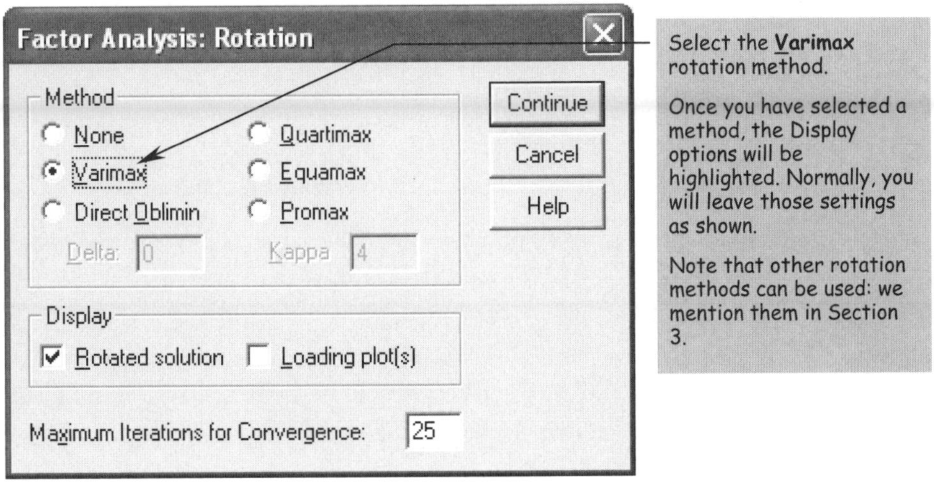

Factor Analysis: Rotation

Method
- ○ None
- ⦿ Varimax
- ○ Direct Oblimin
  - Delta: 0
- ○ Quartimax
- ○ Equamax
- ○ Promax
  - Kappa: 4

Display
- ☑ Rotated solution
- ☐ Loading plot(s)

Maximum Iterations for Convergence: 25

Continue

Cancel

Help

Other options in the **Factor Analysis: Rotation** dialogue box will be described in Section 3. Click on the **Continue** button to return to the **Factor Analysis** dialogue box.

Clicking on [Options...] brings up a dialogue box that allows you to specify how to treat missing values. It also allows you to control the appearance of part of the output; we will describe that in Section 3. Use of the dialogue box from [Scores...] will not be described until Section 3.

Finally, click on [OK]. The annotated output is shown on the next several pages.

OUTPUT FROM FACTOR ANALYSIS USING PRINCIPAL COMPONENT EXTRACTION AND VARIMAX ROTATION

Obtained Using Menu Items: **Analyze > Data Reduction > Factor...**

Descriptive Statistics

	Mean	Std. Deviation	Analysis N
celandine	5.2200	1.56870	50
rose	5.2200	1.51577	50
cornflower	5.4600	1.66856	50
primrose	5.3800	1.39810	50
poppy	6.1200	1.25584	50
bluebell	5.7200	1.29426	50
buttercup	5.3400	1.63645	50
wisteria	5.3200	1.42055	50
daisy	5.6200	1.29189	50
speedwell	5.9600	1.21151	50
sweetpea	5.2800	1.57843	50
delphinium	4.3800	1.71298	50
aster	5.4000	1.55183	50
lavender	5.9400	1.50387	50
hellebore	3.9000	1.85439	50

This table is produced by the **Univariate Descriptives** option in the **Factor Analysis: Descriptives** dialogue box.

Remember that in a real factor analysis you should aim to test a minimum of 200 participants.

TIP The descriptives table above is the only part of the output with a note of the number of participants that you entered into the factor analysis, so we recommend that you always request this table, for reference purposes.

The contents of this table are produced by the **Coefficients** and **Significance levels** options in the **Factor Analysis: Descriptives** dialogue box. Here the whole table is shown shrunk to fit. On the next page there is an annotated section of the upper matrix.

Correlation Matrix

		celandine	rose	cornflower	primrose	poppy	bluebell	buttercup	wisteria	daisy	speedwell	sweetpea	delphinium	aster	lavender	hellebore
Correlation	celandine	1.000	.099	.194	.566	.111	.785	.519	.206	.697	.660	.205	.014	.072	.110	-.126
	rose	.099	1.000	.355	.104	.672	.136	.027	.744	.398	.272	.554	.525	.743	.543	.516
	cornflower	.194	.355	1.000	.378	.694	.344	.188	.531	.405	.393	.725	.145	.440	.735	.279
	primrose	.566	.104	.378	1.000	.206	.782	.656	.164	.692	.612	.256	.015	.070	.186	-.142
	poppy	.111	.672	.694	.206	1.000	.235	.019	.699	.406	.379	.724	.453	.572	.868	.461
	bluebell	.785	.136	.344	.782	.235	1.000	.653	.227	.667	.722	.319	-.015	.189	.243	-.122
	buttercup	.519	.027	.188	.656	.019	.653	1.000	.154	.468	.511	.089	.048	.106	.025	-.204
	wisteria	.206	.744	.531	.164	.699	.227	.154	1.000	.524	.458	.687	.603	.811	.678	.562
	daisy	.697	.398	.405	.692	.406	.667	.468	.524	1.000	.851	.584	.334	.352	.366	.214
	speedwell	.660	.272	.393	.612	.379	.722	.511	.458	.851	1.000	.582	.253	.323	.301	.180
	sweetpea	.205	.554	.725	.256	.724	.319	.089	.687	.584	.582	1.000	.458	.620	.721	.512
	delphinium	.014	.525	.145	.015	.453	-.015	.048	.603	.334	.253	.458	1.000	.556	.397	.719
	aster	.072	.743	.440	.070	.572	.189	.106	.811	.352	.323	.620	.556	1.000	.649	.532
	lavender	.110	.543	.735	.186	.868	.243	.025	.678	.366	.301	.721	.397	.649	1.000	.444
	hellebore	-.126	.516	.279	-.142	.461	-.122	-.204	.562	.214	.180	.512	.719	.532	.444	1.000
Sig. (1-tailed)	celandine		.246	.088	.000	.222	.000	.000	.076	.000	.000	.076	.462	.309	.224	.192
	rose	.246		.006	.236	.000	.173	.427	.000	.002	.028	.000	.000	.000	.000	.000
	cornflower	.088	.006		.003	.000	.007	.095	.000	.002	.002	.000	.158	.001	.000	.025
	primrose	.000	.236	.003		.076	.000	.000	.128	.000	.000	.036	.458	.315	.098	.162
	poppy	.222	.000	.000	.076		.051	.447	.000	.002	.003	.000	.000	.000	.000	.000
	bluebell	.000	.173	.007	.000	.051		.000	.056	.000	.000	.012	.458	.094	.045	.198
	buttercup	.000	.427	.095	.000	.447	.000		.143	.000	.000	.270	.371	.232	.431	.078
	wisteria	.076	.000	.000	.128	.000	.056	.143		.000	.000	.000	.000	.000	.000	.000
	daisy	.000	.002	.002	.000	.002	.000	.000	.000		.000	.000	.009	.006	.004	.068
	speedwell	.000	.028	.002	.000	.003	.000	.000	.000	.000		.000	.038	.011	.017	.106
	sweetpea	.076	.000	.000	.036	.000	.012	.270	.000	.000	.000		.000	.000	.000	.000
	delphinium	.462	.000	.158	.458	.000	.458	.371	.000	.009	.038	.000		.000	.002	.000
	aster	.309	.000	.001	.315	.000	.094	.232	.000	.006	.011	.000	.000		.000	.000
	lavender	.224	.000	.000	.098	.000	.045	.431	.000	.004	.017	.000	.002	.000		.001
	hellebore	.192	.000	.025	.162	.000	.198	.078	.000	.068	.106	.000	.000	.000	.001	

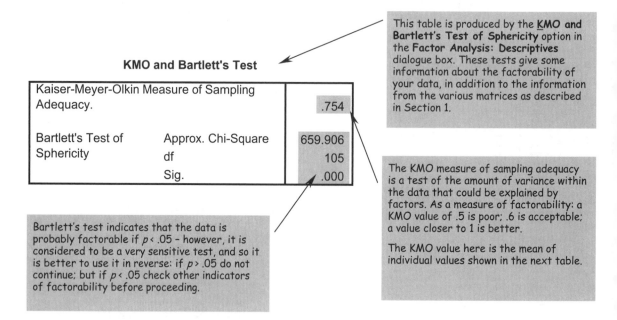

A section of the matrix of correlation coefficients (from the table above): these are the observed correlations, which will later be compared with the reproduced correlations.

		celandine	rose	cornflower	primrose	poppy
Correlation	celandine	1.000	.099	.194	.566	.111
	rose	.099	1.000	.355	.104	.672
	cornflower	.194	.355	1.000	.378	.694
	primrose	.566	.104	.378	1.000	.206
	poppy	.111	.672	.694	.206	1.000
	bluebell	.785	.136	.344	.782	.235
	buttercup	.519	.027	.188	.656	.019
	wisteria	.206	.744	.531	.164	.699
	daisy	.697	.398	.405	.692	.406
	speedwell	.660	.272	.393	.612	.379
	sweetpea	.205	.554	.725	.256	.724
	delphinium	.014	.525	.145	.015	.453
	aster	.072	.743	.440	.070	.572
	lavender	.110	.543	.735	.186	.868
	hellebore	-.126	.516	.279	-.142	.461

Above the diagonal, and mirrored below it, are the observed correlations. Some of the correlations are quite large, indicating that the variables have factorability (.3 is normally considered to be the lower cut-off). If you do the analysis yourself you will be able to see the other correlation coefficients in the complete matrix.

If you selected the **Inverse** option in the **Factor Analysis: Descriptives** dialogue box, then that table would appear here. It is not required for principal components analysis, so we will show it in Section 3.

KMO and Bartlett's Test

Kaiser-Meyer-Olkin Measure of Sampling Adequacy.		.754
Bartlett's Test of Sphericity	Approx. Chi-Square	659.906
	df	105
	Sig.	.000

This table is produced by the **KMO and Bartlett's Test of Sphericity** option in the **Factor Analysis: Descriptives** dialogue box. These tests give some information about the factorability of your data, in addition to the information from the various matrices as described in Section 1.

The KMO measure of sampling adequacy is a test of the amount of variance within the data that could be explained by factors. As a measure of factorability: a KMO value of .5 is poor; .6 is acceptable; a value closer to 1 is better.

The KMO value here is the mean of individual values shown in the next table.

Bartlett's test indicates that the data is probably factorable if $p < .05$ – however, it is considered to be a very sensitive test, and so it is better to use it in reverse: if $p > .05$ do not continue; but if $p < .05$ check other indicators of factorability before proceeding.

This table is produced by the **Anti-image** option in the **Factor Analysis: Descriptives** dialogue box. The upper matrix contains negative partial covariances and the lower matrix contains negative partial correlations. This is the whole table shrunk to fit. Underneath is an annotated section of the lower matrix.

Anti-image Matrices

		celandine	rose	cornflower	primrose	poppy	bluebell	buttercup	wisteria	daisy	speedwell	sweetpea	delphinium	aster	lavender	hellebore
Anti-image Covariance	celandine	.210	-.019	-.043	.091	.021	-.110	.004	-.017	-.076	.005	.055	-.033	.043	-.008	.044
	rose	-.019	.214	.050	-.012	-.096	.005	-.008	-.026	-.036	.068	-.019	.047	-.106	.076	-.049
	cornflower	-.043	.050	.225	-.074	-.036	.036	-.056	-.030	.029	.020	-.106	.112	-.011	-.025	-.061
	primrose	.091	-.012	-.074	.174	.001	-.091	-.058	.022	-.083	.028	.050	-.037	.025	.007	.037
	poppy	.021	-.096	-.036	.001	.112	-.008	.033	-.023	.023	-.047	.004	-.049	.073	-.087	.035
	bluebell	-.110	.005	.036	-.091	-.008	.133	-.041	.021	.044	-.045	-.025	.046	-.035	-.014	-.016
	buttercup	.004	-.008	-.056	-.058	.033	-.041	.398	-.036	.024	-.049	.050	-.098	-.007	.004	.098
	wisteria	-.017	-.026	-.030	.022	-.023	.021	-.036	.190	-.025	-.009	.012	-.027	-.080	.001	-.011
	daisy	-.076	-.036	.029	-.083	.023	.044	.024	-.025	.112	-.071	-.039	-.011	.021	-.024	-.003
	speedwell	.005	.068	.020	.028	-.047	-.045	-.049	-.009	-.071	.152	-.047	.030	-.029	.055	-.035
	sweetpea	.055	-.019	-.106	.050	.004	-.025	.050	.012	-.039	-.047	.187	-.044	-.009	-.017	.005
	delphinium	-.033	.047	.112	-.037	-.049	.046	-.098	-.027	-.011	.030	-.044	.296	-.046	.018	-.187
	aster	.043	-.106	-.011	.025	.073	-.035	-.007	-.080	.021	-.029	-.009	-.046	.179	-.071	.020
	lavender	-.008	.076	-.025	.007	-.087	-.014	.004	.001	-.024	.055	-.017	.018	-.071	.129	-.019
	hellebore	.044	-.049	-.061	.037	.035	-.016	.098	-.011	-.003	-.035	.005	-.187	.020	-.019	.329
Anti-image Correlation	celandine	.667ᵃ	-.090	-.200	.473	.138	-.654	.013	-.085	-.497	.029	.278	-.133	.222	-.050	.168
	rose	-.090	.714ᵃ	.226	-.062	-.618	.028	-.028	-.127	-.234	.379	-.093	.186	-.543	.454	-.184
	cornflower	-.200	.226	.752ᵃ	-.373	-.225	.210	-.187	-.146	.184	.109	-.517	.434	-.057	-.145	-.226
	primrose	.473	-.062	-.373	.660ᵃ	.007	-.597	-.222	.122	-.593	.170	.279	-.162	.142	.044	.156
	poppy	.138	-.618	-.225	.007	.712ᵃ	-.062	.156	-.156	.208	-.358	.027	-.269	.513	-.720	.183
	bluebell	-.654	.028	.210	-.597	-.062	.710ᵃ	-.179	.132	.361	-.313	-.157	.229	-.224	-.105	-.078
	buttercup	.013	-.028	-.187	-.222	.156	-.179	.812ᵃ	-.130	.115	-.198	.184	-.285	-.026	.019	.270
	wisteria	-.085	-.127	-.146	.122	-.156	.132	-.130	.922ᵃ	-.175	-.053	.061	-.114	-.432	.007	-.045
	daisy	-.497	-.234	.184	-.593	.208	.361	.115	-.175	.743ᵃ	-.542	-.267	-.061	.151	-.196	-.017
	speedwell	.029	.379	.109	.170	-.358	-.313	-.198	-.053	-.542	.770ᵃ	-.279	.143	-.174	.395	-.156
	sweetpea	.278	-.093	-.517	.279	.027	-.157	.184	.061	-.267	-.279	.855ᵃ	-.187	-.050	-.111	.019
	delphinium	-.133	.186	.434	-.162	-.269	.229	-.285	-.114	-.061	.143	-.187	.702ᵃ	-.199	.090	-.598
	aster	.222	-.543	-.057	.142	.513	-.224	-.026	-.432	.151	-.174	-.050	-.199	.742ᵃ	-.465	.082
	lavender	-.050	.454	-.145	.044	-.720	-.105	.019	.007	-.196	.395	-.111	.090	-.465	.754ᵃ	-.094
	hellebore	.168	-.184	-.226	.156	.183	-.078	.270	-.045	-.017	-.156	.019	-.598	.082	-.094	.780ᵃ

ᵃ. Measures of Sampling Adequacy(MSA)

A section of the anti-image correlation matrix.

Anti-image Correlation						
	celandine	.667ᵃ	-.090	-.200	.473	.138
	rose	-.090	.714ᵃ	.226	-.062	-.618
	cornflower	-.200	.226	.752ᵃ	-.373	-.225
	primrose	.473	-.062	-.373	.660ᵃ	.007
	poppy	.138	-.618	-.225	.007	.712ᵃ
	bluebell	-.654	.028	.210	-.597	-.062
	buttercup	.013	-.028	-.187	-.222	.156
	wisteria	-.085	-.127	-.146	.122	-.156
	daisy	-.497	-.234	.184	-.593	.208
	speedwell	.029	.379	.109	.170	-.358
	sweetpea	.278	-.093	-.517	.279	.027
	delphinium	-.133	.186	.434	-.162	-.269
	aster	.222	-.543	-.057	.142	.513
	lavender	-.050	.454	-.145	.044	-.720
	hellebore	.168	-.184	-.226	.156	.183

Above the diagonal, and mirrored below it, are the negative partial correlations. Many of these values are small, indicating that there is likely to be a factor structure underlying the variables.

a. Measures of Sampling Adequacy(MSA)

The on-diagonal values in the anti-image correlation matrix are the KMO values for each variable. Thus for the variable "primrose", KMO = .660. If any variable has a KMO value of less than .5, consider dropping it from the analysis. If you carry out the analysis you will see that the KMO for "primrose" is the smallest, so none of the variables need be dropped. The single KMO value, in the KMO and Bartlett's Test table above, is the mean of the KMO value for each of the variables.

The matrices above were all described in Section 1. The remaining tables in this factor analysis output are mostly new to you.

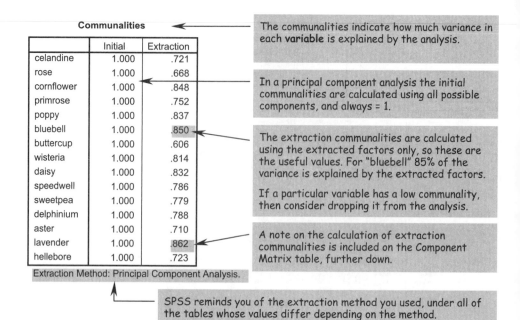

Communalities

	Initial	Extraction
celandine	1.000	.721
rose	1.000	.668
cornflower	1.000	.848
primrose	1.000	.752
poppy	1.000	.837
bluebell	1.000	.850
buttercup	1.000	.606
wisteria	1.000	.814
daisy	1.000	.832
speedwell	1.000	.786
sweetpea	1.000	.779
delphinium	1.000	.788
aster	1.000	.710
lavender	1.000	.862
hellebore	1.000	.723

Extraction Method: Principal Component Analysis.

The communalities indicate how much variance in each **variable** is explained by the analysis.

In a principal component analysis the initial communalities are calculated using all possible components, and always = 1.

The extraction communalities are calculated using the extracted factors only, so these are the useful values. For "bluebell" 85% of the variance is explained by the extracted factors.

If a particular variable has a low communality, then consider dropping it from the analysis.

A note on the calculation of extraction communalities is included on the Component Matrix table, further down.

SPSS reminds you of the extraction method you used, under all of the tables whose values differ depending on the method.

This table summarises the total variance explained by the solution to the factor analysis. Here it is shrunk to fit; each third of it is reproduced below, and annotated.

This is the first part of the output that gives a clear indication of the solution, in terms of how many factors explain how much variance. The previous tables and matrices are important, though, for indicating whether the solution is likely to be a good one.

Total Variance Explained

Component	Initial Eigenvalues			Extraction Sums of Squared Loadings			Rotation Sums of Squared Loadings		
	Total	% of Variance	Cumulative %	Total	% of Variance	Cumulative %	Total	% of Variance	Cumulative %
1	6.810	45.403	45.403	6.810	45.403	45.403	4.355	29.036	29.036
2	3.540	23.602	69.004	3.540	23.602	69.004	3.718	24.787	53.823
3	1.226	8.176	77.180	1.226	8.176	77.180	3.504	23.357	77.180
4	.716	4.773	81.953						
5	.591	3.937	85.890						
6	.419	2.793	88.683						
7	.381	2.538	91.221						
8	.299	1.995	93.216						
9	.252	1.683	94.899						
10	.233	1.555	96.454						
11	.189	1.261	97.716						
12	.139	.924	98.639						
13	.108	.717	99.356						
14	.052	.347	99.703						
15	.045	.297	100.000						

Extraction Method: Principal Component Analysis.

TIP In this type of table the rows relate not to variables but to factors/components.

The three sections of the Total Variance Explained table

Component	Initial Eigenvalues		
	Total	% of Variance	Cumulative %
1	6.810	45.403	45.403
2	3.540	23.602	69.004
3	1.226	8.176	77.180
4	.716	4.773	81.953
5	.591	3.937	85.890
6	.419	2.793	88.683
7	.381	2.538	91.221
8	.299	1.995	93.216
9	.252	1.683	94.899
10	.233	1.555	96.454
11	.189	1.261	97.716
12	.139	.924	98.639
13	.108	.717	99.356
14	.052	.347	99.703
15	.045	.297	100.000

Extraction Method: Principal Component Analysis.

The left-most third of the table contains initial eigenvalues: the eigenvalues for all possible **components**. The components are ranked in order of how much variance each accounts for.

There are 15 possible components: the same as the number of variables entered into the analysis, but that does not mean that each variable is a component.

For each component, the total variance that it explains on its own (its eigenvalue) is followed by the variance that it explains expressed as a percentage of all the variance, then by the cumulative percentage.

Extraction Sums of Squared Loadings		
Total	% of Variance	Cumulative %
6.810	45.403	45.403
3.540	23.602	69.004
1.226	8.176	77.180

The three extracted components together explain 77.2% of the variance.

The middle third of the table contains information for those components with eigenvalue > 1.0: in this example there are three such components.

These values are called extraction values, because they are calculated after extraction of components. Note that in principal component analysis these values are the same as the initial values for these components (the first three rows above).

Rotation Sums of Squared Loadings		
Total	% of Variance	Cumulative %
4.355	29.036	29.036
3.718	24.787	53.823
3.504	23.357	77.180

The right-most third of the table shows the values for the extracted components after rotation has been carried out. (This part of the table will be absent if you did not request rotation.)

Note that the eigenvalues and the relative percentages have changed, but the cumulative percentage of variance explained by all of the extracted components is the same as before rotation.

TIP   The fact that three components have been extracted is nice; to that extent the factor analysis might support our hypothetical aesthete's view. We do not yet know, however, what the factors represent: for example, they could represent not type of flowers but the **colour** of the flowers (pink, blue, and yellow). Nor do we yet know which variables will be associated with which of the factors. So rejoicing should be postponed.

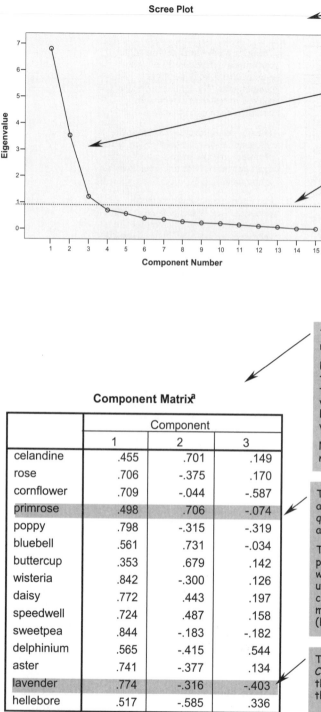

Scree Plot

This graph is produced by the **Scree plot** option in the **Factor Analysis: Extraction** dialogue box. It can be used as an alternative to eigenvalues > 1.0, to decide on which components should be extracted.

In the scree plot the eigenvalues are plotted, in decreasing order. It is called a scree plot because the shape of the curve is reminiscent of the profile of scree that accumulates at the foot of steep hills.

This dotted line, that we have superimposed, indicates the point at which the scree plot "breaks" between the steep and shallow parts of the slope: components above that point would be chosen. In this example, that concurs with the choice made on the basis of selecting factors with eigenvalues greater than 1.
There is some difference of opinion over also including the next factor: see Cooper (2002, p. 124-125) for discussion.

This is a table of the factor loadings **before** the rotation is carried out.

Each column shows the loading of each variable on that component. The loading can be thought of as the correlation between the component and the variable: thus the larger the number, the more likely it is that the component underlies that variable.

Note that some loadings are positive and some negative: we will mention this issue in Section 3.

Component Matrix^a

	Component		
	1	2	3
celandine	.455	.701	.149
rose	.706	-.375	.170
cornflower	.709	-.044	-.587
primrose	.498	.706	-.074
poppy	.798	-.315	-.319
bluebell	.561	.731	-.034
buttercup	.353	.679	.142
wisteria	.842	-.300	.126
daisy	.772	.443	.197
speedwell	.724	.487	.158
sweetpea	.844	-.183	-.182
delphinium	.565	-.415	.544
aster	.741	-.377	.134
lavender	.774	-.316	-.403
hellebore	.517	-.585	.336

Extraction Method: Principal Component Analysis.

a. 3 components extracted.

The variable "primrose" has:
a medium loading (.498) on the first component;
quite a strong loading (.706) on the second;
and a very low loading (-.074) on the third.

These loadings may be useful for seeing the pattern of which variables load most strongly onto which factors: almost always a rotation will be used, however, and then the pattern becomes clearer. In particular, the negative loadings here may be an artefact of the method of calculation (Kline, 1994, p. 39).

The extraction communalities, in the Communalities table above, are calculated using the formula Σx^2, where x is the factor loadings in this table. Thus for "lavender":

$$(.774)^2 + (-.316)^2 + (-.403)^2 = .862$$

As stated above, the size of the communality indicates how much of that variable's variance is explained by the solution to the factor analysis.

This table is produced by the **Reproduced** option in the **Factor Analysis: Descriptives** dialogue box. The upper matrix contains the reproduced correlations and the lower matrix contains the residuals. This is the whole table shrunk to fit. Underneath is an annotated section of each matrix.

Reproduced Correlations

		celandine	rose	cornflower	primrose	poppy	bluebell	buttercup	wisteria	daisy	speedwell	sweetpea	delphinium	aster	lavender	hellebore
Reproduced Correlation	celandine	.721[b]	.084	.205	.711	.095	.763	.658	.192	.692	.694	.229	.048	.093	.071	-.125
	rose	.084	.668[b]	.417	.074	.627	.116	.019	.728	.412	.355	.634	.647	.688	.597	.642
	cornflower	.205	.417	.848[b]	.366	.766	.386	.137	.536	.412	.399	.713	.099	.463	.799	.195
	primrose	.711	.074	.366	.752[b]	.199	.798	.645	.198	.683	.693	.305	-.052	.093	.193	-.180
	poppy	.095	.627	.766	.199	.837[b]	.228	.023	.726	.414	.374	.789	.408	.667	.846	.490
	bluebell	.763	.116	.386	.798	.228	.850[b]	.690	.249	.750	.756	.346	-.005	.136	.217	-.149
	buttercup	.658	.019	.137	.645	.023	.690	.606[b]	.112	.602	.609	.148	-.005	.025	.002	-.167
	wisteria	.192	.728	.536	.198	.726	.249	.112	.814[b]	.542	.483	.743	.669	.754	.696	.653
	daisy	.692	.412	.412	.683	.414	.750	.602	.542	.832[b]	.806	.535	.360	.432	.378	.207
	speedwell	.694	.355	.399	.693	.374	.756	.609	.483	.806	.786[b]	.494	.293	.374	.343	.143
	sweetpea	.229	.634	.713	.305	.789	.346	.148	.743	.535	.494	.779[b]	.454	.671	.785	.483
	delphinium	.048	.647	.099	-.052	.408	-.005	-.005	.669	.360	.293	.454	.788[b]	.648	.349	.718
	aster	.093	.688	.463	.093	.667	.136	.025	.754	.432	.374	.671	.648	.710[b]	.639	.649
	lavender	.071	.597	.799	.193	.846	.217	.002	.696	.378	.343	.785	.349	.639	.862[b]	.450
	hellebore	-.125	.642	.195	-.180	.490	-.149	-.167	.653	.207	.143	.483	.718	.649	.450	.723[b]
Residual [a]	celandine		.016	-.010	-.145	.016	.022	-.139	.014	.005	-.035	-.024	-.034	-.021	.039	-.001
	rose	.016		-.063	.030	.045	.020	.008	.016	-.015	-.084	-.080	-.122	.055	-.054	-.126
	cornflower	-.010	-.063		.012	-.072	-.041	.051	-.005	-.007	-.006	.012	.045	-.024	-.064	.084
	primrose	-.145	.030	.012		.007	-.016	.011	-.035	.009	-.081	-.049	.067	-.024	-.007	.038
	poppy	.016	.045	-.072	.007		.006	-.003	-.027	-.007	.005	-.065	.045	-.096	.022	-.029
	bluebell	.022	.020	-.041	-.016	.006		-.037	-.021	-.083	-.035	-.027	-.011	.053	.026	.026
	buttercup	-.139	.008	.051	.011	-.003	-.037		.042	-.134	-.097	-.060	.052	.081	.023	-.037
	wisteria	.014	.016	-.005	-.035	-.027	-.021	.042		-.018	-.025	-.055	-.065	.057	-.018	-.091
	daisy	.005	-.015	-.007	.009	-.007	-.083	-.134	-.018		.045	.049	-.026	-.079	-.012	.007
	speedwell	-.035	-.084	-.006	-.081	.005	-.035	-.097	-.025	.045		.089	-.040	-.051	-.042	.037
	sweetpea	-.024	-.080	.012	-.049	-.065	-.027	-.060	-.055	.049	.089		.004	-.051	-.064	.029
	delphinium	-.034	-.122	.045	.067	.045	-.011	.052	-.065	-.026	-.040	.004		-.092	.048	.001
	aster	-.021	.055	-.024	-.024	-.096	.053	.081	.057	-.079	-.051	-.051	-.092		.010	-.117
	lavender	.039	-.054	-.064	-.007	.022	.026	.023	-.018	-.012	-.042	-.064	.048	.010		-.006
	hellebore	-.001	-.126	.084	.038	-.029	.026	-.037	-.091	.007	.037	.029	.001	-.117	-.006	

Extraction Method: Principal Component Analysis.

a. Residuals are computed between observed and reproduced correlations. There are 35 (33.0%) nonredundant residuals with absolute values greater than 0.05.

b. Reproduced communalities

	celandine	rose	cornflower	primrose
celandine	.721[b]	.084	.205	.711
rose	.084	.668[b]	.417	.074
cornflower	.205	.417	.848[b]	.366
primrose	.711	.074	.366	.752[b]
poppy	.095	.627	.766	.199
bluebell	.763	.116	.386	.798
buttercup	.658	.019	.137	.645

This is part of the reproduced correlations matrix. Compare this value, of .711 for "primrose" with "celandine", with the **observed** correlation of .566 between those two variables (see Correlation Matrix table above). The values are not very similar. Another point to note is that the factor analysis gives a stronger relationship between the two.

The diagonal holds the reproduced communalities. They are the same values as the extraction communalities in the Communalities table above.

celandine		.016	-.010	-.145
rose	.016		-.063	.030
cornflower	-.010	-.063		.012
primrose	-.145	.030	.012	
poppy	.016	.045	-.072	.007
bluebell	.022	.020	-.041	-.016
buttercup	-.139	.008	.051	.011

Rather than do the comparison suggested above, one can simply inspect the residuals. The residual for "primrose" with "celandine" is -.145 (the negative sign indicates that the reproduced correlation is the stronger as mentioned above.) That is a fairly large residual but if you inspect the other residuals in the whole matrix on your own screen, you will see that they are mostly small. The small size of most of the residuals is another indication of factorability, and it is also an indication of a good factor analysis solution.

TIP Note that the contents of the Reproduced Correlations table are calculated after the factor extraction has been carried out and so the values will vary depending on how many factors were extracted.

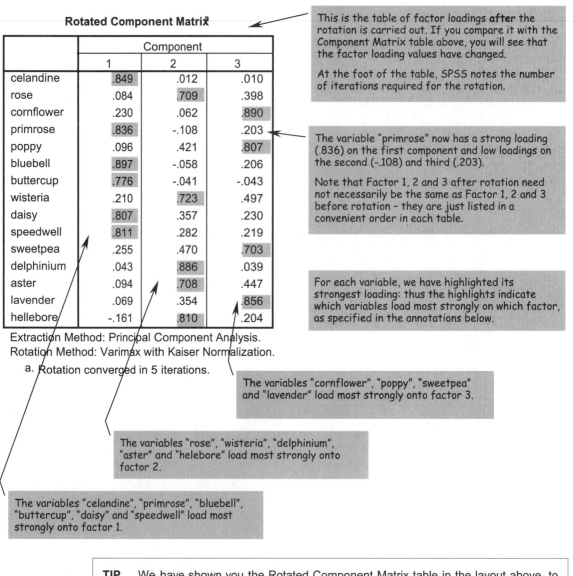

Rotated Component Matrix

	Component		
	1	2	3
celandine	.849	.012	.010
rose	.084	.709	.398
cornflower	.230	.062	.890
primrose	.836	-.108	.203
poppy	.096	.421	.807
bluebell	.897	-.058	.206
buttercup	.776	-.041	-.043
wisteria	.210	.723	.497
daisy	.807	.357	.230
speedwell	.811	.282	.219
sweetpea	.255	.470	.703
delphinium	.043	.886	.039
aster	.094	.708	.447
lavender	.069	.354	.856
hellebore	-.161	.810	.204

Extraction Method: Principal Component Analysis.
Rotation Method: Varimax with Kaiser Normalization.

a. Rotation converged in 5 iterations.

This is the table of factor loadings **after** the rotation is carried out. If you compare it with the Component Matrix table above, you will see that the factor loading values have changed.

At the foot of the table, SPSS notes the number of iterations required for the rotation.

The variable "primrose" now has a strong loading (.836) on the first component and low loadings on the second (-.108) and third (.203).

Note that Factor 1, 2 and 3 after rotation need not necessarily be the same as Factor 1, 2 and 3 before rotation – they are just listed in a convenient order in each table.

For each variable, we have highlighted its strongest loading: thus the highlights indicate which variables load most strongly on which factor, as specified in the annotations below.

The variables "cornflower", "poppy", "sweetpea" and "lavender" load most strongly onto factor 3.

The variables "rose", "wisteria", "delphinium", "aster" and "helebore" load most strongly onto factor 2.

The variables "celandine", "primrose", "bluebell", "buttercup", "daisy" and "speedwell" load most strongly onto factor 1.

TIP We have shown you the Rotated Component Matrix table in the layout above, to demonstrate all of the factor loadings. SPSS will, however, display output in a more easily interpretable layout. See description of **Options** dialogue box in Section 3.

Component Transformation Matrix

Component	1	2	3
1	.521	.586	.621
2	.836	-.499	-.230
3	.175	.639	-.749

Extraction Method: Principal Component Analysis.
Rotation Method: Varimax with Kaiser Normalization.

This table is for information only; it shows the factor transformation matrix that was used to carry out the rotation used to derive the rotated factors. The mathematical/algebraic aspects are beyond the scope of this book. See texts recommended in Section 1.

Under this and the previous table, SPSS reminds you of the rotation method that you used.

Once you have inspected the Rotated Component Matrix table, above, to see which variables load on which factors, you can decide on a suitable name to describe each factor. The extracted factors may, or may not, be the same as the factors that you suggested before you started the survey. If we now compare the pattern of loadings in the table with the aesthete's initial suggestion we can see that there is close agreement, with just one variable on a different factor. Use caution, however: the dimensions that were suggested (liking for **types** of flower) may not be the true factors. To be more sure you should very carefully check the characteristics of the questions/items that measure your variables, and consider all possibilities and alternative explanations. In the results section of a report, you could write about the outcome of the analysis as shown below. You could incorporate more tables (e.g., the rotated component matrix) or values (e.g., the factor loadings; KMO) to illustrate your points as necessary. If you have used principal component analysis, then do ensure that you refer to that and not factor analysis in your report.

In the report you could write: The data were analysed by means of a principal component analysis, with varimax rotation. The various indicators of factorability were good, and the residuals indicate that the solution was a good one. Three components with an eigenvalue of greater than 1.0 were found; the scree plot also indicated three components. The components can be thought of as representing liking for different types of flowers: component 1 – wild flowers; component 2 – formal garden flowers; component 3 – cottage garden flowers. The components and the variables that load on them are shown in Table 11.1.

Table 11.1
The components found by the principal component analysis, and the variables that load on them.

Component 1	Component 2	Component 3
celandine	rose	cornflower
primrose	wisteria	poppy
bluebell	delphinium	sweetpea
buttercup	aster	lavender
daisy	hellebore	
speedwell		

> **TIP** Remember that the survey we used to illustrate factor analysis is fictitious, and we do not know what you would find if you carried out this study.

Section 3: Other aspects of factor analysis

OTHER OPTIONS FROM DESCRIPTIVES DIALOGUE BOX

Determinant

This option is in the Correlation Matrix section of the **Factor Analysis: Descriptives** dialogue box. If you select it, the value of the determinant will be printed underneath the Correlation Matrix table, as shown below. Its value is an indication of whether factor analysis methods other than principal component analysis can be used. Its value must not be zero. If it is zero, the correlation matrix cannot be inverted: see below.

delphinium	.462	.000
aster	.309	.000
lavender	.224	.000
hellebore	.192	.000

a. Determinant = 2.29E-007

> The determinant will be printed at the bottom left of the Correlation Matrix table. NOTE: the determinant may be printed to three decimal places, instead of in exponential format. Thus this determinant would appear as .000. See Tip

> **TIP**   Whether the determinant is printed to three decimal places or in exponential format depends on the setting on the **Edit**, **Options**, General tab, EXCEPT that in Version 12, the determinant is printed to three decimal places regardless of that setting.

Inverse

This option produces the Inverse of Correlation Matrix, a complete matrix for all the variables. A section of it is shown below.

Inverse of Correlation Matrix

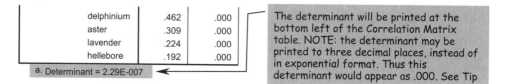

	celandine	rose	cornflower	primrose	poppy	bluebell	buttercup	wisteria
celandine	4.755	-.425	-.918	2.469	.897	-3.904	.046	-.425
rose	-.425	4.672	1.030	-.323	-3.984	.165	-.097	-.627
cornflower	-.918	1.030	4.450					704
primrose	2.469	-.323	-1.885					670
poppy	.897	-3.984	-1.414					070
bluebell	-3.904	.165	1.213					326
buttercup	.046	-.097	-.625					474
wisteria	-.425	-.627	-.704					260
daisy	-3.244	-1.513	1.158					197
speedwell	.162	2.102	.588	1.044	-2.737	-2.198	-.805	-.313

The values in this table (obtained by inverting the correlation matrix) are used in the calculations of many methods of factor extraction other than principal component analysis. If this table cannot be obtained (see above) then those methods cannot be applied.

The details of matrix determinants and inverses are not covered in this book. See Tabachnick and Fidell (2001, pp. 913–14).

OTHER OPTIONS FROM EXTRACTION DIALOGUE BOX

Method

You can choose from the various methods of extracting factors that SPSS allows. To make a sensible choice you will need to read up about each of the methods. Here we make just a few points.

Principal component analysis, shown in Section 2, tends to be the most robust method. Remember, though, that components are distinct from factors (Kline, 1994) and that principal component analysis and factor analysis are somewhat different things. Nonetheless, with large matrices there is little difference between the solutions from different methods (Kline, 1994). Furthermore, if a factor analysis solution is stable, then you should obtain similar results regardless of the extraction method used (Tabachnick and Fidell, 2001). Cooper (2002), however, stresses that as principal component analysis always gives larger loadings than other methods, some rules of thumb may be misleading with this method.

The SPSS output from each of the other methods looks very similar to the output from principal component analysis. The values in the particular tables that show the results of the factor extraction will, of course, differ at least slightly between methods. Some other differences and similarities are:

1. The word "component" is replaced by the word "factor" for all other methods.
2. The same tables are produced, except that for both generalised least squares and maximum likelihood methods, SPSS prints a Goodness-of-fit Test table that can be used to test hypotheses about the number of factors. See Kline (1994) for information about the goodness-of-fit test. If you change the number of factors to be extracted, then you may also need to increase the **Maximum Iterations for Convergence** in the **Factor Analysis: Extraction** dialogue box to allow the Goodness-of-fit Test table to be produced.
3. Communalities table:
   a. Initial communalities have a value of 1.0 in principal component analysis. In all other methods they are less than 1.0, because those methods explain the variance that is shared between all the variables (common variance) and attempt to eliminate other variance (error variance and unique variance).
   b. Extraction communalities are calculated from the factor matrix in the same way as they are from the component matrix, except for generalised least squares.
4. Total Variance Explained table:
   a. The Initial Eigenvalues part of the table will hold the same values for **all** methods of extraction because it shows how **all** of the variance can be explained.

b. In the Extraction Sums of Squared Loadings part of the table, for principal component analysis the row values are identical to the Initial row values for each component because that method explains all of the variance for the extracted factors. For the other methods the row values here differ from the Initial row values because these methods explain common variance and eliminate other variance.

Extract options

Two mutually exclusive options by which you can affect how many factors will be extracted are presented in the lower half of the **Factor Analysis: Extraction** dialogue box. The first option is to change the minimum eigenvalue, normally set at 1. The eigenvalue varies according to the number of variables entered, so it is not a robust guide for the number of factors to extract. The second option is to set the number of factors (you could do that after inspecting the scree plot).

Either of these options may be useful for your final analysis or for the purpose of obtaining information on more of the initial factors. You will need to use one of those options if you wish to inspect "extracted factor" information (e.g., the factor loadings) for more factors than the default values will extract. That information may also be useful if you want to compare factors from your data with those obtained in previous research on the same variables. In any report you should comment on how the number of factors to be extracted was decided upon.

OTHER OPTIONS FROM ROTATION DIALOGUE BOX

Method

The default setting is **None**, for no rotation. The technique of rotation, however, was devised in order to simplify the solution to the factor analysis. Thus, you would normally select one of the rotation methods that SPSS allows, from the **Factor Analysis: Rotation** dialogue box. A broad distinction is between orthogonal rotation methods (**Varimax**, **Eqamax**, and **Quartimax**) and oblique rotation methods (**Direct Oblimin** and **Promax**). Orthogonal methods give factors that are not correlated with one another, whereas oblique methods do allow correlations between factors. Again, to make a sensible choice you will need to read up about each of the methods.

If in doubt, select **Varimax**. It is normally thought to give rotated factors that are most easy to interpret. Kline (1994) points out that psychology constructs may well be correlated with one another. He recommends, if you do need one of the oblique rotation methods, using **Direct <u>O</u>blimin**. The output for **Direct <u>O</u>blimin** varies somewhat from that for **<u>V</u>arimax**:

1. In Total Variance Explained table, the Rotation section only has a Total column.
2. The Rotated Component Matrix table is replaced by two tables, the Pattern Matrix and the Structure Matrix. The Pattern Matrix is the easier to use when determining which variables load most strongly on which component/factor. For more information, use Results Coach from those tables (see end of Section 3, Chapter 12).

Display

If you select a rotation method, then **<u>R</u>otated solution** is also selected; you can unselect it, but it provides the tables that contain the solution!

If you select **<u>L</u>oading plot(s)**, SPSS draws a graph of the variables on the factor axes (up to a maximum of three factors). If you have requested a rotation, then the axes represent the rotated factors.

FACTOR ANALYSIS: OPTIONS DIALOGUE BOX

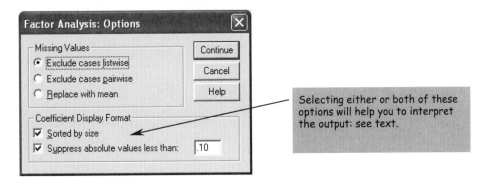

Coefficient Display Format

Two useful options here can make the output much more easy to interpret. If you select **<u>S</u>orted by size** then, in the Component/Factor Matrix and the Rotated Component/Factor Matrix tables, the variables will be sorted according to their factor loading size for each factor. If you select **<u>S</u>uppress absolute values less than**, then small factor loadings will be omitted from those tables. Once you have selected that option the number can be changed, but the default of .10 seems sensible. You could try those options, and compare your output with the tables we have shown in Section 2.

NEGATIVE AND POSITIVE FACTOR LOADINGS

Just as bivariate correlation coefficients can be positive or negative, so can factor loadings. A trivial example is when an item that taps a particular psychological construct is reversed (to avoid participant response bias). Such items should be reversed before analysis (see Chapter 6, Section 10). For factor loadings after rotation, you should note whether they are negative or positive. Before rotation, negative loadings may be an artefact of the method of calculation used to extract factors (Kline, 1994, p. 39).

R FACTOR ANALYSIS

R factor analysis is regular factor analysis, carried out on correlations between variables, as we have described in this chapter. There are other types of factor analysis in which other things are factored. For example, Q factor analysis uses correlations between participants (the rows and columns in the data file have to be reversed). More information on this and other types of factor analysis can be found in Kline (1994).

Section 4: Reliability analysis for scales and questionnaires

Anyone can produce a scale, and if the guidelines on writing items available in the literature are followed then the individual items should be acceptable. There are many existing psychological scales, however, and it is unlikely that you cannot find one that assesses the construct/s in which you are interested. Moreover, it is considered better to use an existing scale than to produce another, as researchers can then compare findings from different samples and situations. For many existing scales, reliability information has been published. Nonetheless, cultural differences, or changes in language over time, or simply sample and situation differences, may affect a scale. Thus whether you are constructing a scale or using an existing one, it is good practice to analyse the data for reliability and dimensionality. Many issues surrounding use of scales are beyond the scope of this book. We recommend: Cooper (2002, particularly Chapters 4 and 17); Fife-Schaw (2000); Hammond (2000); and John & Benet-Martinez (2000). Here we only consider measurement of reliability, and of dimensionality (Section 5).

Test/retest reliability involves testing the same participants with the same scale on two separate occasions, and obtaining the correlation between the two sets of scores. It assesses the stability across time of a scale. Parallel forms, or parallel tests, describes the situation in which more than one version of a scale is available, designed to measure the same construct. To assess how similar they are, one would administer them to the same participants at the same time and correlate the scores. Internal consistency is the type of reliability that we are concerned with in this Section.

INTERNAL CONSISTENCY

If items within a scale are intended to measure aspects of the same construct, then they should all be fairly strongly correlated with each other. One way of assessing this is to correlate every item with each of the other items and inspect the matrix. Measures of internal consistency have been developed, however, which **greatly** simplify this process. *Split-half reliability* is an early measure, in which responses for two halves of the items are summed and then the correlation between them is calculated. Which items should go in which half, however, is a matter of debate. *Cronbach's alpha*, also called coefficient alpha, became easy to obtain with increasing computer power. It is related to the mean correlation between each pair of items and the number of items in the scale. It is the most commonly reported measure, with a rule of thumb that a scale should have a minimum Cronbach's alpha value of .7. It does have drawbacks, however. For example, even if a scale does have a high alpha, individual items may be poorly correlated with the others. Thus we should also inspect other information in the SPSS output. In the annotations below we describe how to use three particular values, which are provided for each item. Firstly, the *part-whole correlation* (or *item-total correlation*) which is the correlation between each item and the sum of the other items. Secondly, the *squared multiple correlation* for each item: that is, the R^2 obtained if the item is entered into a multiple regression as the criterion variable with all the other items as predictor variables. Thirdly, the value of Cronbach's alpha for the scale if a particular item is deleted.

In addition to reliability, one should also assess whether a scale is uni-dimensional (see Section 5).

HOW TO PERFORM A RELIABILITY ANALYSIS

Before you start on this Section, you should run through Chapter 6, Section 10. You will need data file ScaleV3.sav, saved in the last exercise in that Section. Remember that normally you would need many more cases.

We have demonstrated the use of two ways of measuring reliability.

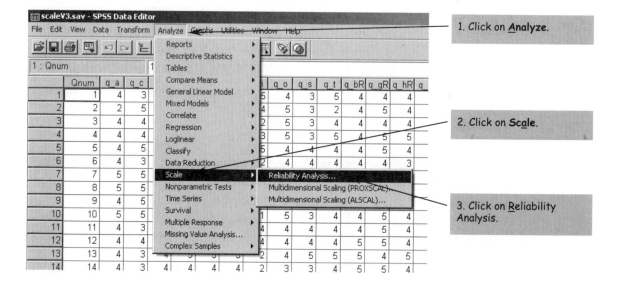

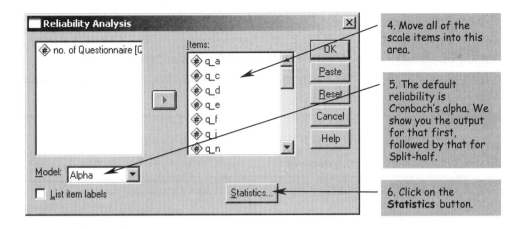

4. Move all of the scale items into this area.

5. The default reliability is Cronbach's alpha. We show you the output for that first, followed by that for Split-half.

6. Click on the Statistics button.

TIP The **Reliability Analysis: Statistics** dialogue box has a number of useful options for the purpose of checking scales. Otherwise SPSS only gives output for the reliability measure that you request under **Model**.

---

7. Select the options shown.

Note: we have selected the Inter-Item: Correlations as this generates useful output in addition to the correlation matrix itself. We will not show the matrix.

8. Click on **Continue**, then on **OK**. The output is shown on the next page.

Obtained Using Menu Item: **Sc**<u>a</u>**le** > **<u>R</u>eliability Analysis** (Model = Alpha)

Reliability

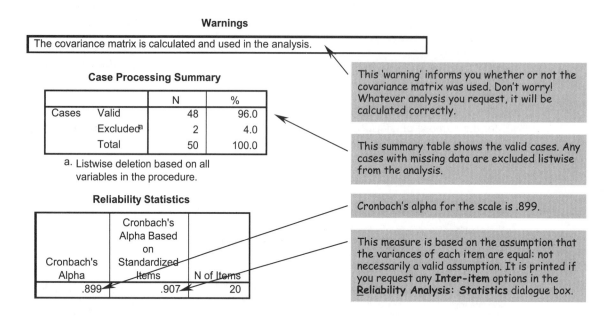

Warnings

The covariance matrix is calculated and used in the analysis.

This 'warning' informs you whether or not the covariance matrix was used. Don't worry! Whatever analysis you request, it will be calculated correctly.

Case Processing Summary

		N	%
Cases	Valid	48	96.0
	Excluded^a	2	4.0
	Total	50	100.0

a. Listwise deletion based on all variables in the procedure.

This summary table shows the valid cases. Any cases with missing data are excluded listwise from the analysis.

Reliability Statistics

Cronbach's Alpha	Cronbach's Alpha Based on Standardized Items	N of Items
.899	.907	20

Cronbach's alpha for the scale is .899.

*This measure is based on the assumption that the variances of each item are equal: not necessarily a valid assumption. It is printed if you request any **Inter-item** options in the **Reliability Analysis: Statistics** dialogue box.*

*The subsequent tables are obtained from options in the **Reliability Analysis: Statistics** dialogue box.*

Item Statistics

	Mean	Std. Deviation	N
q_a	3.96	.849	48
q_c	3.90	1.036	48
q_d	4.27	.707	48
q_e	4.46	.651	48
q_f	4.02	1.062	48
q_j	4.33	.883	48
q_n	3.69	1.114	48

*This table (a section only shown here) is from the **Descriptives for: Item** option.*

*We requested Inter-Item: Correlations in the **Reliability Analysis: Statistics** dialogue box above. A table called the Inter-Item Correlation Matrix is produced, and would normally appear here. We have omitted it, but you could inspect those correlations.*

Item-Total Statistics

	Scale Mean if Item Deleted	Scale Variance if Item Deleted	Corrected Item-Total Correlation	Squared Multiple Correlation	Cronbach's Alpha if Item Deleted
q_a	72.85	107.106	.546	.726	.894
q_c	72.92	106.418	.465	.842	.897
q_d	72.54	108.041	.605	.783	.893
q_e	72.35	108.617	.618	.700	.894
q_f	72.79	101.147	.710	.751	.889
q_j	72.48	105.148	.635	.813	.892
q_n	73.13	114.707	.062	.380	.910
q_o	72.58	108.248	.530	.821	.895
q_s	73.46	112.466	.240	.378	.902
q_t	72.94	106.060	.467	.785	.897
q_bR	72.85	106.766	.515	.720	.895
q_gR	72.42	106.121	.710	.769	.891
q_hR	73.02	106.489	.678	.794	.892
q_iR	73.23	105.329	.550	.761	.894
q_kR	73.21	102.722	.590	.869	.893
q_lR	72.90	103.797	.600	.733	.892
q_mR	73.79	103.530	.555	.782	.894
q_pR	72.85	106.425	.630	.695	.892
q_qR	73.81	105.219	.554	.771	.894
q_rR	73.31	106.517	.601	.615	.893

For item "q_n", there are strong indications that it is not a consistent part of the scale: the part-whole correlation is very low (.062), R^2 is also low (.38), and Cronbach's alpha is increased to .91 when this item is deleted. Thus this item would be a very strong candidate for either being deleted from the scale, or being rewritten.

Note: Cronbach's alpha including "q_n" is .899 (shown in output above). That is well above the rule of thumb of .7 for a reliable scale. Thus this example is a good illustration of the point that Cronbach's alpha alone may be insufficient to be sure of reliability.

Scale Statistics

Mean	Variance	Std. Deviation	N of Items
76.81	117.432	10.837	20

This table of descriptives, for the sum of responses for the whole scale for each participant, is from the **Descriptives for: Scale** option.

Acting on the results

If this was the final scale, you could write: Cronbach's alpha for the ATR scale from the current sample was .899. If you were assessing the scale, you would also describe other attributes from the SPSS output. For these results, however, you would consider deleting or rewriting item "q_n", probably item "q_s", and possibly others. If you delete items, you must repeat the reliability analyses on the remaining items. Additionally you should consider dimensionality of the scale (Section 5).

Obtained Using Menu Item: **Sc<u>a</u>le** > **<u>R</u>eliability Analysis** (Model = Split-half)

At Step 5 above, select Split-half instead of Alpha. Only those tables that differ from the output previously illustrated are shown here.

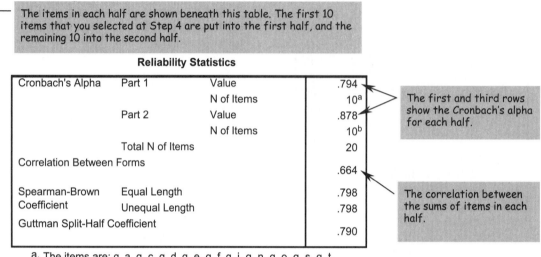

The items in each half are shown beneath this table. The first 10 items that you selected at Step 4 are put into the first half, and the remaining 10 into the second half.

Reliability Statistics

Cronbach's Alpha	Part 1	Value	.794
		N of Items	10[a]
	Part 2	Value	.878
		N of Items	10[b]
	Total N of Items		20
Correlation Between Forms			.664
Spearman-Brown Coefficient	Equal Length		.798
	Unequal Length		.798
Guttman Split-Half Coefficient			.790

The first and third rows show the Cronbach's alpha for each half.

The correlation between the sums of items in each half.

a. The items are: q_a, q_c, q_d, q_e, q_f, q_j, q_n, q_o, q_s, q_t.

b. The items are: q_bR, q_gR, q_hR, q_iR, q_kR, q_lR, q_mR, q_pR, q_qR, q_rR.

TIP You can control which items go into which half by moving the variable names across one at a time, at Step 4 above, in the order you wish. This procedure can be very useful if you wish to compare different combinations of items. For reliability, however, Cronbach's alpha is the most commonly used.

The Scale Statistics table holds descriptives for the sum of responses from each half, in addition to those for the whole scale.

Scale Statistics

	Mean	Variance	Std. Deviation	N of Items
Part 1	40.08	29.142	5.398	10[a]
Part 2	36.73	41.904	6.473	10[b]
Both Parts	76.81	117.432	10.837	20

a. The items are: q_a, q_c, q_d, q_e, q_f, q_j, q_n, q_o, q_s, q_t.

b. The items are: q_bR, q_gR, q_hR, q_iR, q_kR, q_lR, q_mR, q_pR, q_qR, q_rR.

Section 5: Dimensionality of scales and questionnaires

We will describe two ways in which you can use an analysis of the dimensionality of a scale. Relevant references are given at the beginning of Section 4. Firstly, if you want a scale in which all items assess a single construct, you can assess how strongly each item loads onto a single component. Weakly loading items would be discarded or rewritten. Secondly, to assess whether there is more than one construct underlying the scale, you can carry out a component or factor analysis to determine the structure. You could then use the items that load strongly on separate components as sub-scales. (You would need to assess the reliability of each sub-scale separately.) Ensuring that a scale is uni-dimensional, or that sub-scales are identified, is an aspect of construct validity.

Before you work through this section, you should be familiar with the content of Sections 1 to 3 in this chapter. Also, if you have not yet done so, you should run through Chapter 6, Section 10, as you will need data file ScaleV3.sav, from the last exercise in that Section. We will show you the procedure with principal component analysis, but it may be more appropriate to use a factor analysis; for example, alpha factoring. Remember that normally you would need many more cases, and with the data file that we are using alpha factoring does not converge when one factor is requested.

TO IDENTIFY THOSE ITEMS THAT LOAD ON A SINGLE COMPONENT

Enter the items into a principal component analysis (Section 2 above). For this purpose, the only settings you need to make are as follows.
1. in the **Factor Analysis: Extraction** dialogue box set the **Number of factors** to 1.
2. in the **Factor Analysis: Options** dialogue box, select for **Sorted by size**.
   The two tables important for this purpose are shown next.

Total Variance Explained

Component	Initial Eigenvalues			Extraction Sums of Squared Loadings		
	Total	% of Variance	Cumulative %	Total	% of Variance	Cumulative %
1	7.654	38.272	38.272	7.654	38.272	38.272
2	2.416	12.081	50.353			
3	1.463	7.313	57.666			

Note: the largest component explains only 38% of the variance.

Component Matrix^a

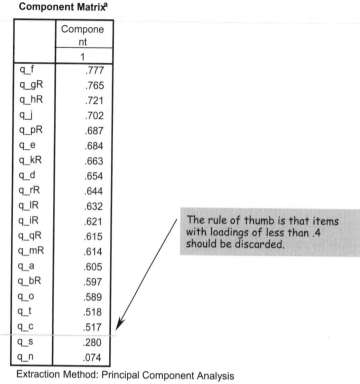

	Component
	1
q_f	.777
q_gR	.765
q_hR	.721
q_j	.702
q_pR	.687
q_e	.684
q_kR	.663
q_d	.654
q_rR	.644
q_lR	.632
q_iR	.621
q_qR	.615
q_mR	.614
q_a	.605
q_bR	.597
q_o	.589
q_t	.518
q_c	.517
q_s	.280
q_n	.074

The rule of thumb is that items with loadings of less than .4 should be discarded.

Extraction Method: Principal Component Analysis

a. 1 components extracted.

Acting on the results

From this analysis, we would either discard items "q_s" and "q_n", or rewrite them. Note that these items were also identified in the reliability analysis (Item-Total Statistics table above).

If items are **discarded**, another analysis should be carried out on the data for the remaining items, as factor loadings will change somewhat. For these data, you will find that the variance explained by the largest component increases to 42%, and the loadings of the 18 items remain above .5. You could then use the scale data (for the 18 items) in other analyses, as long as you cite the reliability and dimensionality results in your report. You must be aware, however, that another sample may give different reliability and dimensionality results.

If items are **rewritten**, data from a new sample must be collected with the new version of the scale. Data from the new version must then be subjected to reliability and dimensionality analyses. Thus scale construction/modification is an iterative process.

Enter all 20 items into a principal component analysis or factor analysis. For this purpose, we carried out the analysis in the way described in Section 2, except that in the **Factor Analysis: Options** dialogue box, we selected for **Sorted by size**. Only some of the tables from this analysis are shown here: see Section 2 for a description of all of the output.

Check the indicators of factorability (described in Section 2). Some of them are reasonable. The KMO value, however, is only .594. Also some of the individual KMO values, in the diagonal of the Anti-Image Correlation matrix, are well below the value of .5 that indicates poor performance of individual items.

The sections, below, of the Total Variance Explained table shows that there were six components with eigenvalue greater than one. It also shows the percentage of variance explained by each component after rotation.

Total Variance Explained

Component	Extraction Sums of Squared Loadings			Rotation Sums of Squared Loadings		
	Total	% of Variance	Cumulative %	Total	% of Variance	Cumulative %
1	7.654	38.272	38.272	4.337	21.683	21.683
2	2.416	12.081	50.353	3.433	17.164	38.847
3	1.463	7.313	57.666	2.669	13.346	52.193
4	1.185	5.924	63.590	1.747	8.736	60.929
5	1.099	5.495	69.085	1.432	7.158	68.087
6	1.059	5.297	74.381	1.259	6.295	74.381

The Scree plot shows just two components above the break between the steep and shallow parts of the curve.

Scree Plot

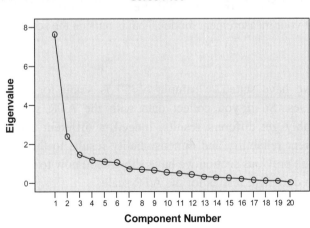

In the Rotated Component Matrix table, below, the heaviest loadings for each item are highlighted. Fourteen of the 20 items load most strongly on one of the first two components, with three items on the third. The last three components each have only one item with heaviest loading: note that items "q_n" and "q_s" are here.

Rotated Component Matrix^a

	Component					
	1	2	3	4	5	6
q_hR	.836	.107	.165	.321	-.109	.034
q_iR	.820	.012	.019	.282	.140	-.087
q_bR	.735	.296	.048	-.110	-.001	-.239
q_f	.698	.233	.362	.166	.065	-.022
q_mR	.690	.411	-.183	-.020	.130	.257
q_qR	.674	-.024	.371	-.061	.364	-.014
q_gR	.508	.305	.478	.032	.297	.126
q_rR	.175	.783	.133	.027	.084	.249
q_kR	.602	.626	.015	-.109	-.193	-.059
q_a	.044	.613	.255	.496	-.047	-.054
q_pR	.241	.608	.178	.152	.428	-.001
q_j	.333	.589	.302	.189	-.032	-.166
q_d	.056	.579	.303	.570	-.009	.140
q_lR	.198	.483	.364	.067	.206	.380
q_o	.244	.006	.805	.266	.040	.075
q_c	-.023	.329	.768	.019	-.024	.182
q_e	.118	.476	.643	.128	.222	-.151
q_t	.225	.094	.110	.875	.182	.105
q_s	.061	.053	.062	.101	.891	-.050
q_n	-.128	.067	.107	.096	-.078	.881

Extraction Method: Principal Component Analysis.
Rotation Method: Varimax with Kaiser Normalization.
a. Rotation converged in 17 iterations.

Acting on the results

If you obtained such results with a sufficient sample size, then you could check the content of those items loading on the first two components, and assess whether they may represent two distinct sub-scales. You should collect data from a new sample to assess whether the results are replicable. You could use exploratory factor analysis as described above, or you could use confirmatory factor analysis to test hypotheses about your measurement model. That is outside the scope of this book.

Important!

As we have stated, a sample of 50 is small for reliability and dimensionality analyses. So if you collect data with the ATR scale (Larsen, 1995), you will probably get different results. Indeed, a different sample that we analysed gave different reliability and dimensionality results to those shown above. Thus in this and the previous section we have shown you how to use these analyses; we have not given definitive results for the ATR scale.

Chapter Twelve

Beyond the basics

The Syntax window
Option settings in SPSS
Getting help in SPSS
Printing from SPSS
Incorporating SPSS output into other documents
Graphing tips
Interactive charts

Section 1: The Syntax window

The dialogue boxes you have been using to control SPSS form an interface which allow the user to specify the analysis they require. When you click on the ![OK] button, this interface translates all your selections into a series of commands telling SPSS what to do. The SPSS processor executes this series of commands. The language in which these commands are expressed in is called the SPSS syntax. Below is an example of the syntax needed to perform the one-way analysis of variance described in Chapter 7, Section 2.

```
ONE-WAY
      Score BY group
      /STATISTICS DESCRIPTIVES
      /MISSING ANALYSIS.
```

It is these commands that SPSS executes to perform the oneway ANOVA. This syntax will be very familiar to anyone who used an old, pre-Windows version of SPSS. In these early versions of SPSS the user had to communicate with the SPSS processor by writing lines of syntax directly. Users had to remember obscure rules of syntax that governed the exact structure of the command lines, and even the smallest error, such as missing a full stop, would result in a string of equally obscure error messages. The greatest strength of the Windows versions of SPSS is that for most operations the user doesn't need to write or understand lines of syntax. However, occasionally it is useful to go back to the old methods and control SPSS directly. It is a bit like programming your videocassette recorder (VCR) at home. Usually you will use the code number published in the newspapers to control which program the VCR records, but sometimes, however, you want to do something a bit different – perhaps recording only the second half of a program. In this situation, you will want to talk directly to the VCR and independently set the channel and start and stop times. In this section, we describe how to control SPSS directly using syntax. When used appropriately the techniques described here can save a great deal of time and effort.

THE PASTE BUTTON AND THE SYNTAX WINDOW

You may have noticed that the dialogue boxes used to execute an analysis (those that include the ![OK] button) also contain a button marked ![Paste]. If you click on the paste button, the analysis is not executed, but control is switched to a new window called the Syntax window, and the command lines needed to execute your analysis are pasted into this window. You could now select a second analysis, (perhaps a *t*-test comparing two of the groups included in the ANOVA) and click on the [Paste] button again. In this way you can build up a sequence of commands in the Syntax Editor window, without executing any of them. Finally, when you have selected all the analyses you want, you can execute or "Run" the commands. This might seem like an odd thing to do, but there are at least three reasons for working in this way.

Repeating actions

You may choose to work in the Syntax Editor window because you need to repeat a complex command several times. For example, when analysing the data from the adoption survey described in Chapter 6, we might need to compute 20 new variables, each of which is the mean of ten existing variables. This would be a tedious procedure using the dialogue boxes, but would be easy to perform using syntax commands (this example is demonstrated later in this section).

Keeping a record of your analysis

Another reason for working with syntax files is to keep a record of your analysis. For example, you may need to repeat an analysis after updating your data file. This is easy to do if you saved the lines of syntax needed to execute your analysis. Alternatively, if you are working with a complex data set then it is likely that you will make errors where you either undertake the wrong analysis or use the correct command but forget to select the right options and as a result the output window will fill up with useless output. One solution is to use the syntax window as a notepad in which to record the details of the successful analyses. When you have the analysis working the way you want it you can save the details to the syntax window. In this way you can build up a permanent record of the analysis which you can then rerun to produce a "clean" set of output.

Tweaking the parameters of a command

Another reason for choosing to work in the Syntax Editor window is that some of the options or parameters associated with certain commands can only be accessed using the syntax commands. In order to keep the number of buttons manageable the SPSS programmers have pre-set certain features of the commands. Occasionally you might want to alter one of these settings. This can only be done using the command syntax. Details of the additional features of a command that can be accessed only via the Syntax window are described in special help screens that can be accessed via the **Help** button on the dialogue box (see next page).

To access details of the features of a command available only via the command syntax

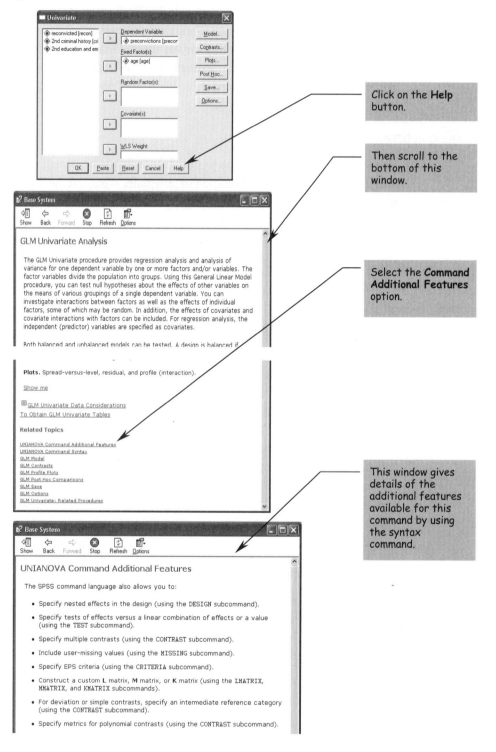

Click on the **Help** button.

Then scroll to the bottom of this window.

Select the **Command Additional Features** option.

This window gives details of the additional features available for this command by using the syntax command.

THE SYNTAX WINDOW

The Syntax Editor window (the Syntax window) is used to build up the syntax commands and to execute them. This window acts like a very simple word processor that allows you to edit the syntax for the commands you want to execute. The **Edit** menu provides access to all the normal text editing functions such as cut, paste, find and replace. Careful use of these functions can allow you quickly to build up a long and complex set of syntax commands. The tool bar across the top of the Syntax window includes a number of useful buttons. The use of some of the special buttons is described below.

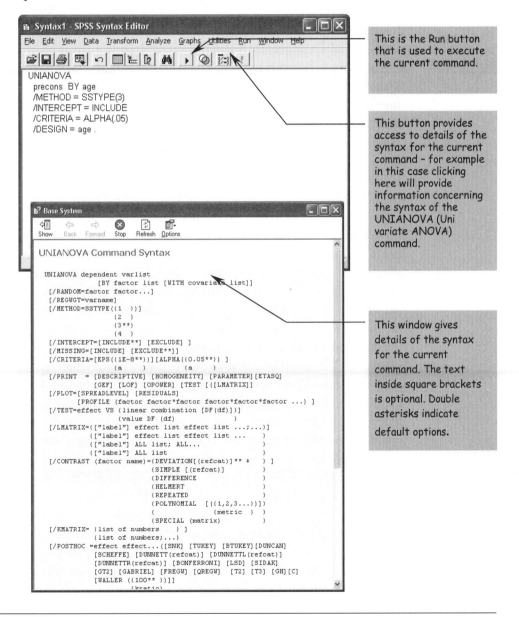

This is the Run button that is used to execute the current command.

This button provides access to details of the syntax for the current command – for example in this case clicking here will provide information concerning the syntax of the UNIANOVA (Uni variate ANOVA) command.

This window gives details of the syntax for the current command. The text inside square brackets is optional. Double asterisks indicate default options.

There are a few rules you need to remember when starting to write syntax commands.

1. Each new command must start on a new line of text. In practice, leaving several blank lines between commands makes the text easier to understand.
2. Each command must end with a full stop or period mark (.).
3. Sub-commands or options are usually separated by the forward slash mark (/). It is a good idea (but not essential) to start each sub-command on a new line and to indent it slightly.
4. You can split a command over several lines – it is safest to break the line at the start of a new sub-command.
5. It is useful to include notes to help you remember what the syntax means. These notes are called comments. A comment must start with an asterisk (*) and must end with a full stop. A comment can be split over more than one line of text.
6. Make sure that you spell your variable names correctly (i.e., exactly as they appear in the Data Editor window). Misspelling a variable name is one of the most common sources of errors when running syntax commands.
7. A set of commands must end with the command "Execute" followed by a full stop.

In practice, it is quite rare to write a piece of syntax "from scratch". It is more usual to use the dialogue boxes to select an analysis and set the options, and then to write this syntax into the Syntax window using the Paste button. This syntax can then be copied and edited before being run. Using this approach, you can be sure that the syntax and spelling will be correct. By careful use of the **Find** and **Replace** commands (available from the **Edit** menu) you can copy the syntax of a command, and change the variable(s) very quickly and accurately to build up a series of analyses. An example is given below. In this example we are seeking to compute 20 new variables. Each of these variables is the mean of a block of 10 questionnaire responses. The original variables were given names that reflect the block and question number. For example, B1Q3 is the third question in the first block, while B9Q8 is the eighth question in the ninth block. We could use the dialogue boxes to perform all these computes, but this would be a very laborious task, and if we would not be able to repeat the computes if, for example, some of our data were changed. Because of the way the variables have been named, it would be much easier to produce a series of syntax commands to perform these computes. This could be done as follows:

1. Using the Compute dialogue box, enter the details needed to compute the new variable "b1mean" (see Chapter 6 for details of the compute command).
2. Click on the Paste button to paste the syntax commands into the Syntax Editor window (see below).

3. Select (highlight) this block of text and copy it once.

4. Move the cursor to the start of the second block and use the **Replace** function to change all instances of the string "b1" to "b2" (click on the **Find Next** button, and then click the **Replace** button repeatedly until all the changes are made – do not use the **Replace All** button).

5. Paste a new copy of the command into the window (you can do this using the keyboard by typing "<Ctrl> V"). Now repeat step 4 to replace "b1" with "b3".

6. Continue in this way until you have ten blocks of syntax each instructing SPSS to compute the mean of the 10 variables in that block.

7. Move the cursor to the top of the Syntax Editor window and select all the text in the window.

8. Click on the **Run** button. The 10 new variables will be computed and appended to your data file.

This Run button can be used to execute any highlighted commands.

This is the first block of syntax pasted in using the dialogue boxes. Note that we have used the MEAN function.

This second block has been edited so that "b1" has been replaced by "b2". Note the blank line we have inserted between commands.

We are about to edit the third block to replace "b1" with "b3". Note that the cursor should be positioned at the start of the third block.

SAVING AND OPENING SYNTAX FILES

Once completed, a syntax file can be saved to disk. If the Syntax window is the active window (i.e., if you are currently working in this window), you can simply save the contents of the window as a syntax file by selecting **Save As** from the **File** menu. SPSS will automatically add the suffix ".sps" to the end of the file name. We strongly recommend that you accept this default suffix.

> **TIP** It is a good idea to use the same root name for all the files relating to one project. For example, in the case of the adoption survey described in Chapter 5 the data file might be called "ADOPT.SAV". The output files produced from the analysis of this file might be saved as "ADOPT1.LST", "ADOPT2.LST" etc, and a syntax file for this research might be called "ADOPT.SPS". In this way, it is easy to see which files relate to each other. Never change the default suffix file names that SPSS uses for the different file types. If you do, SPSS will not recognise them.

RUNNING COMMANDS IN THE SYNTAX WINDOW

Once you have written and saved your syntax commands you can execute, or run them, using either the **Run** button or by selecting one of the options from the **Run** menu. Note that if you have several procedures in the Syntax window, clicking on the **Run** button will only execute the current procedure which is determined by the position of the cursor within the file. It is safer to select all of the commands you want to run and then choose the **Selection** option from the **Run** menu. The available options in the Run menu are:

All – this option executes all of the commands in the Syntax window;
Selection – this option executes any commands that are selected or highlighted;
Current – this option executes only the current command (defined by the position of the cursor;
To End – this option runs all commands from the current command to the end of the Syntax window.

Remember to ensure that the block of syntax that you select and run ends with an "Execute." command (including the full stop). The chosen commands will then be executed as if you had used the dialogue boxes.

SYNTAX FILES AND THE PRODUCTION FACILITY

The production facility allows you to preprogram jobs in SPSS. The production facility runs specified syntax files and directs output towards specified files. This facility is designed for very large analyses that are performed regularly on a changing data file (e.g., an analysis of that day's sales data for a large supermarket chain) and is not likely to be of use to psychologists.

THE JOURNAL FILE

SPSS records all the analyses you undertake during a session in a special file called a journal file. The journal file for a session will include the full syntax of all the commands you have executed, together with any error messages or warnings that SPSS might have issued. By default, SPSS saves the journal file at the end of each session using the file name "spss.jnl" (usually located in the C:\temp directory). This can be another useful source of syntax for insertion into a syntax file.

Before opening the file, check that someone has not altered the default location or name of the file (or even switched the journal off). To do this select **Options** from the **Edit** menu and click on the **General** tab. You can now see (and if you wish change) the name and location of the journal file. You should also check that the **Record syntax in journal** option is selected (the box should contain a tick). You can also choose whether the file should be appended (the default option) or over-written.

Open the journal file by selecting **Open** from the **File** menu, and then select **Syntax** from the sub-menu. Enter the full file name and path into the **File Name** box (e.g., C:\temp\spss.jnl). You can now edit this file. For example, you might wish to copy some of the command syntax from this file into the Syntax window.

> **TIP**   An alternative to using the "paste" button to produce the lines of syntax is to run the command(s) from the dialogue boxes and then open the journal file and copy the lines syntax from the journal file into the syntax window.

Multiple Viewer and Syntax windows

It is possible to simultaneously open multiple Viewer and Syntax windows. When more than one window is open, SPSS will direct the output or syntax towards what is called the designated window. You designate a window by clicking on the button marked by an exclamation point (on the tool bar of the Syntax and Viewer windows).

> **TIP**   It might sound useful to have several Output windows open at the same time, but in our experience you always end up with the output in the wrong window. It is probably easier to work with just one window and then edit the output into two separate files once the analysis is complete.

Section 2: Option settings in SPSS

There are a number of options that can be set in SPSS. These control such things as the appearance of the various windows, the way variables are listed in dialogue boxes, the appearance of output and the location of files. In this section we describe how to access these options and highlight a few that you might like to alter.

> **TIP**   If your screen looks different from the screen-shots included in this book, this may be because some of these options settings are different. In particular, if your variables are always listed differently from ours, it may be that the Variable Lists options in your copy of SPSS are set differently to ours (see below).

CHANGING OPTION SETTINGS

The option settings can be accessed from any of the various SPSS windows. Select **Edit** > **Options**. This will bring up the **Options** dialogue box shown below. This style of dialogue box has a series of tabs across the top (rather like the tabs on index cards). The various options available are grouped together, and clicking on a tab presents you with one of these groups of options.

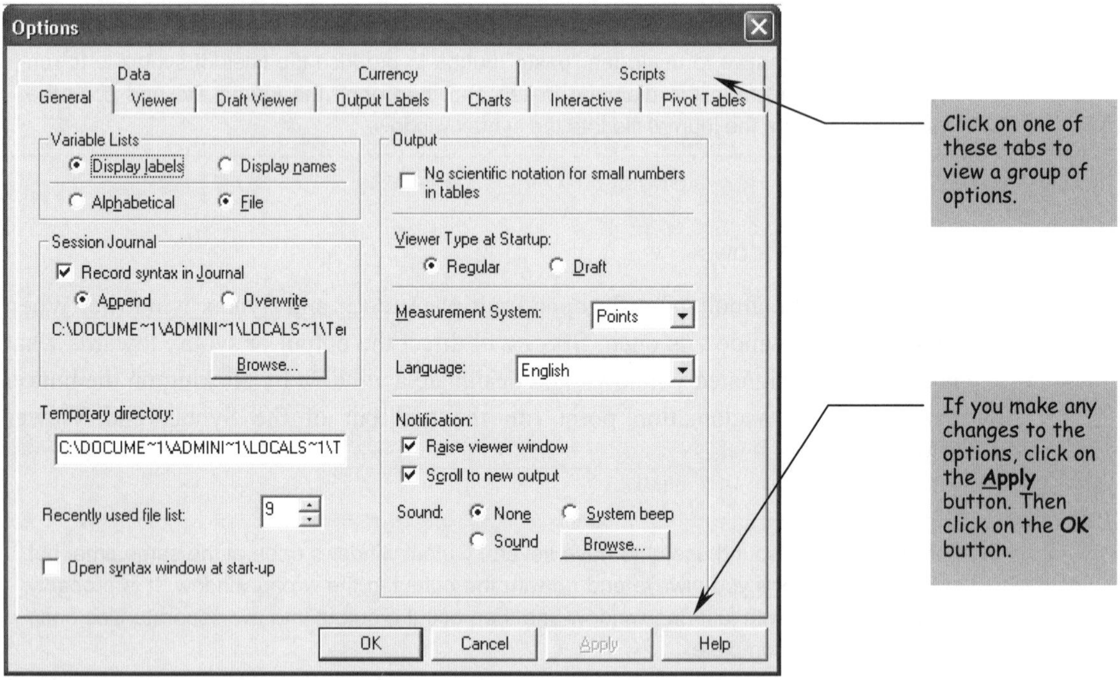

Click on one of these tabs to view a group of options.

If you make any changes to the options, click on the **Apply** button. Then click on the **OK** button.

SOME USEFUL OPTION SETTINGS

Below are just a few of the more useful options. We will leave you to explore all the others for yourself (use the **Help** button if you require an explanation of an option).

The General Tab

Most of the useful options are on this tab. In particular you might want to change the Variable Lists settings. These alter the way in which variables are listed in the dialogue boxes.

Selecting the **Display labels** option will cause SPSS to list the variable labels (with the variable name given in brackets). If a variable does not have a label then the name is listed. When the **Display names** option is selected, only the variable names are listed in the dialogue boxes. The **Alphabetical** and **File** options control the order in which the variables are listed. Most users prefer to have the variables listed in File order – the order they appear in the data file, however, when working with very large data files (e.g., from a survey), having the variables listed in alphabetical order can help you locate a particular variable quickly.

The Data Tab

The **Display Format For New Numeric Variables** on the Data Tab allows you to alter the default settings of the width and number of decimal places used to display a new variable. It might be useful to change this setting if you needed to create a large number of variables using the same settings. Remember, this setting alters only the way the number is displayed on screen, not the number of decimal places used when performing calculations.

The Output Labels Tab

Here you can select whether you want variable labels, variable names, or both variable labels and variable names to appear in output. Similarly, you can choose to display either value labels, values, or both value labels and values. You might like to experiment with these settings.

Section 3: Getting help in SPSS

It might seem odd to wait until the last part of the book before describing how to use the SPSS Help system, but we hope that up to now our instructions will have provided all the assistance you needed! However, from now on you are on your own, and will probably need to make use of the extensive Help files provided with SPSS when trying to use functions or commands not covered in this book.

SPSS comes with several different sources of help.

WHAT'S THIS?

One of the easiest and most useful ways of accessing help is using the right mouse button. This is particularly useful if you need some help to understand output. In the Output window, select a table by double-clicking on it (a hatched outline will appear to show it is selected). You can now move the mouse over any of the column or row titles in the table and click the right hand mouse button. Select **What's This?** from the menu of options that will appear. A brief explanation of that feature of the output is provided (see below).

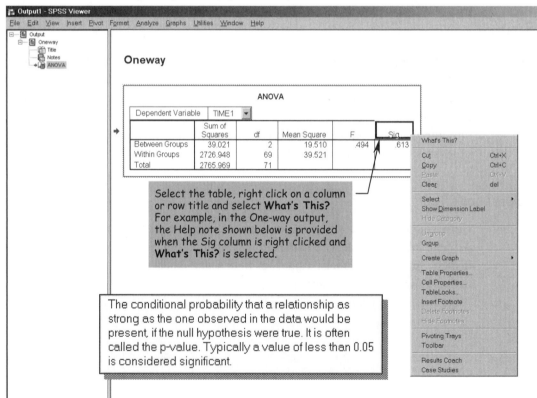

The same technique often can be applied to get help when using Dialogue boxes. For example, when using the one-way dialogue box you can right-click on the **Dependent List** and select **What's This?** (see below).

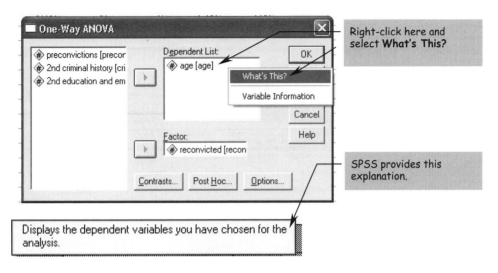

Right-click here and select **What's This?**

SPSS provides this explanation.

Displays the dependent variables you have chosen for the analysis.

THE HELP BUTTON IN DIALOGUE BOXES

Each dialogue box includes a **Help** button. Click on this button to view a Help window containing a more detailed description of the statistical procedure and the options available within SPSS. This Help window will include a number of links to related help pages including a link to the command syntax as described earlier in this chapter.

THE HELP MENU

The **Help** menu gives access to several sources of help. To search for help on a particular topic select **Topics**, and then select the Search tab and enter the first few letters of the topic into the search box. For example, if you search for "chi-square" SPSS will find a long list of related help files. Double-click on the one you want to read (see below).

If the tabs on the left hand side of the window are not visible, click on this button (which will be labelled **Show**).

Select the **Search** tab and then enter one or more words to search for.

Double click on a title to display the help text.

The help text is displayed in the right hand side of the window.

Other Help topic tabs

The other tabs available in this help dialogue box (**Contents** and **Index**) provide various different routes to access the Help information.

The Statistics Coach

This is a slide-show style presentation available from the **Help** menu. The **Statistics Coach** asks a number of questions about your data and the type of analysis you want to perform. It then suggests a suitable statistical procedure. This can act as a useful reminder of suitable procedures, but is no substitute for a basic knowledge of these procedures.

The Results Coach

When viewing output in the Output window, double-click on a table to select it. Now select **Results Coach** from the **Help** menu. SPSS will open a slide-show style tutorial explaining the output. Work through this help using the **Next** button.

Section 4: Printing from SPSS

In this section we provide some information on how to print output in the form of tables and charts, data and syntax files.

PRINTING OUTPUT FROM THE OUTPUT VIEWER WINDOW

The Output Viewer window displays the results of your analysis in the form of text, tables and charts, so this is likely to be the first thing you want to print out. To do this, first make the Output Viewer the active window (if it is not already) by selecting it from the **Window** menu. Now either click on the printer icon on the tool bar across the top of the page, or select **Print** from the **File** menu. The **Print** dialogue box contains several options.

1. The **All visible output** option prints any output that you could see by scrolling up or down in the Output window (i.e., not hidden output).
2. The **Selection** option prints only the output that is selected or highlighted. To select a section of output click and drag the mouse over it or hold down the shift key while moving the cursor up or down.

The first of these options is the default setting (unless output has been selected). The **Selection** option can be very useful and can save you from printing out large amounts of unwanted analysis – especially from some of the more complex procedures such as a within-subjects analysis of variance.

Adjusting the appearance of the output

Selecting **Page Setup** from the **File** menu will bring up the **Page Setup** dialogue box. You can use this dialogue box to set the paper size and margins, and to select whether you want to print in landscape or portrait orientation. This last option can be useful if you have wide tables that you would like to be printed without being split.

The **Options** button on the **Page Setup** dialogue box allows you to include text in the headers or footers of the printout. If you share a printer, it might be useful to have your name and/or the name of the project on every page of output. The default setting is to have the page number appearing in the footer. We recommend that you retain this feature – it can be very useful when you drop a pile of printout!

The changes you make in the **Page Setup** dialogue box affect only the output produced from the Output Viewer window. If after changing these settings you save the output your settings will be retained with the file.

> **TIP** It may be worth checking the appearance of your output before you commit it to paper. You can do this by selecting **Print Preview** from the **File** menu.

PRINTING OUT A DATA FILE

It is sometimes useful to keep a printed record of your data file. You may be required to include a printed copy of the raw data in an appendix to a report, and researchers should keep the data from any published study for several years after publication.

To obtain a printed copy of your data first make the Data Editor window the active window then select **Print** from the **File** menu. The data file is printed as it appears in the Data Editor window. If you have elected to display value labels then these will be printed in place of the numerical values.

> **TIP** The **Fonts** option under the **View** menu allows you to change the size and appearance of the font used to both display and print the data. It might be possible to squeeze a file containing a large number of variables onto a single sheet of paper by reducing the font size.

PRINTING A SYNTAX FILE

When the Syntax window is active, a syntax file can be printed out either by clicking on the printer icon on the toolbar or by selecting **Print** from the **File** menu.

SPECIAL OUTPUT OPTIONS FOR PIVOT TABLES

If you double-click on a pivot table (the name SPSS gives to a table of results displayed in the Output Viewer window), the table will become highlighted with a special shaded border. Once a pivot table is selected in this way, a special set of pivot table menu items will be displayed at the top of the window. These menus can be used to adjust the appearance of the table prior to printing it. A huge number of options are available, including rotating the table (swapping rows and columns) adding or removing grid lines and scaling the table to fit the size of paper being used. Below we have described a few of the most useful actions.

1. From the **Pivot** menu select **Transpose Rows and Columns** to swap the rows and columns of a table.

2. From the **Format** menu select **Table Properties**. The tab-style dialogue boxes displayed will allow you to alter the appearance of the table. The Printing tab contains two very useful options (**Rescale wide table to fit page** and **Rescale long table to fit page**), which force SPSS to automatically adjust the size of print so that the table will fit the page without being split.

3. From the **Format** menu select **TableLooks**. You can now select a style for your table from a list of preprogrammed styles. You can also edit the existing styles to suit your exact requirements. This new style can be saved and applied to any table.

> **TIP**   The academic styles are particularly appropriate for a research report.

4. From the **Format** menu select **Autofit**. This will resize the columns and rows of the table to a size that is appropriate for their contents. This usually makes the table slightly smaller and much neater.

> **TIP**   Before using either of the rescale options (described in point 2 above), you could apply the Autofit option. This will remove any redundant spaces from the table before it is rescaled.

5. From the **Insert** menu select **Caption**. This will allow you to insert a text caption inside the table.

6. From the **View** menu select **Gridlines** to either add or remove gridlines from the table.

7. Select a set of table cells by clicking and dragging over them. From the **Format** menu select **Cell Properties** to adjust the way values are displayed in a cell. Alternatively, select **Set Data Cell Widths** to set the width of the cells.

> **TIP**   Once a pivot table is selected, it is possible to adjust the width of a column by clicking on and dragging the grid line dividing the columns. Double-clicking on a cell allows you to change the cell contents. This is useful if you want to edit the value labels used in a table, but otherwise should be used with caution!

Section 5: Incorporating SPSS output into other documents

The output produced by recent versions SPSS is of such a high quality that you might want to incorporate it directly into your word-processed research report, particularly if you have formatted it as described in Section 4.

COPYING AND PASTING OBJECTS INTO WORD PROCESSOR DOCUMENTS

It is very easy to paste a pivot table or a chart (graph) from SPSS into another application such as a word processing package. Here we describe how to copy between SPSS and Microsoft Word. Pivot tables can be copied into a word document either as a table or as a picture. If a pivot table is copied as a table within Word, it can be edited and amended within Word using all the normal table functions. If the pivot table is copied as a picture it can be resized or moved but not edited. Which of these options you choose will depend on whether you are satisfied with the appearance of the table in SPSS or whether you want to edit it further.

To copy a pivot table or a chart as a picture select it by clicking on it once and then either choose **Copy Objects** from the **Edit** menu or right click the object and select **Copy Object**. Now switch to your word processor, move the cursor to the correct point in the document, and either select **Paste** from the **Edit** menu or right click and chose the **Paste** option. A picture of the SPSS output will be pasted into your document. You can now adjust the format settings of the picture (right-click on it and select **Format Picture**) or resize it using the "handles" (see Tip box).

To copy an SPSS pivot table into a Word table, select the pivot table and then right click and choose **Copy**. Now paste the table into Word in the same way as described above. You can now edit and format the table using all the standard Microsoft Word table formatting options.

> **TIP** You can adjust the size of the picture you have pasted by dragging the "handles". It is best to use the corner handles so that you do not change the aspect ratio of the table. If the aspect ratio changes (that is if you stretch the table out of shape) the text will probably not fit into the cells correctly.

Section 6: Graphing tips

SPSS is capable of producing very high quality charts. Chart production facilities were further enhanced in Version 8 of SPSS when a new type of chart – the interactive chart – was introduced.

Rather than include a separate chapter covering the production of charts, we have described how to produce the three most common types of charts in the chapters covering the analysis of the data linked to these chart types.

1. The production of scattergrams was introduced in Chapter 4, which also covered the analysis of data from correlational designs, and scattergrams were also covered in Chapter 9.
2. The production of bar graphs was introduced in Chapter 5 for nominal data and also in Chapter 7 where we described one-way analysis of variance.
3. The production of more complex line graphs was also covered in Chapter 7 alongside a description of how to undertake within-subjects analysis of variance.

These charts were all produced using the standard chart facility in SPSS. In the final section of this chapter, we will introduce you to interactive charts.

SELECTING THE CHART TYPE

SPSS provides a variety of useful mechanisms to help you select the appropriate chart type for your graph.

To access this help, from the **Graphs** menu select **Gallery**. If you know the type of chart (bar, line, pie, etc.) you want to produce, click on the appropriate chart icon. Alternatively, if you are not sure which type of chart is best to display your data, select **Chart Galleries By Data Structure**. You can now select the option that best describes your data set and follow the instructions to produce the chart. These two options are illustrated on the following pages.

If you know what type of chart to produce, but need help to produce it

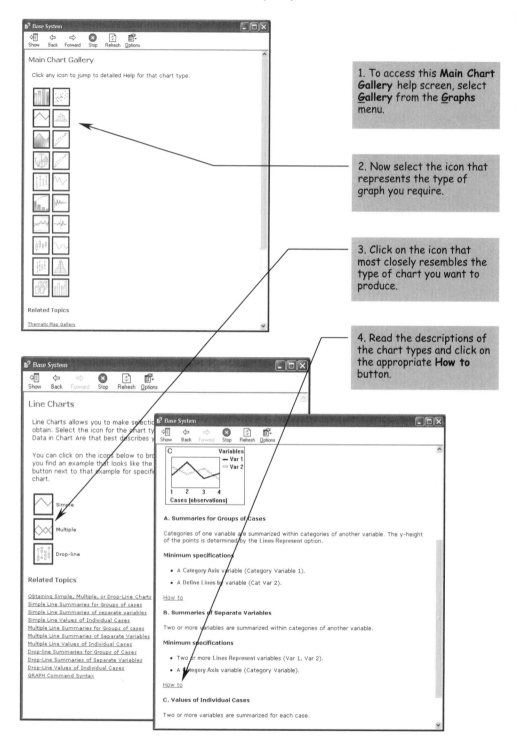

1. To access this **Main Chart Gallery** help screen, select **Gallery** from the **Graphs** menu.

2. Now select the icon that represents the type of graph you require.

3. Click on the icon that most closely resembles the type of chart you want to produce.

4. Read the descriptions of the chart types and click on the appropriate **How to** button.

If you need help to choose an appropriate type of graph for your data

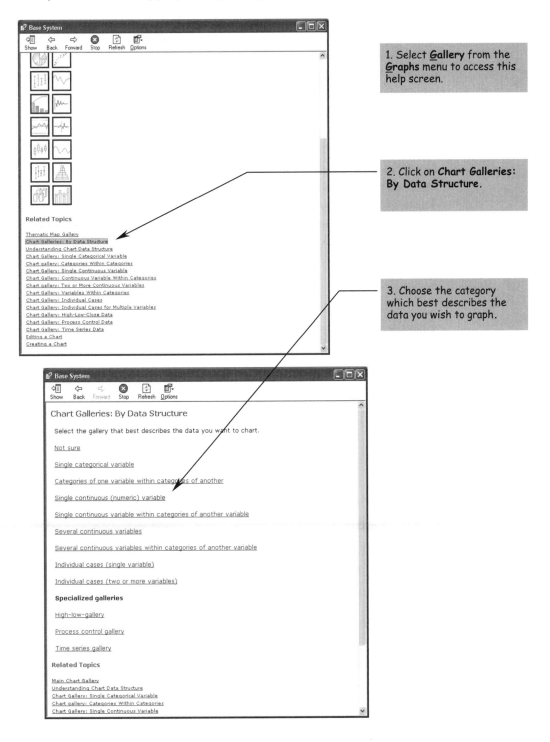

1. Select **Gallery** from the **Graphs** menu to access this help screen.

2. Click on **Chart Galleries: By Data Structure**.

3. Choose the category which best describes the data you wish to graph.

Most chart types require you to define what is to be displayed in the chart. For example, the relevant dialogue box for line charts is illustrated below. If your research employed a repeated measures or within-subjects design, you will have a different SPSS data variable for each level of the independent variable. In these circumstances the **Summaries of separate variables** option is likely to be the most appropriate as it plots the values for two or more data variables on one chart. If, on the other hand, your study employed an independent groups or between-subjects design, you will want to compare the average level of the dependent variable for one group of participants with the average level for another group. In such cases the **Summaries for groups of cases** option is the most appropriate. The third option, **Values of individual cases**, is not very likely to be of use in psychological research. This option allows you to plot the value of one or more variables for each of your participants. This chart type is often sketched by psychology students despite the fact that it tells us almost nothing and generally should be avoided!

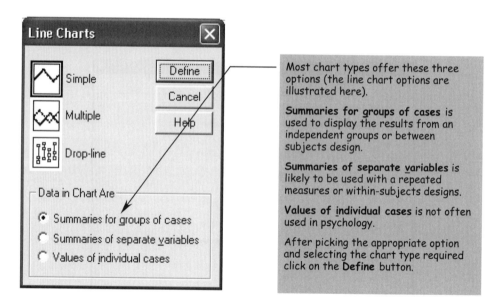

Most chart types offer these three options (the line chart options are illustrated here).

Summaries for groups of cases is used to display the results from an independent groups or between subjects design.

Summaries of separate variables is likely to be used with a repeated measures or within-subjects designs.

Values of individual cases is not often used in psychology.

After picking the appropriate option and selecting the chart type required click on the **Define** button.

Next you are asked to decide which data variables are to be assigned to which axis of the chart. In the above example, if we selected the **Multiple** chart type and the **Summaries for groups of cases** options, then the dialogue box shown below would be presented.

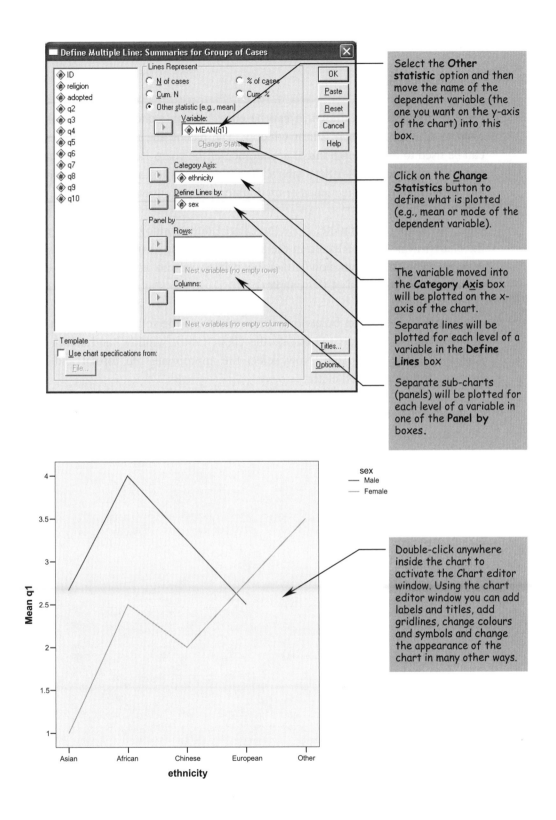

Select the **Other statistic** option and then move the name of the dependent variable (the one you want on the y-axis of the chart) into this box.

Click on the **Change Statistics** button to define what is plotted (e.g., mean or mode of the dependent variable).

The variable moved into the **Category Axis** box will be plotted on the x-axis of the chart.

Separate lines will be plotted for each level of a variable in the **Define Lines** box

Separate sub-charts (panels) will be plotted for each level of a variable in one of the **Panel by** boxes.

Double-click anywhere inside the chart to activate the Chart editor window. Using the chart editor window you can add labels and titles, add gridlines, change colours and symbols and change the appearance of the chart in many other ways.

EDITING AND USING A CHART

Once a chart has been drawn, it can be edited. Double-click anywhere inside the chart to activate the Chart Editor window. The menus and tool bar in this window can be used to improve the initial appearance of the chart. Items such as chart titles, sub-titles, legends, axis titles, labels, line characteristics and markers can all be altered either through the menus or by double-clicking directly on the item.

Once the editing is complete, close the Chart Editor window. The changes made to the chart will now be reflected in the appearance of the chart in the Output Viewer window. This chart can now either be printed or cut and pasted into another document (see Section 5 of this chapter).

Alternatively, charts can be exported in a variety of file formats. To export a chart double-click on the chart to activate the Chart Editor window, and select **Export Chart** from the **File** menu. Now select the appropriate file format and enter a filename for the exported chart.

By employing all these options, it is possible to produce a very high quality chart to incorporate into a research report.

Section 7: Interactive charts

THE DIFFERENCE BETWEEN INTERACTIVE CHARTS AND STANDARD CHARTS

Interactive charts are a relatively new development in SPSS. At present not all of the standard types of chart (those listed under the **Graphs** menu) can be produced as interactive charts. However, the most common chart types can be produced as interactive charts, and there are some advantages producing charts in this way.

The main differences between standard and interactive charts are as follows:

1. Interactive charts are more flexible. With standard charts, once you have defined the chart all that you can change is the appearance of the elements. With an interactive chart you can change everything. You can even change your mind about the type of graph you want or which variables you want to use.
2. If you edit a standard chart, a new Chart Editor window is opened, whereas an interactive chart is edited in the Output Viewer window.
3. In an interactive chart right-clicking on a chart or element of a chart gives access to special functions (in standard charts right-clicking accesses the **What's This?** help function).
4. In interactive charts you can choose whether SPSS lists variables by name or by label.
5. In interactive charts, variables can be "dragged and dropped" (in all other parts of SPSS, variables must be highlighted and then moved by clicking on the appropriate arrow button).
6. Interactive charts can be embedded into other applications or exported, or cut and pasted into another document. Standard charts cannot be embedded.
7. All types of interactive charts can be produced as 3-D charts and can be rotated in all three dimensions.
8. Interactive charts utilise the distinction between Scale, Ordinal and Nominal variables that can be indicated when a variable is being defined (see Chapter 2). SPSS allows Ordinal or Nominal variables to be treated as Categorical variables within interactive charts. In addition, these categorical variables can be used as panel variables. A panel variable is used to create a group of multiple charts. Each chart in the group includes data from only one level of the panel variable. For example, if we were plotting the data from the three-way mixed ANOVA shown in Chapter 7, Section 5, then we might decide to produce two graphs showing the interaction of orientation by negation. One graph would display this interaction for the primed group and the other for the un-primed group. In this case group would be the panel variable.

Glossary

Here we give a description of many of the terms used in the book. In the descriptions, any term in italics has an entry in this glossary. If you need further information about statistical or experimental design concepts then you should consult a statistics text.

Analysis of covariance (ANCOVA)

An inferential statistical procedure used to analyse data from *ANOVA* designs in which one *dependent variable* is measured and in addition at least one covariate (a variable that covaries with the dependent variable) is measured. Compare with *multivariate analysis of variance*.

ANOVA

Abbreviation of Analysis of Variance: an *inferential statistical test* that allows analysis of data from designs with more than two experimental *conditions* and/or with more than one *factor*. The term is often also used to refer to the *experimental design* used to obtain the data. The statistical test is intended for analysis of *parametric* data. The absence, however, of *nonparametric* equivalents for two-or-more-factor designs means that ANOVA is often used in such circumstances. Fortunately, it is said to be robust to the assumptions for parametric tests not being entirely met, provided that the *cell* sizes are equal.

Introduction to ANOVA
One-way *between-subjects* ANOVA (also see *Kruskal–Wallis*)
One-way *within-subjects* ANOVA (also see *Friedman*)
Multi-way between-subjects ANOVA
Multi-way within-subjects ANOVA
Multi-way *mixed* ANOVA

Association

See *correlation* and *chi-square*.

Asymptotic significance

The *p* value calculated on the assumption that the data is a large sample and has an asymptotic distribution. For the vast majority of *inferential statistical tests*, the *p* value given by SPSS is the asymptotic significance. For many tests SPSS now gives an option to also calculate the *exact significance*.

Bar chart

A graph used to display summary statistics for a number of SPSS variables: for example, the mean of data from two or more conditions. Also see *chart* and *interactive chart*.

Also available from the Charts button in the *Frequencies* dialogue box: that version will plot the frequencies or percentages of values in a single SPSS variable.

Between-subjects design

An *experimental design* in which all *factors* are between-subjects factors; that is, when no *participant* takes part in more than one *level* of a factor. This term is part of *ANOVA* terminology. Also see *independent groups design* and *natural independent groups design*.

Bivariate

Analysis of data in which two *variables* are measured: for example, *correlation*. Also see *univariate* and *multivariate*.

Case

Normally, a single *participant* in an experiment. The main exception in psychology is for *matched-subjects designs*, when the matched participants are the case. Each case should be entered into a separate row in the SPSS *data window*. For some studies, the cases will not be people. For example, we may be interested in the average "A" level points for pupils from different schools: the cases would then be the schools.

Cell

An element in the *data window* table, into which a *value* is entered.

In *ANOVA* and *chi-square*, the combination of one *level* of one *factor* and one level of another factor. The cell size is the number of *cases* (normally *participants*) that fall into that cell.

Chart

The name that SPSS gives to a graph. A wide range of graph types is available from the **Graphs** *menu item*. Additionally, some graphs are available through the *Frequencies* command. See also *interactive charts*.

Chart editor window

The SPSS window which appears if you double click on a *chart* in the *output window*. *Interactive charts*, however, are edited in the output window. The chart editor window has to be used to add a regression line to a *scattergram*.

Chi-square

An *inferential statistical test* that is used to analyse *frequencies* of nominal data (see *levels of measurement*). It allows comparison between the observed frequencies in the data and the frequencies that would be expected by chance. The chi-square most often used in psychology is the multi-dimensional chi-square. It can be thought of as a test of association between two *variables*, or as a test of differences between two independent groups.

The chi-square distribution is used to assess *significance* for some other statistical tests: for example, *Friedman* and *Kruskal–Wallis*.

Compute

An SPSS procedure by which a new *variable* can be computed (calculated) from one or more old variables.

Condition

See *Level*.

Confidence Interval

A pair of values which define a range within which we expect the *population parameter*, such as the mean to fall. In the case of the 95% confidence interval these values define the range within which there is a 95% probability that the parameter will fall.

Confounding variable

Any *variable* which changes systematically over the *levels* of the *independent variable* or *factor*. If there is a confounding variable, then you do not know whether the results of an experiment are due to the independent variable alone, to the confounding variable alone, or to some interaction between those two variables.

Correlation

A term used to describe a linear relationship, or association, between two *variables* (measured on ordinal, interval, or ratio *level of measurement*). *Pearson's r*, *Spearman's rho*, and *Kendall's tau* are *inferential statistical tests* of correlation. See also *scattergram*.

Count

An SPSS procedure by which the number of times that a particular value occurs, in one or more *variables* in the *data window,* can be counted.

Data editor window

The SPSS window in which data is entered and edited. It has the appearance of a spreadsheet window.

Data handling

Manipulation of data after it has been entered into SPSS. The different types of data handling are accessed through the *menu items* **Data** and **Transform**. See also *compute, count, rank cases, recode, select cases, sort cases, split.*

Degrees of freedom

A number related to the number of *participants* who took part in an experiment (t-test, *ANOVA*) or to the number of *factors* (*independent variables*) in an experiment (ANOVA, *chi-square*). The degrees of freedom are required when using statistical tables of *significance*. Although SPSS gives the exact *p* value, degrees of freedom should still be reported as shown on the annotated output pages of those *inferential statistical tests.*

Dependent variable

The *variable* that is measured in an experiment, and whose values are said to depend on those of the *independent variable* (or *factor*).

Descriptive statistics

Procedures that allow you to describe data by summarising, displaying or illustrating it. Often used as a general term for summary descriptive statistics: *measures of central tendency* and *measures of dispersion*. Graphs (see *chart*) are descriptive statistics that are used to illustrate the data.

Dialogue box

A box that appears on the screen, normally after you have clicked on a sequence of *menu items*. Windows computer packages use dialogue boxes to ask you for instructions. We show dialogue boxes in all the chapters, annotated to describe their use.

Discriminant analysis

An inferential statistical procedure used to determine which *variables* will predict membership of (or discriminate between) different categories of another variable.

Effect size

A measure of the magnitude of an effect. Can be expressed in the units used to measure the *dependent variable*, or in standardised units such as Cohen's *d*.

Error bar graph

A graph in which the *mean* of each *condition* is plotted with a vertical bar that denotes one *standard error* above the mean and one standard error below the mean. SPSS allows you to alter what the vertical bars represent (e.g., three *standard deviations* from the mean; the 90% confidence interval).

In SPSS it is available for plotting the means for *levels* of one *factor* only, although the *interactive chart* procedure allows you to plot a panel for each level of a second factor.

Exact significance

The *p* value calculated on the assumption that the data is a very small sample and/or does not have an asymptotic distribution. For many tests SPSS now gives an option to calculate the exact significance in addition to the default *asymptotic significance*. The Fisher's Exact Test, an alternative in *chi-square*, is a test that only gives the exact *p* value.

Experimental design

A term used to describe specific methods by which experiments are carried out and which are intended to prevent *participant irrelevant variable*s from *confounding* the experiment: for example, *repeated measures design*; two-way between-subjects *ANOVA*. Basic designs are described in Chapter 1, and other designs are described where relevant for particular statistical tests.

The term is also used in a more general sense to describe the way in which an experiment is to be carried out, including how *situational irrelevant variables* are to be prevented from confounding the experiment.

Factor

In *ANOVA*:
Another term for *independent variable*. Factor is used particularly when discussing *ANOVA* statistical tests and designs, whereas independent variable is used more often for *two-sample designs*. Also see *between-subjects design* and *within-subjects design*.

In *factor analysis*:
A dimension (or a psychological construct) that underlies several measured variables.

Factor analysis

A statistical procedure used to identify whether a *factor* structure underlies *correlations* between a number of *variables*.

F-ratio

The statistic obtained in *ANOVA* calculations. It can be described as the variance due to manipulation of the *factor* divided by the variance due to error.

Frequency/ies

The number of times a particular event or value occurs. Also an SPSS command available from the *menu item* **Analyze** (Version 9) or **Statistics** (Version 8) that will produce tables of frequencies showing the number of times that a particular value occurs in each *variable*. Some *charts* are available through a button on the Frequencies dialogue box. See also *bar chart*.

Friedman

A *nonparametric* equivalent of the one-way within-subjects *ANOVA*.

Graph

See *Chart*.

Grouping variable

An SPSS *variable* that specifies which *level* a participant carried out in an *independent groups design* or for a *between-subjects* factor. Each level is given a number as a code. For example: 1 for male and 2 for female; or 1 for rehearsal condition, 2 for mnemonic condition and 3 for elaboration condition (in a memory experiment). *Value labels* should be used when defining a grouping variable.

Help

You can obtain help in a number of ways while using SPSS: for example, the **Help** button on dialogue boxes, right clicking, and the **Help** *menu item*.

Hypothesis

A prediction about the outcome of an experiment. The experimental hypothesis predicts that a difference between *conditions* will occur, that a relationship will be found, or that an *interaction* will occur. The null hypothesis predicts that there will be no difference between conditions, that a relationship will not be found, or that an interaction will not occur.

Independent groups design

An *experimental design* in which a *participant* takes part in only one *level* of the *independent variable*. This term is usually used for designs with two levels of one independent variable. See also *natural independent groups design* and *between-subjects designs*.

Independent variable

A *variable* either: that is systematically manipulated by the experimenter to have different values (true experiments); or, the values of which are chosen by the experimenter (*natural independent groups designs*). Each value of the independent variable is called a *level*. See also *factor*.

Inferential statistical tests

Procedures that allow you to draw inferences from the data collected. The outcome of an inferential statistical test gives you the probability of obtaining the results by chance if the *independent variable* had no effect. If that probability is low ($p \leq 0.05$ in psychology) then the experimental *hypothesis* is accepted; otherwise it is rejected. Various inferential statistics are covered in this book.

Interaction

An interaction is present in a two- or more-way *ANOVA* if each *level* of one *factor* has a different effect on each level of another factor.

Interaction graph

A *line graph* showing the effects of each *level* of two *factors*. The *dependent variable* is on the y-axis and the levels of one factor on the x-axis; the levels of a second factor are indicated by individual lines drawn in the graph. See also *chart* and *interactive chart*.

Interactive chart

A type of SPSS *chart* that allows you much greater flexibility in specifying the appearance of the chart, and allows some features not available in standard charts.

Irrelevant variable

Any *variable* other than the *independent variable* or *factor/s* and the *dependent variable/s*. Good *experimental design* should ensure that no irrelevant variable becomes a *confounding variable*.

Kendall's tau

An inferential statistical test of correlation used to analyse *nonparametric* data.

Kruskal–Wallis

A *nonparametric* equivalent of the one-way between-subjects *ANOVA*.

Level

The term for each value of an *independent variable* or *factor*. There may be two or more levels of each factor. If there is only one factor, then its levels are equivalent to the conditions of the experiment. For two or more factors, the conditions are a combination of one level from each of two or more factors.

Levels of measurement

The type of scale used to measure *variables*. The four types are: nominal, ordinal, interval, and ratio. The first two are classified as *nonparametric* levels of measurement, and the last two as *parametric* levels of measurement. SPSS uses the term 'Scale' to describe both interval and ratio variables.

Line graph

A graph in which the points plotted are joined by a line. The points could each represent the *mean* of one sample, or they could represent the *frequency* of particular values in an SPSS *variable*. See also *interaction graph*, *chart* and *interactive chart*.

Mann–Whitney

An inferential statistical test used to analyse *nonparametric* data from *two-sample independent groups designs*.

Matched-subjects design

An *experimental design* in which each *participant* is matched closely with another participant, to give a participant pair. Each member of the pair is then allocated, by a random process, to different *levels* of the *independent variable*. Also called matched pairs design. It is a type of *related design*.

Mean

A *measure of central tendency*: the scores are summed and the total is divided by the number of scores.

Measure of central tendency

The average or typical score for a sample. See *mean*, *median*, and *mode*.

Measure of dispersion

How variable the scores in a sample are. See *range*, *standard deviation*, *standard error*, and *variance*.

Median

A *measure of central tendency*: the scores are put into rank order and the middle score is the median

Menu items

The items (words) in the bar in Windows packages, normally across the top of the screen, that give you access to the drop-down menus. In SPSS the menu bar varies slightly between the different windows, and some of the drop-down menus may vary. For example, in the *viewer window* compare the **Help** menu before and after you have double clicked on one of the results tables.

Mixed subjects design

A design in which at least one *factor* is *between-subjects* and at least one is *within-subjects*. This term is part of *ANOVA* terminology.

Mode

The most common value in a sample of scores: a *measure of central tendency*. NB: if a sample of scores has more than one mode SPSS shows the lowest value only.

Multiple regression

An inferential statistical procedure used to investigate linear relationships between three or more *variables*. It indicates the extent to which one variable can be explained or predicted by one or more of the other variables. (See also *regression*.)

Multivariate

Analysis of data in which:
either two or more *variables* are measured and there is at least one *factor,* for example, *multivariate analysis of variance*;
or in which three or more *variables* are measured, for example, *multiple regression.* Also see *univariate, bivariate* and *dependent variable.*

Multivariate analysis of variance

An inferential statistical procedure used to analyse data from designs in which two or more *dependent variables* are measured and there is at least one *factor.* Also see *ANOVA.*

Natural independent groups design

An *independent groups design* or *between-subjects design* in which the groups are chosen by the experimenter from existing (natural) groups. For example: male and female; smoker, ex-smoker, and non-smoker. The results of natural groups studies cannot be used to draw conclusions about cause-and-effect relationships, but only about differences or associations that might be a result of variables other than those used to define the natural groups.

Nonparametric

A term used to denote:
1. nominal and ordinal *levels of measurement*;
2. data that may be measured on ratio or interval scales but do not meet the other assumptions (equality of *variance* and normality of distribution) underlying *parametric* statistical tests;
3. the *inferential statistical tests* used to analyse nonparametric data.
   Nonparametric statistics make use of rank order, either of scores or of the differences between scores, unlike parametric statistical tests. Because non-parametric tests make no assumptions about normality of distribution in the data, they are sometimes called "distribution-free tests".

Options

Options in *dialogue boxes* can be set to request additional statistics or to control the appearance of *charts.*

Additionally, selecting **Opti<u>o</u>ns** from the **<u>E</u>dit** *menu item* allows you to set options that will be applied more generally.

Output window

See *Viewer window*.

Parameters

A characteristic of an entire population, such as the mean. Normally we estimate a population parameter based on the statistics of the *sample*.

Parametric

A term used to denote:
1. ratio and interval *levels of measurement*;
2. data that are measured on one of those scales and also meet the two other requirements (equality of *variance* and normality of distribution) for parametric statistical tests;
3. the *inferential statistical tests* used to analyse parametric data.

Parametric statistics make use of the actual values of scores in each sample, unlike *nonparametric* statistical tests.

Participant

People who take part in an experiment. Previously the word "subject" was used, and still is in many statistics books. The word "subject" is often still used to describe *ANOVA* experimental designs and analyses (e.g., " 2*2 within-subjects") as it is in this book.

Participant irrelevant variable

Any *irrelevant variable* that is a property of the *participants* in an experiment. In text books the term "subject irrelevant variables" is often still used.

Pearson's r

An *inferential statistical test* of *correlation* used to analyse *parametric* data.

Pivot table

The name that SPSS gives to a table of results displayed in the *output viewer window*. The appearance of a pivot table can be altered for the purposes of presentation in a report

Planned comparisons

A group of statistical tests used to compare *conditions* from *ANOVA* designs, when the comparisons to be made were decided upon before data is collected. If used inappropriately, then the frequency of *Type 1 error* will increase. See also *unplanned comparisons*.

Population

The total set of all possible scores for a particular variable.

Power

The power of an inferential statistical procedure is the probability that it will yield a statistically significant result.

Print

The content, or a selection, of all SPSS windows can be printed by selecting **Print** from the **File** *menu item* while the appropriate window is open.

Quantitative research

In psychology today this term is used to describe research that requires *variables* to be measured on any of the four *levels of measurement*, in contrast to qualitative research (not covered in this book).

Note that the term quantitative data is sometimes used in the literature to describe data measured on ratio, interval or ordinal scales, and the term qualitative data is then used to describe data measured with nominal scales.

Range

A *measure of dispersion*: the scores are put into rank order and then the lowest score is subtracted from the highest score.

Rank cases

> An SPSS procedure by which a new *variable* containing ranks for the values in an existing variable can be produced.

Recode

> An SPSS procedure by which the value/s in a *variable* can be changed into different value/s.

Regression

> If two *variables* have been measured, as in a *correlation* design, then regression can be used to allow prediction of a participant's score on one variable from his or her score on the other variable. If three or more variables have been measured, then *multiple regression* can be used to analyse the data.

> A regression line is the line drawn using the regression formula, and represents the "best fit" to the data points in a *scattergram*.

Related designs

> A term that includes both *repeated measures* and *matched subjects designs*. This term is usually used for designs with two *levels* of one *independent variable*. Also see *within-subjects designs*.

Repeated measures design

> An *experimental design* in which every *participant* takes part in both *levels* of the *independent variable*. It is a type of *related design*.

Sample

> A sub-set of a *population*. A smaller set of scores which we hope is representative of the population.

Scattergram

> Sometimes called a scattergraph, and in SPSS it is called a scatterplot. A graph in which one point is plotted for each *case*, used to display the data whenever a test of *correlation* is carried out. A single point represents the value of the x-axis *variable*

and the value of the y-axis variable for a single case. See also *chart* and *interactive chart*.

Select cases

An SPSS procedure by which certain *cases* can be selected on the basis of the *values* in a *variable*; subsequent analyses will only be performed on the selected cases.

Significance level

The level of probability (p) that the results are due to chance, at which we reject the null *hypothesis* and accept the experimental hypothesis. By convention in psychology, p must be less than or equal to 0.05.

Situational irrelevant variable

Any *irrelevant variable* that is to do with the situation in which an experiment is carried out or with the experimenter.

Skewed data

If a data sample is not normally distributed but instead has a "tail" of *cases* that are **either** particularly low **or** particularly high compared to most of the scores, then the sample is said to be skewed. Such a sample does not meet the assumption of normality of distribution (see *parametric*).

Sort cases

An SPSS procedure by which the *cases* in the *data window* can be sorted into a desired order based on the values of one or more *variables*.

Spearman's rho

An *inferential statistical test* of *correlation* used to analyse *nonparametric* data.

Split

An SPSS procedure by which the *cases* in the *data window* are split into groups on the basis of the values in a *grouping variable*; subsequent analyses will be performed separately for each group.

Standard deviation

A *measure of dispersion*: it indicates the average, or standard, deviation of scores away from the *mean*. SPSS uses N-1, not N, as the denominator, giving the standard deviation for the sample rather than for the population.

Standard error

A *measure of dispersion*: its value is equal to the *standard deviation* divided by the square root of N. In this sense the full name is "standard error of the mean".

(The "standard error of differences between means" is obtained as part of calculations for the t-*test*; the "standard error of the estimate" is used in regression.)

Statistics

A general term for procedures for summarising or displaying data (*descriptive statistics*) and for analysing data (*inferential statistical tests*). A characteristic of a *sample*, such as the mean, used to estimate the *population parameters*.

Syntax

The program language commands that underlie the instructions that, in Windows, you give to SPSS by means of the *dialogue boxes*. Only advanced users will need to use syntax. Syntax commands may appear in the *output window* (depending on the settings for SPSS on your PC). Syntax commands can be pasted into and edited in the *syntax window*.

Syntax window

The syntax editor window: a window in SPSS that shows *syntax*. This window does not normally appear. Only advanced users will ever need it.

t-test

An *inferential statistical test* used to analyse *parametric* data from *two-sample* designs. There are two versions: the independent t-test for *independent groups designs*, and the paired t-test for *related designs*.

Two-sample designs

Experimental designs with two *levels* of one *independent variable*. Also see *independent groups design* and *related design*s.

Type 1 error

The situation in which the experimental *hypothesis* is accepted in error. If the *significance level* is set at 0.05 (as it is in Psychology), then even with an excellent experimental design, a Type 1 error will occur on one in 20 occasions, on average. If the significance level is reduced then the chance of Type 1 errors will fall, but the chance of *Type 2 errors* will rise. If more than one *inferential statistical test* is carried out on the data from one experiment, then the chance of Type 1 errors will increase. See also *planned* and *unplanned comparisons*.

Type 2 error

The situation in which the experimental *hypothesis* is rejected in error. The frequency of occurrence depends partly on the *significance level* and partly on the power of the *inferential statistical test*. (The concept of "power" is beyond the scope of this book, but it is briefly explained in Chapter 1, Section 2, and Chapter 3, Section 4.)

Univariate

Analysis of data in which one *dependent variable* is measured for one or more *factors*: for example, *Mann–Whitney, paired t-test,* and *ANOVA*. Also see *bivariate* and *multivariate*.

Unplanned comparisons

A group of *inferential statistical tests* that may be used to make all of the possible comparisons between *conditions* from *ANOVA* designs, as they control for the increased chance of obtaining *Type 1 errors*. See also *planned comparisons*.

Value label

The label that you can give to a value in an SPSS *variable* when you define the variable. It should always be used for nominal *level of measurement* (including values in a *grouping variable*). It can contain spaces, and can be up to 60 characters, although it is best to use a few words at most. Value labels are printed in *output*, and help you to interpret it.

Variable

In *experimental design*, anything that varies; that can have different values at different times or for different *cases*. See also *confounding variable*, *dependent variable*, *independent variable*, *irrelevant variable*.

In SPSS, the contents of a single column in the *data window*.

Variable label

The label that you can give to an SPSS *variable* when you define it. It can contain spaces, and can be very long, although a few words are best. When you put the cursor on the variable name in the data window, SPSS will show the variable label. Also, the variable label is printed in *output*, and often is shown in *dialogue boxes*.

Variable name

The name of eight or fewer characters that you give to an SPSS *variable* when you define it. It will appear at the top of the column in the *data window*, and may appear in the *output*.

Variance

A *measure of dispersion*: it is equal to the square of the *standard deviation*. Equality of variance between the samples is one of the requirements for using *parametric* statistical tests. SPSS will test for equality of variance (e.g., when performing the independent t-*test*). A rule-of-thumb is that the larger variance should be no greater than three times the smaller variance.

Viewer window

The window in SPSS that displays the output from any statistical procedure that you have requested. Also referred to as the output window.

Wilcoxon matched-pairs signed-ranks test

An *inferential statistical test* used to analyse *nonparametric* data from *two-sample related designs*.

A design with one or more *factors* when every *participant* takes part in all *levels* of all factors (or when *matched subjects* take part in each level). This term is part of *ANOVA* terminology. Also see *repeated measures design* and *related designs*. If you have a design with two or more factors, each within-subjects, but each participant only takes part in the levels for one factor, then that cannot be analysed as a multi-way within-subjects ANOVA. It must be analysed as a series of one-way within-subjects ANOVAs or, if appropriate, as a mixed design counting the different factors as different levels of one factor.

References

APA (2001). *Publication Manual of the American Psychological Association* (5th ed.). Washington, DC: American Psychological Association.

Bird, K.D. (2004). Analysis of variance via confidence intervals. London: Sage.

Cohen, J. (1969). Statistical power analysis for the behavioral sciences. New York: Academic Press.

Cohen J (1977) Statistical Power analysis for the behavioral sciences (rev ed.). New York: Academic Press.

Cooper, C. (2002). *Individual Differences (*2nd ed.). London: Arnold.

Fife-Schaw, C. (2000). Questionnaire design. In G.M. Breakwell, S. Hammond, & C. Fifeshaw. (Eds.), *Research Methods in Psychology* (2nd ed., Chapter 12). London: Sage.

Giles, D.C. (2002). *Advanced Research Methods in Psychology.* Hove, UK: Routledge.

Hammond, S. (2000). Using psychometric tests. In G.M. Breakwell, S. Hammond, & C. Fifeshaw. (eds.), *Research Methods in Psychology* (2nd ed., Chapter 13). London: Sage.

Hartley, J. (1991). Sex differences in handwriting: a comment on Spear. *British Educational Research Journal, 17*, 141–145.

Hollin, C.R., Palmer, E.J. & Clark, D.A. (2003). The Level of Service Inventory–Revised profile of English prisoners: a needs analysis. *Criminal Justice and Behavior, 30*, 422–440.

Howell, D.C. (1987). *Statistical Methods for Psychology (*3rd ed.). Belmont, California: Duxbury Press.

* Howell, D.C. (2002). *Statistical Methods for Psychology* (5th ed.). Belmont, California: Duxbury Press.

John, O.P. & Benet-Martinez, V. (2000). Measurement: reliability, construct validation, and scale construction. In H.T. Reis & C.M. Judd (Eds.), *Handbook of Research Methods in Social and Personality Psychology* (Chapter 13). Cambridge: CUP.

Kemp R.I., McManus, I.C. & Pigott, T. (1990). Sensitivity to the displacement of facial features in negative and inverted images. *Perception*, *19*, 531–543.

Kline, P. (1994). *An Easy Guide to Factor Analysis*. London: Routledge.

Larsen, K.S. (1995). Environmental waste: recycling attitudes and correlates. *The Journal of Social Psychology*, *135*, 83–88.

Mason, R.J., Snelgar, R.S., Foster, D.H., Heron, J.R. & Jones, R.E. (1982). Abnormalities of chromatic and luminance critical flicker frequency in multiple sclerosis. *Investigative Ophthalmology & Visual Science*, *23*, 246–252.

Newlands, P. (1997). *Eyewitness Interviewing: Does the cognitive interview fit the bill?* Unpublished PhD Thesis, University of Westminster, London.

Siegel, S. & Castellan, N.J. (1988). *Nonparametric Statistics for the Behavioral Sciences* (2nd ed.). New York: McGraw-Hill.

* Tabachnick, B.G. & Fidell, L.S. (2001). *Using Multivariate Statistics*, (2nd ed.). New York: HarperCollins.

Towell, N., Burton, A. & Burton, E. (1994). The effects of two matched memory tasks on concurrent finger tapping. *Neuropsychologia, 32,* 125–129.

Towell, N., Kemp, R. & Pike, G. (1996). The effects of witness identity masking on memory and person perception. *Psychology, Crime and Law, 2,* 333–346.

* Earlier edition/s of these texts will also be useful.

Appendix I: Data files

These data files are also available to download from the Internet (http://www.palgrave.com/psychology/ brace/data.htm).
We recommend that you enter the first few data files to become skilled at entering data. You can then download the remaining files if you wish.

DATA FILES FOR:

independent *t*-test
paired *t*-test
Mann–Whitney U test
Wilcoxon matched-pairs signed-ranks test
Pearson's r correlation
Spearman's rho correlation
chi-square test
McNemar test
data handling exercises
scale exercise
one-way between-subjects ANOVA
two-way between-subjects ANOVA
one-way within-subjects ANOVA
two-way within-subjects ANOVA
three-way mixed ANOVA
Kruskal–Wallis test and Friedman test
multiple regression
ANCOVA
MANOVA
discriminant analysis and logistic regression
factor analysis

DATA FOR INDEPENDENT *T*-TEST

GROUP 1 = mnemonic condition 2 = no mnemonic condition	SCORE
1	11
1	14
1	17
1	18
1	18
1	18
1	19
1	20
1	20
1	20
1	20
2	9
2	10
2	12
2	12
2	14
2	14
2	15
2	16
2	19
2	20

LARGE SIZE DIFFERENCE	SMALL SIZE DIFFERENCE
936	878
923	1005
896	1010
1241	1365
1278	1422
871	1198
1360	1576
733	896
941	1573
1077	1261
1438	2237
1099	1325
1253	1591
1930	2742
1260	1357
1271	1963

DATA FOR MANN–WHITNEY U TEST

SEX 1 = male 2 = female	RATING
1	4
1	6
1	5
1	8
1	5
1	2
1	4
1	4
1	5
1	7
1	5
1	4
1	3
1	3
1	5
1	3
1	3
1	8
1	6
1	4
2	4
2	2
2	7
2	4
2	6
2	7
2	5
2	2
2	6
2	6
2	6
2	6
2	3
2	5
2	7

SEX 1 = male 2 = female	RATING
2	4
2	6
2	6
2	7
2	8

DATA FOR WILCOXON MATCHED-PAIRS SIGNED-RANKS TEST

E-FIT RATING 1 (from memory)	E-FIT RATING 2 (from photograph)
3	6
3	4
3	5
5	6
2	3
4	3
5	3
5	3
4	3
3	3
2	3
6	6
5	3
4	3
3	3
3	5
4	5
3	2
4	5
3	5
3	2
5	6
3	4
4	3
4	4
4	2
4	5
3	3
5	3
4	3
3	2
3	3
6	4
3	3
3	2
3	3

E-FIT RATING 1 (from memory)	E-FIT RATING 2 (from photograph)
2	4
2	5
5	6
3	5
6	4
2	3
5	5
4	2
3	5
3	2
5	6
4	2

DATA FOR PEARSON'S R CORRELATION

AGE (in years)	CFF
41	34.9
43	30.5
25	35.75
42	32.3
51	28.0
27	42.2
27	35.1
48	33.5
58	25.0
52	31.0
58	23.2
50	26.8
44	32.0
53	29.3
26	35.9
65	30.5
35	31.9
29	32.0
25	39.9
49	33.0

CONFI-DENCE	BELIEVA-BILITY	ATTRACT-IVENESS
4	4	2
4	3	3
4	6	4
4	6	4
4	4	3
4	4	4
4	3	2
5	5	4
4	4	3
6	5	4
4	6	4
4	5	5
4	4	3
6	5	4
5	5	4
4	5	3
2	4	3
6	4	4
3	5	3
3	3	3
2	5	5
5	5	4
5	6	4
5	4	4
4	5	4
5	5	4
5	5	4
4	4	5
4	4	4
3	5	4
5	6	4
5	5	4
1	5	3
5	5	4
5	5	4
5	6	4
5	5	5
4	5	4

CONFI-DENCE	BELIEVA-BILITY	ATTRACT-IVENESS
4	5	4
4	5	4
5	5	4
4	5	4
5	5	3
4	4	2
5	6	5
4	5	3
6	5	2
3	5	4
3	5	4
4	4	3
4	3	3
6	6	4
3	5	2
4	4	3
5	5	4
3	1	3
5	6	4
5	5	4
4	5	4
4	4	4
6	1	1
5	5	4
5	5	4
6	6	5
5	5	3
6	6	5
5	5	2
2	4	4
3	4	4
3	4	4
4	4	4
4	5	4
5	5	4
5	5	3
3	4	4

Data continued on next page

CONFI-DENCE	BELIEVA-BILITY	ATTRACT-IVENESS
2	3	5
6	5	5
4	5	3
5	4	4
4	5	4
4	5	4
4	4	4
4	4	4
4	5	4
4	5	5
5	4	4
4	6	4
5	5	3
6	5	4

DATA FOR CHI-SQUARE TEST

BACKGROUND 1 = Asian 2 = Caucasian 3 = other	MOTHER'S EMPLOYMENT 1 = full time 2 = none, 3 = part time	SCHOOL 1 = comprehensive 2 = private	TENDENCY TO ANOREXIA 1 = high 2 = low
2	1	1	1
2	1	1	1
2	1	1	1
2	3	1	1
2	3	2	1
2	3	2	1
2	2	2	1
2	2	2	1
2	2	2	1
2	1	2	1
2	1	2	1
2	1	2	1
2	3	2	1
2	3	2	1
2	3	2	1
2	3	2	1
2	2	2	1
2	2	2	1
2	2	2	1
2	3	2	1
2	3	2	1
1	3	2	1
1	1	2	1
1	1	2	1
1	1	2	1
3	2	2	1
3	3	2	1
3	2	2	1
3	2	2	1
3	1	2	1
3	1	2	1
3	1	2	1
3	1	2	1
3	1	2	1

Table continued on next page.

BACKGROUND 1 = Asian 2 = Caucasian 3 = other	MOTHER'S EMPLOYMENT 1 = full time 2 = none, 3 = part time	SCHOOL 1 = comprehensive 2 = private	TENDENCY TO ANOREXIA 1 = high 2 = low
3	2	2	1
3	2	2	1
3	2	2	1
2	2	1	2
2	1	1	2
2	1	1	2
2	3	1	2
2	3	1	2
2	2	1	2
2	2	1	2
2	2	1	2
2	2	1	2
2	3	1	2
2	3	1	2
2	3	1	2
2	3	1	2
2	3	1	2
2	3	1	2
2	3	1	2
2	3	1	2
2	2	1	2
2	2	1	2
2	2	1	2
2	3	1	2
2	3	1	2
2	2	1	2
2	2	1	2
2	2	1	2
2	2	1	2
2	3	1	2
2	1	1	2
2	1	1	2
2	1	2	2
2	1	2	2
2	1	2	2
2	1	2	2

Table continued on next page.

BACKGROUND 1 = Asian 2 = Caucasian 3 = other	MOTHER'S EMPLOYMENT 1 = full time 2 = none, 3 = part time	SCHOOL 1 = comprehensive 2 = private	TENDENCY TO ANOREXIA 1 = high 2 = low
2	1	2	2
2	1	2	2
2	1	2	2
1	1	2	2
1	1	2	2
3	1	2	2
3	1	2	2
3	1	2	2
3	1	2	2

DATA FOR MCNEMAR TEST

NORMAL HANDWRITING 1 = correct 2 = incorect	HANDWRITING AS IF OPPOSITE SEX 1 = correct 2 = incorect
2	2
1	1
1	1
1	2
1	1
2	2
1	1
1	2
2	2
1	1
2	2
1	2
2	2
2	2
1	1
2	2
1	1
2	2
1	2
2	2
1	2
1	2
1	2

NORMAL HANDWRITING	HANDWRITING AS IF OPP. SEX
1	2
1	1
1	2
1	2
2	1
1	2
1	1
1	1
1	2
1	2
2	2
1	1
1	1
1	1
2	2
2	1
1	2
2	2
1	1
1	2
1	1
1	1
2	2
1	1
1	2
2	2

DATA FOR DATA HANDLING EXERCISES:

Chapter 6, Sections 1-9

id	sex	ethnicity	religion	adopted	q1	q2	q3	q4	q5	q6	q7	q8	q9	q10
1	2	2	3	1	4	4	4	5	2	4	3	5	2	2
2	1	2	3	0	4	1	5	5	1	3	2	3	1	5
3	2	4	2	1	2	3	2	2	1	2	1	1	1	1
4	2	3	2	0	2	1	1	3	3	3	3	1	1	1
5	2	2	6	0	4	5	3	4	4	2	4	5	4	3
6	2	5	5	0	2	1	9	1	2	1	1	1	1	1
7	1	4	3	4	1	1	1	2	1	1	1	3	2	5
8	1	1	6	4	1	2	2	1	1	1	2	2	3	1
9	2	2	3	2	1	1	2	1	1	2	1	1	1	1
10	2	3	3	3	2	2	1	2	3	2	2	3	2	2
11	2	4	5	0	5	4	5	5	5	5	5	5	5	5
12	1	4	5	1	4	4	3	2	4	3	4	3	4	3
13	2	4	3	1	3	3	3	3	2	3	3	2	3	4
14	1	1	6	2	2	3	5	4	2	3	4	1	3	5
15	1	3	3	1	9	1	2	1	1	1	1	2	3	2
16	2	4	1	4	1	2	1	2	2	2	1	2	2	2
17	2	5	2	0	5	4	4	4	3	4	3	4	5	5
18	1	1	3	2	5	4	9	4	4	3	3	2	4	4
19	2	1	2	4	1	1	1	2	1	2	2	1	1	1
20	2	2	3	9	1	2	3	2	3	2	2	2	3	3

Qnum	q_a	q_b	q_c	q_d	q_e	q_f	q_g	q_h	q_i	q_j	q_k	q_l	q_m	q_n	q_o	q_p	q_q	q_r	q_s	q_t
1	4	2	3	4	4	4	2	2	2	4	2	2	3	5	4	3	5	3	3	5
2	2	2	6	3	4	4	1	2	3	4	2	2	4	4	5	3	3	3	3	2
3	4	2	4	4	4	5	2	2	2	5	3	2	3	2	5	2	3	3	3	4
4	4	2	4	5	5	5	1	1	2	5	2	1	1	3	5	1	2	2	3	5
5	4	2	5	4	5	4	1	2	2	2	3	2	2	5	4	2	2	2	4	4
6	4	2	3	3	4	3	2	3	2	4	3	2	3	2	4	3	3	3	4	4
7	5	1	5	4	5	5	1	2	2	5	2	1	2	4	5	2	2	2	4	4
8	5	2	5	5	4	4	2	2	3	5	3	2	2	5	5	1	3	3	3	4
9	4	1	5	5	4	4	2	1	2	5	1	1	3	5	5	2	4	1	1	5
10	5	2	5	5	5	5	1	2	2	4	2	2	3	1	5	3	3	3	3	4
11	4	2	3	4	5	5	1	2	2	4	2	2	2	4	4	2	2	2	4	4
12	4	1	4	4	4	4	1	2	2	5	2	1	2	4	4	2	2	2	4	4
13	4	1	3	4	5	5	2	1	1	5	1	3	2	2	4	2	2	3	5	5
14	4	1	3	4	4	4	1	2	2	4	1	1	2	3	1	4	3	3	3	4
15	4	3	3	4	4	4	1	3	2	5	2	2	3	4	4	2	3	3	3	4
16	5	2	5	5	5	5	1	2	2	5	2	1	2	5	4	1	3	1	4	4
17	4	3	4	4	5	2	2	3	3	4	5	2	5	4	4	2	4	3	3	3
18	2	2	3	3	5	4	1	3	2	4	4	3	4	2	5	2	2	4	3	2
19	4	2	5	5	5	3	1	3	3	5	1	2	3	2	4	1	3	1	4	4
20	4	2	5	5	5	5	1	2	2	5	2	1	3	5	5	2	2	2	5	5
21	4	1	4	4	5	4	2	2	2	5	1	3	2	3	4	2	3	2	3	3
22	4	2	3	4	4	3	2	2	2	4	3	4	3	4	4	3	3	3	2	4
23	4	2	5	5	5	5	1	2	1	5	1	1	2	5	5	2	2	2	3	5
24	5	1	4	5	5	5	1	1	1	5	1	1	1	3	4	2	3	3	3	3
25	5	1	5	5	5	5	1	3	3	4	3	1	5	2	5	2	4	2	4	4
26	3	2	3	4	4	4	2	3	2	4	2	2	3	4	2	2	3	3	3	3
27	2	4	2	2	2	1	4	4	5	1	5	5	5	4	2	5	5	5	2	1
28	3	2	3	4	4	4	3	3	4	3	3	4	5	3	3	4	4	3	2	2
29	4	2	4	5	5	4	2	2	2	4	2	3	2	5	4	3	2	3	4	9
30	3	2	4	4	4	3	2	2	2	4	2	2	4	4	4	2	3	2	4	4
31	4	2	5	5	5	5	1	2	2	5	3	3	4	5	5	1	2	3	4	5
32	4	3	5	5	5	9	3	3	4	4	4	4	4	3	3	4	4	4	2	4
33	3	2	3	5	4	4	1	2	2	2	5	2	2	4	5	2	3	3	5	5
34	4	2	2	5	5	4	2	2	3	5	3	4	5	4	4	2	5	3	4	4
35	4	2	5	4	4	4	2	2	4	4	2	2	4	4	4	2	2	4	4	4

Table continued on next page

Qnum	q_a	q_b	q_c	q_d	q_e	q_f	q_g	q_h	q_i	q_j	q_k	q_l	q_m	q_n	q_o	q_p	q_q	q_r	q_s	q_t
36	4	3	4	5	5	5	1	2	2	5	1	1	2	5	5	3	4	2	3	4
37	4	2	5	4	5	3	2	2	3	5	2	2	4	4	5	3	3	3	3	4
38	5	2	3	4	4	4	2	2	2	4	2	3	2	3	3	2	3	2	3	4
39	5	1	4	5	5	5	1	1	1	5	1	4	3	2	4	1	1	2	3	5
40	4	1	4	4	4	3	2	2	2	4	2	2	3	4	4	2	3	2	4	4
41	4	4	4	4	4	2	4	4	4	4	4	2	4	3	4	2	5	3	3	5
42	5	1	4	5	5	5	1	3	5	5	1	1	1	5	4	1	3	1	3	1
43	5	1	5	5	5	5	1	1	1	5	1	1	2	5	5	1	2	1	3	5
44	4	2	3	4	4	5	2	2	2	5	3	1	3	4	4	2	2	3	5	5
45	2	4	2	4	4	3	2	3	3	4	3	3	3	4	3	2	4	2	3	3
46	5	4	5	5	5	5	1	2	3	4	4	2	4	5	5	2	2	3	2	5
47	3	2	5	3	5	4	2	2	2	5	2	2	3	3	5	1	2	2	4	2
48	4	2	2	4	4	5	1	2	3	5	3	1	3	3	5	2	3	2	3	5
49	3	2	2	4	3	3	2	2	2	4	3	4	2	3	4	2	3	3	3	3
50	5	5	5	5	5	1	2	4	5	4	4	2	5	5	4	2	5	2	4	4

DATA FOR ONE-WAY BETWEEN-SUBJECTS ANOVA

PRESENTATION CONDITION 1 = unmasked 2 = greyblob 3 = pixelated 4 = negated	MEMORY
1	68
1	75
1	65
1	69
1	70
1	72
1	65
1	66
1	58
1	59
2	56
2	58
2	59
2	54
2	61
2	54
2	57
2	58
2	48
2	52
3	58
3	59
3	62
3	63
3	52
3	53
3	55
3	56
3	68
3	51
4	69
4	70

PRESENTATION CONDITION 1 = unmasked 2 = greyblob 3 = pixelated 4 = negated	MEMORY
4	67
4	65
4	72
4	74
4	68
4	63
4	66
4	58

SEX DIFF. 1 = same sex as defendant 2 = opposite sex as defendant	ATTRAC-TIVENESS 1 = attractive 2 = unattractive 3 = no picture	SENTENCE (in years)
1	1	6
1	1	8
1	1	7
1	1	9
1	1	5
1	1	7
1	1	10
1	1	9
1	1	9
1	1	5
2	1	5
2	1	11
2	1	7
2	1	5
2	1	8
2	1	5
2	1	9
2	1	10
2	1	10
2	1	5
1	2	7
1	2	9
1	2	12
1	2	14
1	2	11
1	2	11
1	2	9
1	2	12
1	2	13
1	2	14

SEX DIFF. 1 = same sex as defendant 2 = opposite sex as defendant	ATTRAC-TIVENESS 1 = attractive 2 = unattractive 3 = no picture	SENTENCE (in years)
2	2	8
2	2	9
2	2	9
2	2	13
2	2	11
2	2	9
2	2	10
2	2	13
2	2	13
2	2	8
1	3	13
1	3	15
1	3	16
1	3	15
1	3	14
1	3	16
1	3	14
1	3	13
1	3	13
1	3	16
2	3	12
2	3	12
2	3	15
2	3	14
2	3	16
2	3	13
2	3	12
2	3	12
2	3	13
2	3	16

DATA FOR ONE-WAY WITHIN-SUBJECTS ANOVA

INCONGRUENT	CONGRUENT	NEUTRAL
13	9	11
13	10	12
16	9	13
13	8	9
14	9	10
15	10	11
14	8	12
13	9	10
16	8	12
17	9	11

h1s1 right hand/ word	h1s2 right hand/ position	h2s1 left hand/ word	h2s2 left hand/ position
-5.52	-1.10	0	1.66
1.48	11.11	4.10	22.96
2.40	-4.19	8.14	4.49
13.78	6.74	11.78	5.57
-.61	-4.91	2.86	-2.45
8.11	11.11	3.85	9.61
8.14	7.49	5.97	5.21
4.07	1.74	9.66	0
-4.10	-3.47	.34	4.73
7.09	6.04	1.66	1.84
9.47	6.51	7.58	6.21
19.06	7.02	17.27	12.04
15.68	5.91	5.40	.77
1.15	.57	3.64	4.31
3.61	.60	-2.07	2.71
11.44	.29	14.03	1.47
4.09	1.75	.35	-.88
9.87	9.87	17.82	14.4
3.73	1.02	-.36	3.73
4.53	8.27	2.05	10.93
14.55	.61	7.95	-6.06
-1.42	2.84	2.13	2.84
17.44	8.90	10.04	10.32
3.80	3.16	2.39	1.58

DATA FOR THREE-WAY MIXED ANOVA

GROUP 1 = unprimed 2 = primed	n1o1 normal/upright	n2o1 negative/upright	n1o2 normal/inverted	n2o2 negative/inverted
2	54.17	70.83	58.33	54.17
2	62.5	75	62.5	45.83
2	66.67	58.33	50	70.83
2	66.67	83.33	54.17	66.67
2	83.33	66.67	75	62.5
2	66.67	66.67	83.33	66.67
2	70.83	66.67	70.83	62.5
2	66.67	58.33	75	66.67
2	79.17	75	83.33	66.67
2	62.5	75	87.5	79.17
2	70.83	75	70.83	54.17
2	54.17	83.33	54.17	62.5
2	58.33	62.5	54.17	62.5
2	66.67	79.17	58.33	75
2	70.83	79.17	66.67	75
2	66.67	58.33	58.33	62.5
2	62.5	75	75	54.17
2	75	70.83	79.17	66.67
2	41.67	66.67	66.67	66.67
2	58.33	66.67	58.33	58.33
2	45.83	62.5	58.33	66.67
2	70.83	70.83	58.33	66.67
2	83.33	70.83	79.17	62.5
1	66.67	70.83	83.33	70.83
1	66.67	58.33	54.17	79.17
1	79.17	62.5	75	75
1	62.5	79.17	62.5	66.67
1	70.83	58.33	50	41.67
1	62.5	62.5	50	62.5
1	62.5	58.33	54.17	66.67
1	66.67	83.33	79.17	75
1	62.5	70.83	75	66.67

Table continued on next page

GROUP 1 = unprimed 2 = primed	n1o1 normal/upright	n2o1 negative/upright	n1o2 normal/inverted	n2o2 negative/inverted
1	70.83	66.67	58.33	58.33
1	54.17	62.5	70.83	70.83
1	58.33	79.17	70.83	58.33
1	62.5	66.67	58.33	66.67
1	62.5	66.67	70.83	62.5
1	66.67	66.67	79.17	75
1	50	62.5	54.17	75
1	79.17	75	75	79.17
1	58.33	45.83	54.17	70.83
1	45.83	41.67	58.33	50
1	83.33	79.17	79.17	79.17
1	54.17	58.33	54.17	62.5
1	70.83	66.67	66.67	70.83
1	58.33	70.83	83.33	58.33
1	66.67	45.83	50	62.5
1	62.5	62.5	54.17	54.17
1	66.67	45.83	58.33	50
1	66.67	75	75	58.33
1	75	79.17	66.67	62.5
1	58.33	58.33	37.5	70.83
1	54.17	54.17	75	75
1	66.67	58.33	75	70.83
1	66.67	58.33	75	58.33
1	70.83	62.5	70.83	50
1	75	70.83	62.5	70.83
1	62.5	70.83	79.17	66.67
1	70.83	62.5	75	70.83
1	58.33	58.33	50	54.17
1	58.33	66.67	62.5	58.33

DATA FOR KRUSKAL–WALLIS TEST AND FRIEDMAN TEST

CONDITION 1 = cognitive int. 2 = visualisation 3 = standard int.	BEFORE INTERVIEW CONFIDENCE	AFTER INTERVIEW CONFIDENCE	IDENTIFICATION CONFIDENCE
1	2	4	4
1	3	3	3
1	2	4	4
1	2	2	4
1	3	3	4
1	1	5	2
1	2	4	4
1	1	3	2
1	2	4	4
1	2	6	4
1	1	4	4
1	1	4	4
1	2	3	3
1	1	4	4
1	2	4	6
1	2	3	5
1	1	4	3
1	2	5	3
1	2	3	5
1	1	4	1
2	1	2	3
2	2	1	6
2	1	2	4
2	3	2	4
2	1	1	7
2	2	2	4
2	2	1	3
2	1	3	3
2	2	1	5
2	3	2	6
2	2	2	5
2	1	1	6
2	1	2	4
2	1	3	4
2	3	1	3
2	2	2	4

Table continued on next page

CONDITION 1 = cognitive int. 2 = visualisation 3 = standard int.	BEFORE INTERVIEW CONFIDENCE	AFTER INTERVIEW CONFIDENCE	IDENTIFICATION CONFIDENCE
2	1	1	6
2	3	2	4
2	1	1	1
2	3	1	4
3	1	3	5
3	2	3	5
3	1	4	3
3	2	3	4
3	2	2	3
3	1	4	1
3	2	3	5
3	2	4	2
3	1	3	3
3	3	3	5
3	1	3	4
3	1	2	3
3	2	4	6
3	2	4	2
3	1	6	6
3	2	2	1
3	2	4	5
3	2	4	4
3	3	5	5
3	3	4	6

DATA FOR MULTIPLE REGRESSION

AGE (in months)	READING AGE (in months)	STANDARDISED READING SCORE	STANDARDISED SPELLING SCORE	% CORRECT SPELLING
93	71	80	104	67
81	76	95		44
84	88	104	107	40
93	71	71	105	50
87	72	86	112	63
92	71	81	100	33
88	83	96	106	48
87	71	75	106	33
86	72	86	103	31
92	97	105	101	58
86	38	131	125	94
83	71	79	104	23
83	71	86	95	31
82	108	125	127	92
86	113	121	122	81
83	99	115		46
92	108	114	114	83
83	90	106	126	75
92	97	105	106	85
82	90	109	110	46
88	96	110	118	71
87	79	93		31
91	71	80		
92	95	102	119	79
85	114	125	120	75
92	72	82	96	44
81	84	103	120	67
97	127	119	118	90
100	95	95	107	77
96	71	79	101	29
95	147	127	141	96
94	114	117	126	92
95	71	71	85	23
96	76	83	109	77
100	87	88	118	83
102	71	69	81	38
93	98	105	104	63
95	114	114	127	94
95	71	79		31
99	83	84	94	52
97	71	79	100	44
100	71	74	75	25
93	77	85	92	42
95	95	99	123	83
101	147	121	128	98

Table continued on next page

AGE (in months)	READING AGE (in months)	STANDARDISED READING SCORE	STANDARDISED SPELLING SCORE	% CORRECT SPELLING
105	88	84	76	23
107	120	105	106	67
106	92	87	114	81
112	71	69	76	23
97	71	76	92	46
104	82	80	94	44
102	102	100	100	50

DATA FOR ANCOVA

GROUP 1 = stooge 2 = no stooge 3 = control	TIME1 Covariate	TIME2 Dependent variable
1	72.5	62.5
1	66	51
1	59.5	46
1	68	59.5
1	58	35
1	66.5	43.5
1	69	50
1	58	48
1	57.5	40
1	68	37.5
1	67.5	51.1
1	70	58
1	55	34.5
1	60	36
1	68	51
1	72	51
1	60	39
1	68	42
1	69	56
1	60	45
1	56	31
1	71	55
1	62.5	35
1	65	36
2	65	52.5
2	57.5	35
2	66	60
2	57.5	54
2	70	62.5
2	62	47.5
2	60	58.5
2	66	62
2	75	68
2	67.5	62.5
2	62.5	50
2	63	52.5
2	65	50

GROUP 1 = stooge 2 = no stooge 3 = control	TIME1 Covariate	TIME2 Dependent variable
2	68	60
2	48	42
3	50	42
2	60	52
2	58	52.5
2	62	56
2	65	52.5
2	65	50
2	68	42
2	57.5	35
2	67.5	50
3	59	45
3	57	52
3	52	46.5
3	70	60
3	67.5	62.5
3	65	58
3	72	62.5
3	65	55
3	58	54
3	65	56
3	67.5	47.5
3	57	52
3	67	45
3	72.5	63
3	60	42
3	67.5	50
3	62	58
3	72.5	62.5
3	59	45
3	45	35
3	75.5	65
3	62.5	52.5
3	60	54
3	56	34.5

DATA FOR MANOVA

GROUP 1 = victim several times 2 = victim once 3 = never been victim	SECURITY No. of security measures	OUTINGS No. of times per week went out alone	REPORT Score on self-report measure
1	5	2	16
1	4	1	14
1	6	2	15
1	3	3	18
1	7	4	19
1	5	3	17
1	3	1	16
1	4	0	14
1	2	0	15
1	1	5	16
2	5	2	13
2	4	3	15
2	3	5	16
2	2	4	12
2	7	0	10
2	8	6	12
2	5	7	14
2	5	3	10
2	4	5	11
2	3	6	12
3	4	5	8
3	5	6	9
3	2	7	10
3	3	4	7
3	7	2	6
3	8	6	11
3	6	7	8
3	5	8	9
3	2	3	6
3	1	7	8

DATA FOR DISCRIMINANT ANALYSIS AND LOGISTIC REGRESSION

age	precons	recon 1 = reconvicted 0 = not	crimhis2	educemp2
28	15	0	6	7
30	0	1	9	8
48	0	1	6	7
32	0	0	1	1
23	6	1	10	7
31	4	1	8	2
38	0	1	4	3
34	0	0	2	3
28	2	1	5	4
30	0	0	1	0
33	11	1	7	6
26	21	1	8	9
30	3	0	5	4
51	3	0	5	3
40	0	0	4	3
46	7	1	4	3
63	0	0	2	2
52	0	0	1	5
24	0	1	9	3
24	0	0	2	1
33	0	1	1	3
32	1	0	4	6
41	0	0	1	2
29	12	0	1	2
24	1	0	2	3
26	0	0	6	2
38	0	0	6	5
28	0	0	7	1
38	2	0	7	5
31	5	0	1	4
27	1	0	6	4
54	0	0	2	4
33	0	1	11	6
59	9	0	3	5
40	0	0	4	3
27	4	0	7	2
26	16	1	7	7
31	0	0	10	6
49	1	0	2	7
33	3	0	4	3
41	14	0	7	5
41	12	1	8	5
20	1	1	3	2
21	9	1	9	7
19	9	1	10	9
21	0	0	3	2
20	2	1	7	9
20	6	1	6	3
21	11	1	7	4
19	4	1	6	9
22	8	1	10	9
20	2	1	8	10
19	4	1	10	6
19	1	1	1	3
21	5	1	9	5
21	1	0	6	6
20	4	1	10	7
20	0	0	6	6
21	10	1	9	3
19	6	1	9	5
20	0	0	5	3
19	1	0	3	3
19	2	0	6	6
19	1	0	4	3
20	4	1	4	5
20	11	0	8	10
17	6	0	2	4
18	0	0	4	1
21	14	0	3	5
20	14	0	10	7
19	4	0	8	6
18	8	1	4	9
19	7	0	10	6
20	0	0	4	4
19	1	0	1	10
21	3	0	10	9
20	12	1	10	7
19	2	0	10	9
20	13	1	9	5
19	0	0	1	1
19	4	1	9	9
19	0	0	8	10
20	12	1	6	8
21	1	0	4	2
21	10	1	10	7
19	8	0	6	7
19	9	0	5	4
18	0	0	11	10
19	8	0	9	9
21	13	0	10	9
15	4	0	8	8
20	0	0	1	2
20	1	0	4	7
20	12	1	11	9
19	10	1	10	9
20	10	0	5	7
20	1	0	2	3
20	1	1	2	1
20	0	0	1	4
19	10	0	8	9
20	0	0	2	3
20	6	0	9	9
18	1	1	4	8
20	9	0	6	6
19	0	0	2	1
21	11	0	10	9
20	0	0	5	7
18	0	0	1	2
19	15	0	9	3
21	4	0	7	8
19	1	0	8	5
20	22	1	8	3
20	13	1	1	2
21	0	0	6	5
20	17	0	9	10
21	8	0	2	0

Continued on next page

age	precons	recon 1 = reconvicted 0 = not	crimhis2	educemp2
20	5	0	6	2
19	0	0	3	1
19	0	0	1	3
17	9	1	4	7
20	5	0	3	3
19	1	0	4	7
17	2	1	10	10
18	9	1	4	3
34	8	0	8	6
24	2	0	3	0
23	15	0	2	0
34	12	0	9	9
26	1	0	5	1
25	10	0	11	2
37	8	0	9	8
26	6	1	7	9
41	14	1	9	6
65	0	0	7	2
54	0	0	3	8
26	0	1	11	9
35	17	0	10	8
30	8	1	10	5
26	2	0	9	2
23	0	0	3	7
71	0	0	3	2
25	0	1	11	7
41	1	0	4	7
25	13	1	8	9
23	17	1	10	8
41	20	0	11	7
59	23	0	10	8
33	10	0	10	8
25	0	0	4	4
29	7	1	9	6
29	1	0	3	8
51	0	0	6	5
43	9	0	8	8
39	2	1	3	0
22	11	0	10	8
41	11	0	6	3
36	9	0	9	8
25	16	1	11	9
27	21	0	11	8
27	17	1	12	4
27	0	0	2	3
31	4	0	6	2
22	1	0	4	8
48	0	0	4	3
37	0	0	10	0
34	0	0	1	7
30	5	0	5	1
35	0	0	2	4
39	2	0	6	3
43	1	0	1	5
51	7	0	6	2
35	0	0	1	3
29	0	0	3	1
54	16	0	10	8
31	0	1	7	5
48	8	1	8	4
32	22	0	11	9
47	9	0	1	4
26	4	0	5	3
44	22	0	11	8
35	2	0	3	1
40	14	0	7	4
25	2	0	4	2
41	0	0	1	1
56	0	0	7	1
32	6	0	7	4
30	0	1	4	3
47	0	0	9	2
60	10	0	12	3
34	5	0	7	4
35	1	0	4	7
54	1	0	8	3
38	4	0	7	2
26	1	0	2	1
44	5	0	9	2
31	11	0	7	3
40	3	0	4	0
33	8	0	7	5
58	8	0	10	5
38	5	0	1	1
62	0	0	2	0
39	6	0	6	4
32	4	0	9	8
29	0	0	9	9
31	0	0	1	1
75	0	0	2	4
53	0	0	6	7
29	1	0	8	2
44	15	1	11	8
35	28	1	8	9
40	24	0	8	6
28	5	0	11	9
32	9	0	9	9
38	15	0	7	7
37	9	1	11	7
28	0	0	7	8
38	32	0	10	7
51	24	0	9	4
23	0	0	8	9
35	24	1	10	9
29	14	0	2	1

DATA FOR FACTOR ANALYSIS

Participant	Sex (1=M, 2=F)	Celandine	Rose	Cornflower	Primrose	Poppy	Bluebell	Buttercup	Wisteria	Daisy	Speedwell	Sweetpea	Delphinium	Aster	Lavender	Hellebore
1	1	5	6	6	5	7	7	6	6	5	5	7	6	7	7	6
2	2	6	6	6	6	6	6	6	6	6	6	6	2	6	6	1
3	1	4	7	7	5	7	5	6	7	6	6	7	7	7	7	7
4	1	6	4	6	6	6	6	6	4	6	6	4	4	4	5	4
5	2	5	4	7	5	7	7	7	4	5	7	6	4	5	7	4
6	2	3	4	7	4	7	4	4	5	5	6	6	4	4	7	4
7	2	7	6	7	7	7	7	7	7	7	7	6	5	6	7	5
8	2	6	6	6	3	7	6	4	6	5	6	6	3	7	7	3
9	1	7	7	7	7	7	7	7	7	7	7	7	7	7	7	5
10	1	6	7	6	2	7	4	1	7	6	6	7	7	7	7	7
11	2	1	1	1	1	1	1	1	1	1	1	1	1	1	1	1
12	2	2	7	6	3	7	2	3	7	5	5	6	7	7	6	7
13	2	7	6	6	6	7	7	6	6	7	7	7	6	6	6	6
14	1	6	6	6	7	6	6	7	6	7	7	6	6	6	6	6
15	2	7	2	7	7	7	7	7	5	7	7	6	4	2	7	1
16	1	5	7	2	3	7	5	4	7	7	7	7	7	7	7	7
17	1	6	7	7	6	7	6	6	7	7	7	7	2	6	7	5
18	2	4	4	5	6	6	6	6	4	5	5	4	3	3	5	3
19	2	3	2	4	4	5	4	5	4	3	5	4	4	4	5	4
20	1	7	7	7	7	7	7	7	7	7	7	7	7	7	7	3
21	2	3	6	7	5	7	5	5	6	5	6	6	6	6	7	6
22	1	6	4	2	7	3	7	7	5	7	7	3	5	5	3	4
23	2	4	4	3	5	5	5	5	3	4	6	3	2	4	3	1
24	1	6	7	7	6	7	6	6	7	6	6	7	7	7	7	7
25	1	7	6	6	7	7	7	6	6	7	7	6	6	7	7	5
26	2	7	4	3	6	4	7	6	3	6	7	3	3	3	2	2
27	2	6	5	5	5	6	5	5	5	5	5	5	3	5	5	2
28	2	6	5	5	7	6	6	7	5	6	7	5	4	3	4	2
29	2	7	2	7	7	5	7	7	5	7	7	5	2	6	7	2
30	1	5	4	6	5	6	5	5	3	5	5	5	4	5	7	3

Table continued on next page

Participant	Sex	Celandine	Rose	Cornflower	Primrose	Poppy	Bluebell	Buttercup	Wisteria	Daisy	Speedwell	Sweetpea	Delphinium	Aster	Lavender	Hellebore
31	2	5	4	5	5	6	5	6	5	5	5	4	3	4	5	3
32	1	6	6	7	7	7	7	7	6	7	7	7	3	7	7	2
33	2	6	5	7	5	6	6	6	7	5	5	4	4	7	7	3
34	2	5	7	2	5	7	5	5	6	5	5	2	6	6	7	3
35	2	4	5	3	5	6	5	3	4	4	3	2	4	4	5	2
36	1	6	5	6	4	6	6	5	6	4	6	4	3	6	6	5
37	1	3	5	7	6	7	5	2	6	6	6	7	6	7	7	5
38	1	6	5	4	6	5	6	6	4	7	7	4	4	5	4	4
39	2	2	6	6	6	6	5	5	4	4	4	5	4	6	7	5
40	1	4	5	5	5	7	6	4	7	5	7	7	7	7	7	6
41	1	7	5	7	7	7	7	1	4	7	7	7	2	3	7	5
42	2	4	6	5	4	7	4	4	4	4	4	4	4	4	7	4
43	1	6	4	3	5	4	6	7	3	5	6	5	4	5	4	1
44	2	4	6	5	5	6	5	6	6	6	6	5	5	6	5	5
45	2	6	4	4	4	4	6	5	4	4	5	3	3	4	4	4
46	2	6	4	4	6	5	6	6	5	6	6	5	4	5	6	4
47	1	4	7	7	6	7	7	5	6	5	6	6	1	7	7	1
48	1	3	7	7	5	7	5	5	7	6	6	7	5	7	7	5
49	2	7	7	7	7	7	7	7	6	7	7	6	5	6	7	4
50	1	7	5	5	6	5	7	7	5	7	7	5	4	4	5	1

RELIABILITY AND DIMENSIONALITY OF SCALES AND QUESTIONNAIRES

The data is given above, under Data Handling Exercises. Read Chapter 6, Section 10 before using the data.

Appendix II: Defining a variable in SPSS Versions 8 and 9

Defining a variable in SPSS Versions 8 and 9

Before you can enter your data, the Data Editor window must be set up so that it is ready to receive your data. SPSS needs to know the name of each of your variables so that these names can be inserted at the top of the columns of the data table. In addition, you need to give SPSS other important information about each of your variables. This process of defining the variables is described below

THE DEFINE VARIABLE DIALOGUE BOX

Double-click on the grey header (which will probably be labelled **var**) at the top of the column you wish to define (see below). SPSS will present you with the **Define Variable** dialogue box containing information about this column.

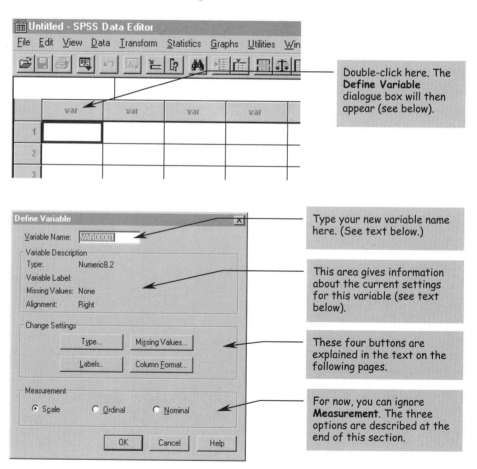

Double-click here. The **Define Variable** dialogue box will then appear (see below).

Type your new variable name here. (See text below.)

This area gives information about the current settings for this variable (see text below).

These four buttons are explained in the text on the following pages.

For now, you can ignore **Measurement**. The three options are described at the end of this section.

Variable name

The first thing you need to do is to give the variable a meaningful name. At the moment the box labelled **<u>V</u>ariable Name** will probably contain the default variable name VAR00001. If you start typing a new variable name, the default name will disappear and be replaced by your new name. You should choose a variable name that makes sense to you and you are not likely to forget. Variable names must not be more than 8 characters long, and must start with a letter of the alphabet (i.e., not a number). Variable names cannot contain spaces or any special characters such as full stops, colons, hyphens or commas (the @, #, $ and _ characters are allowed). If you enter an invalid variable name SPSS will warn you later.

CHANGE SETTINGS

In the **Define Variable** dialogue box (shown on the previous page) there are four buttons labelled **<u>T</u>ype, <u>L</u>abels, Mi<u>s</u>sing Values,** and **Column <u>F</u>ormat.** Clicking on these buttons allows you to change some of the characteristics of the variable. We will now describe each of these buttons in turn.

The type button

From the **Define Variable** dialogue box, click on the **T<u>y</u>pe** button. You will be presented with a new dialogue box titled **Define Variable Type** (see below). This allows you to select whether your data is in the form of numbers (**<u>N</u>umeric**) or letters (**St<u>r</u>ing**), or one of a number of other formats. We strongly recommend that, until you are an experienced user, you only use numeric variables.

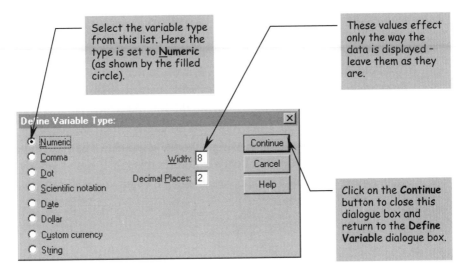

Select the variable type from this list. Here the type is set to **Numeric** (as shown by the filled circle).

These values effect only the way the data is displayed – leave them as they are.

Click on the **Continue** button to close this dialogue box and return to the **Define Variable** dialogue box.

This dialogue box also allows you to set the **Width** of the variable. This is the number of characters before and after the decimal place used to display the variable in the Data Editor and Output Viewer windows. This setting does not affect the way the value is stored or the number of decimal places used in statistical calculations. With numeric data the default settings are for a total **Width** of 8 with 2 **Decimal Places** (e.g., 12345.78). If you attempt to input a data value that will not fit into this width, then SPSS will round it in order to display the value. However, the value you entered is stored by SPSS and used in all calculations. One effect of this is that unless you set **Decimal Places** to zero, all values, even integers (whole numbers without decimal places), will be displayed with 2 decimal places. Thus if you enter a value of "2" in the Data Editor window SPSS will display "2.00". This might look a little untidy, but is of no consequence and it is probably not worth altering these settings to stop this happening.

You can now click on the **Continue** button on the right hand side of the dialogue box. This will close the **Define Variable Type** dialogue box and return you to the **Define Variable** dialogue box.

The labels button

From the **Define Variable** dialogue box, click on the **Labels** button. You will be presented with the **Define Labels** dialogue box (see below). This dialogue box gives you the opportunity to attach two types of label to a variable: variable labels and value labels.

A **Variable Label** is simply a phrase that is associated with the variable name and which helps you to remember what data this variable contains. This label is useful because the variable name itself is limited to 8 characters. If you have called a variable something like "sex", then you probably do not need to be reminded about what it is describing. If, however, you have a large number of variables, then variable labels can be very useful. For example, if you are entering the data from a questionnaire, you might have a variable named "q3relbef". In this case a variable label might be invaluable, as it could remind you that this variable coded the responses to question 3 on your questionnaire which asked about religious belief. You can type in any phrase using any characters that you like, but it is best to keep it fairly short. SPSS will not try to interpret this label; it will simply insert it into the output next to the appropriate variable name when you perform any analysis.

To add a variable label, type it in to the box marked **Variable Label**.

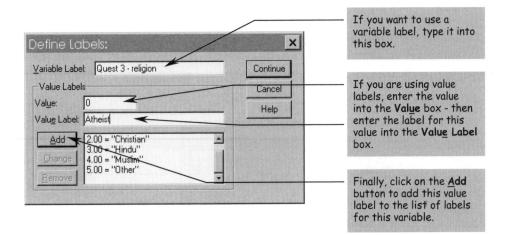

If you want to use a variable label, type it into this box.

If you are using value labels, enter the value into the **Value** box - then enter the label for this value into the **Value Label** box.

Finally, click on the **Add** button to add this value label to the list of labels for this variable.

A **Value Label** is a label assigned to a particular value of a variable. You are most likely to use value labels for nominal or categorical variables as shown in the dialogue box above. A second use for value labels is with a grouping or independent variable. For example, you might want to compare the reaction time of participants who were tested under one of several different doses of alcohol. You could use a value label to remind yourself that group 1 received no alcohol, group 2 received 1 unit of alcohol and group 3, 2 units. Value labels will be inserted into the SPSS output to remind you what these values mean. Above we show you how to add value labels. When you are happy with all your label settings, click on the **Continue** button to return to the **Define Variable** dialogue box. Do not forget to click the **Add** button after typing the last label. If you do, SPSS will warn that "Any pending add or change operations will be lost" when you click on the **Continue** button.

The missing values button

Sometimes you will not have a complete set of data. For example, some participants might decline to tell you their religion or their age, or you might lose or be unable to collect data from some participants (e.g., as the result of equipment failure). These gaps in the data table are known as missing values.

When we have a missing value we need to be able to tell SPSS that we do not have valid data for this participant on this variable. We do this by choosing a value that cannot normally occur for this variable. In the religion example above, we might choose to code religion as 9 when the participant does not state their religion. Thus,

9 is the missing value for the variable religion. The missing value can be different for each variable. For age it could be 99 (unless you are testing very old people).

To specify a missing value click on the **Missing Values** button in the **Define Variable** dialogue box. The **Define Missing Values** dialogue box will appear (see below).

To include up to three different missing values click on this circle (so that it becomes filled) then enter your missing value(s) in the box(es).

Click on the **Continue** button to return to the **Define Variable** dialogue box.

SPSS allows you to specify the missing values in several ways:
1. **No missing values**: This is the default setting for this dialogue box. If this option is selected, SPSS will treat all values for this variable as valid.
2. **Discrete missing values**: This option allows you to enter up to three discrete values. For example, 7, 9 and 11 could all be set as missing values by selecting this option and entering the values in the three boxes. If you have only one missing value enter it into the first of the three boxes.
3. **Range of missing values**: This option allows you to indicate that a range of values is being used as missing values. For example, selecting this option and entering the values 7 and 11 in the **Low** and **High** value boxes would instruct SPSS to treat the values 7, 8, 9, 10 and 11 as missing values.
4. **Range plus one discrete missing value**: This option allows you to set a range of values plus one additional value as missing (e.g., 7–11 plus 0).

In practice we rarely need more than one missing value for a variable (occasionally you might want more than one – for example you might wish to distinguish between an unanswered question and an illegible answer as both are missing values). You will therefore almost always want to enter your missing value into the first of the **Discrete missing values** boxes. To do this, simply click on the circle next to the words **Discrete missing values** and then enter your missing value into the first of the three boxes. Now click on the **Continue** button to return you to the **Define Variable** dialogue box.

The column format button

From the **Define Variable** dialogue box, click on the **Column Format** button to bring up the **Define Column Format** dialogue box (see below).

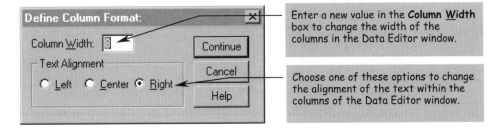

The column format specification does not affect the data values. It only affects the width of the column and the position of the data in the cell in the Data Editor window. You can therefore leave these settings as they are unless you want to change the appearance of the data window. You may, for example, want to fit more columns onto the screen in order to see more variables without having to scroll. In this case you could reduce the width of each column. We recommend that if you need to change the column width, set it equal to no less than the number of characters in the variable name. When you have finished adjusting the column format settings press the **Continue** button to return to the **Define Variable** dialogue box.

Completing the variable definition

When you have made the changes you require to the variable name, type, labels, missing values and column format, you will notice that the new settings are reflected in the information displayed in the **Define Variable** dialogue box (see below). This acts as a useful note of the settings for each variable.

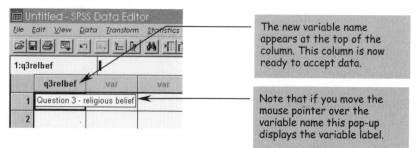

Define Variable

Variable Name: q3relbef

Variable Description
Type: Numeric8.2
Variable Label: Question 3 - religious belief
Missing Values: 9
Alignment: Right

Change Settings
[Type...]   [Missing Values...]
[Labels..]   [Column Format...]

Measurement
(•) Scale   ( ) Ordinal   ( ) Nominal

[OK]   [Cancel]   [Help]

> The new settings are reflected in the details given in the **Variable Description** portion of the dialogue box.

> Click on the **OK** button to accept these settings for this variable.

Click on the **OK** button to accept this variable definition. After a short delay you will see the name of your new variable appear at the top of the appropriate column of the Data Editor window (see below). If you have made an error or if you want to change anything, simply double-click on the variable name and adjust the setting.

Untitled - SPSS Data Editor

File Edit View Data Transform Statistics

1:q3relbef

	q3relbef	var	var
1	Question 3 - religious belief		
2			

> The new variable name appears at the top of the column. This column is now ready to accept data.

> Note that if you move the mouse pointer over the variable name this pop-up displays the variable label.

You must now repeat this process for each of the variables in your data files. Once all the variables are defined you are ready to enter your data.

A NOTE ON THE DEFINE VARIABLE DIALOGUE BOX

At the bottom of the **Define Variable** dialogue box there is a box titled **Measurement** that contains three options, **Scale**, **Ordinal** and **Nominal**. These options are used to indicate the level of measurement of the variable. SPSS does not distinguish between interval and ratio data and uses the term **Scale** to cover a variable measured using either of these levels of measurement.

Select the **Scale** option for variables measured using either an interval or ratio scale.

Select the **Ordinal** option for variables measured using an ordinal scale.

Select the **Nominal** option for nominal variables (e.g., "sex" or "group").

Appendix III: Adding regression lines to scattergrams in versions earlier than 12

Simple scattergram (Chapter 4, Section 2)

Scattergram with multiple groups (Chapter 9, Section 2)

Section 1: Simple scattergram (Chapter 4, Section 2)

HOW TO OBTAIN A SCATTERGRAM WITH REGRESSION LINE

Click on **Graphs** on the menu bar, and then from the menu select **Scatter**. In the **Scatterplot** dialogue box, shown below, click on the **Simple** display, then click on the **Define** button.

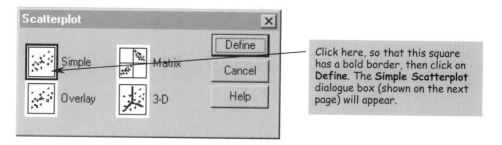

The other options in the **Scatterplot** dialogue box produce more complex graphs, which you can explore in the future. We will only be describing the **Simple** command. After you have clicked on the **Define** button, the **Simple Scatterplot** dialogue box will appear. It is shown below.

In the **Simple Scatterplot** dialogue box, shown above, move the variable names, one into the box labelled **X Axis**, and one into the **Y Axis** box. You can use the **Titles** button and the **Options** button if you wish. When you have finished, click on **OK**. The Output Window will open, containing the scattergram: a part of that window is shown on the next page. To add the regression line, you have to edit the graph: start by double-clicking in the scattergram, and the SPSS Chart Editor window, shown below the Output window, will appear.

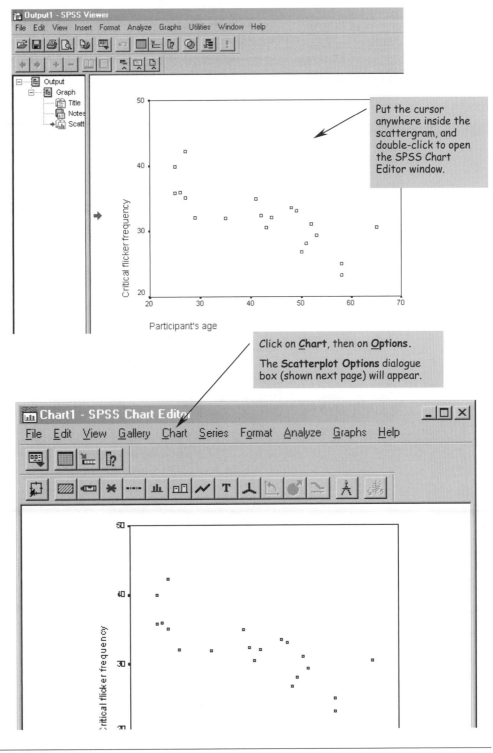

Put the cursor anywhere inside the scattergram, and double-click to open the SPSS Chart Editor window.

Click on **Chart**, then on **Options**.

The **Scatterplot Options** dialogue box (shown next page) will appear.

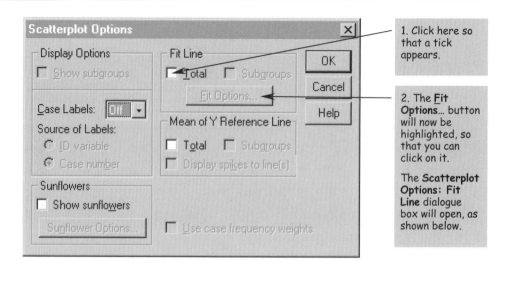

When you have clicked on **OK** in the **Scatterplot Options** dialogue box, the SPSS Chart Editor window will display the regression line in the scattergram, as shown on the next page. To use the scattergram in other packages, click on **Edit**, **Copy Chart**: the scattergram will be placed on the Clipboard, and may be pasted into word processing documents. You can then add a figure legend below the figure: see Chapter 4 for guidance.

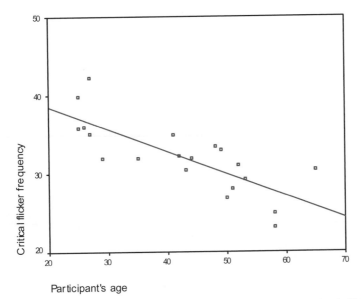

Figure 4.3 Scattergram produced by SPSS, showing critical flicker frequency (in Hz) plotted against the age (in years) of the participants.

Section 2: Scattergram with multiple groups (Chapter 9, Section 2)

HOW TO CHECK FOR LINEAR RELATIONSHIP BETWEEN COVARIATE AND DEPENDENT VARIABLE

Click on **Graphs** ⇒ **Scatter**
You will then see the **Scatterplot** dialogue box.

Select **Simple** and then click on the **Define** button.

Select the dependent variable "time2" and move it across into the **Y Axis** box. Select the covariate "time1" and move it across into the **X Axis** box. Finally, select your factor "group" and move it across into the **Set Markers by:** box. Then click here on the **OK** button.

> **TIP** The **Set Markers by** option in the **Simple Scatterplot** dialogue box can have other uses. For example, you may have carried out a correlational study with participants who are from different backgrounds and you might wish to separate out those from urban and those from rural backgrounds.

A graph will appear in the Viewer window, but this will not include the regression lines. To obtain these, double click on the graph itself in the output window. This will bring up the **SPSS Chart Editor** window.

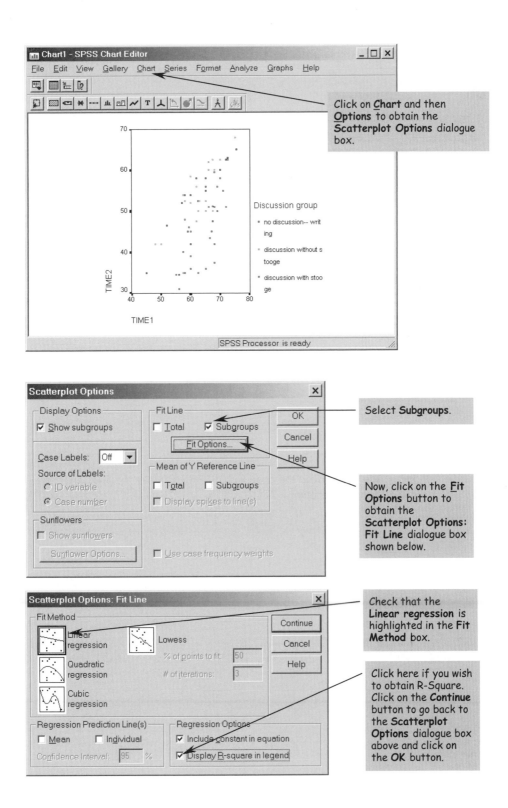

Click on **Chart** and then **Options** to obtain the **Scatterplot Options** dialogue box.

Select **Subgroups**.

Now, click on the **Fit Options** button to obtain the **Scatterplot Options: Fit Line** dialogue box shown below.

Check that the **Linear regression** is highlighted in the **Fit Method** box.

Click here if you wish to obtain R-Square. Click on the **Continue** button to go back to the **Scatterplot Options** dialogue box above and click on the **OK** button.

Graph

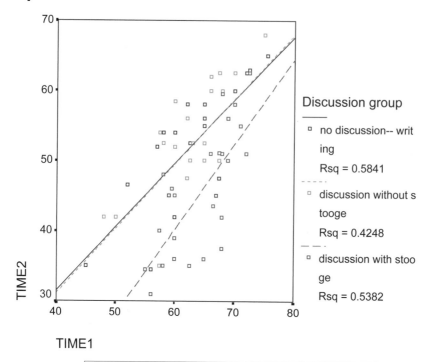

Discussion group

□ no discussion-- writing
Rsq = 0.5841

□ discussion without stooge
Rsq = 0.4248

□ discussion with stooge
Rsq = 0.5382

TIME2

TIME1

> **TIP** We have edited the chart within SPSS to make the lines and case markers more distinct from one another

Index

In this Index, numerals in italic format are page references for a glossary entry for the term.